MANHUNT

ALSO BY PETER L. BERGEN

THE LONGEST WAR

THE OSAMA BIN LADEN I KNOW

HOLY WAR, INC.

MAN

PETER L. BERGEN

HUNT

The Ten-Year Search for Bin Laden
from 9/11 to Abbottabad

CROWN PUBLISHERS   NEW YORK

Library of Congress Cataloging-in-Publication Data

Bergen, Peter L., 1962–
Manhunt : the ten-year search for Bin Laden from 9/11 to Abbottabad / Peter L.
Bergen. — 1st ed.
Includes bibliographical references and index.
1. Bin Laden, Osama, 1957–2011. 2. Qaida (Organization) 3. Terrorists—Saudi
Arabia. 4. Fugitives from justice—United States. 5. Terrorism—United States—
Prevention. 6. Special operations (Military science)—United States. 7. War on
Terrorism, 2001–2009. I. Title.

HV6430.B55B473 2012
363.325'16092—dc23

                                              2012004258

ISBN 978-0-307-95557-9
eISBN 978-0-307-95558-6

PRINTED IN THE UNITED STATES OF AMERICA

Maps by Gene Thorp
Jacket design by Ben Wiseman
Jacket art by Universal History Archive/Getty Images
Author photograph: CNN/Brent Stirton

10 9 8 7 6 5 4 3 2 1

FIRST EDITION

For Pierre Timothy Bergen,
born November 17, 2011

CONTENTS

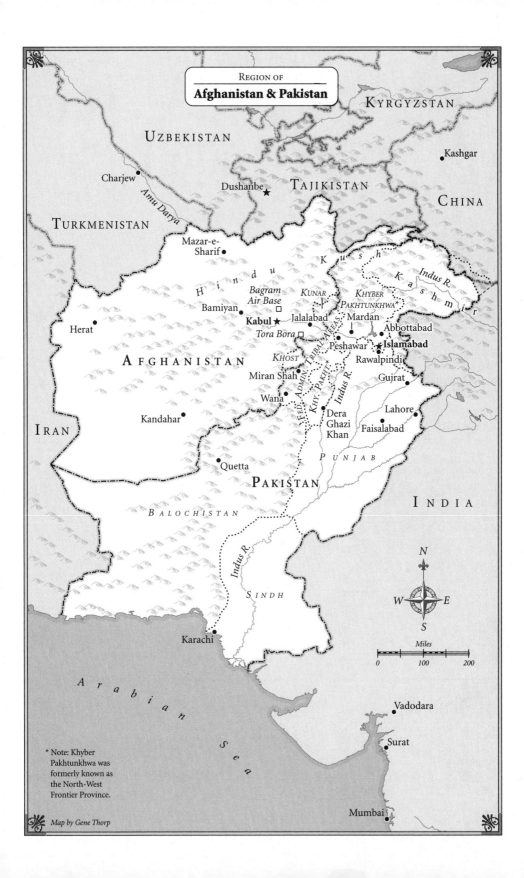

REGION OF
Afghanistan & Pakistan

KYRGYZSTAN

UZBEKISTAN

Kashgar

Charjew

Dushanbe ★   TAJIKISTAN

CHINA

Amu Darya

TURKMENISTAN

Mazar-e-Sharif

H i n d u   K u s h

Indus R.

Kashmir

Bagram Air Base □   KUNAR

KHYBER
PAKHTUNKHWA*

Bamiyan

Herat

Kabul ★   Jalalabad   Mardan

Tora Bora □

Abbottabad

Peshawar   ★Islamabad

AFGHANISTAN

KHOST

Rawalpindi

Miran Shah   Gujrat

Wana

Lahore

Kandahar

Dera
Ghazi
Khan   Faisalabad

IRAN

P U N J A B

Quetta

PAKISTAN

INDIA

B A L O C H I S T A N

Indus R.

Indus R.

KHY. PAKHT.

FED. ADMIN. TRIBAL AREAS

N

W   E

S

S I N D H

Miles

0   100   200

Karachi

A
r
a
b
i
a
n

S
e
a

Vadodara

Surat

* Note: Khyber
Pakhtunkhwa was
formerly known as
the North-West
Frontier Province.

Mumbai

Map by Gene Thorp

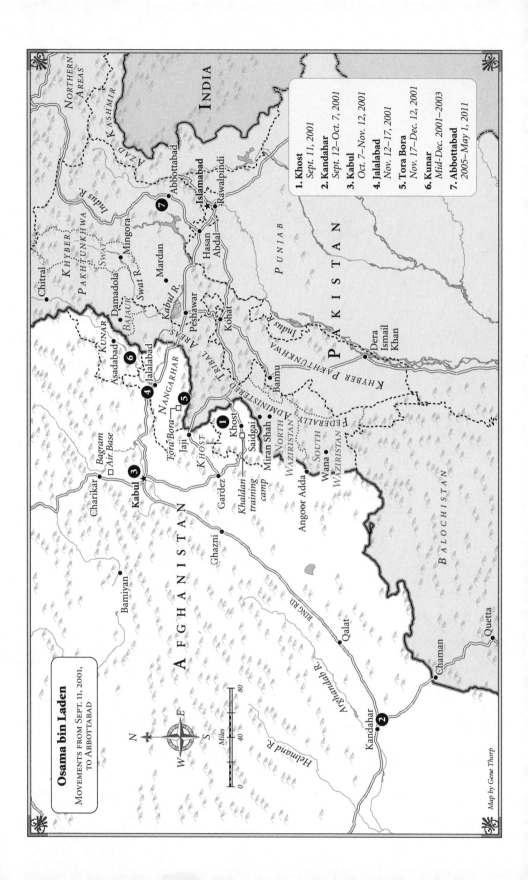

Osama bin Laden

MOVEMENTS FROM SEPT. 11, 2001, TO ABBOTTABAD

1. Khost
Sept. 11, 2001

2. Kandahar
Sept. 12–Oct. 7, 2001

3. Kabul
Oct. 7–Nov. 12, 2001

4. Jalalabad
Nov. 12–17, 2001

5. Tora Bora
Nov. 17–Dec. 12, 2001

6. Kunar
Mid-Dec. 2001–2003

7. Abbottabad
2005–May 1, 2011

Map by Gene Thorp

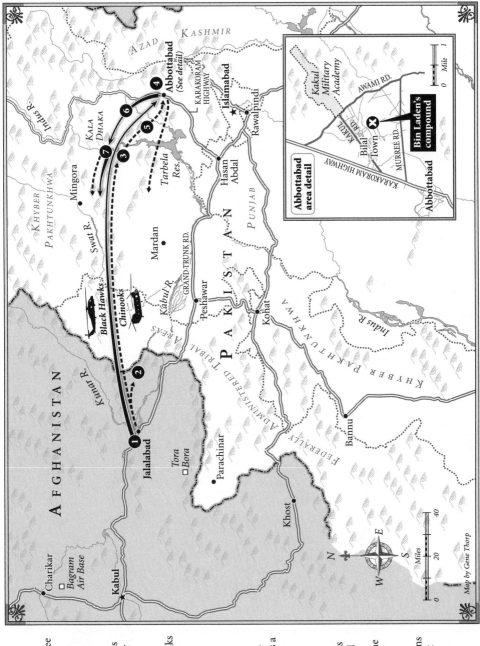

U.S. Navy SEAL
Raid on Abbottabad

1. Two Black Hawks and three Chinook helicopters leave Jalalabad on a raid to bin Laden's compound in Abbottabad.

2. One of the Chinooks stops before crossing the border into Pakistan.

3. The remaining two Chinooks land on the banks of the Indus River at Kala Dhaka as backup for the Black Hawks.

4. The SEALs in the Black Hawks assault the compound, killing bin Laden. In the process, one of the Black Hawks makes a hard landing and must be destroyed.

5. One Chinook leaves Kala Dhaka and flies to Abbottabad, where it picks up bin Laden's corpse and the SEALs from the destroyed Black Hawk. The chopper then returns directly to Jalalabad.

6. The other Black Hawk joins the remaining Chinook at Kala Dhaka and refuels.

7. Both choppers return to Jalalabad.

Map by Gene Thorp

MANHUNT

We sleep soundly in our beds because rough men stand ready in the night to visit violence on those who would do us harm.

—WINSTON CHURCHILL

It is not the critic who counts; not the man who points out how the strong man stumbles or where the doer of deeds could have done better. The credit belongs to the man who is actually in the arena, whose face is marred by dust and sweat and blood, who strives valiantly, who errs and comes up short again and again, because there is no effort without error or shortcoming, but who knows the great enthusiasms, the great devotions, who spends himself for a worthy cause; who, at the best, knows, in the end, the triumph of high achievement, and who, at the worst, if he fails, at least he fails while daring greatly, so that his place shall never be with those cold and timid souls who knew neither victory nor defeat.

—THEODORE ROOSEVELT

A NOTE ABOUT THIS BOOK

I FIRST MET Osama bin Laden in the middle of the night in a mud hut in the mountains of eastern Afghanistan in March 1997. I was there to produce his first television interview for CNN. In person bin Laden was not the table-thumping revolutionary I had expected, presenting himself as a low-key cleric. But while his manner was mild, his words were full of a raw hatred of the United States. Bin Laden surprised us by declaring war on the United States on camera; it was the first time he had done so before a Western audience. That warning, of course, was not sufficiently heeded, and four years later came the 9/11 attacks.

In a sense, I have been preparing to write this book ever since. While the exact timing of bin Laden's capture or death could not be predicted, it was all but inevitable that he would eventually be tracked down. The book you are about to read is the full story of how that happened.

After bin Laden was killed, I traveled to Pakistan three times, on my last visit making an extensive tour of the Abbottabad compound in which he lived his final years. I was the first outside observer to be granted entry by the Pakistani military, which controlled all access, and two weeks after my visit, in late February 2012, the complex was demolished.

The visit to the compound helped me form a much better understanding of the way al-Qaeda's leader and his family and followers lived there for years undetected, and of the U.S. Navy SEAL raid that killed bin Laden. I stood in the room where bin Laden lived for almost six years of his life and where he finally died. I also spoke to a variety of Pakistani security and military officials who investigated the SEAL raid and who were privy to the debriefings of his wives and children who were living on the compound.

On the U.S. side, I spoke to almost every senior official at the White House, Defense Department, CIA, State Department, National Counterterrorism Center, and Office of the Director of National Intelligence who was responsible for building and assessing the intelligence on bin Laden, weighing the possible courses of action in response to the suspected bin Laden compound, and overseeing the execution of the raid. Many of these officials are quoted by name in the book, but several could not be quoted directly due to the sensitivity of aspects of the mission. In the cases where a CIA official's name has not been made public I have used a pseudonym. (No one, including myself, has interviewed the U.S. Navy SEALs who were on the mission.) The SEALs recovered some six thousand documents at the bin Laden compound in Abbottabad. At the White House, I was allowed to review a number of those just-declassified, unpublished documents in mid-March 2012.

The anti-secrecy website WikiLeaks proved another very useful source of information. By consulting leaked, classified documents about Guantánamo, I was better able to map out bin Laden's movements after the 9/11 attacks and to reconstruct how CIA officials were able to zero in on the courier who led them to the al-Qaeda leader's front door. Just because a U.S. government document is secret does not, of course, guarantee that it is accurate, and so I did my best to cross-reference those documents with a variety of other accounts and sources.

This reporting was supplemented by additional interviews with former CIA officials and U.S. military officers involved in the hunt for bin Laden in the decade after 9/11, and multiple trips to Afghanistan to retrace bin Laden's footsteps at the Battle of Tora Bora, where he managed to evade the grasp of the United States during the winter of 2001.

When I met bin Laden back in 1997, it was outside the Afghan city of Jalalabad and close to the mountains of Tora Bora—the region from which, four years later, just months after 9/11, he would stage one of history's great disappearing acts and become the subject of the most intensive and expensive manhunt of all time. It was perhaps fitting that, a decade later, on the moonless night of May 1, 2011, bin Laden's final reckoning would begin with helicopters launched from Jalalabad Airfield. As they ascended, the Navy SEALs on board could see through the pixilated green glow of their night-vision goggles the mountains of Tora Bora only thirty miles to the south, rising fourteen thousand feet to the sky: the last place that a small group of American Special Operations Forces had bin Laden in their sights. This time, they vowed, bin Laden would not escape America's grasp.

PROLOGUE **A COMFORTABLE RETIREMENT**

I T WAS A PERFECT HIDING PLACE.

Squint a little and the neat houses that climb up the green hills and compact mountains that surround Abbottabad are reminiscent of Switzerland, or maybe Bavaria. This Pakistani city of some five hundred thousand souls sits at four thousand feet in the foothills of the Himalayas, which march in ranks toward the border with China. The town was founded in 1853 by James Abbott, an English officer who was a bit player in the Great Game that pitted the British and Russians against each other as they struggled for mastery in Central Asia. Somewhat unusually for an administrator of the Raj, Major Abbott was beloved by the inhabitants of Abbottabad. Abbott even penned an awkward but heartfelt poem to the town when he departed for England:

I remember the day when I first came here.
And smelt the sweet Abbottabad air . . .
I bid you farewell with a heavy heart
Never from my mind will your memories thwart.

Vestiges of Abbottabad's colonial past can be seen in the Anglican church of St. Luke's, which looks like it was airlifted in from Sussex, and the occasional sets of low-slung nineteenth-century buildings lining the main roads that once housed the administrators of the Empire.

Abbottabad is known today as the "City of Schools" and is home to a number of excellent prep schools and Pakistan's leading military academy. U.S. Special Forces soldiers were posted there in 2008 to help with the training of recruits.

Enticed by its relatively cool summers and negligible crime rate, a mix of retired army officers and civil servants, as well as some who have made good working in the Persian Gulf, have been drawn to live in Abbottabad. The vacation high season begins in June, when families from the hot plains of Pakistan travel there to cool off and to revel in its soft mountain breezes. The golfers among them can play on one of the country's finest courses. The overall vibe is a little more country club than the rest of Pakistan's heaving, teeming, smog-filled cities.

Despite Abbottabad's relative obscurity, foreigners are not unknown here. Western adventurers drawn by the Karakoram Highway, which wends its way through the city before heading north toward China, three hundred miles away, occasionally stop off to stock up on camping supplies or linger at an ice-cream shop. And wealthy Afghan refugees fleeing the instability in their country have built large walled compounds to hide their womenfolk.

It was to the placid environs of Abbottabad half a decade after his great victory on 9/11 that Osama bin Laden decided to retire. It was one of the last places in Pakistan that anyone would have suspected he might be living—far enough from the tribal regions of Pakistan, where pretty much every observer believed he was based, so that he would be hard to find, yet not so far away that he couldn't communicate relatively easily by courier with his key lieutenants, many of whom lived in those regions. It was also close to Pakistan-held Kashmir and the Kashmiri militant groups to which bin Laden had long allied himself, a support network that might come in handy.

By the spring of 2011 the terrorist mastermind was in his sixth year of hiding out in the Bilal Town neighborhood of Abbottabad. It isn't the city's glitziest address, but with its porticoed white villas interspersed with small shops selling fruits and vegetables, it is certainly a reasonably pleasant place to live.

Seven years earlier, the man whom bin Laden had entrusted with his life, someone known within al-Qaeda by the alias Abu Ahmed al-Kuwaiti—"the Kuwaiti who is the father of Ahmed"—had begun assembling some small parcels of agricultural land on the fringes of Bilal Town. The Kuwaiti purchased the land over the course of four transactions in 2004 and 2005, paying about $50,000 and buying most of the plots from a local doctor, Qazi Mahfooz Ul Haq. Haq recalls the Kuwaiti as a "very simple, modest, humble type of man" who spoke the local language, Pashto, dressed in traditional Pashtun clothing, and said that he was buying the land for an uncle.

The Kuwaiti hired an architect at Modern Associates, a family-run firm in Abbottabad, to design a residential compound suitable for a family of a dozen or more. The specs for the building were not unusual for these parts: two stories with four bedrooms on each floor, each with its own private bathroom. "One of my students could have done the design," recalls Junaid Younis, the owner of Modern Associates. The architecture firm submitted the drawings of the house to the local planning board, and permission for its construction was duly granted.

Sometime in 2005, bin Laden's compound began rising from what were once open fields. Locals estimate that the sprawling one-acre complex cost in the low hundreds of thousands of dollars to build. During its construction, a third floor was added to the building. No planning permission was sought for this addition, a common enough dodge in a part of the world where paying property taxes is regarded as a sucker's game. But there was a more compelling reason to keep this alteration as secret as possible: the unauthorized floor was for the exclusive use of Osama bin Laden and his newest and youngest wife, a spirited Yemeni named Amal.

The third floor, where bin Laden would live with Amal, was a little different from the others. Unlike the floors below it, it had windows on only one of its four sides, and they were opaque. Four of the five windows were just small slits well above eye level. A tiny terrace leading off the floor was shielded from prying eyes by a seven-foot-high wall designed to conceal even someone as tall as the six-foot-four bin Laden.

Habitually dressed in light-colored flowing robes, a dark vest, and a prayer cap, bin Laden rarely left the second and third floors of the house during the more than five years he lived there. When he did, it was only to take a walk in the compound's kitchen garden. A makeshift tarpaulin over a section of the garden was designed to keep even those walks a secret from the all-seeing American satellites that traversed the skies overheard.

It must have been quite confining for an outdoorsman like bin Laden, who routinely boasted of his ability to ride a horse for forty miles without a break, and who regularly took his sons on arduous hikes through the Afghan mountains that could last for more than twelve hours. Bin Laden was also an avid soccer player, and quite adept at volleyball. Before the fall of the Taliban, one of his great satisfactions had been to take his various wives and children out for expeditions into the vast deserts of southern Afghanistan to practice shooting and toughen them up for the life on the run that he firmly believed would one day be their collective lot.

A COMFORTABLE RETIREMENT

Now bin Laden was living in Abbottabad in a prison of his own making. But there were some compensations. For one thing, he was a long way from the American drone strikes that were steadily picking off many of his longtime aides, the cream of al-Qaeda, in Pakistan's tribal regions some two hundred miles to the west. And he certainly wasn't cowering in a dank cave, as many of the "infidels" imagined. Nor was he suffering from debilitating kidney disease, as was often reported in the West. In fact, he was in fine fettle, graying and slowing down only a little as he approached the middle of his fifth decade. Most important for a committed family man, he was surrounded by three of his wives and a dozen of his children and grandchildren.

Bin Laden's first wife, his tall, beautiful Syrian cousin Najwa, was not among them. They had married in 1974, when he was seventeen and she was fifteen, and she had faithfully stuck with him as he embarked on a life of jihad that took him to Pakistan and Afghanistan during the 1980s, and later Sudan and Afghanistan again in the late 1990s. But after living for five years in grim Taliban-controlled Afghanistan, Najwa had had enough. During the summer of 2001, she started insisting that she wanted to go home and see her family in Syria. She had, after all, given bin Laden eleven children and almost three decades of her life, a good portion of which she had spent with him in exile, and so he eventually agreed to her request. But he allowed her to take only three of their as-yet-unmarried children with her to Syria, insisting that their eleven-year-old daughter, Iman, and seven-year old son, Ladin, stay with him.

Bin Laden was the absolute monarch of his household, and there was nothing Najwa could do to protest this decision. As she was leaving Afghanistan, bin Laden told her—sensing perhaps that this would be the last time he would see her—"I will never divorce you, Najwa. Even if you hear I have divorced you, it is not true." Najwa left Afghanistan on September 9, 2001, the same day that bin Laden's assassins murdered Ahmad Shah Massoud, the leader of the few Afghan forces then still fighting the Taliban, and only forty-eight hours before al-Qaeda's attacks on Washington and New York. Perhaps bin Laden knew that the gentle Najwa, who had married him long before he had devoted his life to the rigors of holy war, wouldn't be able to handle the aftermath of the attacks on America.

Still, a decade after 9/11—even with his first wife long gone—bin Laden had the satisfaction of having his three other wives living with him in his Abbottabad hideaway. They ranged in age from the twenty-nine-year-old Amal to the sixty-two-year-old Khairiah, who had recently and happily reappeared in bin Laden's life quite unexpectedly after an absence of nine years.

Bin Laden had married Khairiah in 1985, when he was twenty-eight and she was thirty-five, an inordinately late age in Saudi Arabia for a woman to get married. Bin Laden's motivation to marry Khairiah was in part religious. He believed that marrying a "spinster" was something that Allah would regard favorably because, should they have children, it would increase the number of Muslims in the world. Before her marriage, Khairiah had had something of an independent career as a teacher of deaf-mute children. She also held a PhD and hailed from a wealthy, distinguished family that claims descent from the Prophet Mohammed. Khairiah had taken the position of bin Laden's second wife only because she wanted to be married to a man she believed to be a true holy warrior, whose exploits fighting the Soviets in Afghanistan were becoming well known in Saudi Arabia in the mid-1980s. Four years after she married bin Laden they had a boy, Hamza, and from then on, Khairiah was known as Um Hamza, "the mother of Hamza."

As the Taliban regime was imploding during the fall of 2001, Khairiah fled Afghanistan for neighboring Iran, together with her beloved Hamza and several of bin Laden's children from his other wives. For years they all lived under some form of house arrest in the Iranian capital of Tehran. Their conditions were not uncomfortable, with time for shopping trips, PlayStation video games, and visits to swimming pools, but they were still in a cage, albeit a gilded one. The Iranian regime likely saw bin Laden's family members as useful bargaining chips in the event of some kind of peace deal with the United States.

However, by the time al-Qaeda militants abducted Heshmatollah Attarzadeh-Niyaki, an Iranian diplomat, in late 2008 near his home in the western Pakistani city of Peshawar, the Iranian regime had long given up on making any accommodation with the United States. After holding the diplomat for more than a year, the militants quietly released him back to Iran in the spring of 2010. This was part of a deal that finally allowed bin Laden's family to end their years of house arrest in Iran.

Sometime during the blazing summer of 2010, Khairiah, now in her early sixties, managed to travel from western Iran to North Waziristan, a flinty, remote tribal region of Pakistan that lies more than fifteen hundred miles to the east of Tehran; the journey took her across tough mountain ranges and through some of the harshest deserts on Earth. She then traveled on to Abbottabad to reunite with her husband after almost a decade. Her one disappointment was that her only child, Hamza, who had traveled with her from Iran, remained in the remote Pakistani tribal regions that were then home to many of al-Qaeda's leaders.

The next wife in seniority in the bin Laden compound was Siham bin Abdullah bin Husayn, an exact contemporary of the fifty-four-year-old al-Qaeda leader, who, like his oldest wife, Khairiah, hailed from a distinguished Saudi family that claimed descent from the Prophet. For bin Laden, who tried—at least in his own mind—to model his life on that of the Prophet, this direct connection to the founder of Islam through his wives no doubt had special meaning. Living in the Abbottabad compound with his mother and father was Siham's first son, Khalid, age twenty-three.

Siham had been a student at King Abdulaziz University in the holy city of Medina, pursuing a degree in religious studies, when bin Laden first proposed marriage to her in the mid-1980s. She insisted on completing her education as a condition of accepting his proposal, a request that bin Laden acceded to only reluctantly. Siham's parents opposed the match because bin Laden already had other wives, but she went ahead with the marriage anyway because she had a steadfast belief in bin Laden's burgeoning jihad project, fighting the Soviets in Afghanistan. By the time they were married, bin Laden was well on his way to becoming an authentic jihadist war hero; Siham found this intriguing. When bin Laden gave her the gold jewelry that is traditional for the wedding dowry, Siham donated it all to the Afghan jihad.

Siham went on to obtain her MA while studying in Medina, and later her PhD in Koranic grammar while she was living with bin Laden in Sudan in the mid-1990s. A poet and an intellectual, she would often edit bin Laden's writings. As a result of her husband's only grudging acceptance of her pursuit of a graduate education, she dedicated her PhD dissertation not to him, but to her children. Her brother says that she was "chained" to bin Laden only because of her intense love for them.

The slot for the fourth wife that is sanctioned by Islamic law had opened up for bin Laden when he was living in Sudan in the mid-1990s. One of his more senior wives, a Saudi named Khadija, confronted him in the flyblown Sudanese capital of Khartoum, telling him that she hadn't signed up for the life of jihad and poverty-stricken exile that the Saudi billionaire's son had recently adopted, and that she wanted a divorce. Bin Laden granted her request, and soon started thinking about the qualities he was looking for in his new wife.

According to the Yemeni cleric who made the match, "She had to be religious . . . and young enough not to feel jealous of the Sheikh's [bin Laden's] other wives." The cleric told bin Laden he had in mind someone to whom he had given religious instruction. She was very pious, he said; she came from a modest family, so she could deal with the hardships that life with the leader of al-Qaeda would obviously entail; and she "really believed that being a dutiful and obedient wife would give her a place in heaven." Her name was Amal Ahmed al-Sadah.

Bin Laden sent an envoy in 1999 to speak to Amal's mother in her home in the provincial backwater of Ibb, a small town some one hundred miles south of the Yemeni capital. At first the marriage proposal was couched as coming from a businessman from the Yemeni province of Hadramaut. There was an element of truth to this, as the bin Laden family owns a major construction business in the Middle East and originally hails from Hadramaut, but as the marital negotiations continued, the envoy let it be known that the suitor was in fact Osama bin Laden. This didn't elicit much reaction, for bin Laden wasn't yet a household name and al-Qaeda had not yet dispatched a bomb-laden boat to try to sink the USS *Cole* as it anchored off the coast of Yemen, as the organization would do a year later.

Amal, a pretty, pale, smiling teenager with an unruly mop of black hair and little in the way of education, eventually consented to the union with the mysterious Mr. bin Laden, saying, "God has blessed it." Bin Laden dispatched one of his most trusted bodyguards from Afghanistan with a $5,000 dowry, some of which was used to buy Amal gold jewelry and festive clothes. Her cousin later recalled, "We agreed that he could marry Amal because we knew that bin

Laden was a good Muslim, very pious, but we did not know much more," adding that the dowry was "very modest." (This would have been no surprise to anyone who had dealt with al-Qaeda's leader before. As is the case with the offspring of some rich families, he was notoriously cheap.)

In 2000 the excited young bride, together with some of her male relatives, made the long journey from Yemen to Kandahar in southern Afghanistan, where bin Laden was then living. There, bin Laden hosted a well-attended wedding party—all male, of course—where poems were declaimed, lambs were slaughtered for the marriage feast, and fusillades of "happy fire" were shot into the air. The women had their own, more modest party as well.

Initially, bin Laden's other wives were furious about his new consort, who was barely seventeen. Bin Laden had told his family that Amal was a "mature" woman of thirty, who knew the Koran by heart. It is not clear whether the Yemeni cleric who had arranged the match had simply fooled bin Laden, or whether bin Laden was lying to his other wives. Bin Laden's chief bodyguard recalls that in the early days of his marriage to Amal, his boss "dragged around this fourth marriage like a ball and chain," though bin Laden's feelings would later change.

Amal's father traveled from Yemen to Afghanistan to look in on his daughter a year or so before the 9/11 attacks. After waiting in Pakistan, where al-Qaeda members seemed to be checking to see if he had been followed, and then enduring a tortuous trip through Afghanistan, he was taken to a house embedded in a cave system where his daughter was staying, likely in the mountains of Tora Bora, in eastern Afghanistan. On the second day of his visit, his son-in-law dropped by. Bin Laden, who was carrying a gun, seemed jumpy and worried that his father-in-law might be some kind of spy.

Bin Laden regaled his father-in-law with stories of the various assassination attempts he had survived. Once these anecdotes were finished, he thanked Amal's father effusively for the great job he had done raising his daughter, saying, "Thank you for this great up-bringing. I didn't expect an upbringing like this. She is like me." Bin Laden splurged, slaughtering a bull in honor of his father-in-law's visit. And Amal, now fully aware of whom she had married, told her father that she wanted to be a martyr at bin Laden's side.

When she was a teenager, Amal told one of her male cousins that when she grew up she wanted to "go down in history." Her cousin retorted, "Your history is in the kitchen," to which Amal tartly shot back, "You mean history is reserved for you men?" Now, with bin Laden as her husband, she had a real chance at a place in the history books, an opportunity that an obscure town in rural Yemen would never have provided.

Bin Laden married Amal when he was forty-three, but the twenty-six-year age difference between them did not stand in the way of what seemed to be a real love match. Their firstborn, Safia, came into the world a year or so before the 9/11 attacks. Bin Laden told acquaintances that he named her after the Safia who was a seventh-century contemporary of the Prophet Mohammed and had killed a Jew. He explained that he hoped that his daughter Safia would also grow up to kill Jews. Amal went on to bear four more children, including two while she and her husband were living in Abbottabad.

His family life in Abbottabad was a source of genuine solace for bin Laden, who believed deeply that polygamy and procreation were religious obligations. To his close male friends he often repeated a saying attributed to the Prophet Mohammed: "Marry and increase in number because with you I increase the nation [of Muslims]." To other friends, he joked, "I don't understand why people take only one wife. If you take four wives you live like a groom." (This seems to be the only recorded joke bin Laden ever made.)

Life in the Abbottabad compound certainly wasn't luxurious, but for Amal it wasn't much different from the life she had known while growing up in rural Yemen. For their meat consumption, the more than a dozen members of the bin Laden family—together with the trusted Kuwaiti, his brother, and their families—subsisted on two goats a week, which were slaughtered inside the compound. Milk came from cows that were housed in concrete sheds, eggs from some one hundred chickens kept in cages, honey from bees in a hive, and vegetables, such as cucumbers, from the spacious kitchen garden. This homegrown produce was supplemented by cans of Sasso olive oil and cartons of Quaker Oats bought locally.

If their diet was relatively meager, their social life was nonexistent. Separated from other homes by green fields, the compound was approachable by a single dirt road. The building's twelve-foot-high walls, barbed wire, and security cameras gave it the look of a minimum-security prison, and did little to encourage casual visitors. If neighborhood kids accidentally hit a cricket ball over the walls of the compound, they were given fifty rupees (sixty cents) and told to buy a new one. If they summoned the courage to knock on the main gate of the compound, eager to play with the many children who lived inside, they would have to knock for ten or twenty minutes before anyone came out. The children who eventually did come out would not give their names and were notably religious, stopping their play when the call to prayer issued from nearby mosques.

Inside its walls the compound was bare of paint, and in keeping with bin Laden's ultrafundamentalist beliefs, there were no pictures. It had no air-conditioning and only a few rudimentary gas heaters—in an area where summers can top a hundred degrees Fahrenheit and winters mean snow. As a result, the electricity and gas bills for a compound of its size and the two dozen or so who lived there were minuscule, averaging fifty dollars a month. Beds for the various family members were made from boards hammered together. It was as if the compound's inhabitants were living at a makeshift but long-term campsite.

Living an austere life was nothing new for the bin Laden family. For decades al-Qaeda's leader had embraced a survivalist ethic, rejecting all the conveniences of modern life. When bin Laden moved to scorching Sudan, he insisted that his family didn't need air-conditioning, and when he later moved to the deserts of Kandahar, the family compound had no running water. A Libyan militant who was once close to bin Laden remembers the leader of al-Qaeda telling his followers, "You should learn to sacrifice everything from modern life, like electricity, air-conditioning, refrigerators, gasoline. If you are living the luxury life, it's very hard to evacuate and go to the mountains to fight."

With the exception of one of the courier's sons, who attended a madrassa, the children living in the compound did not go to school, so bin Laden's two older wives, both academics, taught them the fine points of Arabic and the Koran in a bedroom on the second floor of the main building, which served as a makeshift classroom. Using a whiteboard, the two wives routinely administered tests of the children's knowledge, and bin Laden, who fancied himself something of a poet, taught them poetry. And almost every day, bin Laden, a strict disciplinarian, delivered an address to all his family about how the children should be brought up, outlined dos and don'ts for family members, and preached a religious sermon.

Bin Laden had long given serious thought to how best to conduct the polygamous life that his hiding place in Abbottabad afforded him. As a university student, he had had lengthy discussions with his best friend about how properly to manage more than one wife and to do so in a God-fearing "Islamic way." The two friends agreed that they would never follow the path that bin Laden's own father had chosen, which was constantly to divorce and remarry—so many times that he ended up having some twenty wives. The friend recalls bin Laden saying that he would marry only the four wives sanctioned by Islam and would treat each one absolutely equally. "You have to be fair, you have to give equal justice between all of them, you have to divide the time, to give each one what is enough for her," the two friends agreed.

By virtue of her age and stern temperament, the oldest wife, Khairiah, was highest in the pecking order, but there was little fighting among bin Laden's spouses. All of them had gone into marriage knowing that it would be a polygamous arrangement, something they believed to be sanctioned by God. To ensure harmony— whether in Saudi Arabia in the 1980s, Sudan in the early '90s, or later in Afghanistan and Abbottabad—bin Laden created a dedicated living space for each wife in all his homes. On the Abbottabad compound, each wife had her own separate apartment with its own kitchen (featuring an exhaust system that was nothing more than an upside-down metal bucket suspended over a stove, with crude pipes funneling kitchen smells to the outside). The third floor of the main building was Amal's domain, while on the floor beneath her lived the two much-older wives.

For someone who maintained ultra-fundamentalist views about the proper role of women in society, bin Laden accorded his wives some respect, telling them that if they found his life of holy war too hard, they could leave him. He approvingly quoted the Koranic verse "Husband and wife should live together equitably, or separate in kindness." And he never raised his voice in anger at his wives, perhaps because, as her only child, he had had an exceptionally close relationship with his mother. As an adult, he still doted on his mother, kissing her hands and feet whenever he saw her, and (when he was still able to do so) calling her often to make small talk about what she was cooking that day.

A clue as to how the fifty-four-year-old bin Laden was able to give each wife "what is enough for her" may be the Avena syrup—a sort of natural Viagra made from wild oats—that was found at the compound after his death. Since bin Laden refused to ingest chemicals in any form, any medicine he took was made of herbs or other natural sources.

Although they lived on the Abbottabad compound with bin Laden, his trusted courier "the Kuwaiti," the Kuwaiti's brother, and their wives and children lived in abject poverty. Bin Laden paid the courier and his brother about 12,000 rupees a month each, a little more than $100, a reflection not only of bin Laden's usual stinginess but also of the fact that al-Qaeda's coffers were nearly empty. In jewelry stores in Abbottabad and in the nearby city of Rawalpindi, one of the brothers occasionally bought and sold gold bangles and rings in transactions totaling about $1,500. No doubt this helped them make ends meet.

A modest one-story building housed the Kuwaiti and his family. A seven-foot-high wall separated it from the main house, where bin Laden lived. The Kuwaiti's wife, Mariam, rarely went into the big house except to do cleaning; only once, in the spring of 2011, did she catch a glimpse of a strange, tall man speaking Arabic in the big house. Her husband had explained to her years earlier that there was a stranger living on the compound and had instructed her never to talk about him. Bin Laden was hiding even from some of the people living on his own compound.

In his top-floor sanctuary, bin Laden whiled away the days with Amal. Whitewashed walls and large glass windows that looked out only over the small, high-walled terrace kept things relatively bright in their bedroom, but the space was cramped for a man as tall as bin Laden. The bedroom ceiling was low, no more than seven feet high. A tiny bathroom off to the side had green tile on the walls but none on the floor; a rudimentary toilet that was no more than a hole in the ground, over which they had to squat; and a cheap plastic shower. In this bathroom bin Laden regularly applied Just for Men dye to his hair and beard to try to maintain a youthful appearance now that he was in his mid-fifties. Next to the bedroom was a kitchen the size of a large closet, and across the hall was bin Laden's study, where he kept his books on crude wooden shelves and tapped away on his computer.

The tight living quarters in Abbottabad somewhat replicated his country retreat in the mountains of Tora Bora, a modest mud house he had built with his own hands and lived in for the latter half of 1996 and several months in early 1997. It was there that bin Laden had seemed happiest. In Tora Bora, about a three hours' bumpy drive from the nearest small city, he and his closest followers had grown their own crops, baked their own bread, and lived a back-to-the-earth lifestyle. But in Tora Bora bin Laden had roamed freely across the mountains, breathing the alpine air, which he told visitors was one of his great satisfactions.

In Abbottabad, bin Laden was now forced to stay indoors and, of course, had a great deal of time to kill. He almost certainly kept up the religious practices of his youth, rising before dawn and praying seven times a day, twice more than is required in traditional Islam. A news junkie, he monitored Al Jazeera television and BBC radio closely. In a bare room on the ground floor of his house, he sat wrapped in a blanket against the winter cold, reviewing old videos of himself on a cheap TV. He also watched press conferences being given by the hated U.S. president Barack Obama, whom the leaders of al-Qaeda despised as much as they had President George W.

Bush. Bin Laden's top deputy, Ayman al-Zawahiri, publicly referred to Obama as a "house Negro," implying that he was a slave who received better treatment from his white masters than that meted out to a slave who worked in the fields.

Bin Laden spent much of his enforced leisure time writing on a variety of themes, particularly Palestine, but also the environment and the global economy. And he voraciously read books hostile to U.S. foreign policy, with titles such as *Rogue State: A Guide to the World's Only Superpower.* Bin Laden particularly enjoyed *Imperial Hubris: Why the West Is Losing the War on Terror,* a blistering critique of Bush's foreign policy, which, in a nice irony, had been written by Michael Scheuer, who had led the CIA's bin Laden unit and spent years assembling the intelligence to find and kill bin Laden. Bin Laden obsessed about the issue of Palestine even when he was in his early teens, so books critical of Israel by President Jimmy Carter and the American political scientists Stephen Walt and John Mearsheimer were also on his reading list.

It was a comfortable, if confining, retirement for al-Qaeda's leader. He was able to indulge his hobbies of reading and following the news, and of course he continued rigorously to observe the tenets of Islam. He was attended by three of his wives and surrounded by many of the children he loved. For the world's most wanted fugitive, it was not a bad life. Not bad at all.

1 9/11 AND AFTER

BIN LADEN WAS FIXATED ON THE IDEA that the United States was weak. In the years leading up to 9/11, he often spoke of its weakness to his followers, citing such examples as the U.S. withdrawal from Vietnam in the 1970s, and from Somalia two decades later, following the Black Hawk Down incident, in which eighteen U.S. servicemen were killed. Bin Laden enjoyed recounting how al-Qaeda had slipped fighters into Somalia in 1993 to help train the Somali clans battling American forces, who were there as part of a UN mission to feed starving Somalis. "Our boys were shocked by the low morale of the American soldier, and they realized that the American soldier was just a paper tiger," bin Laden exulted. His disciples eagerly agreed with the man they loved like a father.

Bin Laden assured his men that the Americans "love life like we love death" and would be too scared to put boots on the ground in Afghanistan. Look at what a drubbing bin Laden and his men had inflicted on the Soviets in Afghanistan! And America was every bit as feeble as the former Soviet Union, bin Laden told his nodding acolytes. Those in his inner circle who had any niggling doubt about this analysis largely kept it to themselves.

As plans for the 9/11 attacks took a more definite shape, some of al-Qaeda's senior officials expressed concern that the coming attacks might anger the Taliban leader Mullah Omar, to whom bin Laden had, at least notionally, sworn an oath of allegiance. During the five years that bin Laden had been the Taliban's honored guest, Mullah Omar and other Taliban leaders had made it clear that al-Qaeda could not use Afghanistan to conduct a freelance war against America. Bin Laden thought he could help inoculate himself against any anger caused by the attacks on the United States by offering the Taliban a highly desirable head on a platter: that of Ahmad Shah Massoud, the storied leader of what remained of the anti-Taliban resistance in Afghanistan. For the Massoud hit, bin Laden recruited two Tunisian Belgian al-Qaeda assassins, who disguised themselves as television journalists keen to interview the legendary guerrilla leader.

During the summer of 2001, while al-Qaeda groomed the Massoud assassins, the leaders of the group were putting the finishing touches on their plans for the spectacular attacks on America's East Coast. Ramzi bin al-Shibh, a key plotter based in Hamburg, sent a message to bin Laden on Thursday, September 6, saying that the attacks on Washington and New York would take place the following Tuesday. And on September 9, bin Laden heard the welcome news that his assassins had mortally wounded Massoud, for whom he had long harbored contempt. Now the stage was set for what bin Laden believed would be his greatest triumph: a spectacular strike on the country that was Islam's greatest enemy because it propped up the godless dictatorships and monarchies of the Middle East and, of course, Israel. With one tremendous blow against America, bin

Laden would get the United States to pull out of the Middle East, and then Israel would fall, as would the Arab autocracies, to be replaced by Taliban-style regimes. This was bin Laden's fervent hope and belief.

FROM THE DAY that President George W. Bush took office, January 20, 2001, every morning, six days a week, CIA official Michael Morell briefed the president about what the intelligence community believed to be the most pressing national security issues. Reed-thin and in his early forties, Morell spoke in terse, cogent paragraphs. On August 6, eight months after Bush was inaugurated, Morell met with the president at his vacation home in Texas to tell him of the CIA's assessment that bin Laden was determined to strike inside the United States. This briefing was heavily colored by the fact that Ahmed Ressam, an Algerian on the fringes of al-Qaeda, had recently pled guilty to charges that he planned to detonate a bomb at Los Angeles International Airport in mid-December 1999. The August 6 briefing noted that the FBI had come across information indicating "preparations for hijackings or other types of attacks." After the briefing, Bush continued to enjoy the longest presidential vacation in three decades.

On the morning of September 11, 2001, in Sarasota, Florida, Morell gave the President's Daily Brief as usual. There was nothing memorable in it. Together with political advisor Karl Rove and press secretary Ari Fleischer, Morell got into the president's motorcade to head to the local elementary school where Bush planned to meet with some students. During the ride over, Fleischer asked Morell if he had heard anything about a plane hitting the World Trade Center. Morell said he hadn't, but would check it out with the CIA Ops Center. Officials at the Ops Center confirmed the news and quickly demolished a widely held perception: it wasn't a small plane that had wandered off course; it was a large commercial jet.

At the elementary school, where Bush was reading a story about a pet goat to a group of second-graders, the news came on TV that a second jet had hit the Trade Center. Bush was hustled out of the school to head to Air Force One, which took off for Barksdale Air Force Base near Shreveport, Louisiana. Fleischer was keeping careful notes that day, and the first time he recorded bin Laden's name was at 10:41 a.m., when Chief of Staff Andy Card said to Bush on Air Force One, "It smells like Osama bin Laden to me." By then, both towers of the Trade Center had collapsed and one of the hijacked planes had plowed into the Pentagon. Bush's blood was boiling, and he vowed to himself, "We are going to find out who did this, and kick their ass."

THAT SAME MORNING, bin Laden told Ali al-Bahlul, a bodyguard who doubled as his media maven, that it was "very important to see the news today." Bahlul was eager to comply with his boss's wishes; bin Laden ruled al-Qaeda just as he lorded over his own household, as an unquestioned absolute monarch. On this day, al-Qaeda's leader was, as always, surrounded by his most trustworthy bodyguards, mostly Yemenis and Saudis. Like other members of al-Qaeda, the bodyguards had sworn a religious oath of personal obedience to bin Laden, rather than to his militant organization. (Similarly, those who joined the Nazi party swore an oath of allegiance to Adolf Hitler, rather than to Nazism.)

Bin Laden had founded al-Qaeda in 1988, and since then he had consolidated more and more power as the unquestioned, absolute leader of the group. The conventional view is that Ayman al-Zawahiri, an Egyptian doctor and al-Qaeda's longtime second in command, was bin Laden's "brain." But in making the most important strategic shift in al-Qaeda's history—identifying the United States as its key enemy, rather than Middle Eastern regimes—bin Laden brushed aside Zawahiri's obsessive focus on overthrowing the Egyptian government. Bin Laden also kept Zawahiri in the dark for years about al-Qaeda's most important operation—the planning for the 9/11 attacks—apprising his deputy only during the summer of 2001.

To his followers bin Laden was truly a hero, someone who they knew had given up a life of luxury as the son of a Saudi billionaire. Instead, he was living a life of danger and poverty in the service of holy war, and in person he was both disarmingly modest and deeply devout. Members of al-Qaeda modeled themselves on the man they called "the Sheikh," hanging on his every pronouncement, and when they addressed him, they asked his permission to speak. His followers *loved* him. Abu Jandal, a Yemeni who was one of his bodyguards, described his first meeting with bin Laden in 1997 as "beautiful." Another of bin Laden's bodyguards characterized his boss as "a very charismatic person who could persuade people simply by his way of talking. One could say that he 'seduced' many young men."

So, on the morning of September 11, bin Laden's crew of bodyguards eagerly set out with the man they regarded as their "father," leaving his main base near the southern city of Kandahar for the mountainous region of Khost, in eastern Afghanistan. Bahlul rigged up a TV satellite receiver in a minibus that was part of bin Laden's caravan of vehicles, but when they reached Khost, he found it hard to get a television signal, so bin Laden tuned his radio to the BBC's Arabic service.

Bin Laden told his followers, "If he [the newsreader] says: 'We have just received this . . .' it means the brothers have struck." At about 5:30 in the evening local time, the BBC announcer said, "I have just received this news. Reports from the United States say that an airliner was destroyed upon crashing into the World Trade Center in New York." Bin Laden told his men to "be patient." Soon came the news of a second jet flying into the South Tower of the Trade Center. Bin Laden's bodyguards exploded with joy; their leader truly was conducting a great cosmic war against the infidels!

About eight hundred miles to the south, in the heaving Pakistani megacity of Karachi, some of bin Laden's most trusted lieutenants had also gathered to watch television coverage of the attacks. They were Khalid Sheikh Mohammed, the portly commander of the 9/11 operation; Ramzi bin al-Shibh, an intensely religious Yemeni who was a key coordinator of the attacks; and Mustafa al-Hawsawi, the Saudi paymaster who had transferred tens of thousands of dollars to the hijackers living in the States for their flight lessons and living expenses.

Also watching TV with the three architects of 9/11 were some other al-Qaeda "brothers." As the television showed the hijacked planes flying into the Trade Center, the brothers started weeping with joy, prostrating themselves, and shouting "God is great!" Bin al-Shibh admonished them, "Patience! Patience! Follow the news! The matter is not over yet!" Then came the attack on the Pentagon and the news of the fourth aircraft, which went down in Pennsylvania. The men from al-Qaeda embraced each other and wept again, this time in sadness for the brothers who had died on the hijacked planes.

Bin Laden was confident that the United States would respond to the attacks on New York and Washington only with cruise missile strikes, as it had done three years earlier, following al-Qaeda's attacks against two American embassies in Africa in 1998. At most, he expected the kind of air strikes that the United States and NATO had employed against the Serbs during the air war in Kosovo in 1999. The paper tiger might bare its fangs, but it wouldn't go in for the kill.

In washington, news soon circulated that a Palestinian terrorist organization, the Democratic Front for the Liberation of Palestine, had claimed responsibility for the attacks. Bush summoned Morell, asking, "What do you make of this?"

Morell replied, "The DFLP has a history of terrorism against Israel, but its capabilities are limited. It does not have the resources and reach to do this."

In the early afternoon, Air Force One headed from Louisiana to Offutt Air Force Base near Omaha, Nebraska, home of the U.S. Strategic Command, which controls America's nuclear missiles. Bush asked to see Morell again, and pushed him for his opinion about who was behind the attacks. "I don't have any intelligence as yet, so what I am going to say is my personal view," Morell said. "There are two terrorist states capable of conducting such a complex operation—Iran and Iraq—but neither has much to gain and everything to lose from attacking the U.S." He added, "The responsible party is almost certainly a nonstate actor, and I have no doubt the trail will lead to bin Laden and al-Qaeda."

"How soon will we know for sure?" Bush asked.

Morell reviewed how long it took for the United States to determine the culprits in several previous terrorist attacks. "We knew it was al-Qaeda within two days of the bombings of the U.S. embassies in Africa in 1998, but it took months in the case of the Cole bombing. Bottom line, sir, we may know very soon or it may take some time," Morell concluded.

In fact, it would be only a matter of hours. When Bush landed in Nebraska at around 3:30 p.m., he spoke for the first time to CIA director George Tenet. Tenet told him that the attacks "looked, smelled, and tasted like bin Laden," particularly because the names of two known al-Qaeda associates, Nawaf al-Hamzi and Khalid al-Mihdhar, had been found on the passenger manifests of one of the crashed planes. For the past several months, as many as sixty CIA employees had known that Hamzi and Mihdhar were living in the United States, but they had inexplicably failed to inform the FBI.

Over the next few days, Bush and his war cabinet set in motion a plan to overthrow the Taliban in Afghanistan—unconventional in that it relied on only some four hundred U.S. Green Berets, Special Operations forces, and CIA personnel on the ground, combined with massive American firepower from the air. And on September 17, Bush signed a highly classified authorization to hunt down and, if necessary, kill the leaders of al-Qaeda, allowing the CIA great leeway as to how to get the job done. One of the top lawyers at the Agency, John Rizzo, who had joined the CIA at the height of the Cold War and who helped draft the authorization, says, "I had never in my experience been part of or ever seen a presidential authorization as far-reaching and as aggressive in scope. It was simply extraordinary." The same day that Bush signed this "finding," he spoke with reporters at the Pentagon, saying, "I want justice. And there's an old poster out West, I recall, that said, 'Wanted, Dead or Alive.'"

ON SEPTEMBER 12, at his office in Islamabad, Jamal Ismail, Abu Dhabi Television's correspondent in Pakistan, received a messenger from bin Laden, who told him, "Jamal, I came last night in a hurry from Afghanistan." The messenger read a statement from bin Laden that, while it did not claim responsibility for the attacks, endorsed them heartily: "We believe what happened in Washington and elsewhere against the Americans was punishment from Almighty Allah, and they were good people who did this. We agree with them." Ismail quickly read this message out on Abu Dhabi TV.

Ismail, a savvy Palestinian journalist long based in Pakistan, had known bin Laden on and off over the course of a decade and a half, having worked as a reporter in the mid-1980s for *Jihad* magazine, an organ funded by bin Laden that publicized the exploits of the Arabs then fighting the Soviets. Ismail had recently resumed his relationship with bin Laden when he interviewed him at length for a documentary profile that aired on Al Jazeera in 1999. Ismail thought that the message from bin Laden about the 9/11 attacks meant that bin Laden likely knew far more than he was publicly saying about the hijackers. "Osama never praised anyone who is non-Muslim. From this I determined he knows something, and he's confident of their identity. They have links," Ismail said.

The Bush administration quickly demanded that the Taliban hand over bin Laden, something that Clinton administration officials had also repeatedly requested, to no avail, in the years following al-Qaeda's attacks on the U.S. embassies in Africa in 1998. Abu Walid al-Misri, an Egyptian living in Kandahar who was close to both al-Qaeda and the Taliban, remembers Mullah Omar pronouncing, "I will not hand over a Muslim to an infidel."

Mullah Omar explained to Taliban insiders, "Islam says that when a Muslim asks for shelter, give the shelter and never hand him over to the enemy. And our Afghan tradition says that, even if your enemy asks for shelter, forgive him and give him shelter. Osama has helped the jihad in Afghanistan, he was with us in bad days and I am not going to give him to anyone."

Rahimullah Yusufzai, one of Pakistan's leading journalists, interviewed Mullah Omar many times in person and on the phone.

Both before and after 9/11, the Taliban leader was adamant on the issue of handing bin Laden over to the Americans, telling Yusufzai, "I don't want to go down in history as someone who betrayed his guest. I am willing to give my life, my regime. Since we have given bin Laden refuge I cannot throw him out now."

Mullah Omar put great store in the power of dreams to guide him. Omar asked Yusufzai, "Have you been to the White House? My brother had a dream that there was a White House in flames. I don't know how to interpret this." Omar was also convinced that Washington's threats of serious consequences if bin Laden weren't handed over were mostly bluster. Mullah Abdul Salam Zaeef, the Taliban's ambassador to Pakistan, says Mullah Omar naïvely believed that the United States would not launch a military operation in Afghanistan: "In Mullah Omar's mind there was a less than ten percent chance that America would resort to anything beyond threats." Zaeef disagreed and told Omar "that America would definitely attack Afghanistan."

Mullah Omar's delusional fanaticism was entirely predictable. When he came to power, he anointed himself the "Commander of the Faithful," a rarely invoked religious title from the seventh century, suggesting that he was the leader not only of the Taliban but of Muslims everywhere. To cement his status as a world-historic Muslim leader, in 1996 Mullah Omar had wrapped himself literally and metaphorically in the "Cloak of the Prophet," a religious relic purportedly worn by the Prophet Mohammed that had been kept in Kandahar for centuries and had almost never been displayed in public. Taking the garment out of storage, Omar ascended the roof of a building and draped the cloak on himself before a crowd of hundreds of cheering Taliban.

The Taliban leader was barely educated and determinedly provincial; in the five years that he controlled Afghanistan, he rarely visited Kabul, his own capital, considering it to be a Sodom and Gomorrah. Other than the Taliban's Radio Sharia, there was no Afghan press to speak of, and so Mullah Omar's understanding of the outside world was nonexistent, a stance he cultivated by assiduously avoiding meeting with non-Muslims. On a rare occasion when he met with a group of Chinese diplomats, they presented him with a small figurine of an animal as a gift. The Taliban leader reacted as if they had handed him "a piece of red-hot coal," so strong was his ultrafundamentalist aversion to images of living beings. In short, Mullah Omar was a dim-witted fanatic with significant delusions of grandeur who believed he was on a mission from Allah. The history of negotiations with such men is not encouraging.

The curtain raiser for how Mullah Omar was going to handle the bin Laden matter was how he had dealt with the issue of the great Buddhas at Bamiyan several months earlier. Looming over the snowcapped central Afghan valley of Bamiyan for more than fifteen hundred years, the two giant Buddhas were carved out of sandstone cliffs, the larger one towering 180 feet above the valley, as high as a fifteen-story building, while the smaller Buddha stood around twelve stories tall. The Buddhas were Afghanistan's most famous tourist attraction. They had survived the Mongolian hordes of Genghis Khan and every wave of invaders since. In May 2001, influenced by al-Qaeda's opposition to any portrayals of the human form, the Taliban announced that they planned to destroy the Buddhas using explosives.

Many countries around the world, including a number of Muslim states, pleaded with the Taliban not to engage in this epic act of cultural vandalism. Their pleas seemed to make Mullah Omar all the more determined to blow up the statues. He told a visiting delegation of Pakistani officials that over the centuries rainfall had formed large holes near the base of the statues, which was God's way of saying, "This is the place you should plant the dynamite to destroy the idols."

Bin Laden himself flew up to Bamiyan from Kandahar in a helicopter to spend half a day helping to wreck the statues. He and an acolyte banged their shoes on the heads of the Buddhas—a great show of disrespect in the Arab world. While bin Laden was in Bamiyan, the Taliban were in the middle of their lengthy effort to destroy the statues, launching a missile at one of the Buddhas, because explosives had not fully destroyed it. Bin Laden then wrote a letter to Mullah Omar congratulating him on the Buddhas' destruction, adding, "I pray to God, after having granted you success in destroying the dead, deaf, and mute false Gods [the Bamiyan Buddhas] that He will grant you success in destroying the living false gods [such as] the United Nations."

A week after 9/11, Mullah Omar convened hundreds of Afghan clerics in Kabul to have them weigh in about what to do with bin Laden. Mullah Omar did not attend the convocation himself, but in a message to the assembly, he said that if the United States had evidence of bin Laden's guilt in the 9/11 attacks, it should be handed over to the Taliban and his fate would then be decided by a group of Afghan religious scholars. At the end of the two-day convention, the assembled clerics called on bin Laden to leave Afghanistan voluntarily so war could be avoided. Bin Laden, of course, didn't accede to this request.

As the convocation of clerics wound down in Kabul, U.S. officials were getting their first break in the hunt for bin Laden, two thousand miles to the southwest of Afghanistan in the Yemeni capital of Sana'a. On September 17, FBI Special Agent Ali Soufan and Robert McFadden, an investigator from the Naval Criminal Investigative Service, began interrogating Abu Jandal, who had served as bin Laden's chief bodyguard for years. Abu Jandal, whose real name is Nasser Ahmed Naser al-Bahri, had been jailed in a Yemeni prison since 2000. The two American investigators, who both spoke Arabic and had significant experience investigating al-Qaeda, used the standard, noncoercive "informed interrogator" approach, in which they pretended to know far more than they did.

The FBI 302s, the official summaries of these interrogations, reveal that Abu Jandal divulged a great deal of information—intelligence that was especially valuable to investigators because it largely concerned the time after 1996 when bin Laden and his followers had moved to Afghanistan, a period of al-Qaeda's history that was then poorly understood. Soufan recalls that the bodyguard "named dozens and dozens of people" in the organization. Abu Jandal explained al-Qaeda's bureaucratic structure, the names and duties of its leaders, the qualifications necessary for membership in the group, the regime in its training camps, the location of its guesthouses in Kabul, and its method of encoded radio communications. He picked out eight of the 9/11 hijackers from photos and he named a dozen members of bin Laden's security detail and revealed that they were armed with SAM-7 missiles, Russian PK machine guns, and rocket-propelled grenades. He explained that al-Qaeda's leader usually traveled in a group of about a dozen bodyguards in a motorcade of three Toyota Hilux pickup trucks, each containing a maximum of five armed guards. And he provided a richly detailed seven-page account of the various machine guns, mortars, mines, sniper rifles, surface-to-air missiles, and radar facilities possessed by al-Qaeda and the Taliban.

Crucially, Abu Jandal told his interrogators that highly effective U.S. Stinger anti-aircraft missiles that had fallen into the hands of al-Qaeda and the Taliban—a legacy of the Afghan war against the Soviets—were chronically short of batteries, vital intelligence for U.S. military planners as they planned for the invasion of Afghanistan.

OVER THE NEXT SEVERAL WEEKS, as the Bush administration planned its response to the 9/11 attacks, the CIA secretly worked to widen existing fissures between the Taliban and al-Qaeda. The Agency was well aware that several Taliban leaders had long been fed up with bin Laden's antics on the world stage. Robert Grenier, the CIA station chief in Pakistan, had intelligence that the number two in the Taliban, Mullah Akhtar Mohammad Osmani, was in particular not a fan of bin Laden's. "We knew how deeply resented the Arabs were. The Afghans were quite conscious, being great manipulators themselves, about the extent to which bin Laden, through selected use of donations, was trying to manipulate them to build up his own loyal following within the Taliban," says Grenier.

In late September, Grenier traveled to the Pakistani province of Balochistan, a sparsely populated desert region the size of Germany, for a clandestine meeting with Mullah Osmani. Mullah Omar himself had sanctioned the meeting between his number two and the CIA officer. For the meeting at the five-star Serena hotel in Quetta, the Baloch capital, Mullah Osmani came with a posse of armed guards festooned with bandoliers. Grenier is not one of the stereotypical CIA operations officers, who tend to be larger-than-life backslappers; he is understated, impeccably dressed, and thoughtful. But his offer to Mullah Osmani was a bold one. Grenier told the Taliban leader, "The Americans are coming. You need to do something to dodge this bullet."

Mullah Osmani, surprisingly, said, "I agree. We have to do something. What's your idea?"

Grenier offered Mullah Osmani a deal—U.S. forces would covertly snatch bin Laden while the Taliban looked the other way—assuring him, "It doesn't get any more simple. You just give us what we need to do it. Step aside; the man disappears. You could claim complete ignorance."

Mullah Osmani took careful notes, saying, "I will go back and I will discuss this with Mullah Omar."

Grenier met with Mullah Osmani again in Quetta on October 2 and presented him with an even more radical proposal: the CIA would assist with a coup against Mullah Omar, with the quid pro quo that bin Laden be handed over after the removal of the Taliban leader. Grenier suggested that Mullah Osmani seize Mullah Omar, cut off his ability to communicate, take control of the radio stations, and read out an announcement along the lines of "We are taking necessary action to save the Taliban movement because the Arabs have failed to meet their obligations as good guests and have perpetrated violence. The Arabs are no longer welcome and should immediately depart the country."

Mullah Osmani listened to all this and said, "The whole idea is very interesting. I'll think about it. Let's set up communication so that we can talk to each other." He seemed buoyed by the discussion and sat down for a robust lunch with the CIA officer. In the end, though, Mullah Osmani didn't go through with the coup idea. Grenier thought perhaps Osmani just could not conceive of himself as the overall leader of the Taliban.

At the same time, bin Laden shuttled between his headquarters in Kandahar and al-Qaeda's guesthouses in Kabul. Once it was obvious that the United States was readying an attack on Afghanistan, bin Laden wrote to Mullah Omar on October 3 to alert him to a recent survey showing that seven out of ten Americans were suffering from psychological problems following the 9/11 attacks. In the letter, bin Laden asserted that an American attack on Afghanistan would begin the United States' self-destruction, causing "long-term economic burdens which will force America to resort to the former Soviet Union's only option: withdrawal from Afghanistan, disintegration, and contraction."

ON OCTOBER 7, as the U.S. Air Force started bombing Taliban positions, bin Laden was in Kandahar meeting with Mullah Mansour, a top Taliban official. Bin Laden and his entourage quickly decamped for Kabul, likely calculating it would be safer there since there were fewer Taliban leadership targets and a larger civilian population. The same day, al-Qaeda's leader made a surprise appearance in a videotape that was shown around the world. Dressed in a camouflage jacket with a submachine gun propped at his side, bin Laden, in his first public comments since 9/11, said that the attacks were revenge for the long-standing Western humiliation of the Muslim world.

"There is America, hit by God in one of its softest spots," bin Laden said. "Its greatest buildings were destroyed, thank God for that. There is America, full of fear from its north to its south, from its west to its east. Thank God for that. What America tastes now is something insignificant compared to what we have tasted for scores of years. Our nation [the Islamic world] has tasted this humiliation and this degradation for more than eighty years."

Despite his approving remarks, bin Laden's initial stance was total denial of his role in the attacks. In late September, for example, al-Qaeda's leader told a Pakistani newspaper, "As a Muslim, I try my best to avoid telling a lie. I had no knowledge of these attacks." The truth is, bin Laden was in something of a bind: if he admitted to his role in the attacks, the Taliban defense that there was no evidence that he was involved would be rendered moot, and Mullah Omar wouldn't have much choice but to hand him over to the United States. Still, bin Laden's ego demanded that he take *some* credit for what he believed to be his greatest accomplishment, and once the United States started to bomb Taliban targets in Afghanistan, he began asserting more ownership of the 9/11 attacks.

Tayseer Allouni of Al Jazeera television was one of the only international correspondents the Taliban had permitted to work in Afghanistan in the years before 9/11. Bin Laden sat down with Allouni for a lengthy interview on October 21. For reasons that Al Jazeera never convincingly elucidated, the network did not air this interview for a year. At one point Al Jazeera explained that the decision not to broadcast the interview was because it wasn't "newsworthy," an explanation that was risible. As this was his only post-9/11 television interview, it would have been news if bin Laden had simply read from the phone book. It seems likely that the Qatari royal family, which owns Al Jazeera, caved to Bush administration pressure not to air the interview, at a time when Bush officials were also putting pressure on American broadcasters not to air "propaganda" from bin Laden.

In fact, the Al Jazeera interview was both wide-ranging and newsworthy, as became apparent three months later, when CNN obtained and broadcast it without Al Jazeera's permission. During the interview, bin Laden appeared relaxed, and for the first time publicly, he explicitly linked himself to the 9/11 attacks. Allouni asked him, "America claims that it has proof that you are behind what happened in New York and Washington. What's your answer?" Bin Laden replied, "If inciting people to do that is terrorism, and if killing those who are killing our sons is terrorism, then let history be our judge that we are terrorists. . . . We practice the good terrorism."

9/11 AND AFTER

Allouni followed up with a key question: "How about the killing of innocent civilians?" Bin Laden countered: "The men that God helped [on September 11] did not intend to kill babies; they intended to destroy the strongest military power in the world, to attack the Pentagon. . . . [The World Trade Center is] not a children's school." Bin Laden gloated as he recounted to the Al Jazeera correspondent the large economic consequences of the attacks: Wall Street stocks lost 16 percent of their value, airlines and air freight companies laid off 170,000 employees, and the hotel chain Intercontinental fired 20,000 workers.

In a meeting with a toadying Saudi supporter a few weeks after 9/11 that was filmed by al-Qaeda's media arm, bin Laden showed that he well understood the propaganda value of the attacks when he explained that the hijackers "said in deeds, in New York and Washington, speeches that overshadowed all other speeches made everywhere else in the world. The speeches are understood by both Arabs and non-Arabs—even by Chinese." He added that 9/11 had even resulted in unprecedented conversions to Islam in countries such as Holland.

By now bin Laden was entering the realm of myth. For his supporters he was the noble "Emir of Jihad," or Prince of Holy War— veneration he did not discourage. Self-consciously mimicking the Prophet Mohammed, who first received the revelations of the Koran in a cave, bin Laden made some of his early videotaped statements from the caves and mountains of Afghanistan. Pro–bin Laden rallies drew tens of thousands in Pakistan, and a beatific image of his face could be found on T-shirts throughout the Muslim world. To his detractors—and there were many, including Muslims—bin Laden was an evil man who had ordered the wanton murder of thousands of civilians in the city many see as the capital of the world. But whether you admired or loathed him, there was little debate that he had become one of the few individuals in modern times who had unequivocally changed the direction of history.

HAMID MIR, the editor of the pro-Taliban Urdu newspaper *Ausaf*, was a natural choice to conduct bin Laden's only print interview following 9/11. On November 6, Mir was taken from his Islamabad office to meet with bin Laden in Kabul. On the way, he was blindfolded and bundled up in a carpet in a van, arriving at an al-Qaeda safe house the morning of November 8. Mir, who had previously been skeptical that bin Laden was behind 9/11, started to change his mind when he saw pictures of Mohammed Atta, the lead hijacker, in the house where the interview took place.

Seemingly unaware that the fall of Kabul was only four days away, bin Laden was in great spirits at their meeting, consuming a hearty breakfast of meat and olives. The Saudi terrorist leader privately admitted everything, reaching over to turn off Mir's tape recorder and saying, "Yes, I did it. Okay. Now play your tape recorder." Mir turned the tape recorder back on, and bin Laden said, "No, I'm not responsible." When Mir asked him how he could justify the killing of so many civilians, bin Laden replied, "America and its allies are massacring us in Palestine, Chechnya, Kashmir, and Iraq. The Muslims have the right to attack America in reprisal."

Mir asked bin Laden to comment on reports that he had tried to acquire nuclear and chemical weapons. Al-Qaeda's leader replied, "I wish to declare that if America used chemical or nuclear weapons against us, then we may respond with chemical and nuclear weapons. We have the weapons as a deterrent." Mir followed up: "Where did you get these weapons from?" Bin Laden responded coyly, "Go to the next question."

After the interview was finished, Mir had tea with bin Laden's deputy, Dr. Ayman al-Zawahiri. "It is difficult to believe that you have nuclear weapons," Mir told Zawahiri.

"Mister Hamid Mir, it is not difficult," Zawahiri replied. "If you have thirty million dollars, you can have these kind of nuclear suitcase bombs from the black market of Central Asia [in the former Soviet Union]."

This claim was entirely nonsensical. Al-Qaeda never possessed anything remotely close to a nuclear weapon, and the supposed black market in Soviet "nuclear suitcase bombs" exists in Hollywood, not in reality. So what was the point of the claim? It seems to have been a clumsy attempt at psychological warfare—an attempt to dissuade the Bush administration from its attacks on Afghanistan. Zawahiri, in particular, was well aware that the American national security establishment was anxious about terrorists acquiring weapons of mass destruction. Indeed, two years earlier, Zawahiri had sanctioned the establishment of al-Qaeda's amateur and poorly funded chemical and biological weapons program precisely because the United States seemed to be so worried about those weapons.

Around the same time that Mir was interviewing al-Qaeda's leaders, another outsider was admitted to meet with members of al-Qaeda's inner circle: Dr. Amer Aziz, a prominent Pakistani surgeon. Dr. Aziz, a Taliban sympathizer who had treated bin Laden in 1999 for a back injury, was summoned to Kabul in early November 2001 to treat Mohammed Atef, a former Egyptian policeman who served as the military commander of al-Qaeda. While examining Atef, Dr. Aziz again met with bin Laden. For years there had been reports that the al-Qaeda leader suffered from kidney disease, but Dr. Aziz said those reports were false: "He was in excellent health. He was walking. He was healthy. I didn't see any evidence of kidney disease. I didn't see any evidence of dialysis."

MANHUNT

As the American bombing campaign intensified and U.S. Special Forces began arriving in small numbers in northern Afghanistan, bin Laden had to start making serious contingency plans for the possibility that the Taliban and his al-Qaeda foot soldiers would soon be on the run. It was a kind of planning that he had neglected to do when he authorized the 9/11 attacks. In mid-October he met with Jalaluddin Haqqani, arguably the most effective military commander of the Taliban, whom bin Laden had known since the early days of the jihad against the Soviets. Together they discussed the possibility of waging a long guerrilla war against the infidel Americans, as they had with the Soviets. Haqqani was sure that the Americans were "creatures of comfort" who would be defeated in the long term. Around the same time, another warlord from the anti-Soviet war, Yunis Khalis, invited bin Laden to move into his territory surrounding Jalalabad in eastern Afghanistan, the region where bin Laden had long maintained his Tora Bora country retreat.

On the same day as the Mir interview, bin Laden attended a memorial ceremony for an Uzbek militant leader who had just been killed in a U.S. air strike. The next day, the Uzbek city of Mazar-e-Sharif, the largest city in northern Afghanistan, fell to the Northern Alliance and a small team of U.S. Special Forces. Twenty-four hours later, a bin Laden security advisor, Dr. Amin ul-Haq, met with tribal elders in the area around Jalalabad and gave them each $10,000 and a horse, in exchange for which the elders agreed to provide refuge to the members of al-Qaeda who soon would be streaming toward Jalalabad, close to the border with Pakistan.

On November 12, Kabul also fell to the Northern Alliance forces. Just ahead of them, bin Laden and his followers hastened from Kabul down the steep, narrow, and winding road to Jalalabad.

A few days later, Mohammed Atef was killed in a U.S. Predator drone air strike. Atef had been not only al-Qaeda's military commander but also bin Laden's chief executive officer, working around the clock to manage al-Qaeda's personnel and operations. He had been bin Laden's closest collaborator in al-Qaeda since the group was founded in 1988. A Saudi member of al-Qaeda recalls that Atef's death "shocked us deeply, because this was the candidate to succeed bin Laden."

Fearing for their safety, bin Laden's son-in-law Muataz made arrangements for three of bin Laden's wives and a number of their younger children to leave Kandahar and cross over the border into Pakistan.

Two months after 9/11, bin Laden had lost his longtime military commander, much of his family was fleeing into exile, and the regime that had provided him his sanctuary was on life support. Instead of goading the United States into departing the Arab world, he was now facing a massive and relentless American bombing campaign and a reinvigorated Northern Alliance, allied to small groups of highly effective U.S. Special Forces and CIA officers. It was a disaster the scale of which bin Laden was only beginning to grasp. He had only one plan now, to flee to Tora Bora, a place he had known intimately since the mid-1980s, and mount there some kind of final stand before slipping away to fight another day.

2 TORA BORA

DESPITE HIS RETREAT, bin Laden seemed undaunted. In the small city of Jalalabad, al-Qaeda's leaders and foot soldiers regrouped, and bin Laden gave rousing pep talks to his men and to local supporters. Around the beginning of the holy month of Ramadan, on November 17, he and Ayman al-Zawahiri and a contingent of bodyguards set off on the bumpy three-hour ride over a narrow mud-and-stone track to the mountains of Tora Bora, where they planned to dig in and face the coming American onslaught.

Tora Bora was an ideal base for guerrilla warfare. The Afghan mujahideen had routinely mounted hit-and-run operations against the Soviets from there during the 1980s because it had easy escape routes by foot to Parachinar, a region of Pakistan that juts like a parrot's beak into Afghanistan. And bin Laden had fought his first major battle against the Soviets in 1987 at Jaji, a valley some twenty miles west of Tora Bora. Although Tora Bora had been the object of several offensives by the Russians, one of them involving thousands of soldiers, dozens of helicopter gunships, and several MiG fighter jets, so solid are the caves that riddle the Spin Ghar Mountains surrounding Tora Bora that the Soviet offensives were held off by a force of not much more than a hundred Afghans.

In 1987, bin Laden started opening a crude road from Jaji to Jalalabad, which was then occupied by the Soviets; it went directly through the mountains of Tora Bora. It was a challenging task, for which he used bulldozers provided by his family's construction company. It took more than six months to build the road, which only four-wheel-drive vehicles could navigate.

When bin Laden was exiled from Sudan in 1996, he chose to live in the Tora Bora settlement of Milawa, high up in the mountains, in an Afghan-style mud house encircled by lookout posts. He told visitors to his Tora Bora retreat, "I really feel secure in the mountains. I really enjoy my life when I'm here." It was in Milawa that bin Laden took his older sons on all-day hiking expeditions, admonishing them, "We never know when war will strike. We must know our way out of the mountains."

His three wives and more than a dozen children did not share bin Laden's joy in living the life of medieval peasants in a place where the only light at night was from gas lanterns and the moon, and the only heat—in a place where fierce blizzards were common—was from a wood-burning metal stove. Hunger was a frequent companion to the bin Laden children, who lived on a subsistence diet of eggs, salty cheese, rice, and bread. Even honored guests, such as leading Palestinian journalist Abdel Bari Atwan, were fed a diet of salty cheese, fried eggs, and bread invariably caked with sand.

Almost a decade and a half after the Battle of Jaji, bin Laden would put his intimate knowledge of Tora Bora and its mountain passes to good use. Once it was obvious that the United States was planning a serious attack on Afghanistan, he envisioned Tora Bora as the place where he could reenact his heroic stand against the Soviets. During the 1987 Jaji engagement, which had also taken place during the holy month of Ramadan, bin Laden and some fifty Arab fighters had held off a much larger group of Soviet soldiers, including Soviet Special Forces, in a battle that lasted about a week before bin Laden and his colleagues were forced to retreat. Bin Laden's stand at the Battle of Jaji received considerable attention in the Arab world, marking his ascension from mere financier of jihad to military commander and becoming a central part of his heroic self-image.

Before traveling to Tora Bora, bin Laden had dispatched Walid bin Attash, one of the planners of the bombing of the USS *Cole* in Yemen, to prepare for his arrival. Around the beginning of November a number of bin Laden's bodyguards started stockpiling food and digging trenches and tunnels between some of the small caves that dot the mountains of Tora Bora.

At the same time, the CIA was closely monitoring bin Laden's whereabouts. The Agency's top official on the ground at that time was Gary Berntsen, a CIA operations officer who spoke Dari, one of the local languages. Shortly after the fall of Kabul, Berntsen received a stream of intelligence reports indicating that bin Laden and a group of his followers had retreated from Kabul to the Jalalabad area. A few days later Berntsen got "multiple hits" from sources on the ground that bin Laden had moved on to the cave complexes of Tora Bora.

The information that a large contingent of al-Qaeda fighters had moved to Tora Bora was relayed back to the Counterterrorist Center at CIA headquarters in Virginia, where it was fed into an electronic map that overlaid data of the Taliban and al-Qaeda positions and the locations of American Special Forces soldiers and CIA officers on the ground, and of allied Afghan forces. That map was then duplicated at Central Command (CENTCOM), the U.S. military headquarters in Tampa, Florida, which was coordinating the war effort. The CIA now predicted that "bin Laden would make a stand along the northern peaks of the Spin Ghar Mountains" at a place called Tora Bora.

In the last week of November, bin Laden gave a speech to his men holed up at Tora Bora, telling them it would be a "grave mistake and taboo to leave before the fight was over." Al-Qaeda's leader again gave a speech along similar lines to his followers in Tora Bora in early December. As his Tora Bora battlefield commander, bin Laden appointed Ibn al-Sheikh al-Libi, a tall, thin Libyan with a regal manner who had fought against the Soviets in Afghanistan and later commanded the Khaldan training camp, where Islamist militants from around the world had trained in the years before 9/11. Bin Laden was convinced that U.S. soldiers would soon land in the Spin Ghar Mountains by helicopter and that his men would inflict heavy losses on them. This never happened. Beyond this vague hope, bin Laden didn't seem to have much of a battle plan, other than somehow to duplicate the mujahideen's successes against the Soviets.

Unlike bin Laden's vision of things, the battle—which took place over an area of some thirty square miles—turned out to be more a series of skirmishes between al-Qaeda's foot soldiers and the ground forces of three fractious local Afghan warlords on the American payroll, punctuated by intense U.S. bombing.

During this time, snow was falling steadily in the mountains, and the temperature at night often dipped below zero. Ayman Saeed Abdullah Batarfi, an articulate Yemeni orthopedic surgeon in his thirties, was asked by bin Laden to treat the injured. Around December 1, Batarfi told bin Laden he would have to send someone back to Jalalabad to get supplies, since he was out of medicine. As the casualties mounted, Batarfi resorted to doing amputations with knives and scissors. He told bin Laden that if they did not leave Tora Bora soon, "no one would stay alive" under the American bombardment. He noted that bin Laden had made few preparations for the Tora Bora battle and seemed preoccupied mostly with making his own escape from the battlefield.

One obstacle to his escape was that he was strapped for cash, money that would be vital if he and his men were to bribe their way out of Tora Bora and pay for shelter and travel expenses. A Yemeni al-Qaeda member traveled into Tora Bora to deliver $3,000 to the al-Qaeda leader. Bin Laden also borrowed $7,000 from a local cleric.

Back in Washington and at CENTCOM in Tampa, there was growing certainty that bin Laden was now trapped at Tora Bora. Lieutenant General Michael DeLong, the deputy commander of CENTCOM, remembers, "We were hot on Osama bin Laden's trail. He was definitely there when we hit [the Tora Bora] caves. Every day during the bombing, [Secretary of Defense Donald] Rumsfeld asked me, 'Did we get him? Did we get him?'" On November 20, Vice President Dick Cheney told ABC News that bin Laden "was equipped to go to ground there. He's got what he believes to be secure facilities, caves underground. It's an area he's familiar with. He operated there during the war against the Soviets in the eighties."

Dalton Fury (a pseudonym), a thirty-seven-year-old major in the elite and secretive Delta Force commandos, led the small Western forces hunting bin Laden at Tora Bora, which comprised about seventy American and British Special Operations soldiers and CIA officers. From the beginning of the operation, Fury had identified the central weakness in the American plan at Tora Bora: there was no one to guard the escape routes into Pakistan. Fury recommended in late November that his own Delta team be dropped into Tora Bora at eight thousand feet or so. Equipped with oxygen, his team would then climb to fourteen thousand feet to reach the tallest peaks in the area—a trek that would take a few days—and from there descend to attack al-Qaeda's positions from above, the direction from which bin Laden's followers would least expect them. Somewhere in the chain of command, that request was turned down.

Despite the casualties they were taking and the extreme weather conditions, al-Qaeda fighters were still able to lay down somewhat effective mortar barrages and small-arms fire. Mohammed Zahir, who commanded a group of thirty Afghan militiamen on the front lines throughout the Battle of Tora Bora, skirmished with Arab and Pakistani militants fighting with rockets and machine guns, a formidable force that could be taken on only with the help of the American bombing raids on al-Qaeda's positions. Muhammad Musa, a commander who led hundreds of Afghan soldiers on the Tora Bora front lines, recalled the fanatical bravery of bin Laden's fighters: "They fought very hard with us. When we captured them, they committed suicide with grenades. I saw three of them do that myself." Al-Qaeda fighters were no doubt buoyed by the fact that they were fighting during the holy month of Ramadan, as it was at the Battle of Badr during Ramadan that the Prophet Mohammed had led a small group of Muslims to victory fourteen centuries earlier, against a much larger army of infidels.

On the morning of December 3, heavy American bombing began, and continued around the clock. It was the beginning of a four-day period during which seven hundred thousand pounds of American bombs rained down on Tora Bora. During this period, bin Laden was videotaped by an al-Qaeda member instructing his followers how best to dig trenches in which to shelter. On the tape a bomb explodes in the distance. Bin Laden comments without evident concern in his voice, "We were there last night."

As the American bombing increased in intensity, bin Laden reminisced fondly with his deputy, Ayman al-Zawahiri, about the nineteen 9/11 hijackers, talking about each one with emotion. Fearing that he would be killed by the American bombardment and wanting to be sure that he had properly memorialized these heroic "martyrs," he wrote out nineteen death certificates for the hijackers.

The Afghan warlords on the ground who were working with the Americans were at odds with one another, and every evening during the battle, they and their foot soldiers retreated to their homes as dusk fell to observe the Ramadan breaking of the fast. On the evening of December 3, realizing that the Afghan ground forces were not up to the job of encircling al-Qaeda's hard core, CIA officer Gary Berntsen sent out a lengthy message to headquarters asking for up to eight hundred elite Army Rangers to assault the complex of caves where bin Laden and his lieutenants were believed to be hiding and to block their escape routes. Berntsen's boss, Henry A. Crumpton, who was by that time "100 percent" certain that bin Laden was bottled up in the Tora Bora mountains, called the CENTCOM commander General Tommy Franks, who had overall control of the Tora Bora operation, to request the additional soldiers. Franks pushed back, pointing out that the American "small footprint" approach had worked well during the overthrow of the Taliban, and also that it would take weeks to get more U.S. soldiers on the ground. Franks never asked Secretary of Defense Donald Rumsfeld for more troops at Tora Bora, and Rumsfeld didn't ask Franks if he needed them.

General Franks also believed the United States could rely on the Pakistanis to cut off fleeing members of al-Qaeda. "I think it was a pretty good determination, to provide support to that operation, and to work with the Pakistanis along the Pakistani border to bring it to conclusion," he said in a 2002 interview. The assumption that the Pakistanis had their side of the border covered was, at best, wishful thinking. Crumpton had repeatedly warned the White House, his own CIA leadership, and CENTCOM that the Pakistanis were not capable of securing their border. President Bush even asked Crumpton directly if the Pakistanis would seal the border, to which he replied, "No, sir."

Delta ground commander Dalton Fury remembers that, to rectify that problem, in early December his squadron commander suggested dropping GATOR antipersonnel mines from the air into the Tora Bora passes leading to Pakistan, mines that disable themselves after a set period of days. This request also died somewhere farther up the chain of command.

The Delta team set up camp near Tora Bora and tried to press closer toward al-Qaeda's positions to get "eyes on target." They directed laser beams on al-Qaeda targets so that accurate air strikes could be called in. By now the latest intelligence placed bin Laden squarely in Tora Bora. On December 9, a U.S. bomber dropped a fifteen-thousand-pound bomb known as a "daisy cutter" on al-Qaeda's positions. That night, al-Qaeda member Abu Jafar al-Kuwaiti was "awakened to the sound of massive and terrorizing explosions very near to us." The following day, members of al-Qaeda received the awful news that the trench of "Sheikh Osama" had been destroyed. But bin Laden had survived, having moved his position just before the daisy cutter strike.

The day after the daisy cutter was dropped, the U.S. National Security Agency picked up an intercept from Tora Bora: "Father [bin Laden] is trying to break through the siege line." At about 4:00 p.m., Afghan soldiers said that they had spotted bin Laden. In Washington, Paul Wolfowitz, the number two official at the Pentagon, told reporters that bin Laden was likely at Tora Bora, saying, "We don't have any credible evidence of him being in other parts of Afghanistan or outside of Afghanistan."

By December 11, bin Laden realized that his only hope was escape. He told his men he was leaving them, and just after nightfall he prayed with his most loyal bodyguards. That same day, al-Qaeda leaders suggested a cease-fire to Hajji Zaman, one of the Afghan warlords on the U.S. payroll, saying that they would surrender the following morning. Much to the anger of his American sponsors, Zaman agreed to the cease-fire, and that night some of the militants holed up in Tora Bora, including bin Laden, began their retreat out of their mountain refuge.

American signals operators on the ground at Tora Bora now intercepted radio transmissions from bin Laden addressing his followers. "I am sorry for getting you involved in this battle. If you can no longer resist, you may surrender with my blessing," he said in one of them. Fury kept a careful log of these intercepted communications, which he typed up at the end of each day and passed on up his chain of command.

A Pentagon official back in Washington, who had been tracking bin Laden intensively since 1997, was monitoring all this in real time. "Everyone in the community who was working on al-Qaeda was absolutely aware of every radio message that was coming in and every sit rep that was coming back from our SOF [Special Operations Forces] guys. There was a lot of attention being paid to it." The official remembers that he and his colleagues were excited because it seemed to them that now bin Laden would make his final stand. They did not think that bin Laden would try to escape because it would so damage his credibility with al-Qaeda and the wider jihadist movement. "Little did we know that this was his farewell message," says the official. It was a miscalculation the Pentagon would come to regret.

The man responsible for the deadliest terrorist attack in U.S. history, along with many of his top lieutenants, was making his escape. Why was there no effort to put more American boots on the ground, beyond the total of several dozen Delta operators, Green Berets,

U.S. Air Force tactical air controllers, and CIA officers already in Tora Bora? Lieutenant General DeLong says the Pentagon did not want to put many American soldiers on the ground because of a concern that they would be treated like enemies by the locals: "The mountains of Tora Bora are situated deep in territory controlled by tribes hostile to the United States and any outsiders. The reality is if we put our troops in there we would inevitably end up fighting Afghan villagers—creating bad will at a sensitive time."

Contributing to the sense that Afghans were implacably opposed to foreign troops on their soil was an article titled "Afghanistan: Graveyard of Empires" in the November 2001 issue of the influential *Foreign Affairs* magazine, by veteran CIA officer Milton Bearden, who had overseen the Agency's effort to arm the Afghan mujahideen against the Soviets. Bearden made the case that large numbers of American boots on the ground would simply replicate the failures of the Soviets in Afghanistan in the twentieth century and the British in the nineteenth century.

The Pentagon was also quite risk-averse at the time, something that is hard now to recall following the years of war in Afghanistan and Iraq. At this stage in the Afghan War, more journalists had died in the conflict than U.S. soldiers, and during the 1999 conflict in Kosovo, not a single American had died in combat. The leaders of the U.S. military seemed to have convinced themselves that the American public could not tolerate casualties—even in pursuit of Osama bin Laden.

There was also the matter of Iraq, which had diverted the Pentagon's attention. In late November, Secretary of Defense Donald Rumsfeld told General Franks that President Bush "wants us to look for options in Iraq." Already in the middle of one war, in Afghanistan, Franks was nonplussed, telling his staff, "Goddam! What the fuck are they talking about?" Yet on December 4, he briefed

Rumsfeld and other top Pentagon officials regarding war plans for Iraq, drawing on the existing contingency plan, an eight-hundred-page document. Rumsfeld did not find the war plans at all satisfactory. "Well, General," he admonished Franks, "you have a lot of work ahead of you." Franks then rebriefed Rumsfeld on the plan for the invasion of Iraq, on December 12, the very same day that al-Qaeda's leaders began their escape from Tora Bora under cover of a cease-fire agreement.

Years later, Franks explained why he did not send more U.S. soldiers to take on al-Qaeda's hard core at Tora Bora:

> My decision not to add American troops to the Tora Bora region was influenced [by] . . . the comparative light footprint of coalition troops in theater, and the fact that these troops were committed to operations ongoing across Afghanistan; the amount of time it would take to deploy additional troops would likely create a "tactical pause" which would run the risk of losing the momentum our forces were enjoying across Afghanistan; [and] uncertainty as to whether bin Laden was in fact in Tora Bora. Intelligence suggested that he was, but conflicting intelligence also reported that he was in Kashmir . . . [and] at a stronghold on the Iranian border.

General Dell Dailey, who headed Joint Special Operations Command, shared some of Franks's concerns: "There was no question it would have taken a huge number of folks to seal Tora Bora. . . . We're talking December. Every hilltop is covered in snow at this point, every location needed logistics support." Dailey's ground commander dismissed the idea of introducing more troops, saying to Dailey, "No fucking way. We have won this war with special operations and CIA without a conventional footprint and without any of the negativeness that comes back with a massive U.S. force. Let's not do it." Brigadier General James N. Mattis, the commander of twelve hundred marines then stationed near Kandahar, traveled up to Bagram Air Base, near Kabul, to discuss with Dailey the idea of putting a force of marines into Tora Bora. In the end, no marines or any other additional U.S. military forces were deployed to Tora Bora.

Susan Glasser, who covered the Tora Bora battle for the *Washington Post*, recalled that initially there were "fifty to seventy journalists; at the height of the battle a week or so in, perhaps one hundred." That was slightly more than the total number of Western soldiers at Tora Bora. Given that scores of journalists made it to the battle, could the Pentagon have deployed additional soldiers to Tora Bora? Yes. There were about two thousand American troops already in the Afghan theater. In Afghanistan's neighbor to the north, Uzbekistan, were stationed some one thousand soldiers of the Tenth Mountain Division. More than one thousand marines were also stationed near Kandahar. And it would have taken less than a week to deploy an additional eight hundred soldiers of the Eighty-Second Airborne Division from their headquarters at Ft. Bragg, North Carolina, to Tora Bora. Of course, such a force would have had to deal with the treacherous weather conditions and high altitudes of Tora Bora and with fierce resistance from al-Qaeda. There was also a limited number of helicopters in theater, which would have made getting more troops into Tora Bora logistically difficult. However, no effort was made to see if these obstacles might be overcome.

Condoleezza Rice, the national security advisor, later said that there were "conflicting reports" about bin Laden's whereabouts at the time, and that President Bush was never asked to make a decision about sending more soldiers into Tora Bora, which Bush confirms. Why this didn't happen remains a mystery that may, in part, be explained by the fact that the Bush administration had just achieved one of the signal military victories of the modern era, overthrowing the Taliban regime in just three weeks with only some three hundred U.S. Special Forces and one hundred CIA officers on the ground. Why change an approach that had worked so well up to that point?

Beginning December 12, with no blocking forces from the marines or any other American military unit to stop them, a group of more than two dozen of bin Laden's bodyguards hiked out of Tora Bora and toward Pakistan. They were arrested in Pakistan on December 15 and handed over to the Americans. Bin Laden was not with them. He and his deputy, Ayman al-Zawahiri, had shrewdly decided to split up and stay in Afghanistan. Zawahiri left the mountainous redoubt with Uthman, one of bin Laden's sons. Bin Laden went to say good-bye to Uthman, not knowing when, or if, he would see him again, saying, "My son, we are keeping our oath, fighting jihad in the path of Allah." Accompanied by some of his guards, al-Qaeda's leader fled with another of his sons, seventeen-year-old Muhammad.

As bin Laden abandoned the battlefield at Tora Bora, he wrote a final testament warning his children away from his path in life: "Forgive me because I have given you only a little of my time since I answered the jihad call. I have chosen a road fraught with dangers and for this sake suffered from hardships, embitterment, betrayal, and treachery . . . I advise you not to work with al-Qaeda." To his wives, he said, "You knew that the road was full of thorns and mines. You left the comfort of your relatives and chose to share the same hardships with me. You renounced worldly pleasure with me; renounce them more after me. Do not think of remarrying and you need only to look after our children."

Bin Laden went to the house of Awad Gul, a trusted ally near Jalalabad, to rest. Before the battle, bin Laden had entrusted Gul with $100,000. Soon after, bin Laden, an accomplished rider, went by horse to the northeast, to Kunar province, an ideal place to disappear. Its twelve-thousand-foot peaks, dense trees, and evergreen shrubs made detection of movement from the air difficult; it had a small population hostile to outsiders; and there was no central government to speak of.

A couple of weeks after the Tora Bora battle had ended, a visibly aged bin Laden released a video in which he contemplated his own death. "I am just a poor slave of God," he said. "If I live or die, the war will continue." He did not move his left side during the half-hour videotape, which suggested that he had sustained some kind of serious injury. A few months later, on an al-Qaeda website, the ten-year-old Hamza bin Laden posted a poem bemoaning the fate that had befallen him and his family: "Oh, Father! Why have they showered us with bombs like rain, having no mercy for a child?" On the same website, bin Laden replied, "Pardon me, my son, but I can only see a very steep path ahead. A decade has gone in vagrancy and travel, and here we are in our tragedy. Security is gone, but danger remains."

On January 4, 2002, at President Bush's vacation ranch in Texas, Michael Morell had the delicate task of informing Bush that it was the CIA's assessment that bin Laden had fought at the Battle of Tora Bora and survived. Bush was incensed at this and became hostile, as if Morell himself were the culprit.

Two and a half years later, during a close election race, Democratic nominee John Kerry made a campaign issue of whether bin Laden could have been finished off at Tora Bora. The notion that there had been a real opportunity to kill bin Laden at that point was a "wild claim," Bush said, and Vice President Dick Cheney termed it "absolute garbage." Nevertheless, from the totality of the available accounts, it is clear that when presented with an opportunity to kill or capture al-Qaeda's top leadership just three months after September 11, the United States was instead outmaneuvered by bin Laden, who slipped away, disappeared from the American radar, and slowly began rebuilding his organization.

3 AL-QAEDA IN THE WILDERNESS

BIN LADEN RETREATED into the mountains of Kunar with his organization on life support. Al-Qaeda, "the base" in Arabic, had just lost the best base it ever had. In Afghanistan, al-Qaeda had run something of a parallel state to that of the Taliban, conducting its own independent foreign policy by attacking American embassies, warships, and the centers of U.S. military and economic power, as well as churning out thousands of militant foot soldiers in its training camps.

This pre-9/11 al-Qaeda was quite bureaucratic, with its various committees for media outreach, military planning, business affairs, and even farming; its top-down CEO; the salaries it paid many of its members; the comprehensive training it provided its recruits; and the detailed application forms that were required to attend its training camps. The group's bylaws, which ran to thirty-two pages in an English translation, covered annual budgets, salaries, medical benefits, policies for al-Qaeda members with disabilities, grounds for dismissal from the group, and vacation allowances.

Al-Qaeda's leaders were the type of micromanagers familiar to anyone who has toiled in the office of a large organization. Mohammed Atef, the group's military commander, once fired off a memo to a subordinate, complaining, "I was very upset with what you did. I obtained 75,000 rupees for your family's trip to Egypt. I learned that you did not submit the voucher to the accountant, and that you made reservations for 40,000 rupees and kept the remainder." In a similar vein, Ayman al-Zawahiri chastised members of al-Qaeda in Yemen who had splurged on an expensive fax machine. For an organization devoted to revolutionary holy war, the pre-9/11 al-Qaeda sometimes had the feel of an insurance company, albeit a heavily armed one.

This bureaucratic structure was demolished by bin Laden's foolhardy decision to attack the United States. In June 2002 an al-Qaeda member wrote a letter to Khalid Sheikh Mohammed (KSM), the operational commander of 9/11, admonishing him, "Stop rushing into action and consider all the fatal and successive disasters that have afflicted us during a period of no more than six months." The writer complained that bin Laden ignored any advice that didn't fit with his view that attacking the United States had been a master stroke: "If someone opposes him, he immediately puts forward another person to render an opinion in his support." Bin Laden, the writer continued, didn't understand what had befallen al-Qaeda since the 9/11 attacks, and kept pushing for action by KSM; meanwhile, jihadist groups in Asia, the Middle East, Africa, and Europe had all suffered tremendous losses. The writer urged KSM to halt completely any further terrorist attacks "until we sit down and consider the disaster we caused."

This internal critique of bin Laden was substantially amplified in public two years later, when Abu Musab al-Suri published on the Internet a fifteen-hundred-page history of the jihadist movement. Suri was a deeply serious Syrian intellectual who had known bin Laden since the 1980s—perhaps the most thoughtful strategist of bin Laden's inner circle. He had spent much of the 1990s living in Spain and later in London, where he wrote for obscure militant jihadist publications. In the year before 9/11 Suri had run his own training camp in Afghanistan, where he advocated a flatter, more networked structure for al-Qaeda, rather than the hierarchical structure then in force.

In hiding after the fall of the Taliban, and knowing that he was likely to be arrested at some point (as he eventually was, in Pakistan in 2005), Suri spent much of his time on the run, writing his massive history of the jihadist movement. It recounts the devastation that al-Qaeda and allied groups suffered following 9/11: "We are passing through the most difficult of circumstances and are living the climax of affliction. . . . The Americans have eliminated the majority of the armed jihadist movement's leadership, infrastructure, supporters, and friends." Suri wrote that common estimates that three thousand to four thousand militant jihadists had been killed or captured since 9/11 were actually on the low side.

He concluded: "America destroyed the Islamic Emirate [of the Taliban] in Afghanistan, which had become the refuge for the mujahideen. They killed hundreds of mujahideen who defended the Emirate. Then America captured more than six hundred Jihadists from different Arab countries and Pakistan and jailed them. The Jihad movement rose to glory in the 1960s, and continued through the '70s and '80s, and resulted in the rise of the Islamic Emirate of Afghanistan, but it was destroyed after 9/11." For a longtime intimate of bin Laden and a major jihadist strategist to say publicly that the attacks on Manhattan and Washington had resulted in the wholesale destruction of much of al-Qaeda, the Taliban, and allied militant groups was quite significant.

Some in al-Qaeda continued to push the idea that 9/11 and its aftermath had been a great success for the movement. In an internal "after-action" report about the attacks on the World Trade Center and the Pentagon, an anonymous al-Qaeda writer applauded the strategic wisdom of the attacks: "Targeting America was a very smart choice strategically because the conflict with America's followers in the Islamic world showed that these followers cannot stay on top of their tyrant regimes without America's support. So why keep fighting the body when you can kill the head." The after-action report also celebrated the media attention that the 9/11 attacks had generated: "The giant American media machine was defeated in a judo-like strike from Sheikh bin Laden. CNN cameras and other media dinosaurs took part in framing the attacks and spreading the fear, without costing al-Qaeda a dime."

Similarly, Saif al-Adel, one of the group's military commanders, explained in an interview published four years after the fall of the Taliban that the attacks on New York and Washington were part of a diabolically clever plan to get the United States to overreact and attack Afghanistan: "Our ultimate objective of these painful strikes against the head of the serpent was to prompt it to come out of its hole. . . . Such strikes will force the person to carry out random acts and provoke him to make serious and sometimes fatal mistakes. . . . The first reaction was the invasion of Afghanistan."

This was a post facto rationalization of al-Qaeda's strategic failure. The whole point of the 9/11 attacks had been to get the United States *out* of the Muslim world, not to provoke it into invading and occupying Afghanistan and overthrowing al-Qaeda's closest ideological ally, the Taliban. September 11, in fact, resembled Pearl Harbor. Just as the Japanese scored a tremendous tactical victory on December 7, 1941, they also set in motion a chain of events that led to the eventual collapse of Imperial Japan. So, too, the 9/11 attacks set in motion a chain of events that would lead to the destruction of much of al-Qaeda and, eventually, the death of its leader.

IT WAS CODE-NAMED GREYSTONE, and was arguably the most expansive covert action program in the history of the CIA. Authorized by President Bush in the wake of 9/11, the program encompassed the aggressive pursuit of al-Qaeda suspects around the globe, dozens of whom were snatched from wherever they were living and then "rendered" in CIA-leased planes to countries such as Egypt and Syria, where they were tortured by the local security services. The program introduced the use of what the CIA called "enhanced interrogation techniques," including waterboarding, and led to the establishment of a secret CIA prison system in eastern Europe for "high-value" prisoners. Top CIA lawyer John Rizzo says, "The consensus of the experts, the counterterrorism analysts, and our psychologists, was that for any interrogation program of high value, senior al-Qaeda officials—and we're talking here about the worst of the worst, the most psychopathic but knowledgeable of the entire al-Qaeda system—that for any interrogation to have any effect, it was essential that these people be held in absolute isolation, with access to the fewest number of people." The presidential authorization also allowed the CIA to kill the leaders of al-Qaeda and allied groups using drones.

The urgency of finding bin Laden was underlined when the CIA discovered that he had met with retired Pakistani nuclear scientists during the summer of 2001 to discuss the possibility of al-Qaeda developing a nuclear device. General Richard Myers, the chairman of the Joint Chiefs, says that six weeks after 9/11, Bush told a meeting of his National Security Council that bin Laden "may have a nuclear device" big enough to destroy half of Washington. In fact, al-Qaeda had nothing of the sort, but in the panicked aftermath of 9/11, such a threat could not be easily discounted.

Famously, President Bush kept a list in a drawer of his desk of the most-wanted al-Qaeda leaders. The list was in the form of a pyramid, with bin Laden at the top. As al-Qaeda leaders were captured or killed, Bush would cross them off the list. For about a year after the fall of the Taliban regime, Bush believed that the leader of al-Qaeda might already be dead. After all, throughout much of 2002 nothing was heard from bin Laden that established "proof of life." "The president thought maybe we got him already. He's dead, and we don't know it. [Killed at] Tora Bora or somewhere else," recalls Bush's press secretary, Ari Fleischer.

The uncertainty about bin Laden's status would begin to change at 10:00 p.m. on November 12, 2002, when Ahmad Zaidan, the Al Jazeera bureau chief in Pakistan, received a call on his cell phone from a strange number. A man with a Pakistani accent said in English, "I have something interesting and a scoop for you. Meet me at Melody Market, behind the Islamabad hotel." Zaidan drove through a heavy rainstorm and parked his car at the market, usually crowded with hawkers and shoppers, but now deserted because of the bad weather and late hour. As soon as he got out of the car, a man with his face wrapped in a scarf approached him and handed him an audiotape, saying, "This is from Osama bin Laden."

Zaidan demanded "Hold on," but bin Laden's messenger vanished as quickly as he had materialized. Zaidan shoved the audiocassette in the tape player of his car and recognized immediately that it was bin Laden's voice, and that what al-Qaeda's leader was saying on the tape was definitive proof that he had survived the Tora Bora battle. It was quite a scoop for Al Jazeera.

AL-QAEDA IN THE WILDERNESS

Back at his office, Zaidan started feeding the bin Laden audio-tape to Al Jazeera's headquarters in Qatar. The news soon flashed around the world: "Bin Laden Alive." On the tape bin Laden celebrated a string of recent terrorist attacks perpetrated by his followers: the bombing of a synagogue in Tunisia, the attack on a French oil tanker off the coast of Yemen, and the suicide bombings at two nightclubs on the Indonesian island of Bali that killed two hundred mostly young Western tourists. This was a comprehensive "proof of life," and any faint hopes that bin Laden might have succumbed to the wounds he sustained at Tora Bora had been dashed. The night the tape surfaced, National Security Advisor Condoleezza Rice called President Bush in his residential quarters at the White House to tell him the bad news that bin Laden was alive and well.

Bin Laden was alive, but where was he? The consensus in the U.S. government for the first few years after 9/11 was that he was hiding in or around Pakistan's tribal areas, where al-Qaeda had started to rebuild itself after the Battle of Tora Bora. Some intelligence officials also thought he might be living in the far north of Pakistan, in the sparsely populated mountains of Chitral. This analysis was based in part on trees native to the region that could be seen in a 2003 video of bin Laden, and on the length of time it seemed to take for audiotapes from bin Laden to make their way to outlets such as Al Jazeera. When bin Laden commented on important news events, it usually took about three weeks for the tapes to make their way to the public. But even that pattern was sometimes upended. After al-Qaeda's Saudi wing attacked the U.S. consulate in Jeddah in early December 2004, killing five employees, bin Laden released an audiotape crowing over this victory that was made public in just over a week. Maybe he wasn't in remote Chitral after all?

———

MANHUNT

AFTER THE FALL OF THE TALIBAN, many of the leaders of al-Qaeda did not, in fact, go to ground in Pakistan's tribal areas. Some slipped into Iran, but most preferred to hide in the anonymity of Karachi, one of the largest cities in the world. One of bin Laden's oldest sons, Saad bin Laden, who had recently taken on something of a leadership role in al-Qaeda, spent the first six months of 2002 living in Karachi. He helped one of his aunts and several of his father's children move from Pakistan to Iran, where they subsequently lived under house arrest for years. Saad joined them in Iran along with a number of other prominent leaders of al-Qaeda, such as Saif al-Adel, a former Egyptian Special Forces officer who had fought against the Soviets in Afghanistan. From Iran, Adel authorized al-Qaeda's branch in Saudi Arabia to begin a series of terrorist attacks in the Saudi kingdom that began in Riyadh in May 2003, a campaign that killed scores.

From one of their safe houses in Karachi, two of the key planners of 9/11, KSM and Ramzi bin al-Shibh, gave an extensive interview to an Al Jazeera reporter in the spring of 2002 that laid out in detail how they had planned the attacks on New York and Washington. Several months later, on the first anniversary of 9/11, bin al-Shibh was arrested in Karachi along with other members of al-Qaeda. Recovered in their safe house were twenty packages of passports and documents belonging to bin Laden's wives and children, underlining the key role that Karachi played for bin Laden's family and inner circle after the fall of the Taliban.

Karachi, the business capital of Pakistan, was also where al-Qaeda did its banking. While bin Laden was strapped for cash in Tora Bora during the winter of 2001, in Karachi the following year, KSM was routinely handling hundreds of thousands of dollars. KSM gave $130,000, for instance, to the Southeast Asian terrorist group

Jemaah Islamiya, after its successful terrorist attacks in Bali in October 2002.

In Karachi, KSM planned a second wave of attacks on the West, dreaming up a plan to crash planes into Heathrow airport and scheming about how to use remote-controlled explosive devices hidden inside Sega game cartridges, which al-Qaeda was then developing. He also hoped to relaunch al-Qaeda's fledgling anthrax research program, discussing the possibility with Yazid Sufaat, a Malaysian who had studied biochemistry at California Polytechnic State University and had previously tried, unsuccessfully, to develop "weaponized" anthrax for al-Qaeda. Sufaat confided to KSM that he had gotten himself vaccinated against anthrax so that he wouldn't be affected by his research for al-Qaeda, but the program never got off the ground.

KSM's plotting came to an abrupt end when he was captured in Rawalpindi on March 1, 2003, in a 3:00 a.m. raid in the city that is home to the headquarters of Pakistan's army. He was caught with the help of an informant who slipped into the bathroom of a house where the terrorist was staying, then text-messaged his American controllers, "I am with KSM." Later that night al-Qaeda's "chief of external operations" was arrested.

THE ARREST OF KSM brought the CIA a trove of intelligence. Not only was he carrying three letters from bin Laden, one of them addressed to family members in Iran, but the CIA also gained hold of his computer. On the 20-gigabyte hard drive, in a document titled "Merchant's Schedule," intelligence officers found a list of the names of 129 al-Qaeda operatives and an accounting of their monthly allowances. Spreadsheets on the computer listed families who had received financial assistance from the terrorist group; there was also a list of wounded and killed "martyrs" and passport photos of operatives.

None of this, however, led the CIA any closer to bin Laden.

In October 2003, bin Laden called for attacks against Western countries whose troops were fighting in Iraq; subsequently, terrorists bombed a British consulate in Turkey and commuters on their way to work in Madrid. And on the eve of the 2004 U.S. presidential election, bin Laden suddenly appeared in a videotape mocking Bush for reading the story about the pet goat at the elementary school in Florida while the 9/11 attacks were in progress. On that tape, bin Laden also responded to Bush's frequent claim that al-Qaeda was attacking the United States because of its freedoms rather than its foreign policy, saying sardonically, "Contrary to Bush's claims that we hate freedom. If that were true, then let him explain to us why we do not attack Sweden?" In December 2004, bin Laden called for attacks on Saudi oil facilities, and a rash of attacks on energy companies and refineries followed.

Despite the taunting videotapes, a number of key al-Qaeda operatives were run to ground between 2002 and 2005. All of them were captured in Pakistan's packed cities. Members of al-Qaeda faced a dilemma: if they stopped using their phones or the Internet, it made them much harder to find, but it also made it more difficult to plan terrorist attacks and communicate with colleagues. In the end, few al-Qaeda operatives threw away their cell phones or stopped using the Internet. The CIA used newly emerging geolocation technologies to home in on those phones and the locations of the IP addresses used by those operatives. KSM was tracked down in part through his use of Swiss cell phone SIM cards, which were popular among al-Qaeda operatives because they carried prepaid minutes and could be purchased without the buyer providing a name.

AL-QAEDA IN THE WILDERNESS

The CIA also used relatively new software to map potential connections between suspected terrorists and suspect cell phone numbers, such as the program called Analyst's Notebook. A Silicon Valley outfit named Palantir became a favorite of U.S. intelligence agencies, doing hundreds of millions of dollars of business every year because of its ability to collate information from multiple databases and put together as complete a picture as possible of a suspect. And a whole new category of job was created at the CIA: that of the "targeter," someone who helped the terrorist hunters by assembling any scrap of information from a suspect's "digital exhaust," that is, from cell phones, ATM transactions, and any other available information. Additional resources devoted to attacking al-Qaeda quickly flowed to the CIA. Within the first year after 9/11, the Counterterrorist Center at the Agency mushroomed from 340 to 1,500 operatives and analysts.

Relations between the CIA and Pakistan's military intelligence service, ISI, were reasonably good during the first years after 9/11. After all, al-Qaeda was a common enemy that was also targeting Pakistan's president, General Pervez Musharraf, the subject of two serious assassination attempts by the terrorist group in December 2003. General Asad Munir, who was in charge of ISI's operations in the North-West Frontier Province in the first years after 9/11, recalls of the CIA, "We had so much trust with all their people. There was nothing hidden." Munir says that on dozens of operations in 2002 he worked closely with the CIA, which had few officers on the ground and needed the manpower ISI could provide.

The al-Qaeda operatives captured in Pakistan's cities in the first years after 9/11 included Abu Zubaydah, who provided logistical support for al-Qaeda; Walid bin Attash, who played a role in the attack on the USS *Cole* in Yemen; Ahmed Khalfan Ghailani, one of the conspirators in the 1998 bombings of the U.S. embassies in Africa;

and Abu Faraj al-Libi, al-Qaeda's number three, who was nabbed by police officers disguised in burqas. All told, Pakistan handed over 369 suspected militants to the United States in the five years after the attacks on New York and Washington, for which the Pakistani government earned bounties of millions of dollars.

The remaining leaders of al-Qaeda faced an existential decision: remain in Pakistan's cities, where they could easily stay in touch with their colleagues in the country and with other militants around the world, or retreat to the safe haven of Pakistan's tribal areas, where communicating with the outside world was quite difficult, but the reach of the CIA and the Pakistani intelligence services was minimal to nonexistent.

Al-Qaeda's leaders now chose survival over effective communications.

4 THE RESURGENCE OF AL-QAEDA

IN THE SPRING OF 2003, as the Iraq War was getting under way, a group of British citizens traveled to Pakistan determined to train with al-Qaeda, intending to fight U.S. and other NATO forces in Afghanistan. Omar Khyam, the cricket-mad son of Pakistani immigrants, was the ringleader. At an al-Qaeda camp on the Afghanistan-Pakistan border, the men learned how to build fertilizer-based bombs. During their training, Abdul Hadi al-Iraqi, one of bin Laden's top lieutenants, sent word to the group that because al-Qaeda already "had enough people . . . if they really wanted to do something they could go back [to the United Kingdom] and do something there." Toward the end of Khyam's stay in Pakistan, an al-Qaeda operative met him and instructed him to carry out "multiple bombings" either "simultaneously" or "one after the other on the same day" in the United Kingdom.

In the fall, Khyam and most of his group returned to the United Kingdom, where they purchased thirteen hundred pounds, more than half a ton, of the fertilizer ammonium nitrate—almost the quantity used to demolish the Federal Building in Oklahoma City in 1995—and hid it in a West London storage locker. The fertilizer plotters considered blowing up a variety of possible targets, including a shopping center, trains, synagogues, and "slags" (loose women) dancing at the well-known London nightclub the Ministry of Sound. In February 2004, Khyam contacted an al-Qaeda operative in Pakistan to check the precise bomb-making instructions he had learned in the camps the previous year. By then a suspicious employee at the storage facility had tipped off police, and British authorities had swapped out the fertilizer for a similar inert material. Khyam was arrested on March 30, 2004, as he was enjoying his honeymoon at a Holiday Inn in Sussex.

Khyam was the first example of a worrisome nexus that developed in the years after 9/11 between British militants and al-Qaeda's leaders based in Pakistan's tribal regions. Al-Qaeda had greater success with the next group of British plotters it trained in bomb making in Pakistan. They were four men, all British citizens, three of them of Pakistani descent. Mohamed Khan, the ringleader, linked up with al-Qaeda when he took time off from his teaching job for a three-month visit to Pakistan in November 2004. While the soft-spoken British schoolteacher was there, al-Qaeda leader Abdul Hadi al-Iraqi tasked him with launching an attack in the United Kingdom. On July 7, 2005, the four men detonated bombs on the London Underground and on a bus, killing fifty-two commuters and themselves. It was the deadliest terrorist attack in British history.

Two months after the London bombings, a videotape of Khan appeared on Al Jazeera, branded with the Arabic logo of al-Qaeda's Pakistan-based media arm, As Sahab ("the Clouds"). On the tape, Khan described Osama bin Laden and his deputy, Ayman al-Zawahiri, as "today's heroes," and Zawahiri himself then made an appearance, explaining that the London bombings were revenge for Britain's participation in the war in Iraq, and came as a result of its ignoring bin Laden's earlier offer of a "truce." Zawahiri asked, "Didn't the lion of Islam the Mujahid, the sheikh Osama bin Laden, offer you a truce? . . . Look what your arrogance has produced."

The London attacks underlined the fact that in Pakistan's tribal areas, al-Qaeda had begun remaking the kind of base it had once enjoyed in Afghanistan under the Taliban, albeit on a much smaller scale. From this new base, al-Qaeda began training Westerners, in particular second-generation British Pakistanis, for attacks in the West. While the London bombings were not remotely on the scale of the 9/11 attacks, they showed the kind of planning, and the ability to hit targets far from its home base, seen in pre-9/11 al-Qaeda attacks, such as the one mounted on the USS *Cole* in Yemen in 2000.

Morale among al-Qaeda militants must also have been buoyed by the CIA's failed drone strike targeting Zawahiri. On January 13, 2006, six months after the London attacks, believing it had Zawahiri in its sights, the CIA launched a drone strike aimed at a group of men sitting down to dinner in the village of Damadola, near the Afghanistan-Pakistan border. The strike killed only local villagers, and two weeks later Zawahiri released a videotape celebrating the fact that he was alive and making disparaging comments about President Bush.

In the summer of 2006 al-Qaeda directed an effort to blow up several passenger jets flying to the United States and Canada from the United Kingdom, recruiting half a dozen British citizens for the job. The ringleader of the plot, twenty-five-year-old Londoner Ahmed Abdullah Ali, made a "martyrdom" video in which he said, "Sheikh Osama warned you many times to leave our lands or you will be destroyed. Now the time has come for you to be destroyed." Luckily, the plot was discovered by British police, and the conspirators were arrested. Michael Chertoff, the cabinet official in charge of the recently created U.S. Department of Homeland Security, said that if the "planes plot" had succeeded, it "would have rivaled 9/11 in terms of the number of deaths and impact on the international economy."

The regrouping of al-Qaeda in Pakistan's tribal areas was the cause of increasing alarm at the CIA and in the Bush administration. This alarm was compounded by the public release of an increased number of tapes featuring bin Laden, beginning in early 2006. Through them, "the Sheikh" was asserting greater strategic control over jihadist militants around the world. In 2007 he called for attacks on the Pakistani state; Pakistan had more than fifty suicide attacks that year. And when the Saudi government surveyed about seven hundred extremists in its custody—men who had been arrested in the half decade after 9/11—participants cited al-Qaeda's leader as their most important role model.

As al-Qaeda resurged, the CIA was no longer capturing al-Qaeda operatives in Pakistani cities and was also having little success in picking off al-Qaeda's leaders with drone strikes in Pakistan's tribal areas. In 2005 the CIA had given President Bush a secret PowerPoint briefing on the hunt for bin Laden. Bush was surprised by the small number of CIA case officers posted to the Afghanistan-Pakistan region. "Is that all there are?" he asked. In June 2005, CIA director Porter Goss said publicly that he had an "excellent idea" where bin Laden was. In fact, no one at the Agency had a clue where he was, though most assumed that he was in the Pakistani tribal region. Art Keller was one of a handful of CIA officers posted in early 2006 in the seven Pakistani tribal areas where al-Qaeda was concentrated. "A great deal of the resources has gone to Iraq. I don't think it's appreciated that the CIA is not really a very large organization in terms of field personnel," Keller said.

The intense focus on Iraq at the CIA had begun in the summer of 2002, when Robert Grenier, the station chief in Islamabad who had tried to negotiate the handover of bin Laden by the Taliban, was summoned back to Washington to begin work at a newly created job at the Agency, that of "Iraq mission manager." Grenier says the resources devoted to Iraq were a "big surge," draining away from Pakistan and Afghanistan the best Agency counterterrorism specialists, case officers, and targeting personnel. For years Iraq also consumed the bulk of President Bush and his national security team's focus and effort. Australian counterinsurgency guru David Kilcullen—who served in Iraq as General David Petraeus's advisor and then worked at the State Department advising Secretary of State Condoleezza Rice—says that, until mid-2007, "they were just all Iraq, all the time."

Keller says that the few CIA officers like him who were working in the tribal areas were constrained by the fact that they lived on a Pakistani military base and had little freedom of movement. "I couldn't go out myself—blond-haired, blue-eyed me. I could do it in Austria, but not in Pakistan." As a result of the mostly indifferent intelligence gathered on the ground in Pakistan's tribal areas during 2006 and 2007, there were a total of six CIA drone strikes there, none of which killed anyone significant in al-Qaeda. CIA director Michael Hayden complained to the White House, "We are zero for '07," and asked for permission to conduct a more aggressive drone program.

Steve Kappes, the deputy director of the CIA, and Michael Leiter, the head of the National Counterterrorism Center, formed a task force in the summer of 2008 that brought together a small, "compartmented," or highly secret, group of key intelligence officials and experts from outside the intelligence community to think of innovative ways to find "Number One" and "Number Two." The plan involved greatly increasing the number of drones flying over the tribal areas, putting more CIA case officers on the ground there, and ramping up cross-border raids by Special Operations Forces.

Bush ordered the CIA to expand its attacks with Predator and Reaper drones, and the U.S. government stopped seeking Pakistani officials' "concurrence" or alerting them when strikes were imminent. As a result, the time taken to identify and shoot at a target dropped from many hours to forty-five minutes. The Predator and Reaper drones were controlled by the CIA and flown out of bases in Afghanistan and Pakistan, but were operated by "pilots" stationed at Creech Air Force Base in Nevada. After a day's work shooting at targets on the other side of the world, the pilots went home to their families. More than two dozen feet in length, the drones lingered over the tribal areas looking for targets and were equipped to drop Hellfire missiles or JDAM (joint direct attack munition) bombs.

In the Pakistani tribal region of South Waziristan on July 28, 2008, a U.S. drone killed Abu Khabab al-Masri, who ran al-Qaeda's crude chemical weapons program, along with two other militants. The assassination of Abu Khabab marked the beginning of a vastly ramped-up program to take out al-Qaeda's leaders using drones in the waning months of the Bush administration, likely a legacy-building effort to dismantle the entire al-Qaeda leadership. Between July 2008 and the time he left office, President Bush authorized thirty Predator and Reaper strikes on Pakistani territory, compared with the six strikes the CIA launched during the first half of the year, a fivefold increase.

Other leading figures in al-Qaeda killed in the drone strikes in the final six months of Bush's second term included Abu Haris, al-Qaeda's chief in Pakistan; Khalid Habib, Abu Zubair al-Masri, Abu Wafa al-Saudi, and Abdullah Azzam al-Saudi, all senior members of the group; Abu Jihad al-Masri, al-Qaeda's propaganda chief; and

Usama al-Kini and Sheikh Ahmed Salim Swedan, who had played key roles in planning the 1998 bombings of the two American embassies in Africa. In half a year the drone attacks had killed half of the leadership of al-Qaeda in the tribal areas and had made the "number three" job in al-Qaeda one of the most dangerous in the world. But none of these drone strikes targeted bin Laden, who had simply vanished. "The whole time along, President Bush would ideally have loved to have been able to have gotten bin Laden," says Ari Fleischer, Bush's press secretary.

At the same time that he gave the green light to the accelerated drone attacks, Bush also authorized Special Operations Forces to carry out ground assaults in the tribal regions without the advance permission of the Pakistani government. On September 3, 2008, a team of Navy SEALs based in Afghanistan crossed the Pakistani border into South Waziristan to attack a compound housing militants in the village of Angoor Adda. Twenty of the occupants were killed, but many of them turned out to be women and children. The Pakistani press picked up on the attack, which then sparked vehement objections from Pakistani officials, who protested that it violated their national sovereignty. Pakistan's chief of army staff, General Ashfaq Parvez Kayani, bluntly said that Pakistan's "territorial integrity . . . will be defended at all costs," suggesting that any future insertion of American soldiers into Pakistan would be met by force. The cross-border missions by Special Operations ceased, but the drone attacks increased in intensity.

5 A WORKING THEORY OF THE CASE

CIA HEADQUARTERS in Langley, Virginia, is a grouping of modern buildings with the air of an upscale office park sprawling over acres of quiet woodland, twenty minutes' drive from downtown Washington, D.C. Casual visits are not encouraged. To reach the main building, you negotiate first the visitors' center—where machines constantly sniff the air for chemical and biological toxins and guards bristling with automatic weapons direct traffic—then walk for fifteen minutes down a narrow road screened off from the surrounding woods by high fencing topped with barbed wire, then pass the CIA's own dedicated water tower and electrical plant. At the end of the road is a seven-story modernist glass-and-concrete building, the main headquarters, erected in the 1950s, its lobby paved with slabs of white marble. Emblazoned in the marble floor is the great seal of the Central Intelligence Agency, and engraved on a wall are words from the Gospel According to John: "And ye shall know the truth and the truth shall make you free."

On one wall of the lobby are dozens of gold stars that represent CIA officers killed on the job since the Agency was founded in 1947.

A WORKING THEORY OF THE CASE

Beneath the gold stars, the names of the fallen are inscribed in black ink in a glass-encased book. In some cases there is only a star and no name in the book, as the officer remains, even in death, undercover. In the decade after 9/11, the names of two dozen CIA officers and contractors who died in the line of duty were added to the honor roll, a reminder that the Agency is much more than just another office complex in the Virginia suburbs.

On the ground floor of the main building is the Counterterrorism Center, which long oversaw the hunt for bin Laden. During the several years after he disappeared at the Battle of Tora Bora, the hunt for bin Laden sputtered, encountering dry hole after dry hole. Any news that came into the Counterterrorism Center about al-Qaeda's leader was only in the form of "Elvis sightings," recall the officials who were tracking him. But all the Elvis sightings still had to be run down, says the founder of the bin Laden unit, Michael Scheuer, "because after 9/11 the senior officers in the Agency and everywhere in the intelligence community were covering their asses. If you got a report that Osama was in Brazil, sunning himself in Rio, you had to at least respond to the cable. And so we were chasing enormous numbers of sightings. And because everybody was afraid something else was coming, we were tracking things down that a normal adult would have never done."

In April 2002, Barbara Sude, a senior Agency analyst who had done her doctorate at Princeton in medieval Arabic thought and had been working full-time on al-Qaeda for years, joined a task force of analysts from various intelligence agencies who would meet regularly over the course of several weeks to brainstorm ideas about how to track down bin Laden. Sude had near-iconic status among the tight-knit group of veteran al-Qaeda analysts in the intelligence community, as she had been the principal author of the highly classified President's Daily Brief delivered to President Bush on August 6,

2001, entitled "Bin Ladin Determined to Strike in the U.S.," which made the case in some detail that al-Qaeda was planning an attack on the homeland. It would be another two years before the 9/11 Commission made that document public and many more years until Sude was first identified as its author. Sude had the reputation of being an "analyst's analyst," with a dispassionate interest in the facts, and of having a near-photographic memory of the many hundreds of reports produced by the intelligence community on al-Qaeda.

Sude remembers that, by early 2002, it was obvious to her and her colleagues that bin Laden's trail had gone cold, so the best hope to find him was to try to map out the relationships of those who knew him best: What were his family connections? What were his links to the Afghan mujahideen groups that had fought the Soviets? Whom else did he trust? The analysts created a baseline assessment of bin Laden's family and associates and a time line of all his activities. They circulated photos of what bin Laden might look like if he shaved off his beard and wore a Western-style pinstriped suit. "He was so weird looking," Sude remembers. They also discussed the reward for bin Laden, which at the time stood at $25 million. Some analysts felt that many in Afghanistan couldn't conceive of that kind of money in a country that was one of the poorest on the planet. Might it make sense actually to *lower* the reward? The reward remained where it was.

The analysts also produced papers examining whether it would be better to kill bin Laden or to capture him. Bin Laden would likely become a martyr in death, which could well provoke retaliatory attacks, but he would, after all, be *dead*. A captured bin Laden would try to turn his trial into a soapbox for his poisonous views. There was also the possibility that bin Laden's followers would try to kidnap Americans around the world as bargaining chips for springing their leader from captivity. And what if he died of some disease while in an American prison? Or was somehow killed by a fellow prisoner? Robert Dannenberg, the head of CIA counterterrorism operations, says that capturing bin Laden was never really on the table because of those concerns: "We wanted to make sure that we didn't find ourselves in a situation where we were obliged to capture, not kill bin Laden. . . . We would much rather give him the five-hundred-pound bomb on his complex and pick up his DNA someplace than put him on trial."

From the founding of the bin Laden unit in December 1995—the first time that the CIA had established a "station" targeting a specific individual—female analysts such as Barbara Sude played a key role in the hunt for al-Qaeda. The founder of the unit, Michael Scheuer, explains, "They seem to have an exceptional knack for detail, for seeing patterns and understanding relationships, and they also, quite frankly, spend a great deal less time telling war stories, chatting, and going outside for cigarettes than the boys. If I could have put up a sign saying, 'No boys need apply,' I would've done it."

Jennifer Matthews, one of Scheuer's top deputies, focused on the all-important Afghanistan-Pakistan border region. Her work was critical to the spring 2002 arrest of Abu Zubaydah, a key al-Qaeda logistician, who provided the first information that it was KSM who had masterminded the 9/11 attacks. This came as a complete surprise to the CIA, where KSM had been largely seen as a peripheral figure in al-Qaeda. Matthews knew Islamic history cold, and how al-Qaeda believed it fit into that history, which made her a formidable interrogator of al-Qaeda detainees, some of whom found the fact that she was a well-informed female particularly disconcerting. After 9/11, in addition to her busy job at the CIA, she was also raising three young children.

Frederica (a pseudonym) was another smart, tough CIA officer who was indefatigable in chasing after al-Qaeda. Scheuer says of her, "If she bites your ankle, if she gets her teeth into your foot, you're done like dinner. You may as well give up. It may take two years, but she's going to get you."

And there was Gina Bennett, who in August 1993, while working at the Bureau of Intelligence and Research, inside the State Department, had authored a paper that was the first strategic warning about a man named "Usama Bin Ladin." When bin Laden was expelled to Afghanistan in May 1996 from the Sudanese capital of Khartoum, Bennett also wrote a prescient analysis, warning, "His prolonged stay in Afghanistan—where hundreds of 'Arab Mujahidin' receive terrorist training and key extremist leaders often congregate—could prove more dangerous to US interests in the long run than his three-year liaison with Khartoum."

In the years after the attacks on New York and Washington, Bennett helped draft the key National Intelligence Estimates on the state of al-Qaeda while at the same time balancing the demands of her five children. She reported to David Low, who recalls how quick she was to absorb complicated information: "I could walk into her office at noon and say, 'I need fifteen pages on X,' and it's there three hours later. She is really fast."

The prominent role that women played in the hunt for bin Laden was reflective of the largest cultural shift at the CIA in the past two decades. Veteran CIA operative Glenn Carle recalls, "When I started, there were to my knowledge four senior operation officers who were females, and they had to be the toughest SOBs in the universe to survive. And the rest of the women were treated as sexual toys." When Scheuer set up the bin Laden unit, Carle remembers the reaction among his fellow operations officers: "What's his staff? It's all female. It was just widely discussed at the time that it's a bunch of chicks. So, the perspective was frankly condescending and dismissive. And Scheuer [and his staff] essentially were saying, 'You guys need to listen to us; this is really serious. This is a big deal, and people are going to die.' And of course they were right."

Scheuer's team had mounted aggressive efforts in the years before 9/11 to take out bin Laden, but they were often beset by a certain amount of confusion. Senior national security officials under President Bill Clinton believed that he had authorized bin Laden's assassination, while the Agency officers implementing the program believed it was a capture bin Laden program in which he might only be killed inadvertently. When the Afghan militia leader Ahmad Shah Massoud was told in 1999—at the same time that he was waging a battle to the death with the Taliban—that the CIA was hoping to partner with him in capturing but *not killing* bin Laden, he responded, "You guys are crazy. You haven't changed a bit."

CIA operatives in Afghanistan had bin Laden in their sights a number of times before 9/11. The exact number is in dispute. Clinton's counterterrorism coordinator Richard Clarke says three times, while Scheuer says there were as many as ten opportunities. But there is little disagreement that the best chance to capture or kill bin Laden came in early February 1999 when he was spotted by CIA assets on the ground in Afghanistan as part of a hunting party outside of Kandahar. The group was hunting desert bustards with falcons in a remote area, so there was little risk of causing civilian casualties during a strike—a consideration that had hampered previous operations to target bin Laden.

On February 9, 1999, satellite imagery confirmed the existence of the hunting camp. Clinton's national security staff started planning to launch cruise missiles at the camp from submarines standing by in the Arabian Sea, or tasking the CIA's Afghan allies to snatch al-Qaeda's leader. This became a much more complicated call when the imagery also revealed the presence of officials of the United Arab Emirates at the camp. A strike at the camp might end up missing bin

Laden and instead kill a group of bustard-hunting Emirati princes, who also happened to be allies of the United States. By February 11, the military was ready to launch a strike, but the operation was called off by both Clarke and CIA director George Tenet because of the concerns about the Emiratis. A day later new intelligence indicated the al-Qaeda leader was no longer in the camp.

Bin Laden was also a hard target. His obsession with security had begun in earnest in 1994 when he was living in Sudan, where he was the target of a serious assassination attempt, in which gunmen raked his Khartoum residence with machine-gun fire. After that attack, bin Laden took much greater care of his security, changing locations often and without warning, always surrounded by his cadre of ultra-loyal bodyguards. To kill bin Laden with cruise missiles in the years before 9/11 was additionally complicated because intelligence about bin Laden's location had to be *predictive*. Once a decision to launch a strike had been made in Washington, it took time for the cruise missiles to spin up in their submarine tubes in the Arabian Sea and then fly the several hours to their targets in Afghanistan, so officials had to know not only where bin Laden was when they made the decision but where he would be twelve hours later. That kind of perfect intelligence was, of course, rarely if ever available in the years before the 9/11 attacks.

In 1997, when I was a producer for CNN, I was one of a team of three that met with bin Laden in eastern Afghanistan to tape his first television interview. We witnessed the Herculean efforts that al-Qaeda members made to protect their leader. My colleagues and I were taken to bin Laden's hideout as night fell; we were made to change vehicles while blindfolded; and we had to pass through three successive groups of guards armed with submachine guns and rocket-propelled grenades. We were thoroughly searched and the guards then ran some kind of electronic scanner over us to see if we were concealing weapons or tracking devices. (In fact, the scanner wasn't working, but bin Laden's advisors thought it was important to fool the CNN team—something they later had a good laugh about.)

DESPITE THE ABSENCE of any good leads in the years after the attacks on New York and Washington, the bin Laden hunters at the CIA continued to think that finding him was a "solvable puzzle" because they had gradually built up a "working theory of the case": what kind of circumstances he might be living in, who might be protecting him, and generally where he might be. Some of this was done through a process of elimination. Early on, analysts concluded that it was quite unlikely that bin Laden had left his old stomping grounds in Afghanistan and Pakistan for a country such as Yemen, the bin Laden family's country of origin. Bin Laden was so recognizable that the trip would have been too dangerous, and his most dependable support networks were in South Asia.

Over the years, the CIA also began eliminating some of bin Laden's old buddies from the Afghan war against the Soviets as his possible protectors. The Haqqanis were a Taliban militia who controlled a chunk of eastern Afghanistan and North Waziristan, in the tribal regions of Pakistan. Bin Laden had known the patriarch of the family, Jalaluddin Haqqani, since the mid-1980s. But counterterrorism officials began to think it was less and less likely that bin Laden was living in the vicinity of the Haqqanis' base in Waziristan. Communications from bin Laden seemed to be going *to* al-Qaeda members living in Waziristan, but not emanating from there. Similarly, Gulbuddin Hekmatyar, a leader of another militant Afghan group that straddled both sides of the Afghanistan-Pakistan border, had been an al-Qaeda ally since the late 1980s. But he had changed sides so often during the series of wars that wracked Afghanistan over the past decades that counterterrorism officials tracking bin Laden assessed Hekmatyar as "untrustworthy" and not someone whom the cagey bin Laden would want to stake his life on.

When he fled Sudan in 1996, bin Laden had been welcomed back to Afghanistan by some old contacts from the Soviet war era, the Khalis family militia in eastern Afghanistan, but there didn't appear to be any evidence that he had kept up those connections in the years after 9/11. The CIA also ruled out the idea that he might be with the Taliban leader Mullah Omar, who himself was a fugitive and was believed to be living in or around the Pakistani city of Quetta.

Bin Laden's trackers minutely examined the audio- and videotapes bin Laden occasionally released, for clues to his health, state of mind, and possible location. On October 29, 2004, bin Laden appeared in his first videotaped address in three years. On the tape, he looked like he had recovered completely from his near-death experience at the Battle of Tora Bora, delivering his "Message to the American People" while dressed in beige and gold robes. He even appeared to be reading from some kind of teleprompter. Addressing himself to American voters five days before they went to the polls in the close race between President Bush and Democratic challenger John Kerry, bin Laden said that it didn't matter whom Americans voted for—that they had to change U.S. foreign policy in the Muslim world if they wanted to avoid further attacks by al-Qaeda.

This elder-statesman-of-jihad pose was quite aggravating for President Bush and his national security team, recalls Bush's top counterterrorism advisor, Fran Townsend, a feisty former federal prosecutor from New York whose bold designer clothes and Christian Louboutin shoes stood out in the sea of gray flannel at the White House. Townsend remembers, "I can still see the picture of bin Laden on the screen looking for all the world like a statesman.

A WORKING THEORY OF THE CASE

He was standing at a podium. It was maddening to see him present himself as though he was some head of state and legitimate representative of an ideology."

Frustratingly, such tapes never gave away much of anything about bin Laden's location. On the more than thirty tapes that bin Laden released after 9/11, no one was ever heard whispering in the background something helpful like "Sure is hot here in Waziristan." Speaking of the bin Laden trackers, Scheuer recalls, "When there were videos, the highest priority was the background. They didn't give a shit about what he was talking about. If he was walking around, they would get geologists in and see if those rocks were particular to one place in Afghanistan." When a bird could be heard chirping on one tape, a German ornithologist was called in to analyze the chirps. If plants were visible, they, too, were analyzed to see if they were unique to a particular place. None of this forensic work on the tapes ever yielded a useful lead.

At the Pentagon, officials were similarly frustrated. On the second anniversary of 9/11, al-Qaeda released a statement celebrating the attacks, along with footage of a gaunt bin Laden walking with the help of a wooden staff through a steep mountainous region. Analysts thought that the area looked similar to the province of Kunar in the northeast of Afghanistan, but analysis of the vegetation visible on the tape was inconclusive.

As at the CIA, Pentagon intelligence officials also had to chase down every bin Laden lead no matter how implausible. One recalls, "Every time a news report said he's in Thailand, or he's in this location, we literally had to set up a little special project we called 'Where's Waldo?' and we did a comprehensive study around the globe of all of the funky, insane mentions of where we saw a tall Arab-looking guy with a beard."

The statements on the various tapes made by bin Laden while he was on the run did yield some clues about his possible living conditions. In 2004 he referred to a sequence in *Fahrenheit 9/11,* a film by the American documentarian Michael Moore, and three years later he recommended the works of Noam Chomsky, the leftist author. The fact that bin Laden was watching DVDs and reading books tended to rule out the notion that he was stuck in a remote cave. Also, in his appearances on videotape his clothes were well pressed and the productions were well lit. Sude, who was often tasked to write analyses of these tapes, remembers the debates they would spark at the Agency: "We didn't necessarily think anybody would be in a cave. But we went back and forth: 'Did they have a curtain up? Are they covering up a cave wall?'"

Officials turned to the study of a number of successful manhunts to see if there were any lessons to be learned. They examined how the Israelis had managed after many years to track down Adolf Eichmann, who had helped send millions of Jews to their deaths in the concentration camps during World War II. After the war, Eichmann escaped Germany for Argentina, where he lived with his family in some comfort in Buenos Aires, under an alias, for a decade and a half. It was Eichmann's son who gave the game away when he bragged to his girlfriend's father about his father's Nazi past. The girlfriend's father, who was half-Jewish, contacted a judge in Germany who had prosecuted former Nazis. Mossad, the Israeli intelligence service, somehow got wind of this and sent operatives to Buenos Aires, where they kidnapped Eichmann and bundled him onto a flight for Israel, where he would stand trial. The lesson for the manhunters at the CIA was that family members could provide inadvertent and important clues to the location of a target.

Another manhunt the CIA examined was the operation to find Pablo Escobar, the brutal Colombian drug lord who dominated the lucrative cocaine trade in the United States during the 1980s, murdering and kidnapping many of Colombia's top politicians and journalists. Unlike bin Laden, Escobar was known to live in one particular place: his hometown of Medellin, in whose sprawling slums the tubby drug lord with penchants for having sex with teenage girls and torturing his enemies to death was something of a folk hero. Yet even though elite Colombian police units working with CIA officials and American Special Operations Forces knew that Escobar was hiding somewhere in Medellin, it still took two years to track him down, and that was with plenty of help from Escobar's rivals, the Cali cartel. Escobar moved around town in nondescript taxis, and when he talked to his associates on a radio-phone, he constantly changed frequencies, which made his location hard to pinpoint.

What finally gave him away was his love for his son. Escobar was careful to speak only briefly on his phone, knowing the prowess of the Americans in signals intelligence, but one day he spoke for several minutes to his sixteen-year-old son, Juan Pablo, and that was long enough for direction-finding technology provided by the CIA to Colombian police units to zero in on the street where he was. The police swarmed Escobar's hiding place and shot him dead.

The two lessons of the Escobar takedown were that love of family can get you caught and that you should never talk on the phone. But as General Mike Hayden, the head of the CIA during much of George W. Bush's second term, observed, "You can throw all your phones away, but you pay a price in speed, you pay a price in agility. So, we find, they don't throw their phones away. They try to be careful, but they don't throw them away." The problem was that bin Laden hadn't talked on a phone since even before 9/11. According to his London-based Saudi media advisor, Khaled al-Fawwaz, bin Laden started avoiding any electronic communications as early as 1997, understanding that they could be intercepted. Also, al-Qaeda's leaders had closely followed the April 1996 assassination of Dzhokhar Dudayev, the Chechen prime minister, who was killed by a Russian missile that homed in on the signal emitted by his cell phone. At the time, Chechnya was a major focus of al-Qaeda's efforts to foment global jihad.

Closer to home, counterterrorism officials looked at the case of Eric Rudolph, who had bombed a park in downtown Atlanta thick with tourists in town for the 1996 Olympics. The nail bomb killed a woman, and Rudolph later went on to firebomb abortion clinics and gay nightclubs. He was soon the subject of one of the most intensive manhunts in FBI history, but for years he gave his pursuers the slip, hiding in the backwoods and mountains of North Carolina, near where he had grown up. Five years passed, and Rudolph's trail went very cold. The fugitive began taking more chances, descending from his hiding places in the Appalachians to score fast food at outlets such as Taco Bell. One day a rookie cop saw a vagrant Dumpster-diving behind a Piggly Wiggly grocery store and arrested him. A fellow deputy thought the suspect looked like Rudolph, so they ran the suspect's prints and realized they had their man. The lesson here was that as fugitives get comfortable over time, some start taking more risks, and then pursuers might just catch a lucky break. But relying on a lucky break wasn't much of a strategy in bin Laden's case.

The manhunt whose features most resembled the hunt for "UBL," as bin Laden was universally known in the U.S. government, was the one that struck closest to home for the CIA. It began with the murder of two Agency employees driving into the main entrance of the CIA's Virginia headquarters on the morning of January 25, 1993. Mir Aimal Kansi, a Pakistani from a prominent family in Quetta, a city near the Afghan border, calmly shot Lansing Bennett, sixty-six, and Frank Darling, twenty-eight, with an AK-47 as he strolled through rush-hour traffic that was backed up waiting to get into the CIA main gate. No one gave chase, and the next day the shooter was on a flight back home to Pakistan.

It took more than four years to find Kansi, who, after the CIA murders, was lionized in the border regions of Afghanistan and Pakistan, where he hid out before being captured. The man who tracked him was FBI special agent Brad Garrett, a former marine who habitually dressed from head to toe entirely in black, accessorized with black shades. The soft-spoken agent, a workaholic who typically got home to his crash pad in Washington at 11:00 p.m. and was back in the gym by 6:00 a.m., had a long string of fugitive scalps under his belt and a PhD in criminology. He was exactly the sort of person you wouldn't want on your tail.

Garrett spent four years chasing the elusive Kansi around the Afghan-Pakistani border region before Kansi made a serious mistake, which was to leave the relative safety of Taliban-controlled Afghanistan and travel to central Pakistan. From a country where there was no American presence to speak of at the time, he entered one where Garrett had developed a good network of sources over the years, many of them informants for the U.S. Drug Enforcement Administration, which was active in Pakistan because of the large role the country played in the heroin trade. Eventually Garrett found some tribal sources who were meeting with Kansi. Motivated at least in part by the sizable reward ($2 million) for anyone willing to give up Kansi, the sources supplied Garrett with a glass Kansi had drunk from, and FBI technicians were able to lift a fingerprint from the glass and got a match with Kansi's prints. Bingo! Garrett finally tracked Kansi down to the city of Dera Ghazi Khan, in central Pakistan, where he was staying in a two-dollar-a-night hotel, and arrested him there in the middle of a sweltering night in mid-June 1997.

For two years after 9/11 no one bothered to talk to Garrett about his role in the Kansi takedown. Finally, in 2003, he got a call from the CIA asking him to come out to Langley to brief officials on the Kansi hunt. Garrett's central advice was blunt: You can't trust the Pakistanis. "Every time we had a conversation with the Pakistanis the information just immediately leaked," he told them. "I remember we had a conversation with them one day and the next day in the *Dawn* newspaper it talked about the agents that had talked to this particular guy and what flight they were going to fly to Lahore the next day to go interview somebody else." Garrett said it was fine to work with the Pakistanis if they simply provided the muscle for the arrest, but otherwise going after al-Qaeda's leaders had to be a unilateral American operation. And he emphasized that the sizable cash reward had really helped in the Kansi case.

The bottom line for those tracking bin Laden, after they had "scrubbed" all the intelligence they had on him and had examined the lessons of other manhunts: there wasn't much to go on. Working with Pakistani officials on a bin Laden takedown could blow the whole operation, so that eliminated a large potential source of help. There was no signals intelligence, or SIGINT, from bin Laden's phones, so that eliminated the vast resources of America's technical spying capabilities. And there was no human intelligence, or HUMINT, from sources in and around al-Qaeda. Finally, there had been large cash rewards advertised for information leading to bin Laden for years before 9/11, but there had never been any takers, because members of al-Qaeda believed bin Laden to be the savior of true Islam and wouldn't rat him out for a cash reward, no matter how large.

By 2005 there was a dawning realization at the CIA that there would be no one magic piece of intelligence that took them straight to bin Laden. Nor would there be a "magic detainee"—one al-Qaeda prisoner who would supply the decisive lead. Meanwhile, al-Qaeda was operating with impunity in Pakistan's tribal regions and was training significant numbers of Westerners for mass casualty attacks in the West. It was also developing "nodes" in Iraq, Yemen, Somalia, North Africa, and Lebanon that were capable of acting autonomously. And the Agency concluded that although it could capture or kill any number of "midlevel managers" in al-Qaeda, the linchpins of the operation remained bin Laden and, to some degree, his deputy, Ayman al-Zawahiri.

With bin Laden having vanished and al-Qaeda resurgent, morale at the CIA's Counterterrorist Center was poor. Also, a new congressionally mandated National Counterterrorism Center was being "stood up" to provide strategic analysis of the threat from terrorism, and it was draining away many talented analysts from the CIA. In 2005 the dedicated bin Laden unit at the CIA was closed, and its analysts and operatives were reassigned. This did not mean that the CIA had suddenly decided that bin Laden was no longer important, but it did mean that a single focus on one man wasn't reflecting how al-Qaeda had changed since the bin Laden unit was founded in December 1995. Philip Mudd, then a senior CIA counterterrorism official, recalls, "It was a reflection of what was happening in the war, which was a globalization of 'al-Qaedaism.' I do remember the sense that we were facing not just bin Laden and core al-Qaeda, but we were facing a bigger global jihad problem." Around this time Mudd authored an influential memo outlining how al-Qaeda the centralized organization was morphing into al-Qaeda the movement, which was spreading into countries such as Iraq and penetrating North Africa.

Mudd, an English literature major in college with the lean physique of an avid runner, had been the number two at the CIA's Counterterrorist Center between 2003 and 2005. He recalls that bin Laden and Zawahiri were not central to the conversations he was then having: "If you sat around the table, both in the Center but also in the conversations we had with Director Tenet, you wouldn't have heard bin Laden or Zawahiri's name very often. You would have heard about operational guys. And there was a strategic reason for that. People in al-Qaeda didn't talk about plots and bin Laden. They talked about KSM or they talked about Abu Faraj al-Libi." Mudd and his team were trying to stop the next attack on the States, and to do that they focused particularly on whoever was "al-Qaeda's number three" at the time, because he was the person who was trying to put together the next attack on the homeland, not bin Laden, who was believed to be more the big-picture guy.

In 2005 an analyst named Rebecca (a pseudonym), who had worked on the bin Laden case for years, wrote an important paper titled "Inroads" that would help guide the hunt in the years to come. Given the absence of any real leads on bin Laden, how could you plausibly find him? she asked. Rebecca then came up with four "pillars" upon which the search had to be built. The first pillar was locating al-Qaeda's leader through his courier network. The second was locating him through his family members, either those who might be with him or anyone in his family who might try to get in touch with him. The third was communications that he might have with what the Agency termed AQSL (Al-Qaeda Senior Leadership). The final pillar was tracking bin Laden's occasional outreach to the media. These four pillars became the "grid" through which CIA analysts would from now on sift all the intelligence that had been gathered on al-Qaeda that might be relevant to the hunt for bin Laden, and also helped to inform the collection of new intelligence.

The most obvious way to find bin Laden was via the delivery of his statements to the media, which often first went to Al Jazeera. The problem with this approach, according to a senior U.S. intelligence official, was that al-Qaeda "didn't use Zawahiri's kid" to deliver these tapes, but rather used a series of "cutouts," that is, several couriers in a chain, each aware only of the courier he received the tape from and the one he delivered it to. And some tapes to Al Jazeera were simply mailed to the station's headquarters in Qatar's capital, Doha.

Over the years, counterterrorism officials developed a better understanding of how bin Laden might be living, reaching some "solid conclusions" by 2006 about his domestic arrangements. By then they had rejected the popular notion that he was living in a cave. They also concluded that he was not moving much, or even at all, and that he wasn't meeting anyone face-to-face in the years after 9/11, because none of the al-Qaeda detainees in custody seemed to have met bin Laden, nor did they describe others as having met him—though, crucially, some of the detainees did describe receiving communications from their leader through couriers. So when there were periodic Elvis sightings of bin Laden—say, that he had given a speech to hundreds of cheering supporters along the Afghan-Pakistani border—those sightings became increasingly easy for the CIA to dismiss.

Officials also concluded that bin Laden "was not making any new friends" while on the run, and that anyone protecting him was likely to have been in his inner circle since well before 9/11. Many of his most loyal bodyguards—a group of thirty guards known to their American interrogators as "the dirty thirty"—had been captured in Pakistan immediately after the Battle of Tora Bora, so bin Laden's trusted circle had gotten smaller from that point on. Analysts also concluded that while he was on the lam, bin Laden wouldn't have many guards, to ensure he didn't have "too big a footprint."

To develop a fuller picture of the man and his habits, CIA analysts mined books about al-Qaeda's leader, such as the 2006 history

MANHUNT

The Osama bin Laden I Know: An Oral History, by this author; the authoritative 2008 biography of his family, *The Bin Ladens,* by Steve Coll; and the 2009 memoir *Growing Up bin Laden,* by his first wife, Najwa, and her son Omar. The analysts noticed how devoted the terrorist leader was to his wives and children and concluded that they might well be living with him, in which case he would likely be settled in a sizable compound suitable for the separate living quarters for each of his wives and her children that mimicked his domestic arrangements in Sudan and Afghanistan.

Over time, counterterrorism officials came to think it less and less plausible that bin Laden was hiding out in the tribal regions of Pakistan, where the CIA had stationed more case officers from the summer of 2006 forward. They had in turn recruited a considerable number of local agents. Those agents never developed any intelligence that indicated that bin Laden was living in the tribal areas.

In *Growing Up bin Laden,* Omar bin Laden recounts that after al-Qaeda bombed U.S. embassies in Kenya and Tanzania in 1998, his father traveled to Kabul to hide from American retaliation, and he notes that bin Laden had safe houses in all the major cities in Afghanistan. This helped to confirm the evolving view at the CIA that bin Laden was likely hiding in a city. Then, too, there was the fact that between 2002 and 2005, all the key al-Qaeda leaders and associates who were captured had been found in Pakistani cities.

By 2009 those tracking bin Laden had become even more certain that he was living in some kind of urban setting. On a flight from Islamabad to Washington in May 2010, the CIA station chief in Pakistan was chatting with a group of Obama's national security officials. One of them asked, "Where's Osama bin Laden? Everybody thinks he's hiding out in Karachi in the middle of the slum somewhere." The station chief replied, "No, he's probably in the outskirts of Islamabad in one of those suburbs. Less than sixty miles outside." This was an inspired hunch, as it would be another three months before the CIA tracked bin Laden's courier to Abbottabad, thirty-five miles north of Islamabad.

There was, of course, always a faint hope at the CIA that they might just catch a lucky break. "We always hoped for a person who said, 'I walked past the same compound every day for seven years and today a door was open and I spotted Osama bin Laden,'" recalls one counterterrorism official. That lucky break never came. Also the CIA was never able to place a spy in al-Qaeda who could tell them where bin Laden was. At the top level of the terrorist group, information was highly compartmented, and the leaders practiced good operational security, so placing a spy in the leadership ranks was just not feasible. Robert Dannenberg, a CIA veteran of the Cold War who ran counterterrorism operations at the Agency after 9/11, explains that the religious fanaticism of members of al-Qaeda made them hard to recruit as spies: "It was much easier to convince a Soviet that your way of life was better. You could take them to Kmart in the United States, or to Wal-Mart, because they were driven by many of the same things that we're driven by: success and taking care of our families. When you're dealing with a man who has religious or extremist views, it's completely different."

Instead, it was the painstaking and cumulative assemblage of information from multiple detainee interviews, from thousands of al-Qaeda documents recovered on the battlefield or following an arrest, and the scouring of open-source reporting about bin Laden that helped build a picture of who his associates were and the circumstances in which he might be living, and with whom.

In the end the Agency returned to the four "pillars" of the hunt: bin Laden's courier network, his family, his communications with other leaders in his organization, and his media statements. Three of the pillars yielded nothing. His family wasn't communicating with him; what communications he had with other leaders were extraordinarily "compartmented," making it impossible to follow them back to bin Laden; and his media statements over time didn't yield any useful clues. That left the CIA with his courier network.

Intelligence analysts created a composite of the ideal courier: he would have to be able to travel in Pakistan without sticking out, he would have to speak Arabic to communicate effectively with al-Qaeda's Arab leadership, and he would have to have been trusted by bin Laden before the 9/11 attacks. Abu Ahmed al-Kuwaiti, the man known as "the Kuwaiti," certainly ticked all those boxes: his family was originally from northern Pakistan, he had grown up in Kuwait, and the Agency believed he had joined al-Qaeda around 1999. But although the Kuwaiti was seen as a player in al-Qaeda, a counter-terrorism official who spent years tracking bin Laden recalls that, for a long time, "there was never a sense: 'This was the guy.'"

6 CLOSING IN ON THE COURIER

THE LONG ROAD TO BIN LADEN'S COURIER began with Mohammed al-Qahtani, the man al-Qaeda was grooming to be the
twentieth hijacker in the months before the 9/11 attacks. Qahtani
was a poorly educated drifter from Kharj, a rural backwater in the
deeply conservative heartland of Saudi Arabia, whose schooling
consisted largely of Koranic studies, so even as an adult he believed
that the sun revolved around the Earth. In the late 1990s, Qahtani
dropped out of agricultural college and moved to the United Arab
Emirates, where he held down a series of menial jobs for a couple of
years. Returning home, he drove an ambulance for a while and later
took a job as a laborer at a power company.

In 2000 the twenty-five-year-old Saudi underwent an intense religious awakening, which gave him a new purpose in life. He quit his
dead-end job at the power company to travel to Afghanistan for the
more glamorous life of fighting alongside the Taliban against their
Northern Alliance enemies—the last force standing between the
Taliban and their total victory in Afghanistan.

In Afghanistan in early 2001, Qahtani trained on the usual panoply of weapons at an al-Qaeda camp and soon met bin Laden, who was by then deep into the planning of the attacks on Washington and New York. Bin Laden told the young Saudi that if he wanted to be of service to Islam he should consult with Khalid Sheikh Mohammed (KSM), the operational commander of the coming attacks on America. In late June 2001, Qahtani met again with bin Laden and told him he was "ready for a mission in the United States." KSM then instructed Qahtani to return to Saudi Arabia to get a new, "clean" passport without any telltale entry stamps for Afghanistan and Pakistan, and also to obtain a visa for the United States, which, as a Saudi citizen, Qahtani could do without the kind of difficulties the citizens of other, poorer Arab countries, such as Yemen, routinely encountered. KSM gave Qahtani about $5,000, and Qahtani flew to Saudi Arabia, where he picked up his new passport and visa for the States and from there traveled on to Orlando, Florida, arriving on August 4, 2001.

Mohammed Atta, the lead 9/11 hijacker, was waiting for him in the parking lot at Orlando airport. Atta planned to induct Qahtani into the 9/11 plot as one of the "muscle" hijackers who would help restrain the passengers and crews. But a sharp U.S. immigration official was suspicious of the fact that Qahtani spoke no English and was traveling on a one-way ticket. Through an interpreter, the immigration official asked Qahtani for details about his stay in the United States, at which point the al-Qaeda recruit became increasingly evasive and angry. After he was told that he was being denied entry to the States, Qahtani threatened, "I'll be back."

Qahtani returned to Afghanistan and, after 9/11, was caught up in al-Qaeda's hasty retreat to Tora Bora during the late fall of 2001. Shortly after bin Laden disappeared from Tora Bora, Qahtani and a group of the al-Qaeda leader's bodyguards retreated over the border to Pakistan, where they were arrested on December 15 and handed over to American custody.

Qahtani was sent to Guantánamo, where at first he told his captors that he had gone to Afghanistan because of his love of falconry, a not-uncommon al-Qaeda cover story. But by July 2002, investigators had matched Qahtani's fingerprints to those of the angry young Saudi man who had been deported from Orlando a year earlier. This prompted a much more intensive interrogation regime for Qahtani, who had become increasingly uncooperative, at one point head-butting one of his interrogators.

Between November 23, 2002, and January 11, 2003, Qahtani was interrogated for forty-eight days, more or less continuously, rousted from bed at 4:00 a.m. for interrogation sessions that went on until midnight. If he dozed off, he was doused with water or given a sharp blast of some especially annoying music by Christina Aguilera. He was forced to perform dog tricks, often exposed to low temperatures, made to stand in the nude, and whenever he seemed to be flagging, he was given drugs and enemas so that the interrogations could continue.

This abusive treatment caused marked changes in Qahtani's behavior. An FBI official later noted that he began "evidencing behavior consistent with extreme psychological trauma (talking to non-existent people, reporting hearing voices, crouching in a cell covered with a sheet for hours on end)." And Qahtani's treatment amounted to torture, according to Susan Crawford, a former federal judge who was appointed to oversee the Guantánamo military commissions by the Bush administration. Crawford determined that the cumulative effects on Qahtani of sustained isolation, sleep deprivation, nudity, and prolonged exposure to cold met the legal definition of torture. As a result, Crawford ruled that Qahtani could never be prosecuted for anything.

From the secret summaries of Qahtani's Guantánamo interrogations made public by WikiLeaks, it appears that it was only after the weeks of abuse that he told interrogators that KSM had introduced him to a man known as Abu Ahmed al-Kuwaiti, who had instructed him how best to communicate covertly with al-Qaeda members once he was in the States. In July 2001 the Kuwaiti had taken him to an Internet café in the buzzing Pakistani city of Karachi and given him some tuition in secret communications, likely instructing him in the "dead drop" method of secure e-mail communication that was then prevalent in al-Qaeda, in which two of the group's members would open a commonly shared password-protected e-mail account and write drafts of e-mails to each other that they never actually sent over the Internet, but that they both could still access in draft form.

The admission from Qahtani that the Kuwaiti had given him training in operational security seems to have been the first time that U.S. officials realized that the Kuwaiti was a player in al-Qaeda and a confidant of KSM's. It's not clear whether Qahtani gave that information up because he had been coercively interrogated or because interrogators had told him that KSM, who had been captured in Pakistan on March 1, 2003, was in American custody and Qahtani thought it was therefore permissible to divulge information relating to KSM's trusted circle. Either way, Qahtani identified the Kuwaiti only after he was subjected to a considerable amount of abuse at the hands of his captors.

American interrogators now knew that the Kuwaiti had helped train potential hijackers for the 9/11 mission, but as yet there was no sense that he might be bin Laden's key courier. And Abu Ahmed al-Kuwaiti was just one of many hundreds of names and aliases of al-Qaeda members and associates that interrogators were learning in 2002 and 2003 from detainees housed at Guantánamo, from captives in CIA secret prisons in eastern Europe, and from documents recovered in Afghanistan after the fall of the Taliban.

When KSM was first arrested, there was a sense at the CIA that his capture might soon lead to bin Laden himself. Michael Scheuer, who had led the dedicated bin Laden unit at the CIA when it was founded in December 1995, was less sanguine than most. He knew that bin Laden had a far better sense of security than KSM and some of the other al-Qaeda leaders who had been captured in the years immediately after 9/11. "Those guys were swashbucklers, they were the first generation, they didn't think there was a bullet made for them," says Scheuer. In fact, the letters and photos found on KSM did not provide any real leads to bin Laden's whereabouts.

Initially KSM was held by the Pakistanis, and he gave them some useful information that the CIA appears to have overlooked, or perhaps wasn't briefed about. A day after he was captured, he told his interrogators that bin Laden might be in Kunar province in Afghanistan. He also told them that the last letter he had received from bin Laden came through a courier, and that his leader had been helped out of Tora Bora by Ahmed al-Kuwaiti and a man named Amin ul-Haq. This was all accurate information. It's not clear how the information was extracted from KSM, but Pakistani interrogators are known to use harsh methods on occasion.

KSM was then transferred to U.S. custody. Despite being waterboarded 183 times and at one point kept up for seven and a half days straight while diapered and shackled at a CIA secret prison in northern Poland, KSM did not confess to the Kuwaiti's key role in al-Qaeda, instead telling his interrogators in late 2003 only that the Kuwaiti was now "retired." But hopes ran so high that KSM might provide the Rosetta Stone to al-Qaeda that senior CIA analyst Frederica traveled from the Agency's headquarters in Virginia to Poland to watch KSM being waterboarded.

KSM's assertion that the Kuwaiti was retired was curious, as not too many members of al-Qaeda were known to have retired. Indeed, information that KSM had given his U.S. interrogators a few months earlier led to the arrest in Thailand of a man known as Hambali, who was a leader of al-Qaeda's virulent Southeast Asian affiliate, Jemaah Islamiya. When CIA officials interrogated Hambali, he said that when he fled Afghanistan after the fall of the Taliban he stayed in an al-Qaeda safe house in Karachi, which was managed by . . . the Kuwaiti.

And shortly after KSM told his interrogators that the Kuwaiti was retired, an al-Qaeda courier by the name of Hassan Ghul told CIA interrogators a quite different story. Ghul, a Pakistani, was arrested in mid-January 2004 in northern Iraq carrying a letter addressed to bin Laden from al-Qaeda's leader in Iraq urging that he be allowed to embark on a full-scale war against Iraq's Shia population. Ghul obviously had access to al-Qaeda's inner circle in Pakistan and so was taken to a secret CIA prison in eastern Europe, where he was subjected to a variety of coercive interrogation techniques, including being slapped, slammed against a wall, forced to maintain stress positions, and deprived of sleep. Ghul's interrogators also requested permission to use nudity, water dousing, and dietary manipulation, but it's not clear if these techniques were actually employed on Ghul. At some point, Ghul told interrogators that the Kuwaiti was bin Laden's courier and frequently traveled with al-Qaeda's leader. He also said that the Kuwaiti was trusted by KSM and by Abu Faraj al-Libi, KSM's successor as the operational commander of al-Qaeda.

Libi had masterminded two serious but ultimately unsuccessful attempts to assassinate Pakistani president Pervez Musharraf in December 2003, and so he became the subject of intense interest from Pakistani security services. Libi was quite recognizable because of a skin disease that disfigured his face with blotchy white patches where he lacked melanin. As a result, Libi held the number-three spot in al-Qaeda for only a couple of years before he was arrested in Pakistan on May 2, 2005, in the city of Mardan, one hundred miles from Abbottabad, where bin Laden himself would soon arrive to live for the next six years.

A month after his arrest, Libi was handed over to the CIA. Coercive interrogation techniques (though not waterboarding) were used on him, and he told his American interrogators that after KSM was captured he, Libi, had received notice from bin Laden through a courier that he had been promoted to KSM's spot as the number three in al-Qaeda. At the time of his promotion, Libi was living in Abbottabad, an early indicator that the city was something of a base for al-Qaeda. It would be another seven years before the CIA would focus on Abbottabad as a likely hiding place for al-Qaeda's leader. Libi also told his interrogators that the Kuwaiti wasn't an important player in al-Qaeda and that it was in fact "Maulawi Abd al-Khaliq Jan" who was the courier who had informed him of his promotion by bin Laden. Counterterrorism officials later concluded that Maulawi Abd al-Khaliq Jan was a made-up name.

Did coercive interrogations lead to bin Laden? Such techniques were used on Qahtani, the twentieth hijacker, and on Ghul, the Pakistani al-Qaeda courier who was captured in Iraq. Both of them subsequently gave interrogators information that led the CIA to focus on the Kuwaiti as a possible avenue to finding bin Laden, which to defenders of these interrogation techniques would seem to prove that they are effective. Critics of the techniques, however, can point out that harsh methods were also used by the CIA to get KSM and Libi to talk, and both those men gave their interrogators disinformation about the Kuwaiti. Since we can't run history backward, we will never know what conventional interrogation techniques alone might have elicited from these four prisoners. And as we shall see, there were other steps along the way to finding bin Laden that had little to do with the information derived from al-Qaeda detainees.

Robert Richer, a veteran covert operations officer who ran the CIA's Near East Division after 9/11, says that, despite the frequent claims of Bush administration officials, information from detainees was not particularly helpful in averting possible terrorist attacks: "If you were to ask me what operations were actually defeated based on the information provided by the detainees, I'd be hard-pressed to give you an operation. I'd say we got some names; we could track some people." Where the detainee interrogations were useful, Richer said, was to fill in what he compares to the largely blank Scrabble board that was the structure of al-Qaeda known to the CIA in the immediate aftermath of 9/11. In combination with other information the CIA derived from documents and phone intercepts, detainee interrogations "could put that last thing in that got us a triple score."

Robert Dannenberg, who ran CIA counterterrorism operations from 2003 to 2004, agrees with this assessment: "Those guys gave a wealth of invaluable information about al-Qaeda. I wouldn't say so much about specific plots—you know, Abu is going to take a bomb and go blow up a train station in New York, no—but who the players are and what their relationships are, what their modus operandi is. . . . It gave us a cartography of al-Qaeda that would have taken us years to assemble had we not had this program in place. And it was an ongoing value. We would run pictures past these guys all the time and they said, 'This is so-and-so and this is so-and-so.'"

Neither KSM nor Libi ever produced any information that could help in the hunt for bin Laden. Counterterrorism officials gradually realized that for the senior al-Qaeda members they had in their custody, any items of knowledge they possessed that might lead to bin

Laden were the "crown jewels" that would be protected by the detainees at all costs.

Because both KSM and Libi had downplayed the Kuwaiti's importance to al-Qaeda, he began to be a subject of real interest at the CIA. But the Kuwaiti was not going to be easy to find, not least because he went by a blizzard of aliases, including "Mohamed Khan" (a name in Pakistan roughly equivalent to John Smith in America), "Arshad Khan," and "Sheik Abu Ahmed," while his real name, Ibrahim Saeed Ahmed, was known to almost no one but his immediate family.

Adding to the confusion, the Kuwaiti came from a large family of brothers, at least one of whom had died in Afghanistan after 9/11. In 2006, interrogators were told by a Mauritanian detainee who had joined al-Qaeda in the first year or so of its existence that the Kuwaiti had died in the arms of another al-Qaeda recruit during the Battle of Tora Bora. This suggested to the CIA that the Kuwaiti might well be a member of al-Qaeda. But was he now dead?

As the years passed after 9/11, President Bush abandoned his early "dead or alive" rhetoric about finding bin Laden and rarely mentioned him in public. If he did, it was to say, as he did in March 2002, that bin Laden had been "marginalized." After all, there was no need to add to the al-Qaeda leader's already-mythic profile by reminding the world that he continued to elude America's grasp.

In private, though, Bush never let the subject go. Michael Hayden, the CIA director during much of Bush's second term, recalls, "As I would walk into the Oval Office about 8 o'clock on a Thursday morning, the President would kind of look up from the desk and say, 'Well, Mike, how're we doing?' And there was no doubt in anyone's mind that was in the Oval, what he was talking about. He was talking about the pursuit of Osama bin Laden." One of the officials leading the hunt for bin Laden recalls drily, "The president's questions were passed down to us."

Hayden has the affability and twinkle of a favorite uncle, but his easy charm masks the steely edge of someone who grew up in a working-class family in Pittsburgh and rose to become a four-star air force general. Before he headed the CIA, Hayden spent years presiding over the ultra-secretive National Security Agency (NSA), which sucks up terabytes of data from phone calls and e-mails around the world. The NSA during Hayden's tenure also controversially, without first obtaining a warrant from a judge, listened in on phone conversations taking place in the United States by those who were suspected to have ties to al-Qaeda.

Hayden recalls that sometime in 2007 counterterrorism officials at the CIA began to brief him on a new approach: pursuing bin Laden through his courier network. "Now, keep in mind, if you're doing this, you're not chasing bin Laden," Hayden says. "This is at best a bank shot. You're putting your energy into identifying and deconstructing the courier network in the belief that it would lead you to bin Laden." Hayden in turn briefed Bush, explaining that the CIA had yet to find bin Laden's key courier but had zeroed in on the Kuwaiti as a possible candidate. "There was still no bated-breath moment about Abu Ahmed al-Kuwaiti," recalls one of the officials hunting bin Laden, but the fact that no al-Qaeda detainee had seen the Kuwaiti for a while made him intriguing.

The group at the CIA whose day-to-day task was to find bin Laden was never larger than two dozen men and women; all of them could fit comfortably into a medium-size conference room. Members of the group would come and go over the decade of the hunt, but many stayed on the bin Laden "account" during the long, lean years when there were no promising leads of any kind. John (a pseudonym), an analyst with the tall, lanky physique of the avid basketball player he had been in both high school and college, was highly regarded by senior officials at the Agency. John joined the Counterterrorism Center in 2003 and stayed there—even though he could have taken promotions to go elsewhere—because he was fixated on finding bin Laden. He had pushed for more drone strikes in the tribal regions of Pakistan in 2007, when he noticed that more Westerners were showing up there for terrorist training. Chuck (a pseudonym) was a careful analyst who had been on the al-Qaeda account since the terrorist group had bombed the two U.S. embassies in Africa in 1998, killing more than two hundred. As the years went by during the hunt for bin Laden, Chuck's hair had gradually turned gray.

Hanging over the veteran members of the team was the knowledge that some of their number could have done more to avert the 9/11 attacks. Certainly the general perception among the public was that there had been some kind of intelligence failure at the CIA. In fact, the intelligence community had done a thorough job of warning the Bush administration of the likelihood of some sort of large-scale anti-American attack during the spring and summer of 2001, as demonstrated by the titles and dates of reports the Agency generated for policymakers: "Bin Ladin Planning Multiple Operations," April 20; "Bin Ladin Public Profile May Presage Attack," May 3; "Bin Ladin Network's Plans Advancing," May 26; "Bin Ladin Attacks May Be Imminent," June 23; "Bin Ladin Threats Are Real," June 30; "Planning for Bin Ladin Attacks Continues, Despite Delays," July 2; "Bin Ladin Plans Delayed but Not Abandoned," July 13; and "Threat of Impending al-Qaeda Attack to Continue Indefinitely," on August 3. Of course, the CIA did not predict the time and place of al-Qaeda's looming attack, but that kind of precise warning information happens more often in movies than in real life.

If there was a fault, it was the failure among key national security officials in the Bush administration to take the CIA's warnings seriously enough.

But if there had not been an intelligence failure at the CIA, there *had* been a major bureaucratic failure, though it became clear only in the years after 9/11. Members of the Agency had failed to "watchlist" two suspected al-Qaeda terrorists, Nawaf al-Hazmi and Khalid al-Mihdhar, whom the CIA had been tracking since they attended a terrorist summit meeting in Malaysia on January 5, 2000. The failure to watch-list the two al-Qaeda suspects with the Department of State meant that they were able to enter the United States under their real names with ease. Ten days after the Malaysian terror summit, on January 15, 2000, Hazmi and Mihdhar flew into Los Angeles. The Agency also did not alert the FBI about the identities of the suspected terrorists, so that the Bureau could look for them once they were inside the United States. An investigation by the CIA inspector general—published in unclassified form in 2007—found that this was not the oversight of a couple of Agency employees, but that a large number of CIA officers and analysts had dropped the ball. "Some fifty to sixty" Agency employees read cables about the two al-Qaeda suspects without taking any action. Some of those officers knew that one of the al-Qaeda suspects had a visa for the United States, and by March 2001 some knew that the other suspect had flown to Los Angeles.

The soon-to-be hijackers would not have been difficult to find in California if their names had been known to law enforcement. Under their real names they rented an apartment, obtained driver's licenses, opened bank accounts, purchased a car, and took flight lessons at a local school. Mihdhar even listed his name in the local phone directory. It was only on August 24, 2001, as a result of questions raised by a CIA officer on assignment at the FBI, that the two al-Qaeda suspects were watch-listed and their names communicated to the Bureau. Even then the FBI sent out only a "routine" notice requesting an investigation of Mihdhar. A month later Hazmi and Mihdhar were two of the "muscle" hijackers on American Airlines Flight 77 that plunged into the Pentagon, killing 189 people.

The CIA inspector general's report concluded that "informing the FBI and good operational follow-through by CIA and FBI might have resulted in surveillance of both Mihdhar and Hazmi. Surveillance, in turn, would have had the potential to yield information on flight training, financing, and links to others who were complicit in the 9/11 attacks." The names of the CIA officers who dropped the ball on the al-Qaeda hijackers remain classified, and no disciplinary action was taken against them; however, most worked at the Counterterrorist Center, and many continued to work on the hunt for bin Laden after 9/11. The knowledge that they could have done more to avert the loss of nearly three thousand lives animated them to work all the harder on finding the man responsible.

7 OBAMA AT WAR

ON THE MORNING OF Tuesday, September 11, 2001, Illinois state senator Barack Obama was driving to a legislative hearing in downtown Chicago when he heard on the radio that a plane had hit the World Trade Center. By the time he arrived at the meeting, a second plane had flown into the Twin Towers. "We were told to evacuate," Obama recalls. Out on the streets, people looked nervously up at the sky, fearing that the Sears Tower, Chicago's landmark skyscraper, was also a possible target. Back at his office, Obama watched the images from New York: "a plane vanishing into glass and steel; men and women clinging to windowsills, then letting go; tall towers crumbling to dust."

Six years later, Obama was a U.S. senator mounting what seemed a quixotic challenge to Hillary Clinton for the Democratic nomination for president. Clinton appeared to hold all the cards: name recognition, the Clinton money machine, the endorsement of many of the Democratic Party's heavy hitters, top political consultants working on her team, and the hopes of many that she would be the first female president of the United States. But Obama thought she was vulnerable, particularly because of her support for the Iraq War, which was by now deeply unpopular, and which he had come out firmly against five years earlier. And Obama impressed a growing number of supporters with his intellect, his cool, and his ability to inspire young people, who flocked to his campaign. An Obama win, some hoped, would also help to heal the American Original Sin of slavery and subsequent racial discrimination.

As Obama's long-shot campaign gathered steam, on July 17, 2007, an unclassified version of a National Intelligence Estimate (NIE) on the state of al-Qaeda was released to the media with a considerable splash. The estimate concluded that al-Qaeda "has protected or regenerated key elements of its homeland attack capability, including: a safe haven in the Pakistan Federally Administered Tribal Areas (FATA), operational lieutenants, and its top leadership." This wasn't exactly news. In the summer of 2005, al-Qaeda had directed the deadliest terrorist attack in British history, killing fifty-two commuters on the London transportation system. And the following summer, there had been a foiled attempt to blow up as many as seven American, Canadian, and British airliners with liquid explosives smuggled onto planes at London's Heathrow airport. The public release of the key findings of the NIE was an official recognition that al-Qaeda had regrouped and was capable again of pulling off significant attacks in the West, and that the Bush administration's policy of giving the Pakistani military dictator Pervez Musharraf a free pass to deal on his own terms with the militant groups based in Pakistan's tribal regions was now over.

A couple of weeks after this NIE was released, Obama was scheduled to give a keynote speech on national security at the Woodrow Wilson Center in Washington. He met with his foreign policy advisors, Susan Rice and Denis McDonough, and speechwriter Ben Rhodes, at the modest two-room offices on Massachusetts Avenue that served as the Obama campaign headquarters in Washington. Together they hashed out a speech that encapsulated the Obama campaign's foreign policy critiques of the Bush administration: that it had diverted too many resources to Iraq and had taken its eyes off al-Qaeda, and that it didn't have a strategy for taking out al-Qaeda's leaders in their bases in Pakistan's tribal regions. Obama and his advisors kicked around exactly what language he would use in the speech. The decision was made to take a harsh line on Musharraf, whom they believed the Bush administration had coddled for too long.

There was a lot riding on the speech at the Wilson Center. The fact was, most of the D.C.-based punditocracy thought Senator Obama was a bit green, especially on national security issues and, in particular, by comparison to Senator John McCain, the presumptive Republican nominee for president, who had already served two decades in the Senate and was a leading member of the powerful Senate Armed Services Committee. Senator Clinton, too, was regarded as someone with credibility on national security issues. She also served on the Armed Services Committee and had traveled to dozens of nations when her husband was president, which had put her on a first-name basis with many world leaders.

The Wilson Center speech did not seem to allay doubts about Obama's experience. Much of the attention that it garnered from the media and other presidential candidates focused on a section about al-Qaeda's leaders in Pakistan, in which Obama declared, "If we have actionable intelligence about high-value terrorist targets and President Musharraf won't act, we will. . . . I will not hesitate to use military force to take out terrorists who pose a direct threat to America."

At a debate for Democratic presidential candidates in Chicago a week after the Wilson Center speech, Obama came under attack from Senator Christopher Dodd of Connecticut, who said Obama's suggestion of a possible American unilateral strike into Pakistan was "irresponsible." Senator Clinton piled on: "I think it is a very big mistake to telegraph that." To large applause, Obama struck back at Dodd and Clinton, who had both voted to authorize the Iraq War, saying, "I find it amusing that those who helped to authorize and engineer the biggest foreign policy disaster in our generation are now criticizing me for making sure that we are on the right battlefield and not the wrong battlefield in the war against terrorism."

Obama's supposed weakness on national security was the subject of Hillary Clinton's most famous campaign ad, which debuted in late February 2008. Over pictures of children sleeping at night and the sound of a ringing phone, a man's voice intoned portentously, "It's three a.m. and your children are safe and asleep. But there's a phone in the White House and it's ringing. Something's happening in the world. Your vote will decide who answers that call. Whether it's someone who already knows the world's leaders, knows the military, someone tested and ready to lead in a dangerous world. It's three a.m. and your children are safe and asleep. Who do you want answering the phone?" At the end of the ad the pictures of sleeping children dissolved to a shot of a composed Hillary Clinton wearing glasses and answering the phone. Obama was never mentioned, but he was clearly the person whom the Clinton campaign was targeting.

Criticism of Obama's presumed bellicosity toward Pakistan was not limited to the Democrats. Republican presidential candidate Mitt Romney ridiculed Obama as a "Dr. Strangelove" who is "going to bomb our allies." John McCain also weighed in: "Will we risk the confused leadership of an inexperienced candidate who once suggested bombing our ally, Pakistan?" When accepting his party's nomination for president in Denver in late August 2008, Obama took a swipe back at McCain, saying, "John McCain likes to say that he'll follow bin Laden to the gates of Hell, but he won't even follow him to the cave where he lives."

After Obama was inaugurated as president he faced a choice. Many of the voters who had elected him had done so because he was the "antiwar candidate" who had spoken out early against the Iraq War. Once in office, Obama could have recast Bush's "Global War on Terror" as a large-scale law enforcement campaign against jihadist terrorists, which many on the left of the Democratic Party believed was a more useful and accurate formulation. Obama did not choose that path. Instead, he publicly declared that the United States was at "war against al-Qaeda and its allies." This framing had a number of advantages: it opened a way for groups such as the Taliban, which might one day choose to distance itself from al-Qaeda, to enjoy peaceful relations with the United States, and it named the enemy rather than continuing the Bush formulation of a vague and open-ended conflict against a tactic that had existed for millennia. For Obama, however, the conflict remained a *war*, and not some kind of global police action.

Perhaps his views on national security had to do with when he came of age. Obama was the first major American politician in decades whose views about national security weren't deeply informed by what he did or didn't do in Vietnam. Too young to have served in Vietnam as the senators John McCain and John Kerry did, he was also too young to have avoided service in Vietnam as Dick Cheney, Bill Clinton, and George W. Bush had. For Obama, Vietnam was a nonissue, and it is possible this fact contributed to his greater willingness to use military power in comparison to an older generation of Democrats. It took Clinton two years to intervene in Bosnia, which was on the verge of genocide, whereas it took Obama only a week or so to intervene in Libya in the spring of 2011, when dictator Moammar Gadhafi was threatening large-scale massacres of his own population.

Obama embraced American "hard power" from the moment he assumed office. Only three days after his inauguration, at his first National Security Council meeting on January 23, 2009, the head of the CIA's National Clandestine Service, Michael J. Sulick, proposed that the United States continue the aggressive campaign of drone strikes in the tribal regions of Pakistan. Obama approved the campaign. That same day, a pair of CIA drone strikes in North Waziristan and South Waziristan reportedly killed ten militants and some dozen bystanders.

On December 9, 2009, Obama went to Norway to accept the Nobel Peace Prize for his "extraordinary efforts to strengthen international diplomacy." Seemingly confounding the expectations of those who awarded him the prize, a little over a week earlier, troubled by the recent resurgence of the Taliban, he had substantially ramped up the Afghan War, authorizing a "surge" of thirty thousand troops, thereby doubling the number of American soldiers in Afghanistan. During his brief time in office, his administration had also authorized an unprecedented forty-five drone strikes aimed at Pakistani Taliban and al-Qaeda networks, killing about a half-dozen leaders of militant organizations—including two heads of Uzbek terrorist groups allied with al-Qaeda, and Baitullah Mehsud, the leader of the Pakistani Taliban—in addition to hundreds of lower-level militants and a smaller number of civilians (about 5 percent of the total), according to reliable press reports.

This policy of the targeted killing and execution without trial of hundreds of people was greeted mostly with silence by the human rights groups and those on the Left who had loudly condemned the Bush administration for its use of coercive interrogations and the lack of due process at Guantánamo.

Obama used the occasion of his Nobel Prize acceptance speech in Oslo to mount a nuanced defense of just wars, in particular the ground war and drone campaign he was waging against al-Qaeda and its allies in Afghanistan and Pakistan. The president acknowledged the great legacies of nonviolent approaches to social change bequeathed to the world by Gandhi and Martin Luther King Jr., but he also made it perfectly clear that his opposition to the Iraq War didn't mean that he embraced pacifism—not at all. Obama declared, "I face the world as it is, and cannot stand idle in the face of threats to the American people. For make no mistake: evil does exist in the world. A nonviolent movement could not have halted Hitler's armies. Negotiations cannot convince al-Qaeda's leaders to lay down their arms. To say that force is sometimes necessary is not a call to cynicism—it is a recognition of history, the imperfections of man, and the limits of reason."

Obama understood that simply because the Bush administration had tended to inflate the threat from al-Qaeda into an existential one similar to that posed by the Nazis or the Soviets, it didn't mean, conversely, that the threat was merely a mirage. In the year before his Nobel acceptance speech, Obama had been reminded about the reality of the threat from terrorists in many ways. Before he was even sworn in, he received some of his first intelligence briefings about the brutal three-day attack in Mumbai, India, in late November 2008, in which ten gunmen had targeted five-star hotels, a railway station, and an American-Jewish community center, killing some 170 people.

On the freezing day of January 20, 2009, when Obama took office as president, the intelligence community was at a high level of alert because of a serious threat to his inauguration by Al-Shabaab, an al-Qaeda-allied militant group based in Somalia. A group of Al-Shabaab terrorists was reported to be arriving in the United States from Canada to detonate a bomb on the Mall in Washington, D.C., where a million people would be gathered to watch Obama take the oath of office. The top counterterrorism aide to George W. Bush, Juan Zarate, says that during the four days before the inauguration, chasing down this threat consumed the attention of top national security officials on both the Bush and Obama teams: "Most of these threats, they wash out fairly early on, because elements of the story don't pan out. I got a call from my deputy, Nick Rasmussen, saying, 'This isn't washing out.'" In the end, the inauguration passed peacefully, and the threat from Al-Shabaab was determined to be a "poison pen," in which one group of Somali militants sought to make mischief for a rival group. But it was a stark reminder to Obama and his national security team that terrorism would be a major focus of their young administration.

Obama was determined, as he put it, to "destroy, dismantle, and defeat al-Qaeda." And what better way to speed that process than to eliminate bin Laden? Shortly after Obama assumed office, he met with CIA director Leon Panetta privately in the Oval Office and asked him, "How's the trail? Has it gone completely cold?" Panetta told the president that there weren't many promising leads. Obama said to him, "We need to redouble our efforts in hunting bin Laden down." In other meetings, Rahm Emanuel, Obama's chief of staff, and other senior members of the administration asked CIA officials point-blank, "Where do you think Osama bin Laden is?" The officials replied that they didn't have a clue, except that he was somewhere in Pakistan.

In late May 2009, Obama received one of his regularly scheduled briefings from his counterterrorism team in the Situation Room, which included an update on the hunt for bin Laden and his deputy Zawahiri. After the meeting, the president asked Panetta and National Security Advisor Tom Donilon to join him privately in the

Oval Office. The president asked them both to sit down and said, "We really need to intensify this effort. Leon, it needs to be your number one goal." On June 2, Obama signed a memo to Panetta that stated, "In order to ensure that we have expended every effort, I direct you to provide me within 30 days a detailed operation plan for locating and bringing to justice" bin Laden.

Five senior U.S. intelligence officials who worked for both Bush and Obama say that the idea that the CIA needed to be pushed to do more on bin Laden is laughable; the Agency was doing as much as it could already. Still, Panetta made updates on the hunt for bin Laden a required element of the three-day-a-week operational updates on counterterrorism and Middle East issues he already received. Woven into that was a weekly update on the hunt for bin Laden. Even if they had nothing, Panetta made it clear to his staff that they should tell him what they knew. It became embarrassing to bring nothing new to these briefings.

One promising lead appeared to be Saad bin Laden, one of the al-Qaeda leader's older sons, who had spent most of the past decade living under some form of house arrest in Iran. Saad was in his late twenties and had already played a minor leadership role in al-Qaeda. Around the time that Obama assumed office, Saad had been quietly released by the Iranians and had made his way to Pakistan's tribal regions. CIA officials tracking Saad hoped that he might try to find his father and so lead them to him. But itchy trigger fingers at the CIA prevailed, and in late July 2009 Saad was killed in an Agency drone strike, which took that lead firmly off the table.

Around the same time, what appeared to be the first real break to penetrate the top leadership of al-Qaeda was brought to Panetta: a Jordanian agent who was willing to spy on the inner circles of the terrorist group in Pakistan. This was of great interest because, despite the hundreds of billions of dollars consumed by American intelligence agencies since 9/11, the United States had never managed to place a spy inside al-Qaeda. Humam al-Balawi was a Jordanian pediatrician in his early thirties who had become radicalized by the Iraq War and had subsequently become an important voice on militant jihadist websites. Balawi was arrested in early 2009 by Jordan's General Intelligence Department (GID), with which the CIA enjoyed exceptionally close relations. After offering the doctor the possibility of earning substantial sums of money, GID officials believed they had "turned" Balawi, who said he was willing to go to the tribal regions of Pakistan to spy on the Taliban and al-Qaeda. The doctor quickly came through. In the early fall of 2009, Balawi sent his handlers at Jordanian intelligence a short video clip of himself sitting with Atiyah Abdul Rahman, one of bin Laden's top aides. Suddenly CIA officials saw the Jordanian doctor as a "golden source." Balawi told his handlers that his skills as a physician meant that he was being introduced to the leaders of al-Qaeda, including Ayman al-Zawahiri, to whom he was providing medical treatment. The CIA became so hopeful that in November 2009, Panetta told the president that the Jordanian doctor might soon lead the Agency to Zawahiri himself.

A jolting reminder of the importance of dismantling al-Qaeda's leadership structure in Pakistan had come just two months earlier. In early September 2009, Najibullah Zazi traveled from Denver to New York "to conduct martyrdom operations" in the Manhattan subway system. Zazi, an Afghan American who had been trained by al-Qaeda in Pakistan, planned to launch what would have been the deadliest terrorist attack in the United States since 9/11, by detonating bombs made with seemingly innocuous hair bleach, a signature of recent al-Qaeda plots. Under heavy FBI surveillance, Zazi was spotted in downtown Manhattan on September 11, 2009, the eighth anniversary of the attacks on the World Trade Center. From the time of Zazi's arrival in New York, Obama had received multiple briefings about the case from his national security team. Eight days later, Zazi was arrested. He was the first genuine al-Qaeda recruit to be discovered living in the United States in six years. On his laptop the FBI discovered pages of handwritten notes about the manufacture of explosives, technical know-how he had picked up at one of al-Qaeda's training facilities in Pakistan's tribal regions in 2008.

On Christmas Day 2009, the Obama administration faced an even larger threat when Umar Farouk Abdulmutallab, a twenty-three-year-old from a prominent Nigerian family, boarded Northwest Airlines flight 253 in Amsterdam, which was bound for Detroit with some three hundred passengers and crew. Hidden in his underwear was a bomb made with a plastic explosive that went undetected at airport security. As the plane neared Detroit, the young man tried to ignite the bomb. Some combination of his own ineptitude, faulty bomb construction, and the quick actions of the passengers and crew, who subdued him, prevented an explosion that might have brought down the plane. Immediately after he was arrested, Abdulmutallab told investigators that the explosive device "was acquired in Yemen along with instructions as to when it should be used."

If Abdulmutallab had succeeded in bringing down Northwest Airlines flight 253, the bombing would not only have killed hundreds but also seriously damaged the U.S. economy, already reeling from the effects of the worst recession since the Great Depression. It would also have dealt a crippling blow to Obama's presidency. According to the White House's own review of the Christmas Day plot, there was sufficient information already known to the U.S. government to determine that Abdulmutallab was likely working for al-Qaeda's affiliate in Yemen. As Obama admitted in a meeting of his national security team after the Nigerian was in custody, "We dodged a bullet."

The Christmas Day plot made the stakes all the higher for the CIA officials who knew of the Jordanian doctor and his promises to execute the first high-level penetration of al-Qaeda since 9/11. However, no one at the CIA had met Balawi, and pressure was mounting to get some Agency eyes on him. That task fell to Jennifer Matthews, the CIA station chief in Khost, in eastern Afghanistan, who had worked for the bin Laden unit almost from its inception. Matthews arranged for the Jordanian doctor to slip over the border from Pakistan's tribal areas to meet with her and a considerable team from the CIA. Determined that this first meeting with the golden source be warm and friendly, Matthews did not have Balawi searched when he entered the CIA section of Forward Operating Base Chapman in Khost on December 30, 2009. She had even arranged for a cake to be made for Balawi, whose birthday had been only five days earlier.

But there was to be no opportunity to celebrate. As he met with the CIA team, the Jordanian doctor began muttering to himself in Arabic, reached inside his coat, and then detonated a bomb that killed Matthews, a forty-five-year-old mother of three, and six other CIA officers and contractors who had gathered to meet him. It was the deadliest single day at the Agency since Hezbollah blew up the U.S. embassy in Beirut in 1983, killing eight CIA employees. The doctor from Jordan had not been spying on al-Qaeda's leaders; he had, in fact, been recruited by them.

John Brennan, who had served at the CIA for decades and was now Obama's top counterterrorism advisor, says the suicide bombing at Khost only deepened the Agency's determination to find the men they termed Number One and Number Two, making it "very personal for a lot of CIA officers." So personal that in the three weeks after Balawi's suicide attack, the CIA launched an unprecedented eleven drone strikes aimed at al-Qaeda and Taliban targets in Pakistan's tribal regions, killing more than sixty militants.

Within the space of a week, al-Qaeda's Yemen branch had almost downed an American commercial jet flying over the United States, and its Pakistan-based core had succeeded in killing seven CIA employees. It was a stark reminder that the Agency had to eliminate the leader of al-Qaeda.

Under Panetta, the CIA began pushing harder to put more Agency officers on the ground in Pakistan. The war in Iraq was winding down, which freed up more assets for the Afghanistan-Pakistan theater, including spies, drones, and satellites. The November 2008 Mumbai attacks, which were carried out by the Pakistan-based Lashkar-e-Taiba group, demonstrated that al-Qaeda was not the only terrorist organization based in Pakistan that was intent on attacking American targets. The State Department's Vali Nasr, a top advisor on Pakistan, explains, "The CIA goes into a completely different mode, almost like Pakistan becomes your Berlin of the 1960s, where you need to have assets, eyes, ears. Not for a specific project, but broadly, because every threat coming at us is probably going to come from here. You have to have your own assets. You have to have your own operations." Shamila Chaudhary, the director for Pakistan at the National Security Council, recalls that in the spring of 2010 there was a backlog of almost four hundred U.S. officials who were requesting visas for Pakistan. Clearly, these were not all conventional diplomats.

At the same time, in their public statements and in private meetings with U.S. officials, leading Pakistani politicians maintained with great conviction that bin Laden wasn't in their country. During an interview on CNN in April 2010, Prime Minister Yousuf Raza Gilani said, "Certainly he is not in Pakistan." Six months earlier Interior Minister Rehman Malik had met with a delegation of members of Congress and assured them that bin Laden wasn't in the area, although he could be in Iran, Saudi Arabia, or Yemen, or even dead.

Despite these denials, the necessity for the CIA to have more of its own assets in Pakistan was dramatically confirmed on May 1, 2010, when Faisal Shahzad, an American of Pakistani descent trained by the Taliban in the Pakistani tribal region of Waziristan, tried unsuccessfully to blow up his SUV in New York City's Times Square on a busy Saturday night. In late May, Panetta traveled to Pakistan to deliver a stern message to Pakistan's civilian and military leaders, making an open-ended threat that "all bets are off" should Pakistan-based terrorists successfully carry out an attack in the United States. Pakistani president Asif Ali Zardari pushed back, saying of Shahzad, "This guy is an American citizen. Why don't you have things more under control on your end?"

Not only did Obama sign off on a large increase in the number of CIA assets on the ground in Pakistan and an intensified campaign of CIA drone warfare there, but he also would come to embrace the use of covert military units in countries where the United States wasn't fighting traditional land wars, such as Libya, Pakistan, Somalia, and Yemen. By 2011, to the dismay of at least some of those who had voted for the "antiwar" president, the United States was waging some kind of war in six Muslim countries simultaneously.

8 ANATOMY OF A LEAD

IT WAS NOT UNTIL 2010 that the CIA had a series of significant breakthroughs regarding the Kuwaiti, the elusive courier. Earlier, with the help of a "third country" that officials won't identify, the Agency had been able to tie him to his real name, Ibrahim Saeed Ahmed. Still, his whereabouts remained unknown.

Then, in June 2010, the Kuwaiti and his brother both made changes in the way they communicated on cell phones that suddenly opened up the possibility of the "geolocation" of their phones. Knowing this, the Agency painstakingly reviewed reams of "captured" phone conversations of the Kuwaiti's family and circle of associates. Around this time the CIA conducted a joint operation with Pakistan's military intelligence service on phone numbers associated with an al-Qaeda "facilitation network." The Pakistanis did not know that some of these numbers were linked to Abu Ahmed al-Kuwaiti, but they could tell that one of the suspects in the network was speaking in a mix of both Arabic and Pashto, the language of northwest Pakistan, which was unusual. This suspect's phones were also switched off most of the time and were turned back on only in and around the city of Peshawar in northern Pakistan, not far from the Afghan border.

Finally, in the summer, the Kuwaiti received a call from an old friend in the Persian Gulf, a man being monitored by U.S. intelligence.

"We've missed you. Where have you been?" asked the friend.

"I'm back with the people I was with before," the Kuwaiti responded elliptically.

There was a tense pause in the conversation as the friend mulled this over. "May God facilitate," the caller finally said, likely realizing that the Kuwaiti was back in bin Laden's inner circle.

CIA officials took this call as confirmation that the Kuwaiti was still likely working with al-Qaeda, something they had not been entirely sure about. The National Security Agency was listening to this exchange and, through geolocation technologies, was able to zero in on the Kuwaiti's cell phone in northwestern Pakistan. But to find out where the Kuwaiti lived by monitoring his cell phone would go only so far. The courier practiced rigorous operational security and was always careful to insert the battery in his phone and to turn it on only when he was at least an hour's drive away from the Abbottabad compound where he and bin Laden were living. And Pakistan was a country of 180 million people.

In August 2010 a Pakistani "asset" working for the CIA tracked the Kuwaiti to Peshawar, where bin Laden had founded al-Qaeda more than two decades earlier. In the years that bin Laden had been residing in the Abbottabad compound, the Kuwaiti regularly passed through Peshawar, the gateway to the Pakistani tribal regions where al-Qaeda had regrouped after 9/11. Once the CIA asset had identified the Kuwaiti's distinctive white Suzuki Jeep with a spare tire on its back in Peshawar, he was able to follow him as he drove home to Abbottabad, more than two hours' drive to the east. The large compound where the Kuwaiti finally alighted immediately drew interest at the Agency because it didn't have phone or Internet service, suggesting that its owners wanted to stay off the grid.

No one at the Agency believed that the courier would actually be *living* with bin Laden. CIA officials thought that they would track the courier to his home and then there would be another round of surveillance to see if he would then lead them to bin Laden's hiding place. But there was something about the Abbottabad compound that piqued their interest. One official remembers her reaction when she first saw the compound: "Holy Toledo! Who in al-Qaeda would the group spend this kind of money on?" Officials calculated that the compound and the land it stood on were worth several hundred thousand dollars—about the cost of the 9/11 operation.

In late August 2010 the top officials in the CIA's Counterterrorism Center briefed Panetta about the new bin Laden lead, telling him, "We've been tracking suspected couriers, people who've got historic ties to bin Laden, and we tracked them back to a place that looks like a fortress." This got Panetta's attention. "A fortress? Tell me about that fortress," he said. The CIA officials described a compound ringed with twelve-foot-high walls, and one section having eighteen-foot-high walls, and a top-floor balcony on one of the buildings shielded by seven-foot-high walls. They told Panetta the residents of the compound burned their own trash.

"This is very strange," Panetta said. "It's very mysterious. It requires deeper investigation. I want every possible operational avenue explored to get inside that compound."

PANETTA BRIEFED PRESIDENT OBAMA and his key national security advisors about this development in the Oval Office, saying, "We have the courier's name and we have his location in a place called Abbottabad and maybe, just maybe, bin Laden might be there as well." Panetta showed the group satellite imagery of the compound and compared the area where the compound sat to Leesburg, Virginia—a pleasant historic town thirty miles northwest of Washington. Obama recalls that Panetta "was cautious in saying that they could say definitively this was where bin Laden was. My feeling at the time was: interested, but cautious."

Tony Blinken, a low-key lawyer who had worked for Bill Clinton on his National Security Council staff and was now Vice President Joe Biden's top national security advisor, recalls both real interest and some skepticism among the officials listening to Panetta. "This wouldn't have been brought to the president if it wasn't serious," Blinken says, "but there had obviously been instances in the past when we really thought we were hot on the trail, and then for one reason or another we weren't. And so I think it was a real interest, but also we didn't want to make too much of it."

Over the next several months, Panetta became increasingly annoyed—some CIA officials even say "pissed"—about what he believed was a lack of creativity among the bin Laden hunters. "I want to know what's going on inside that compound," Panetta demanded. "I don't want to just surveil it from the outside. I want to get inside there, I want to get clarity on what is happening there." Leaders of the Counterterrorism Center were instructed to show Panetta any of the ideas for observing the compound they came up with—even those they discarded. He urged them to consider every form of espionage, including getting into sewage lines and implanting devices, putting a telescope in the mountains two kilometers away, even putting a camera on a tree inside the compound walls. The Counterterrorism Center officials came back to him, dismissing one approach after another as too risky or not workable. A few weeks after Panetta suggested putting a camera on a tree inside the compound, the Kuwaiti chopped down the tree in question.

Finally, in the late fall, Jeremy Bash, Panetta's chief of staff, gathered together the bin Laden hunters at the Agency and said, "Give the director twenty-five operational activities that you could use to get into the compound, or to learn what is happening there, and don't be afraid of making some of them kind of creative." The bin Laden hunters came back with a chart with thirty-eight ideas. Some were outlandish. One idea was to throw in foul-smelling stink bombs to flush out the occupants of the compound. Another was to play on the presumed religious fanaticism of the compound's inhabitants and broadcast from loudspeakers outside the compound what purported to be the "Voice of Allah," saying, "You are commanded to come out into the street!"

Other more plausible ideas included coming up with some technology that would enable the Agency to spy on the occupants using the small satellite dish connected to the compound's sole television, or from a nearby CIA safe house, where agents would pick up the sounds and energy emissions that would result if bin Laden decided to record a new videotape.

After Panetta was confident that the team had exhausted every possible approach, they narrowed it down to three or four avenues. One creative, if ethically questionable, tactic was to recruit Shakil Afridi, a Pakistani doctor from the tribal regions, to mount a bogus vaccination program in and around bin Laden's neighborhood. The idea was to get access to the compound, take samples of the residents' blood, and then match those with known samples of bin Laden family DNA that were in the Agency's possession. In March, Dr. Afridi traveled to Abbottabad, telling locals that he had funds to start a free hepatitis B vaccination drive. So as not to arouse suspicion, Afridi recruited nurses and health workers to administer the vaccinations starting in a poor neighborhood on the outskirts of the city rather than in the more affluent Bilal Town. But Afridi's team was never able to get DNA samples from the bin Laden children.

The analytical case that the Kuwaiti was the key to finding the al-Qaeda leader was first made in a memo by CIA officials in August 2010 titled "Closing In on Usama bin Ladin's Courier." A month later, an even more detailed assessment of all the intelligence on the Kuwaiti was bundled into a document titled "Anatomy of a Lead." It was well understood by the authors of these memos that anything they wrote that focused on bin Laden's location was going to get a great deal of attention, including from the president. A counter-terrorism official explains: "We had a group who weren't afraid to say right out front that we believe this leads to bin Laden, putting themselves on the line."

Almost everyone who was then working on the bin Laden hunt had also worked on the hunt for Ayman al-Zawahiri. And they were keenly aware that seven CIA officers and contractors had died at the forward operating base in Khost, Afghanistan, chasing what at the time seemed to be the most promising lead the Agency had on Zawahiri since 9/11 but turned out to be an al-Qaeda sting opera-tion. Those who died at Khost had been friends and colleagues of the analysts who were now positing that they had the best lead on bin Laden in a decade.

What everyone involved in the bin Laden hunt wanted to avoid at all costs was another weapons of mass destruction (WMD) debacle. The faulty assumption that Saddam Hussein was reconstituting his WMD program, which had been the key justification for the Iraq War, rested in part on a number of dodgy intelligence sources. One of them was an Iraqi defector with the telling alias of "Curveball," who claimed that Saddam possessed mobile bioweapons labs. This became a central exhibit in the Bush administration's assertions that Saddam had a biological weapons program. What wasn't well understood by senior Bush officials and in much of the U.S. intelligence community was the fact that Curveball was an alcoholic and a congenital liar.

The damage done by the fabrications of sources such as Curveball was compounded by the fact that where there were "dissents" about aspects of Iraq's supposed WMD program from any of the sixteen U.S. intelligence agencies, they were generally buried in lengthy reports. Aluminum tubes shipped to Iraq in 2001 were believed by the CIA to be parts for centrifuges in Iraq's uranium-enrichment program, but experts at the Department of Energy were rightly skeptical of this claim, a view that didn't get any real hearing among policymakers.

The intelligence community was determined to learn from these costly mistakes. This time there would be no repeat of CIA director George Tenet's famous "slam dunk" assertion to President Bush that Iraq possessed weapons of mass destruction. The director of terrorism analysis at the CIA, a careful analyst who for four years had been the official who six days every week delivered to President Bush his highly classified President's Daily Brief, was determined to thoroughly kick the tires of the analytical case on the Kuwaiti. The small cadre of analysts at the CIA who were aware of the intelligence on the Kuwaiti subjected it to a formal process of structured analytical techniques, drilling down on key questions: What's the body of evidence that the Kuwaiti is bin Laden's courier? Who else could the Kuwaiti be if he wasn't the courier for al-Qaeda's leader? Was the Kuwaiti even still working for al-Qaeda?

During October 2010, officials came up with several alternative explanations for the intelligence they had been able to gather on the Kuwaiti: that he had stolen money from al-Qaeda and was now keeping a low profile; that he was working for someone else in al-Qaeda; that he was the courier for some criminal unrelated to al-Qaeda; or that bin Laden's family, but not bin Laden himself, was living in the mysterious compound. They concluded that they could not rule out any of these alternative hypotheses. A counterterrorism official recalls, "We put an enormous amount of work in exploring all of these hypotheses so the president and his advisors could make an informed judgment about what they planned to do next." Cognizant of the lessons of the WMD fiasco, officials actively encouraged dissent among the analysts leading the hunt for bin Laden. One official says, "We kept explaining to our group: 'If you see something that doesn't make sense you need to raise your hand now.' "

During the fall, counterterrorism officials continued to watch the Abbottabad compound and track the Kuwaiti's movements around northwestern Pakistan. They now had "high confidence" that the Kuwaiti was still a member of al-Qaeda, but they didn't have any such level of confidence that bin Laden was living in the compound. The Agency listened in to the Kuwaiti's phone conversations and spied on him as he traveled around Pakistan. CIA officials found it telling that when the Kuwaiti and his family visited other family members in Pakistan, they lied about where they were living, saying they lived in Peshawar. They also lied to neighbors about who they were, what they were doing, and where they were going. They also didn't let anybody into the compound, the construction of which seemed to be designed to thwart good surveillance from any angle.

As they observed the comings and goings at the compound, one U.S. official says, "We began to believe bin Laden's family was there. Was bin Laden nearby, given his devotion to them?" A few analysts, such as John, the deputy chief of the Afghanistan-Pakistan section in the Counterterrorism Center, thought that the likelihood of bin Laden being at the compound was as high as 90 percent, but whatever an analyst thought the odds might be, the case that bin Laden was there was always entirely circumstantial.

There continued to be features of the compound that caused some head scratching at CIA headquarters. The first "anomaly" was that the compound was less than a mile from the Pakistani military academy. The second was that it was far from small and obscure, rising fortress-like above many of the neighboring buildings. Third, there were many children living there, a number of whom were old enough to blab about a mysterious "uncle" who never left the compound. And the wives and children of the courier and his brother would regularly take trips to visit family members elsewhere in Pakistan. One of those children, seven-year-old Muhammad, even attended a religious school outside Abbottabad. CIA officials were familiar with the idea of "hiding in plain sight," but the Abbottabad compound seemed to take that concept to a new level.

Robert Cardillo, a veteran intelligence official who briefed President Obama three times a week about national security developments around the world, thought that if bin Laden was indeed living in the compound, it was "nuts" that he hadn't moved in six years. And if bin Laden was living there, how could the Pakistanis not know? After all, he reasoned, this wasn't in some remote, lawless tribal region, but in a well-policed city. Other facets of the case didn't sit well with Cardillo either; there were about twenty adults and children living at the compound, which seemed a big security risk for bin Laden to take. And while the courier and his brother practiced rigorous operational security with their cell phones, there were other cell-phone users at the compound who weren't taking any such precautions. Cardillo had so many nitpicky questions about the intelligence picture surrounding the compound that at one point Michael Vickers, the civilian overseer of Special Operations, said,

ANATOMY OF A LEAD

"You know you're being Debbie Downer around here." Cardillo parried, "Mike, that's my job. Thank you."

In the early fall the CIA set up a safe house in Abbottabad for agents who would survey the compound and built up a "pattern of life" analysis of the people living at the compound. According to a retired senior CIA operations officer who worked in Pakistan after 9/11, Agency officials setting up this type of safe house typically looked for a residence that would attract no attention; everything would have to appear to be perfectly normal. This meant there should be no detectable changes made to the profile of the house and its constituent buildings, meaning no proliferation of antennas, no lights on late at night, and no conspicuous new construction. The routine at the safe house would have to be "non-alerting: no sudden uptick in visitors and no comings and goings at odd hours. Also, the cover story for the residents—who they were, where they came from, what their business was in Abbottabad—would have to be rock-solid. Nothing weird. Nothing unusual. Boring is always best. And, always best to provide answers to questions up front rather than hope that the neighbors will reach the conclusion you want. In a place like Pakistan one easy way to do that is simply to make sure that your own household staff is fed the right cover story. All maids, cooks, and drivers talk in environments like that. It's like a small-town environment. Whatever your maid knows, or thinks she knows, about who you are, where you came from, and what you are up to will be known to every domestic in the neighborhood within days of your arrival."

The CIA agents monitoring the compound initially observed only the two families of the courier and his brother living there. But after further careful monitoring, they determined that there was a third family living at the compound. Members of this third family never seemed to leave the compound, but a careful observation of their movements and the number of men's, women's, and children's garments hung up to dry on clotheslines indicated that this other family consisted of three women, a young man, and at least nine children, all living in the main building. Were these bin Laden's wives, children, and grandchildren? Certainly the composition of this family was consistent with what was known about bin Laden's immediate family.

DESPITE HAVING SPIES on the ground in Abbottabad and NSA satellites orbiting in space above the compound, the Agency was never able to get an image of bin Laden. It did observe that some individual took a walk every day in the vegetable garden of the compound, but someone had cleverly installed a tarpaulin above the area where that person would walk, so spy satellites never got a good look at him. Analysts called the mysterious person "the pacer." The pacer never left the compound, and his daily excursions seemed like those of someone in a jail yard who couldn't leave but was trying to get some exercise. He walked very rapidly in tight circles, then went back inside. Knowing that bin Laden was quite tall, Panetta instructed his team to check the pacer's height by comparing it to that of the nearest wall. By measuring the pacer's shadow, intelligence officials determined that the mystery man could measure anywhere from five foot five to six foot eight. This didn't provide much of a clue.

The CIA went to Congress and successfully lobbied for tens of millions of dollars to be reallocated in the Agency budget to support this ramped-up intelligence effort. Still, officials had what they termed "collection gaps": they couldn't see inside the compound, and they couldn't monitor it around the clock. But counterterrorism officials were wary of becoming more aggressive in their collection efforts, because this might end up "spooking the targets." They were concerned that someone as canny as bin Laden, if he really was the pacer, would have some kind of escape plan in place. They also thought it likely that he would have taken the precaution of putting a local police officer on his payroll—someone who would tip him off if there was any sign of an operation to take down the compound.

In November, Panetta, together with the CIA bin Laden hunters, went to Obama and said, "We think there is a strong possibility that bin Laden is in the Abbottabad compound." The analysts believed this with varying degrees of certainty, with most estimating the probability at 80 percent. The lead analyst, John, was still at about 90 percent, while Michael Morell, the deputy director of the CIA, was at 60 percent.

"Why do people have different probabilities?" Obama asked Panetta, who pitched the question to Morell.

"Intelligence is not an exact science," Morell explained. "Even if we had a source inside the compound saying bin Laden was there, I'd only be at 80 percent because sources are of varying reliability. Those analysts who are at 80 to 90 percent have been tracking al-Qaeda in recent years and have had great success stopping plots and undermining the organization. They are confident. The folks at the lower end of the range are those who lived through intelligence failures, particularly the Iraq WMD issue." At one point Morell told the president that when it came to the sheer volume of data points, "the circumstantial case of Iraq having WMD was actually stronger than the circumstantial case that bin Laden is living in the Abbottabad compound."

Morell's own confidence that bin Laden was at the compound remained steady, at 60 percent, because there was never any direct confirmation that bin Laden was there. On the other hand, there was no good alternative explanation for everything that happened at the compound and the fact that the residents were clearly hiding *something*. Throughout the first weeks of 2011 the circumstantial case that bin Laden was living in the Abbottabad compound remained in a sort of stasis. "We got a lot of information over time that didn't disprove bin Laden was there and didn't corroborate it either," says a counterterrorism official. CIA officers from outside the Counterterrorism Center were brought in to see whether the bin Laden analysts might be missing something. They didn't see anything obvious. A CIA analyst who hunted bin Laden says, "We had pulled on a gazillion threads in the last decade, sometimes a 'sighting' of bin Laden, or some other piece of intelligence, and every time the threads were pulled they quickly unraveled. With this Abbottabad thread, every time you pulled on it, it didn't unravel."

JOHN BRENNAN, the longtime CIA officer who was now Obama's top counterterrorism advisor, met regularly with the analysts working the bin Laden case, many of whom he had known and admired for years. Brennan pushed them to come up with intelligence that disproved the notion that bin Laden was living in the Abbottabad compound, saying, "I'm tired of hearing why everything you see confirms your case. What we need to look for are the things that tell us what's *not* right about our theory. So what's not right about your inferences?"

The analysts came back to the White House one day and started their intelligence update, saying, "Looks like there's a dog on the compound." Denis McDonough, Obama's deputy national security advisor, remembers thinking, "Oh, that's a bummer. You know, no self-respecting Muslim's gonna have a dog." Brennan, who had spent much of his career focused on the Middle East and spoke Arabic, pointed out that bin Laden, in fact, did have dogs when he was living in Sudan in the mid-1990s. (Indeed, when al-Qaeda's leader was living in the Sudanese capital of Khartoum, he had taken an interest in training police dogs.)

As February turned into March, CIA director Leon Panetta asked a veteran counterterrorism official—who had lived through many years of bin Laden leads not panning out—what percentage she now placed on bin Laden being in the compound. "Seventy percent," she said.

The percentages suggested a kind of precision that didn't exist in reality. Bin Laden was either living in the compound or he wasn't. Even after months of observation, no one really knew for sure.

9 THE LAST YEARS OF OSAMA BIN LADEN

BIN LADEN'S LIFE IN THE COMPOUND was not, of course, taken up only by attending to his wives and children, saying his daily prayers, indulging in his hobbies of reading anti-American and anti-Zionist literature, and watching old videos of himself. It was also consumed with the serious business of trying to run al-Qaeda, a difficult task for someone in hiding whose key lieutenants were also on the run.

It was only through Abu Ahmed al-Kuwaiti that bin Laden was able to maintain a semblance of control over his organization. The Kuwaiti and his brother Abrar, both in their early thirties, were bin Laden's sole guards and his only connection to the outside world. At the local general store, they bought rice, lentils, and other groceries. Using their local aliases, Arshad Khan and Tariq Khan, the two brothers would escort the bin Laden children to a local doctor for treatment of the usual stomach upsets, colds, and coughs. The Khans came and went in the neighborhood without fanfare, driving their white Suzuki Jeep and red van as they went about their errands. The two brothers occasionally attended daily prayers at a local mosque but made no small talk. To the inquisitive, they said they worked in the transportation business. This didn't satisfy the curiosity of some locals, who thought they might be drug dealers and complained that even with such a big house they didn't help the poor.

The brothers were in fact longtime al-Qaeda made men whose father had immigrated five decades earlier to Kuwait from a small Pashtun village in the north of Pakistan, some three hours' drive from Abbottabad. This background made the two brothers indispensable to bin Laden because they could easily blend into the Pashto-speaking areas of northern and western Pakistan, where the leaders of al-Qaeda were now hiding, and they also spoke Arabic and so could communicate easily with the Arab leaders of al-Qaeda. The brothers had sworn *bayat* to bin Laden, a religiously binding oath of allegiance to the man they venerated as the emir (prince) of jihad. They would do bin Laden's bidding without question.

Crucially, the Kuwaiti transported letters and computer thumb drives containing instructions from bin Laden to other al-Qaeda leaders. The Kuwaiti practiced careful operational security when he transported these items to Peshawar for later distribution to the nearby tribal regions on the border with Afghanistan, where many of al-Qaeda's leaders were based. Conscious of American and Pakistani abilities to monitor cell phones, the Kuwaiti would turn on his cell only around the small town of Hasan Abdal, an hour's drive southwest of Abbottabad.

Through the messages transported by the faithful Kuwaiti, bin Laden stayed in touch with the organization he had founded and did his best to manage al-Qaeda's far-flung regional affiliates in countries such as Iraq, Somalia, and Yemen. He also continued to plot carnage on a grand scale—weighty matters that he never discussed with his wives.

Bin Laden's principal conduit to his organization was Atiyah Abdul Rahman, a Libyan militant of about forty. Viewed by officials in the West as no more than a mid-tier terrorist, Rahman was actually bin Laden's chief of staff. Privately, bin Laden fretted that Rahman could be heavy-handed and undiplomatic in his dealings with others, but despite those concerns, bin Laden was in frequent contact with the Libyan, far more so than with his more well-known top deputy, the dour Egyptian surgeon Ayman al-Zawahiri. In the years after 9/11, Western counterterrorism officials believed that Zawahiri was the hands-on manager of al-Qaeda, but in reality it was still bin Laden who was deep in the weeds of personnel decisions and plotting for the group.

Through Rahman, bin Laden issued instructions to his regional affiliates: the North African terrorist organization al-Qaeda in the Islamic Maghreb, the Somali militant group Al-Shabaab, al-Qaeda in Iraq, and al-Qaeda in the Arabian Peninsula. In the years after 9/11, Rahman also traveled to Iran to act as a bridge between bin Laden and some longtime leaders of al-Qaeda such as Saif al-Adel, who was living there under a form of house arrest, as were a number of bin Laden's children.

Iraq was a particular concern for bin Laden, who initially had been ecstatic about the opportunities that the 2003 American invasion presented to establish an al-Qaeda affiliate in the Arab heartland. By the time he had moved into the Abbottabad compound two years later, however, he had grown increasingly worried about the brutal tactics of al-Qaeda in Iraq, which included blowing up key Shia mosques and killing fellow Sunnis who didn't follow the group's dictates to the letter. Bin Laden reminded the leaders of his Iraqi affiliate about the mistakes that Islamist militants had made in Algeria in the 1990s, when they launched a civil war so brutal that they eliminated any vestige of popular support they had once enjoyed.

Bin Laden at his one and only press conference, held in 1998, in which he declared war against the U.S. CNN VIA GETTY IMAGES

Doting father Osama bin Laden with son Hamza on January 1, 2001. HAMID MIR/DAILY DAWN/GAMMA-RAPHO VIA GETTY IMAGES

New York police stand near a wanted poster for bin Laden in the financial district of New York on September 18, 2001. JEFF HAYNES/AFP/GETTY IMAGES

A cave in Tora Bora where al-Qaeda militants sheltered during the Battle of Tora Bora in December 2001. REZA/GETTY IMAGES

Two Afghan anti-Taliban fighters in Tora Bora on December 6, 2001, as the battle against al-Qaeda reached its height. ROMEO GACAD/AFP/GETTY IMAGES

In December 2001, in his first video statement since the 9/11 attacks, bin Laden delivered a message to the American people.

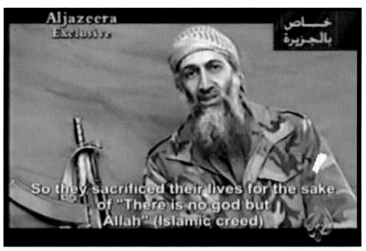

In this video, shot six years later in 2007, bin Laden's beard has been trimmed and dyed.

 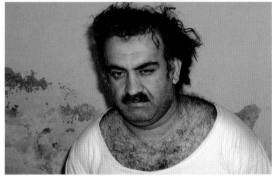

Mohammed al-Qahtani, originally recruited to be a muscle hijacker on 9/11 (left), and Khalid Sheikh Mohammad, the mastermind of the 9/11 attacks (right), were captured in 2001 and 2003 respectively. Coercive interrogations of the men yielded contradictory information about "the Kuwaiti," bin Laden's courier. DEPARTMENT OF DEFENSE/MCT VIA GETTY IMAGES [AL-QAHTANI]; ASSOCIATED PRESS [KSM]

Between 2003 and 2008, Major General Stanley McChrystal transformed Joint Special Operations Command (JSOC) into a commando force of unprecedented agility and lethality, paving the way for Operation Neptune Spear.
PAULA BRONSTEIN/ GETTY IMAGES

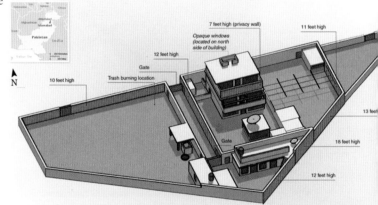

CIA graphic of bin Laden compound in Abbottabad. CIA

7 feet high (privacy wall)
Opaque windows (located on north side of building)
11 feet high
12 feet high
Gate
N
10 feet high
Trash burning location
13 feet
Gate
16 feet high
12 feet high

A satellite image of the bin Laden compound in Abbottabad.
DIGITALGLOBE VIA GETTY IMAGES

General James "Hoss" Cartwright (right) laughs with CIA director Leon Panetta. ALEX WONG/GETTY IMAGES

Undersecretary of Defense for Policy Michèle Flournoy testifies before members of Congress alongside Admiral Mike Mullen, chairman of the Joint Chiefs of Staff. ALEX WONG/GETTY IMAGES

President Barack Obama shakes
hands with Admiral Mike Mullen
in the Green Room of the
White House, following his
statement detailing the mission
against bin Laden on May 1, 2011.
OFFICIAL WHITE HOUSE PHOTO
BY PETE SOUZA

The architect of the raid on bin Laden's
Abbottabad compound, Vice Admiral
William McRaven.
WIN MCNAMEE/GETTY IMAGES

Assistant Secretary of Defense
for Special Operations and Low
Intensity Conflict Michael Vickers.
CHIP SOMODEVILLA/GETTY IMAGES

President Barack Obama makes a point during a meeting in the Situation Room of the White House about the mission against bin Laden. National Security Advisor Tom Donilon is next to the president.
OFFICIAL WHITE HOUSE PHOTO BY PETE SOUZA

Director of the National Counterterrorism Center Michael Leiter, who led a Red Team to review the intelligence on the Abbottabad compound just a few days before the raid. CHIP SOMODEVILLA/GETTY IMAGES

CIA Director Leon Panetta and his chief of staff, Jeremy Bash, watch a screen intently during the Navy SEAL raid that killed bin Laden. CIA

President Obama and Vice President Biden in the White House, May 1, 2011. Seated, from left, are Brigadier General Marshall B. "Brad" Webb, Deputy National Security Advisor Denis McDonough, Hillary Clinton, and Secretary of Defense Robert Gates. Standing, from left, are Admiral Mike Mullen, National Security Advisor Tom Donilon, Chief of Staff Bill Daley, National Security Advisor to the Vice President Tony Blinken, Director for Counterterrorism Audrey Tomason, Assistant to the President for Homeland Security John Brennan, and Director of National Intelligence James Clapper. OFFICIAL WHITE HOUSE PHOTO BY PETE SOUZA

THE LAST YEARS OF OSAMA BIN LADEN

In November 2005, as bin Laden was settling into his new life at the Abbottabad compound, Rahman wrote a seven-page letter to the leader of al-Qaeda in Iraq, the astonishingly cruel Abu Musab al-Zarqawi, who had made a habit of personally beheading his hostages and videotaping the results for global distribution on the Internet. Rahman's letter, which clearly reflected the views of bin Laden, was a polite but blistering critique of Zarqawi, who had recently directed suicide bombings at American hotels in Amman, Jordan, that had killed sixty people, almost all of them Jordanian civilians attending a wedding. The bombings had severely tarnished al-Qaeda's image in the Arab world and came on top of Zarqawi's indiscriminate slaughter of any Muslim who didn't precisely share his views. Like a dissatisfied boss delivering a performance review, Rahman told Zarqawi that he should henceforth follow instructions from bin Laden and cease counterproductive operations such as the hotel bombings in Jordan.

When Zarqawi was killed in an American air strike six months later, bin Laden's subsequent public statements of admiration for him were only because Zarqawi had taken the fight to the Americans in Iraq in a manner that bin Laden himself could only dream of. Privately, bin Laden was worried that Zarqawi had grievously harmed the al-Qaeda brand, and in October 2007, al-Qaeda's leader even issued an unprecedented public apology for the behavior of his followers in Iraq, scolding them for "fanaticism."

As bin Laden's stay in Abbottabad lengthened into years, his central focus always remained attacking the United States. By early 2011 he was keenly aware that almost a decade had passed since a successful attack on America. As the tenth anniversary of his great victory against the Americans approached, bin Laden wrote messages to al-Qaeda's franchises in Algeria, Iraq, and Yemen reminding them that America was still their main enemy, and admonishing

139

them not to be distracted by local fights. He schemed about assassinating President Obama and General David Petraeus, who had inflicted such heavy losses on al-Qaeda's affiliate in Iraq, although he observed that killing Vice President Joe Biden would likely be a waste of time because he was not a sufficiently important target. To his team, bin Laden emphasized the continued importance of targeting major American cities such as Chicago, Washington, New York, and Los Angeles. Rahman frequently had to remind bin Laden that al-Qaeda simply didn't have the resources to carry out his ambitious plans. Some of bin Laden's other lieutenants pointed out to him that it would be much more realistic to focus on fighting American soldiers in Afghanistan rather than trying to attack the United States itself, advice bin Laden simply ignored.

Writing in his journal, bin Laden, a meticulous note taker, tallied up how many thousands of dead Americans it would take for the United States to withdraw finally from the Arab world. He mused about attacking trains by putting trees or cement blocks on railroad tracks in the United States, and he suggested that al-Qaeda enlist non-Muslim American citizens opposed to their own government, citing disaffected African Americans and Latinos as potential recruits. Al-Qaeda enjoyed only modest success with this tactic, recruiting Bryant Neal Vinas, an unemployed Hispanic American from Long Island, who participated in an attack on a U.S. base in Afghanistan in 2008 before he was arrested by the Pakistanis and handed over to American custody.

Bin Laden exhorted his followers to plan an attack on the United States to coincide with the tenth anniversary of 9/11 or with holidays such as Christmas, and he advocated attacks on oil tankers as part of a wider strategy to bleed the United States economically. He ordered Rahman also to focus on recruiting jihadists for attacks in Europe. Al-Qaeda's last successful European attacks had been the four suicide bombings on London's transportation system on July 7, 2005, which killed fifty-two commuters. Rahman was in touch with a group of Moroccan militants living in Düsseldorf, and in the fall of 2010, al-Qaeda's leaders were impatient to pull off an attack with multiple gunmen somewhere in Germany, though this plan fizzled out.

In one of his more blue-sky moments, bin Laden considered changing the name of al-Qaeda, which he believed had developed something of a branding problem. He worried that the full name of the group, al-Qaeda al-Jihad, which means "The Base for Holy War," was being lost in the West, where the group was known, of course, simply as al-Qaeda. Bin Laden believed that lopping off the word *jihad* had allowed the West to "claim deceptively that they are not at war with Islam." Bin Laden mulled over some decidedly uncatchy alternative names: the Monotheism and Jihad Group and the Restoration of the Caliphate Group.

Bin Laden paid a great deal of attention to his relatively new but quite promising Yemen-based affiliate, al-Qaeda in the Arabian Peninsula. It was this affiliate that had managed to smuggle a bomb onto an American passenger jet in the underwear of Umar Farouk Abdulmutallab, the Nigerian recruit who tried, unsuccessfully, to detonate the device as the plane flew over Detroit on Christmas Day 2009. Bin Laden gave tactical advice to the group, which published *Inspire*, an English-language webzine aimed at recruiting militants in the West. In one issue of *Inspire* a writer proposed that jihadists turn a tractor into a weapon by outfitting it with giant blades and then driving it into a crowd. Bin Laden tut-tutted that such indiscriminate slaughter did not reflect al-Qaeda's "values." And bin Laden made important personnel decisions for the group. When the leader of al-Qaeda in the Arabian Peninsula suggested appointing the American-born cleric Anwar al-Awlaki to head the organization, because his name recognition in the West would help with fund-raising, bin Laden nixed the idea, saying that he didn't know Awlaki and was quite comfortable with the leadership already in place. Bin Laden also offered strategic advice to his Yemeni followers, warning that there wasn't yet enough "steel" in al-Qaeda's support in the region to try to impose a Taliban-style regime there.

His key lieutenants wrote to bin Laden about the problems they were facing; chief among them was the campaign of American drone strikes in Pakistan's tribal regions. The U.S. drone campaign had begun there in 2004, under President Bush, but, as we have seen, President Obama had massively expanded the program. Under Bush, there had been one strike every forty days; under Obama, the tempo increased to one every four days. The strikes had made the position of al-Qaeda's "number three" one of the world's most perilous. In May 2010, down a dirt road from Miran Shah, the main town in the tribal region of North Waziristan, a missile from a drone killed Mustafa Abu al-Yazid, along with his wife and several of their children. Yazid was a founding member of al-Qaeda who served as the group's number three and oversaw the group's plots, recruitment, fund-raising, and internal security. In the past two years, bin Laden had also lost to drone strikes his chemical weapons expert, his chief of operations in Pakistan, his propaganda chief, and half a dozen other key lieutenants.

Rahman wrote to bin Laden that al-Qaeda was getting hammered by the drones, and asked whether there were alternative locations where the organization might rebase itself. Bin Laden instead approved the formation of a counterintelligence unit to root out the spies in the tribal areas who were providing pinpoint-accurate information to the Americans about the locations of his lieutenants. In 2010, however, he received a complaint that the counterintelligence shop could barely function on its small budget of a few thousand dollars. A particular worry for both bin Laden and Rahman was the fact that cash flow at al-Qaeda headquarters had by then slowed to a trickle. They corresponded about ways to refill the group's depleted coffers, focusing in particular on kidnapping diplomats in Pakistan.

Conscious of the pressures that al-Qaeda was now under—its dire financial situation, its decimated leadership bench, and its long-time inability to carry out any attack in the West—bin Laden started casting about for ways to reinvigorate his group. In the spring of 2011 he contemplated a new effort to negotiate a grand alliance of the various militant groups fighting in Afghanistan and Pakistan. In exchanges with his aides, he also considered brokering some sort of deal with the Pakistani government: al-Qaeda would halt its attacks in Pakistan and would in turn receive official Pakistani protection. There's no evidence that this deal ever happened, and it was, in any event, quite a naïve idea. No Pakistani government would make a peace deal with al-Qaeda; bin Laden and his top deputies had for many years publicly and repeatedly called for attacks on Pakistani officials and, as noted ealier, had on two occasions in 2003 tried to assassinate Pakistan's president, General Pervez Musharraf.

To the world, of course, bin Laden tried to present a very different image from that of the aging leader of a troubled terrorist group that he had become. Bin Laden once told the Taliban leader Mullah Omar that up to 90 percent of his battle was fought in the media. Indeed, he took his media campaign seriously, and in the videotapes he shot in a makeshift studio in the Abbottabad compound he dyed his whitening beard jet black and dressed in his finest beige robes trimmed with gold thread. In these videos, he sometimes sat behind a desk and no longer had the gun that had invariably been beside him, a prominent feature of many of his earlier videotaped appearances.

In 2007, bin Laden released a half-hour videotape that received considerable attention in the West because it was the first time he had appeared on video in three years. On the tape, he spoke directly to the American people from behind a desk in a jihadist parody of a presidential address from the Oval Office. He made no explicit threat of violence but instead urged Americans to convert to Islam and, in a meandering indictment of the United States, invoked the atomic bombings of Hiroshima and Nagasaki; the extermination of Native Americans; the baleful influence of U.S. corporations; and America's poor record on climate change, as demonstrated by its failure to sign the Kyoto agreement on global warming. These seemed more the musings of an elderly reader of *The Nation* than the leader of global jihad.

Bin Laden also recorded an average of five audiotapes a year from his Abbottabad lair, which were passed by courier to As Sahab, al-Qaeda's propaganda arm. As Sahab would dress up the audio files with photos of bin Laden, graphics, and sometimes sub-titled translations and then upload the results to jihadist websites or deliver them to Al Jazeera. On the audiotapes, bin Laden, ever the news junkie, would comment on events both large and small in the Muslim world. In March 2008 he denounced the publication five years earlier of cartoons of the Prophet Mohammed by a Dan-ish newspaper as a "catastrophe." Three months later, an al-Qaeda suicide attacker bombed the Danish embassy in Islamabad, killing six. After a nine-month silence, bin Laden released an audiotape in March 2009 condemning the recent Israeli invasion of Gaza. In late 2010 he weighed in on France's decision to ban Muslim women from wearing the all-enveloping burqa in public, and threatened revenge. Around the same time, he released a tape lambasting the Pakistani government's slow response to the massive flooding that had dis-placed twenty million Pakistanis during the summer of 2010.

Bin Laden's eloquence on every issue of interest to the Muslim world made his public silence about the events of the Arab Spring of 2011 all the more puzzling. After all, here was what he had long dreamed of: the overthrow of the tyrannical regimes of the Middle East. His silence on the issue is likely explained by the fact that his foot soldiers and his ideas were notably absent in the revolutions that roiled the Middle East. No protestors held aloft pictures of bin Laden or spouted his virulent anti-American rhetoric, and few were demanding Taliban-style theocracies, bin Laden's preferred political end state. The protests also undercut two of bin Laden's key claims: that only violence could bring change to the Middle East, and that only by attacking America could the Arab regimes be overthrown. The protestors in Tunisia and Egypt who overthrew their dictators were largely peaceful and were not inspired by al-Qaeda's attacks on the West; rather, they were ordinary Tunisians and Egyptians fed up with the incompetence and cruelty of their rulers.

How to respond to all this must have been confounding for bin Laden, whose love for the limelight was intense and whose total irrelevance to the most important development in the Middle East since the collapse of the Ottoman Empire was painfully obvious. In late April 2011 he taped an audio message, which was not released before he was killed, in which he welcomed the Tunisian and Egyptian revolutions, saying, "We watch this great historic event and we share with you joy and happiness and delight." On the tape, bin Laden said that Sharia law should govern the new Egypt and Tunisia, but strangely did not mention the revolts that were then also spreading in Bahrain, Libya, Syria, and Yemen.

Bin Laden was still revered by his family and followers living on the Abbottabad compound, but by the spring of 2011, as he embarked on his sixth year of residing there, he had become increasingly irrelevant to the Muslim world. The religious Robin Hood image he had projected in the years immediately after 9/11 had largely evaporated, and most Muslims had rejected al-Qaeda because of its long track record of killing Islamic civilians. Perhaps most fatal to his ambitions, bin Laden never had anything to offer in the way of real solutions to the economic and political problems that continued to plague the Arab world.

10 THE SECRET WARRIORS

Several hundred miles off the coast of Somalia, as dusk deepened over the Indian Ocean, on the sweltering evening of April 13, 2009, three shots rang out. All the bullets found their targets: three Somali pirates in a small lifeboat bobbing on the darkening sea.

For the past five days the pirates had held hostage Richard Phillips, the American captain of the container ship *Maersk Alabama*. President Obama had authorized the use of deadly force if Phillips's life was in danger. Unbeknownst to the pirates, days earlier a contingent of Navy Sea, Air, and Land (SEAL) teams had parachuted at night into the ocean near the USS *Bainbridge*, which was shadowing the pirates. The SEALs had taken up positions on the fantail of the *Bainbridge* and were carefully monitoring Phillips while he was in the custody of the pirates. One of the pirates had just pointed his AK-47 at the American captain as if he were going to shoot him. That's when the SEAL team commander on the *Bainbridge* ordered his men to take out the pirates. Three SEAL sharpshooters fired simultaneously at the pirates from a distance of thirty yards in heaving seas at nightfall, killing them all.

Obama called Vice Admiral William McRaven, the leader of Joint Special Operations Command and of the mission to rescue Phillips, to tell him, "Great job." The flawless rescue of Captain Phillips was the first time that Obama—only three months into his new job—had been personally exposed to the capabilities of America's "Quiet Professionals," the secretive counterterrorism units of Special Operations, whose well-oiled skills he would come to rely upon increasingly with every passing year of his presidency.

It was not always so. Joint Special Operations Command was born out of the ashes of an American defeat in the deserts of Iran three decades before Obama assumed the presidency. When fifty-two Americans were held hostage at the U.S. embassy in Tehran in 1979 by fervent followers of the ayatollah Ruhollah Khomeini, President Jimmy Carter authorized a mission to rescue them. The mission was never going to be easy: it entailed flying almost one thousand miles into a remote desert region of Iran, traveling undetected to Tehran, and then rescuing the hostages, who were guarded by Iran's fanatical Revolutionary Guard.

Operation Eagle Claw, sometimes referred to as Desert One, was doomed almost as soon as it started. Three of the eight helicopters that flew the mission developed mechanical problems because of sand storms. The mission was aborted, and then one of the five remaining working helicopters collided with an American transport plane during a refueling in the Iranian desert, killing eight American servicemen. It was, in U.S. military parlance, "a total goat fuck." Back in Washington, a rising CIA official in his early forties named Robert Gates was at the White House watching with mounting dismay as the whole disaster unfolded.

A Pentagon investigation found myriad problems with Operation

THE SECRET WARRIORS

Eagle Claw: Interservice rivalries meant that the army, air force, navy, and marines all wanted to play a role in this important operation, and even though the four services had never worked together before on this kind of mission, each service got a piece of the action. An overemphasis on operational security prevented the services from sharing critical information with one another and also prevented the entire plan from being written down so that it could be studied overall. The navy allowed poor maintenance of the mission helicopters, the air force pilots who flew the mission had no experience in commando operations, and there was no full-scale rehearsal of all the elements of the plan.

Something needed to be fixed. The fix was the creation in 1980 of the Joint Special Operations Command (JSOC, pronounced "JAY-sock"), located at Ft. Bragg in North Carolina, so that the "Special Operators" of the various services could start to work together more seamlessly. The key components of JSOC are secret, "black," Navy SEAL units, the army's Delta Force and 75th Ranger Regiment, the helicopter pilots of the 160th Special Operations Air Regiment, and the air force's Special Tactics Squadron. (The primary mission of "white" Special Forces units, which operate quite openly and are known as the Green Berets, is to train indigenous military forces.)

The top officers who ran the U.S. military were often suspicious of the "snake eaters" in Special Operations, whom they tended to regard as cowboys. Then came the debacle at Mogadishu, Somalia, in early October 1993. A daytime helicopter assault by pilots of the Special Operations Air Regiment and elements of Delta Force, SEAL Team 6, and the 75th Rangers with the goal of snatching Somali clan leaders who were attacking U.S. troops stationed in Somalia, turned into a fiasco in which two Black Hawk helicopters were shot down by rocket-propelled grenades (RPGs), and eighteen American servicemen died.

Unknown to anyone in the U.S. government at the time, al-Qaeda had sent some of its top trainers from its then base in Sudan into Somalia to train the Somali clansmen fighting the Americans in how best to bring down helicopters using RPGs. This is far from easy to do, as RPGs are designed to be antitank weapons; hitting a flying object with an RPG is difficult to pull off, given the powerful recoil of the RPG launcher.

Scarred by the Battle of Mogadishu, the Pentagon was resistant to using Special Operations Forces to take on al-Qaeda in Afghanistan once the terrorist group had rebased itself there in 1996. President Bill Clinton pushed the Pentagon to deploy the elite units of JSOC into Afghanistan to take out bin Laden, telling General Hugh Shelton, his top military advisor, "You know it would scare the shit out of al-Qaeda if suddenly a bunch of black ninjas rappelled out of helicopters into the middle of their camp. It would get us enormous deterrence and show the guys we are not afraid." Michael Scheuer, the head of the bin Laden unit at the CIA at the time, says, "I don't carry a brief at all for President Clinton. But, numerous times, he asked the military to use commandos or Special Forces to try to kill bin Laden. And General Shelton, who was the chairman of the Joint Chiefs at that time, always brought him plans back for those operations that looked like the invasion of Normandy!" President Clinton was looking for a covert operation, not a large-scale military assault.

After the 9/11 attacks, Secretary of Defense Donald Rumsfeld was deeply frustrated that the first American boots on the ground in Afghanistan were from the CIA and not the highly trained counterterrorism units of JSOC. On October 17, 2001, ten days after the U.S. campaign against the Taliban had started, Rumsfeld wrote a secret memo to the chairman of the Joint Chiefs, General Richard Myers, expressing his irritation: "Does the fact that the Defense

Department can't do anything on the ground in Afghanistan until CIA people go in first to prepare the way suggest that the Defense Department is lacking a capability we need? Specifically, given the nature of our world, isn't it conceivable that the Department [of Defense] ought not to be in a position of near total dependence on CIA in situations such as this?"

Officials working for Rumsfeld commissioned Richard Shultz, a historian of Special Forces, to find out why JSOC units were not deployed to hit al-Qaeda before the attacks on New York and Washington. After all, fighting terrorists was why these units were founded in the first place. Shultz concluded that in the years before 9/11, the senior officers at the Pentagon had become "Somalia-ized." As a result, they tended to recommend "big-footprint" operations involving as many as several hundred soldiers, "showstoppers" that made the missions politically impossible at a time when the American public was believed to have no tolerance for U.S. casualties. Another showstopper: before launching an operation, the Pentagon demanded high-quality "actionable intelligence," which simply didn't exist in Taliban-controlled Afghanistan. Special Operations boss General Peter Schoomaker recalled, "Special Operations were never given the mission. It was very, very frustrating. It was like having a brand-new Ferrari in the garage and nobody wants to race it because you might dent the fender."

The attacks on the World Trade Center and the Pentagon allowed Rumsfeld to push Special Operations to the center of the "Global War on Terrorism." In a sign of where Rumsfeld wanted to take the military, in the summer of 2003 he took the unprecedented step of asking General Schoomaker to come out of retirement to become the chairman of the Joint Chiefs. And on September 6, 2003, Rumsfeld signed an eighty-page order that empowered JSOC to hunt al-Qaeda in as many as fifteen countries. It wasn't a blanket permission, since in a number of those countries the president or State Department would still have to sign off on the missions, but it allowed JSOC considerable latitude to operate independently.

Crucially, JSOC—unlike the CIA—would not have to brief Congress about its actions in those fifteen countries. That was because JSOC operated under Title 10 of the U.S. Code, which outlined the rules under which the U.S. military operated, unlike the CIA, which operated under Title 50, and was required to brief Congress whenever it conducted covert operations overseas. This might seem like no more than a typical bureaucratic loophole, but it would have a significant result: JSOC was now empowered to mount covert actions in many countries around the world with less accountability than the CIA. JSOC's overseas operations were all classified, so it also received very little scrutiny from the media or public. For many years the Pentagon didn't even acknowledge that JSOC existed.

In the decade after 9/11, JSOC mushroomed from a force of eighteen hundred to four thousand, becoming a small army within the military. It had its own drones, its own air force (known as the Confederate Air Force), and its own intelligence operations. The rise of JSOC was inextricably linked to the vision of Major General Stanley McChrystal, a brilliant workaholic from a military family who was beloved by his men and who during the Iraq War would go out with them on missions to capture/kill insurgents. Depending on your perspective, this was either foolhardy or brilliant leadership— or maybe a little of both—given that killing a two-star American general would have been a significant propaganda coup for Iraq's insurgents.

It was McChrystal who took the Special Operations Ferrari out of the garage and drove it to become a killing machine of unprecedented agility and ferocity. The Iraq War provided the opportunity to make that change because, to prevail against the insurgency, Special Operations would need to be geared for not only one-off missions but also an entire campaign. McChrystal said that Special Operations had to go from being just "a bookseller to being Amazon.com."

McChrystal realized that the most lethal of the Iraqi insurgent groups, in particular "al-Qaeda in Iraq," were not fighting like Saddam Hussein's tank-based army—which fought as every other hierarchical military had done before it—but comprised, rather, loose networks of fighters who operated in largely independent bands.

Unlike satellite imagery of Saddam's tank formations, intelligence about the insurgents was both fleeting and highly perishable. JSOC would have to become more like al-Qaeda if it was going to defeat al-Qaeda; it would take "a network to defeat a network," in McChrystal's formulation. A major part of McChrystal's strategy was to go after not just the leaders of the insurgency but also the midlevel insurgents who were keeping the trains running. (It is one of history's little ironies that al-Qaeda itself was set up as a JSOC-like group. The main trainer of al-Qaeda in the years before 9/11 was Ali Mohamed, an Egyptian American army sergeant who had served at Ft. Bragg, the headquarters of JSOC. In the 1980s, Mohamed taught courses on the Middle East and Islam at the Special Warfare Center at the army base. During his leave from the army, he trained al-Qaeda operatives in Afghanistan using Special Forces manuals he had pilfered from Ft. Bragg. His life as an al-Qaeda double agent was not discovered until 1998.)

To make JSOC more like al-Qaeda meant making it "flat and fast," two qualities rarely mentioned in the same sentence as "the U.S. military." To get JSOC as flat and fast as the insurgents, McChrystal made a number of key decisions. In the summer of

2004 he set up his base of operations in a group of aircraft hangars at Balad Air Base in central Iraq. This was a long way from the stultifying embrace of Washington and the Pentagon, and even a ways from Baghdad, and it would allow JSOC to get outside all the typical bureaucratic restraints that made quick decisions impossible. Then, to break down the "stovepipes" that existed between JSOC and the intelligence community, McChrystal started recruiting CIA and National Security Agency (NSA) analysts to work at Balad, and he also sent Colonel Michael T. Flynn, his top intelligence officer, to work at the CIA station in Baghdad for eight months in 2004. Gradually, other potential bureaucratic rivals were co-opted into McChrystal's enterprise, so he could quickly and easily draw on the resources of key intelligence agencies such as the CIA and the NSA.

McChrystal also harnessed technology to transform JSOC's operations. Through the aggressive and early adoption of video teleconferences (VTCs), McChrystal tied together JSOC's far-flung operations, which stretched from Balad to Ft. Bragg to Tampa (the headquarters of Special Operations Command), to other key bases, such as at Bagram in Afghanistan, which managed JSOC's Afghan and Pakistan missions. Gradually, these daily ninety-minute VTCs became worldwide briefings about the fight against al-Qaeda and its allies that also drew in the CIA and State Department officers. The discussions ranged across Africa, the Middle East, and South Asia, and McChrystal wanted to hear from anyone with real expertise, regardless of rank. One of the senior leaders in the Pentagon who began to listen in on these videoconferences was the chief of naval operations, Admiral Michael Mullen.

At first JSOC had only one Predator drone in Iraq. So it improvised and leased a couple of small aircraft to which cameras were affixed. As the command grew, JSOC acquired its own dedicated drones so that it could maintain an "unblinking eye" 24/7 over targets.

The natural tendency of the intelligence community is to hoard information. McChrystal made his teams share intelligence, creating a JSOC intranet that everyone in the command could access, and he teamed with an obscure military intelligence unit in Washington, the National Media Exploitation Center, to turn the large volume of papers, CDs, thumb drives, computers, and other "pocket litter" that his operators were picking up on the battlefield into "actionable intelligence." JSOC built computer infrastructure so that when units on the battlefield captured anything of interest, they would get it to Balad and the material would then be quickly uploaded to the States, where the staff at the National Media Exploitation Center worked around the clock to turn it into usable intelligence. "We got to a point where they were able to turn things that were large quantities in about twenty-four hours, whereas before it would get lost in the ether," says one of McChrystal's deputies. All this required massively increased bandwidth, which JSOC acquired on commercial satellites, building up over the years a significant "farm" of satellite dishes at its headquarters in Balad.

For JSOC, every mission now became what McChrystal termed a "fight for intelligence." The intelligence was used to get inside the "decision cycle" of the insurgents so that information picked up on one raid could be used to launch still other raids. Sometimes intelligence recovered from one location led to an assault on another insurgent hideout in the same night.

JSOC techs were creative. They designed an "electronic divining rod" that would ping only when it was near a cell phone linked to a particular insurgent. The base at Balad was awash in cell phones used by insurgents that had been picked up on raids. But because the base was shielded from electronic eavesdropping, the cell phones were no longer receiving incoming calls, calls that could have provided important clues to other insurgents. So JSOC techs rigged a cell phone base station inside the Balad headquarters so that the phones could start receiving calls again. Once the station was turned on, dozens of the captured phones started ringing and buzzing, netting more leads for JSOC.

All these measures were taken to create a sequence known as "F3EA," in which JSOC would "find, fix, finish, exploit, and analyze" its insurgent targets. Hiding behind ever-shifting anodyne code names such as Task Force 121, which captured Saddam Hussein, JSOC got results. In 2006 it killed Abu Musab al-Zarqawi, the psychopathic leader of al-Qaeda in Iraq. After Zarqawi was killed, President Bush took the unusual step of referring by name to the hitherto shadowy General McChrystal and gushed that JSOC was "awesome."

JSOC's record was not unblemished. In the first year of the Iraq War, at Camp Nama, near Baghdad, a Special Operations task force maintained a prison facility where prisoners were sometimes beaten; thirty-four task force members were disciplined for mistreating prisoners, and the facility was closed in 2004. The same year, McChrystal himself was one of a number of officers who did not disclose that Pat Tillman, the football star turned Army Ranger, was killed in a friendly fire incident in Afghanistan, rather than by the Taliban, as the army had initially portrayed it. The army declined to discipline McChrystal because he did try to warn senior officers that Tillman might have been killed by his comrades.

JSOC went from half a dozen operations a month in Iraq in the spring of 2004 to three hundred a month by the summer of 2006. The work ethic was brutal. At JSOC, the day was "17-5-2"—seventeen hours for work, five hours for sleep, and two hours for everything else. In 2006, McChrystal wrote to all his men: "It will not be about what's easy, or even what we normally associate with conventional military standards. It will not even be about what is effective. It will be about what is the MOST effective way to operate—and we will do everything to increase effectiveness even in small ways. If anyone finds this inconvenient or onerous, there's no place in the force for you. This is about winning—and making as few trips to Arlington Cemetery en route to that objective." McChrystal, who ran JSOC until 2008, saw his wife only one month a year for the five years he was in command. The "battle rhythm" was so brutal that one JSOC officer used to joke, "We lived in Balad and vacationed in Kabul or Bagram."

Accounts of why Iraq came back from the brink of an all-consuming civil war in 2007 typically include the generalship of David Petraeus; a more effective counterinsurgency strategy that got U.S. troops off their giant bases and into Iraqi neighborhoods; al-Qaeda's own spectacular error of enforcing Taliban-style rule on Iraq's unwilling Sunni tribes; the resulting Sunni tribal Awakening movement that rose up against al-Qaeda; and previous sectarian cleansing that had forced more than four million Iraqis to flee their homes, making it harder for sectarian death squads to find their victims. To that list must be added the work of JSOC, which killed the leaders of the militant sectarian groups, both Sunni and Shia, at an industrial rate.

The principal effort of JSOC for almost the entire duration of the Iraq War was in Iraq; Afghanistan and Pakistan were relative sideshows. Indicative of this, when McChrystal took command of JSOC in October 2003, he found only 20 of his men in Afghanistan and 250 in Iraq. And six years later, in the spring of 2009, JSOC was still doing only twenty operations a month in Afghanistan. The army's Delta Force got the main show in Iraq, while the Navy

SEALs got Afghanistan, which was somewhat ironic, given the fact that the country is entirely landlocked.

IT IS NOTORIOUSLY DIFFICULT to become a SEAL. First you have to survive what is generally regarded as the hardest training in the world. The climax of the brutal selection process is the aptly named Hell Week, which involves more or less continuous running, doing push-ups, moving massive logs in teams, swimming considerable lengths in the cold ocean, and sleeping only a few hours over the course of the entire week. Other tests include swimming underwater for fifty yards with your hands tied behind your back and your feet tied together. The dropout rate is 90 percent. Eric Greitens, a Rhodes scholar with a doctorate from Oxford who went on to become a lieutenant commander in the SEALs, recalls of his training, "We had some incredible people come in—high school track stars, intercollegiate water polo players, international-quality swimmers. And a lot of them ended up failing. At the same time, we had guys who had trouble on the runs, guys who had trouble doing push-ups, guys whose teeth would start chattering just looking at the cold ocean, and yet they made it. And one of the reasons why they made it is they had this relentless perseverance."

After Hell Week comes Pool Competency training, in which the SEAL hopefuls swim underwater with scuba gear and are attacked by instructors who tear off their mouthpieces and masks and flip off their oxygen tanks. During this test, those who make the cut have to remain calm and figure out how to reestablish their lines to the life-giving oxygen while their bodies are desperate for air. "The point of all that is you are going to push people as hard as you possibly can. You push them to their mental, physical, and emotional limit so that when combat happens, they are ready," says Greitens.

THE SECRET WARRIORS

If it is quite challenging to enter the SEALs, an even greater challenge is to be selected for the SEALs' premier counterterrorism force, the innocuously named Naval Special Warfare Development Group, based at Dam Neck, Virginia, near the bustling resort town of Virginia Beach. It's known inside the military as DevGru, and more popularly as SEAL Team 6, and is an elite within the SEAL elite. The men of DevGru, about 250 in total, are battle-hardened and are usually in their mid-thirties. DevGru is divided into squadrons that are named by color: Red, Blue, and Gold are the assault squadrons; Gray handles vehicles and boats; and Black is the sniper team. These squadrons scout other SEAL teams, which number around two thousand men, for those with the particular skills they need.

DevGru's base at Dam Neck does not announce itself. Behind the high wire fence that divides the SEALs from the rest of the world is a large dog pound, where the highly trained dogs that accompany the men on their missions live. There is a giant wall to sharpen climbing skills; a hangar full of exceptionally fast boats; other hangars that house experimental dune buggies suitable for driving in the deserts and mountains of Afghanistan, and weapons rooms loaded with exotic firearms.

Even as JSOC became a more agile and deadlier force after 9/11, when it came to sending the SEALs or Delta to kill the leaders of al-Qaeda, political considerations continued to affect decisions about operations. The leaders of the terrorist group were based either in Pakistan, a prickly ally, or in Iran, a sworn enemy, and the political consequences of placing American boots on the ground in either country were large.

As we have seen, Saad bin Laden and a number of other al-Qaeda leaders moved to Iran after the fall of the Taliban regime in Afghanistan. Intelligence indicated they lived in the northern Iranian town of Chalus, on the Caspian Sea. In 2002 a SEAL insertion into Chalus was planned and then rehearsed somewhere along the U.S. Gulf Coast. In the end, the chairman of the Joint Chiefs, General Richard Myers, nixed the operation, which had the potential to be Operation Eagle Claw all over again, because the intelligence about where exactly the al-Qaeda operatives were living in Chalus was never precise.

Three years later, the CIA and JSOC were tracking al-Qaeda's number three, Abu Faraj al-Libi, who drove around Pakistan's tribal regions on a distinctive red motorcycle. Intelligence indicated that Libi would be attending a meeting in a small compound in a northern tribal area near the border with Afghanistan, possibly with Ayman al-Zawahiri. A plan was developed to drop in thirty SEALs close to the compound and attack it. McChrystal and CIA director Porter Goss backed the plan, but top Pentagon officials worried about extracting the SEALs and wanted more firepower. The plan mushroomed to include some 150 Army Rangers. As Rumsfeld examined the operation, it began to look more and more like an invasion of Pakistan, something that would be quite politically damaging to Pakistani president General Pervez Musharraf, given the high level of anti-American sentiment in Pakistan. Rumsfeld called off the raid.

The men under McChrystal's command were growing increasingly frustrated with the political impediments preventing them from going over the border into Pakistan, where al-Qaeda's leaders were hiding. In 2006, Frances Townsend, Bush's top counterterrorism advisor, took up McChrystal's standing offer to meet with his officers and senior enlisted men at Ft. Bragg. They sat around a U-shaped table and Townsend told the group, "You can't hurt my feelings. I'm from New York, I don't have any, so this is only going to be worth the trip if you tell me what your concerns are." Their frustrations poured out: the inability to cross the border; the lack of good tactical-level intelligence on al-Qaeda's leaders; and, most fundamentally, the question: "Who's in charge of finding bin Laden?" Was it the CIA, which didn't have much of a capacity to operate in the war zone along the Afghan-Pakistan border? Or was it JSOC, which wasn't being given good intelligence on al-Qaeda's leaders? Townsend told them that outside the theater of war the CIA was in charge, but in the war zone JSOC would necessarily have to take the lead, and concluded by saying, "So it's the difference, in military-speak, between the supporting and the supported command." Townsend could see that the group wasn't buying this explanation. "The fact is that it's difficult for me to explain, how do you think that translates to the guy on the ground? If it's hard to explain here, in the United States, how hard do you think it is to operate in that environment? And by the way, that ought to tell you why we'd not been effective." Townsend went back to the White House and began to push for more CIA officers deploying overseas with the military, and to loosen the rules around the use of drone strikes in Pakistan's tribal areas.

On August 11, 2006, commanders from the Taliban and al-Qaeda met to discuss increasing the tempo of operations in eastern Afghanistan, in particular joint missions the following year in Nangarhar province. In July 2007, JSOC received intelligence that bin Laden himself might cross the border from Pakistan into Afghanistan to go to a summit meeting of militants in Nangarhar in his old stomping ground of Tora Bora. The CIA noticed that there was a significant buildup of al-Qaeda and Taliban forces there. The Pentagon planned an attack involving long-range bombers, but as the B-2 stealth bombers were in flight, commanders ordered them to return because of concerns about both the intelligence on bin Laden and possible civilian casualties from a large-scale bombing raid. Instead, JSOC mounted a smaller operation over the course of three or four days that killed several dozen militants in Tora Bora.

Just as he had in the winter of 2001, bin Laden again seemed to have vanished like a wraith.

11 COURSES OF ACTION

I̶N DECEMBER 2010, CIA director Leon Panetta again briefed President Obama about the "collection" effort in Abbottabad, presenting videos of the compound and an account of what it looked like from the ground based on the observations of those who had seen it. Despite the continuing uncertainties about who was living at the compound—at one point Obama said, "For all we know this could be some sheikh hiding from one of his wives"—the president's interest was by now very much piqued. Obama said, "I want to hear back from you, Director Panetta, when I get back from the holidays. Let's make sure that we pull this string as quickly as possible. If he's there, time is of the essence." President Obama then departed for his usual Christmas vacation in Hawaii.

Obama recalls that he now wanted an even sharper picture about what was happening in the Abbottabad compound and who was living there: "If we were going to embark on any kind of assault on this compound . . . we had to make darn sure that we knew what we were talking about."

In late January 2011, CIA officials were surprised to discover that an Indonesian militant named Umar Patek, one of the conspirators in the 2002 bombings of Bali, had recently shown up in Abbottabad and had been arrested there by Pakistani security services. Patek had gone to Abbottabad to meet someone on the fringes of al-Qaeda who worked in the city post office. What to make of this? After all, al-Qaeda's leaders had paid tens of thousands of dollars to the Bali conspirators. Analysts went back and forth about why Patek had chosen to travel from Southeast Asia to Abbottabad, a relatively obscure Pakistani city. In the end they concluded it was just one of life's strange coincidences.

That same month, the CIA analyst John, who had been at 90 percent for some time, in his confidence that bin Laden was at the compound, concluded that the intelligence had reached a tipping point. He went to Panetta and said, "We have to act now. Abu Ahmed al-Kuwaiti might not be there next month. The intelligence is not going to get any better." Panetta then went to the president and told him that one of his top bin Laden watchers was telling him, "Either we need to move or this particular intelligence might dissipate." Obama told Panetta, "I would like to have options to go against this compound."

Around this time, the National Geospatial-Intelligence Agency used its minute reconnaissance of the compound to produce a digital computer-aided design (CAD) file of the type that engineers use in drawing up blueprints. From that CAD file, a four-by-four-foot model of the suspected bin Laden compound was constructed that was accurate down to the last tree. The model even included two tiny toy cars that represented the white Jeep with a spare tire and the red van that the Kuwaiti and his brother drove. The model became a vital prop at the CIA and White House for discussions about who was living on the compound and in which location, and later for talking through the planning of the various military options. Gen-

COURSES OF ACTION

eral James Cartwright, then the vice chairman of the Joint Chiefs, recalls, "That was a good vehicle for us as we planned the various options to then sit down with that model and say . . . 'This is how we would come at it; this is what would happen in this courtyard or this house. . . . Here's how we would have more than one avenue of approach on what we thought were the target-inhabited buildings.' "

Obama asked the CIA to work up some conceptual options for what to do about the Abbottabad compound. Now that the possibility of military action had entered the picture, Panetta and senior Pentagon official Michael Vickers decided to bring another person into the secret. In late January, Vickers called Vice Admiral William McRaven in Afghanistan, who for the past three years had run JSOC. Vickers and McRaven had known each other for three decades and had worked intensively together for the past four years, as Vickers was the civilian overseer of JSOC.

In Iraq, McRaven had led the shadowy Task Force 121, which tracked down Saddam Hussein in December 2003. Much of the public credit for Saddam's capture went to conventional army units, but it was, in fact, the Special Operations forces under McRaven's command who had done most of the work to find the former Iraqi dictator.

As the Iraq War began to wind down in 2009, David Petraeus, the overall commander of the Afghanistan-Pakistan theater, told McRaven to shift his emphasis from Iraq to Afghanistan. In the summer of 2009, McRaven moved his headquarters from Iraq to Afghanistan, tripled the number of his men there, and greatly increased the level of air support and intelligence operations. As a result, Special Operations missions in Afghanistan went from two hundred a year in 2008 to well over two thousand a year by 2010.

During McRaven's tenure at JSOC, the "jackpot" rate—the

165

rate of missions in which Special Operations forces captured or killed their targets in Afghanistan or Iraq—soared from 35 percent to more than 80 percent. The amount of punishment JSOC was inflicting on the Taliban can be gauged by the fact that, during this period, the average age of Taliban commanders in Afghanistan declined from thirty-five to twenty-five.

McRaven is a strapping, dark-haired, blue-eyed Texan in his mid-fifties. In person, as he chugs a Rip It—a heavily caffeinated beverage popular with American soldiers in Afghanistan—he speaks in well-thought-out paragraphs, but he also peppers his speech with the occasional *doggone*, as well as more robust swear words. A battle-hardened colleague says McRaven reminds him of the comic-book superhero Captain America, while another says he "is reputed to be the smartest SEAL that ever lived. He is physically tough, compassionate, and can drive a knife through your ribs in a nanosecond." Even as a three-star admiral, McRaven went out with his teams on snatch-and-grab missions about once a month in Afghanistan.

In January 2011, McRaven visited CIA headquarters, where he was briefed by Michael Morell, the head of the Special Activities Division, a small and elite paramilitary force within the Agency, and officials from the Counterterrorism Center. McRaven could see immediately that to level a compound the size of the one in Abbottabad was going to take dropping two dozen or so two-thousand-pound bombs on the target. And there was no guarantee that the bombs would land with 100 percent accuracy in what is a good-sized Pakistani city. A Special Operations raid was the more plausible military approach, he believed. But he told colleagues he didn't want to force the idea down anyone's throat—better to let them come to this decision on their own, over time.

"First of all, congratulations on getting such a good lead," McRaven said. "Second, this is a relatively straightforward raid from

JSOC's perspective. We do these ten, twelve, fourteen times a night. The thing that makes this complicated is it's one hundred and fifty miles inside Pakistan, and logistically getting there, and then the politics of explaining the raid, is the complicating factor. I want to think about it a little bit, but my instinct is to put a very seasoned member of a special unit to work directly with you who will come to CIA every day and basically begin to plan and flesh out some options."

McRaven threw out some names of who should be in charge of the operation on the ground. Of one particular SEAL team commander he liked, he said, "He's an experienced operator. They're gonna land on the compound and something is going to go wrong. They're going to have to improvise, change the plan, go to Plan B, or wriggle their way out of a sticky situation."

McRaven tasked a navy captain with developing scenarios for some kind of assault on what was dubbed Abbottabad Compound 1 (AC1). The planning for the operation was done at the CIA, because this was going to be a covert, "deniable" operation, in which the chain of command ran from the president to Panetta and then to McRaven, rather than through the conventional military structure. CIA officials took to referring to AC1 with the code words "Atlantic City" when they e-mailed one another, a nod to the fact that the whole operation was something of a gamble.

In an unmarked office on the first floor of the CIA's printing plant, the navy captain covered the walls with satellite images and topographical maps of Abbottabad and began planning the assault on AC1, together with the commander of Seal Team 6's Red Squadron. McRaven later added a half dozen other planners to think through the air and ground options for the assault. One plan was to land a SEAL team some ways outside Abbottabad and proceed to the compound on foot. Abbottabad's size, however, and the chance of discovery, or of the forces tiring after a long run to the target, nixed that plan.

McRaven had quite literally written the book on Special Operations. He had helped establish a Special Operations curriculum at the Naval Postgraduate School in Monterey, California, and after taking up a job in the Bush White House just weeks after 9/11, he had become one of the principal authors of the Bush administration's counterterrorism strategy. McRaven's 1996 book, *Spec Ops*, is a lucid dissection of eight decisive actions, ranging from the British forces who used midget submarines to badly damage the *Tirpitz*, a key Nazi battleship, in 1943; to the Nazi rescue the same year of the Italian dictator Benito Mussolini from his anti-Fascist captors; to the raid at Entebbe in 1976 that freed Israeli hostages held in Uganda by Palestinian terrorists.

For his book, McRaven interviewed many of the key participants in the raids he examined and traveled to the sites of the operations. After a careful investigation of each raid, he identified six principles that had made these operations a success: repetition, surprise, security, speed, simplicity, and purpose. Repetition meant frequent and realistic rehearsals so that the "friction" of actual battle was reduced. Surprise meant catching the enemy entirely off guard; the Nazi rescuers of Mussolini crash-landed gliders on a mountain near the hotel where the Fascist leader was being held and rescued him without a shot being fired. Security meant, of course, confining the knowledge of the operation to a small circle. Speed meant that "relative superiority" over the enemy needed to be achieved in the first few minutes of the attack, and that the entire mission should be completed in half an hour. Simplicity ensured that the operation was well understood by each of the soldiers involved—"release the hostages" at Entebbe—and purpose meant that the soldiers were completely committed to the mission.

COURSES OF ACTION

There are many heroes in McRaven's book, but the star is Jonathan Netanyahu (the older brother of the Israeli politician Benjamin Netanyahu), who led the raid on Entebbe. An officer who read Machiavelli to relax and was an intense Israeli patriot, Netanyahu was imbued with total responsibility for his men and mission, and involved in the smallest details of any operation. At the time of the Entebbe raid it was virtually unthinkable that a force would fly more than seven hours from Israel to Uganda to launch a rescue operation. Adding to the element of surprise, the Israeli commandos who landed at Entebbe airport wore Ugandan military uniforms, and the lead assault element drove the same type of Mercedes driven by Ugandan generals. From the time the first Israeli transport plane landed at Entebbe, it took only three minutes for the commandos to secure the hostages, but Jonathan Netanyahu was mortally wounded in the assault.

As McRaven formulated the assault on the Abbottabad compound, his planning was deeply informed by the key principles he had laid out in *Spec Ops*. It was a simple plan, carefully concealed, repeatedly rehearsed, and executed with surprise, speed, and purpose.

The McRaven option was not the only "kinetic" (the Pentagon's way of saying "lethal") plan that the Obama national security team gave serious consideration to. Should a B-2 bomber obliterate the compound? Might a drone strike be a better option? And could the operation involve the Pakistanis in some shape or form? Toward the end of February, as all these options received serious consideration, Vickers decided it was now time to read in the Pentagon's top policy thinker, Michèle Flournoy, because each military option came freighted with policy implications, many of them knotty.

As undersecretary for policy, Flournoy was the highest-ranking woman ever to serve at the Pentagon and was often mentioned as the first woman likely to be tapped to be secretary of defense. A mother of three with a graduate degree in international relations from Balliol College, Oxford, and a long history of working on heavyweight national security issues such as the Pentagon's Quadrennial Defense Review, Flournoy is a regal presence in well-tailored pantsuits and pearls. She speaks deliberately, without a hint of bluster, and is typical of the "no drama" officials Obama likes to have around him.

The most nettlesome issue that Flournoy had to help think through was how to deal with the Pakistanis. After all, whether it was a SEAL raid, a bombing run, or a drone strike, all these actions were major violations of the national sovereignty of a country that was, at least nominally, a close ally of the United States. There was a range of options to consider with the Pakistanis: you could clue them in about the Abbottabad compound and they would become partners in the next steps; you could tell them ahead of time about the assault plan, but too late for them to do anything about it; you could tell them at the point of execution; or you could tell them afterward. The downside of involving the Pakistanis was that, based on a decade of dealing with them in other operations against al-Qaeda and the Taliban, it seemed likely that sensitive information might leak.

"We had a very serious debate and set of discussions over the pros and cons of how much to tell the Pakistanis and whether to do this in partnership with them. It was not dismissed lightly at all. That said, we've also had a fair amount of experience with them that suggested they have some significant operational security challenges internally," says Flournoy.

The question about how to handle the Pakistanis was complicated by the fact that U.S.-Pakistani relations—never the warmest—were now at a nadir. The U.S.-Pakistani alliance has always been complex, with recriminations on both sides. The Pakistanis felt that the United States was a "fair-weather friend" that used them instrumentally—whether to defeat the Soviets in Afghanistan in the 1980s or, more recently, to defeat al-Qaeda—only to abandon them when they were no longer of use. For their part, American policymakers were keenly aware that Pakistan was a sanctuary for militant groups killing U.S. soldiers in Afghanistan—groups that enjoyed some kind of support from elements in Pakistan's military.

Just as the intelligence picture at the Abbottabad compound began to sharpen, this history of U.S.-Pakistani mistrust was significantly worsened when Raymond Davis, an American citizen, killed two Pakistanis in the bustling city of Lahore on January 25, 2011. The U.S. government subsequently made a number of shifting and false assertions about Davis's job, but over the course of several weeks it became painfully clear that the muscular Davis—who had calmly shot two Pakistanis he claimed were robbing him in the middle of the day, in front of many eyewitnesses—was, in fact, a CIA contractor. This seemed to confirm every Pakistani conspiracy theory about the country being awash in CIA spies, and many Pakistanis, including some politicians, called for the execution of Davis. The severe tension between the United States and Pakistan after this incident further decreased the already slim chance that the U.S. government would inform any element of the Pakistani government or military about what it had recently learned about the possible location of al-Qaeda's leader.

An additional consideration was that the American war effort in landlocked Afghanistan was highly dependent on supplies coming in through Pakistan; in early 2011, about three-quarters of all NATO and U.S. supplies, including food, fuel, and equipment, had to transit Pakistan. Pakistan also allowed its airspace to be used for the three to four hundred daily flights into Afghanistan by U.S. aircraft supplying the one hundred thousand U.S. soldiers based there.

Cognizant of the fact that the Pakistanis could decide to close off these vital supply routes, Flournoy worked to bolster what the Pentagon termed the Northern Distribution Network, a series of logistical arrangements connecting ports on the Baltic Sea to Afghanistan through its Central Asian neighbors and Russia. "So there was a big push with presidential letters, people going out, signing new agreements, getting things in place, just to make sure we had that network as shored up as possible," says Flournoy. In a speech in St. Petersburg on March 21, Defense Secretary Robert Gates pledged that the United States and Russia would work together to expand the Northern Distribution Network into Afghanistan. That these new arrangements served in part as insurance against any possible fallout from the Abbottabad operation was known to only a handful at the Pentagon.

Secretary of State Hillary Clinton, who had often smoothed things over with the Pakistanis whenever there was one of the frequent crises in the U.S.-Pakistani relationship, made it clear that preserving that relationship was not the priority when it came to getting bin Laden. "I didn't want to miss the opportunity," Clinton said. "I didn't want another Tora Bora, where we overthought it, and we underresponded. And I remember at one point one of the briefers saying, 'This will be considered a gross violation of the Pakistanis' national honor,' and I exploded at that moment and said, 'What about our national honor? And what about going after a man who killed three thousand innocent people?'"

By now Obama was pushing for real courses of action (COAs, pronounced "KO-ahs") against the compound, rather than just additional intelligence gathering. National Security Council official Nicholas Rasmussen recalls that Obama had "decided that the potential for this story to be leaked somehow was of such great importance that we needed to accelerate efforts on this. And then added to that was the sense from Panetta that nothing in the intelligence world was going to bear further fruit over the next three or four months. We might marginally increase our confidence in the CIA's conclusions, but only marginally so. There wasn't any developmental effort under way that would give us the Polaroid shot of bin Laden." (Although the CIA was never able to get a picture of bin Laden, officers did obtain a picture of the Kuwaiti's brother.)

On a Friday evening in late February—a good time for a discreet meeting—a group of black Suburbans pulled up at CIA headquarters carrying Admiral McRaven, Mike Vickers, and General Cartwright. Cartwright, an introverted U.S. Marine aviator with a deep understanding of and love for technology, had endeared himself to some of Obama's inner circle during the discussion of the "surge" of U.S. forces into Afghanistan in the fall of 2009, when he had bucked the prevailing consensus among Gates, Mullen, and Petraeus, all of whom wanted a large-scale troop deployment of forty thousand soldiers for a counterinsurgency campaign. Cartwright had worked with Joe Biden and Tony Blinken to sketch a plan for a contingent of only twenty thousand supplemental forces in Afghanistan that would execute a "counterterrorism plus" mission, rather than a full-scale counterinsurgency campaign. Obama had ended up splitting the difference and authorizing thirty thousand soldiers for the surge, but Cartwright's perceived independence from the Pentagon brass had made him a powerful voice inside Obama's war councils.

McRaven, Vickers, and Cartwright were at headquarters to review with Panetta the possible courses of action for Abbottabad. Over sandwiches and sodas, seated around the massive wooden table in the director's conference room, with the model of the compound in front of them, they discussed the intelligence picture with a small group of officials from the Counterterrorism Center. Then the group talked about four possible COAs: a bombing run by a B-2 bomber, a raid by Special Operations that would be done without informing the Pakistanis, a drone strike, and a joint operation with the Pakistanis. McRaven explained that a Special Operations assault on the bin Laden compound was going to be relatively easy. What was likely to be difficult was dealing with the Pakistani reaction to the raid, whether on the ground or in the air.

After the meeting, which was a dress rehearsal for a detailed discussion with the president in about two weeks, Panetta, Michael Morell, and Jeremy Bash retired to Panetta's office. Panetta was pumped up. Pouring them each a glass of scotch, he said, "I think our folks have developed four really good options. None of them is perfect, they're all really tough, but we've got to stay on this. We've got to really get more intelligence and we have really got to flesh out these options, because I can't imagine at the end of the day, we're not going to do something about this."

ON MARCH 14, 2011, Obama's war cabinet gathered at the White House to brief the president. The COAs presented to Obama orally and also in memo and graphic form included the bombing run by a B-2 bomber, a drone strike, the raid option, and some kind of bilateral operation with the Pakistanis.

The B-2 strike had some attractions. Anyone who was in the compound or in any possible tunnels underneath it would die, and no American forces would be at risk. But a B-2 raid also had significant downsides. To destroy the compound, which sprawled over one acre, would require a large payload of bombs. General Cartwright pointed out that the force of the bombs would be like an earthquake in the area. Such blunt force would certainly incur civilian casualties, not only of the women and children known to be living at the compound but also people in neighboring homes. And of course there would be no proof of bin Laden's death, since all DNA evidence would vanish in the air strike, and with it any proof that he had been living there.

The B-2 bombing option sparked debate. According to Tony Blinken, "Some people said, 'The DNA evidence was not the most important thing. If bin Laden was there, and we knew that with certainty, and we could take him out, taking him definitively off the battlefield was what counted.' But a number of people felt that half—if not more—of the success we would achieve would be the world knowing bin Laden was gone, and you had to be able to prove that, or at least have enough proof to dispel most doubts and conspiracy theories."

One way to limit the number of civilian casualties would be to drop a small bomb directly on the compound, but a bomb with a small payload might not actually kill bin Laden. And because the CIA had no way to see inside the compound, there was also the possibility that bin Laden might shelter in a vault hidden inside the building, or even escape through a tunnel to live another day. Using thermal imaging, the National Geospatial-Intelligence Agency concluded that the water table around the Abbottabad compound was quite high. Indeed, large streams course through the neighborhood in which the compound sits. Given the high water table, analysts discounted the idea that bin Laden might escape through a tunnel, but they were concerned that he might have some kind of safe room or vault in his house.

Proponents of the raid option, who included Panetta, pointed out that as risky as it was to send in the SEALs, if they did raid the compound and bin Laden wasn't found, there was still a pretty decent chance that they could just leave and no one would ever know about the operation. And even if a handful of people in and around the compound did find out about it, the operation could simply be denied. And, in any event, *whoever* was living in that compound wasn't going to create a public stink, as he was clearly trying to keep a low profile. A Special Operations helicopter assault that didn't net bin Laden wouldn't violate Pakistan's sovereignty because it would never be made public, while a bombing raid would be a very public event, so any chance of "plausible deniability" for the operation would go out the window.

Another option was to fly a Predator or Reaper drone over the suspected bin Laden residence and fire a small missile or drop a small bomb on the compound. General Cartwright, Obama's favorite general, was pushing this approach. The idea would be to use a very small munition to hit the mysterious "pacer" whom American satellites were seeing as he took his daily walk. Such a strike required a very high degree of precision, and there was the risk that the drone shot might simply miss its target, as other drone strikes aimed at high-value targets had done in the past, but the risk of civilian casualties was much lower, and the pushback from the Pakistanis would likely be lower than from a conventional air strike. There would still be the problem of proving bin Laden was dead, but there was likely to be subsequent "chatter" about bin Laden's "martyrdom" among the al-Qaeda leadership, which American satellites would be able to pick up. And al-Qaeda almost always eventually confirmed the death of its leaders in communiqués, because they were happy to announce the passing of one of their "martyrs."

Admiral Mike Mullen, Obama's top military advisor, was skeptical of using the small munition as soon as the subject came up. "From my perspective," he says, "it was a system that had not been tested. I think we have hung our hopes on sophisticated new technologies sometimes too soon that don't work out." Instead Mullen favored the raid.

Michèle Flournoy was also one of the proponents of the raid, because "the circumstantial evidence at some point became almost overwhelming in that it was very hard to explain this compound and the presence of certain individuals absent the presence of bin Laden. It just didn't make any sense. Second, I felt that from a symbolic and strategic point of view, capturing or killing Osama bin Laden would have a very powerful effect on al-Qaeda on top of the losses they had already suffered. Third, we expected that there would be an intelligence trove that would help us further understand the network and create further opportunities to take action against the core leadership should we actually go in."

At the March 14 meeting, Admiral McRaven laid out the raid option, telling Obama very directly, "Mister President, we haven't thoroughly tested this out yet and we don't know if we can do it, but when we do, I'll come back to you and I'll tell you straight up."

Obama asked, "How much time do you need?"

McRaven said he would need three weeks to rehearse the mission thoroughly.

Obama observed, "Then you'd better get moving."

The officials in the meeting agreed that a helicopter-borne assault team was a risky option. Would the helicopters be detected in Pakistani airspace? And what would the Pakistanis do if they detected them? There were also refueling issues, since the choppers couldn't go to the target, hover, land, take off, and make it all the way back to Afghanistan. How likely was the refueling site to be detected? Once the Black Hawks were over the compound, what were the potential risks to the helicopters?

Cartwright mentioned an experimental, radar-evading stealth helicopter that would help to lower the possibility that the Pakistanis would detect the raid, but his comments didn't get much traction at the time. When the meeting broke up, many of the participants believed that Obama was leaning toward bombing the compound with a B-2 bomber. Hillary Clinton recalls, "Everybody left those meetings totally drained because of the consequences and the stakes that we were dealing with."

On March 16, Raymond Davis, the CIA contractor who had killed the two Pakistanis two months earlier, was released from jail following an ingenious deal in which the U.S. government paid $2 million of Islam-sanctioned "blood money" to the families of the two victims. This was a significant development for the small group at the White House planning the Abbottabad operation, because there was a real concern that Davis, who was passionately hated in Pakistan, might end up getting killed in his Pakistani prison cell following any kind of U.S. assault on Abbottabad. Now that Davis was a free man, there was one less impediment to taking some kind of military action against the compound.

By the time of the next "principals" meeting with Obama in the White House, on March 29, the B-2 bombing option had been largely discounted. When Pentagon planners assessed what it would take to destroy the one-acre compound, they found that it would require dropping thirty-two 2,000-pound bombs. This not only would incinerate any DNA evidence but also would be a major air strike in a crowded city, obliterating the compound with its more than twenty inhabitants and destroying another building nearby. Bombs might also fall short of the target, killing still more civilians. The president was concerned about the potential number of civilian casualties and lack of certainty about killing bin Laden. There was also the furious Pakistani response that such an attack would assuredly provoke to consider, and there would be no "sensitive site exploitation," which is CIA-speak for the forensic examination of computers, cell phones, and pocket litter that typically is performed following a raid to capture or kill a high-value target.

What remained on the table was a surgical strike by a "stand-off" weapon such as a drone, the helicopter-borne assault option, and a wait-and-see approach that boiled down to trying to gather more definitive intelligence. During this meeting, Obama peppered McRaven with questions such as "What if there is a safe room in the compound?" "What if bin Laden isn't there?" "How do you get bin Laden out of the compound, whether dead or alive?" "What if the helicopters have mechanical problems?" "What happens if we meet resistance at the compound?"

Throughout this planning process, Defense Secretary Robert Gates was consistently one of the most skeptical of the president's advisors. His was a voice that carried great weight, as he had worked for six American presidents; he was working for Nixon's National Security Council when Obama was only thirteen. And Gates had enough experience from his tenure as director of the CIA to know that you could have a pretty strong circumstantial case and still be wrong. In the event of a ground attack on the Abbottabad compound, he was also concerned about the level of risk for U.S. forces and for the American relationship with Pakistan.

Above all, Gates was concerned about a replay of Operation Eagle Claw, the botched effort in 1979 to release the fifty-two American hostages held in the U.S. embassy in Tehran during the Iranian Revolution. The failed rescue operation was a major factor in making Jimmy Carter a one-term president. Eagle Claw was something Gates had lived through in excruciating detail when he was working for then-CIA director Stansfield Turner as his executive assistant. As the disaster unfolded in Iran on November 4, 1979, Gates was with Turner the whole night, shuttling between the CIA and the White House. Gates recalled, "We finally left the White House at about 1:30 in the morning. . . . I had a long, sad drive home."

Now, more than three decades later, another Democratic president was considering putting his presidency on the line with a helicopter assault on the other side of the world in a country that many in the White House considered, at best, a duplicitous ally. Gates repeatedly pressed in White House meetings as the planning continued, "What if you have a helicopter crash?" "What if the Pakistanis respond faster than you think?" "What if guys get pinned down in the compound?" Flournoy says that Gates "didn't drink the Kool-Aid. He was constantly asking the hard questions."

As the helicopter-borne assault by the SEALs became more plausible, Flournoy says that any chance that the Pakistanis would be given a heads-up became increasingly remote: "Even though we both had very shared interests in getting bin Laden, their concerns about having the U.S. come across the border to do it with a raid, we felt that that could create enough ambivalence that we might not get the support we wanted. At the end of the day, this was such a critical objective, and there's such a vital interest at stake, and the risk of Pakistanis either losing control of the information or choosing to oppose it because of sovereignty concerns—it was too great. And the decision was made to go unilaterally, but to tell them at the earliest possible opportunity."

Now that the decision had been made not to bring the Pakistanis into any aspect of the operation, Obama and his team had to think through how best to deal with whatever their reaction might be, particularly on the ground in Abbottabad, should the president greenlight the raid. A senior administration official explains: "McRaven, in some of the earliest briefings, was very sensitive to the idea that we don't want to create, for lack of a better word, a shit storm with the Pakistanis if we don't need to. So if this can be accomplished in a way that did not result in dead Pakistanis, either civilians or security forces, that's the optimal solution."

McRaven initially came up with an assault plan that would have had the SEALs avoiding any kind of firefight with the Pakistanis unless it was absolutely necessary. If the Pakistanis did show up in force at the compound, McRaven's proposal was that the SEALs set up a defensive perimeter and hold them at bay. Meanwhile, senior U.S. officials would explain to their Pakistani counterparts the intelligence case on bin Laden and why the raid had taken place, in the hope that the SEALs would eventually be able to leave without further hindrance.

In the scenario in which the SEALs were surrounded in the Abbottabad compound by hostile Pakistani soldiers, Obama's national security team discussed who would be the best person to make the call explaining the situation to the most powerful man in Pakistan, the chief of army staff, General Ashfaq Parvez Kayani. As this discussion went on without a clear resolution, it was plain that Obama was not at all comfortable with this scenario. "The premium is on the protection of our force, not on keeping the Pakistanis happy," he instructed McRaven. "I want you to plan against a scenario that you have to fight your way out. You have to be able to face active Pakistani opposition and still get out with all your men safe." The short-hand for that approach became the "fight your way out" option.

The Raymond Davis incident helped to shape the thinking of those considering the raid option. What if instead of one American CIA contractor in jail, you ended up having some two dozen Navy SEALs in Pakistani custody because they didn't have the firepower to fight their way out?

Obama did not get into the tactical details of where the Chinook helicopters carrying the backup force should be located, nor how many extra SEALs needed to be added to the attacking force; he just told McRaven the force had to be able to fight its way out. "That was a huge fundamental shift, because Bill McRaven thought he was bringing what people wanted, which was a 'don't piss off the Paks' approach," says a senior administration official. McRaven went back to the drawing board and returned with a variety of ways he could protect the assault team, particularly having a quick reaction force that was deployed deep into Pakistan, rather than on helicopters stationed at the Afghan-Pakistan border, as previously planned. Mullen says, "Obama is the one that put in the Chinook-47s. He is the one that said, 'There is not enough backup.'"

Mullen, who had visited Pakistan twenty-seven times when he was chairman of the Joint Chiefs, had repeatedly told his counterpart, General Kayani, "If we know we can find Number One or Number Two we are going to get them. Period. And we are going to get them unilaterally. Period."

On April 11, Panetta met at CIA headquarters with Lieutenant General Ahmad Shuja Pasha, the head of Pakistan's powerful military intelligence agency, ISI. Pasha, who had forged a personal relationship with Panetta—calling him by his first name, Leon, and inviting him to his home for dinner with his wife when Panetta had visited Pakistan—complained vociferously about the amount of CIA activity going on in Pakistan, which the Raymond Davis affair had underlined. Pasha said, "You have too many CIA agents in this country, and I don't care if they're security officers or case officers or analysts. There are too many of them." Pasha termed the meeting a "shouting match." Panetta described it in gentler terms, but it strengthened his determination to keep the Pakistanis out of the loop on the bin Laden raid, and it increased the pressure on the Agency to act quickly, since it was obvious that ISI was now going to start cracking down on CIA activities in Pakistan.

While the White House continued to debate the various COAs over the course of five days in early April, the SEAL team from DevGru's Red Squadron began its rehearsals on full-scale models of the compound in a secret facility deep in the forests of North Carolina. They practiced on a one-acre replica of the Abbottabad compound, fast-roping down from Black Hawks onto the courtyard of the compound and the roof of its main building. These rehearsals were observed by the overall commander of Special Operations, Admiral Eric Olson, a thoughtful Arabic speaker and former Navy SEAL, and by Mike Vickers from the Pentagon, Admiral McRaven, and Jeremy Bash of the CIA. The rehearsals took place in daytime and didn't include a practice run of the helicopter ride into Abbottabad, focusing only on what the SEAL team would do "on target."

The raid would employ the "stealth" helicopters Cartwright had suggested using, rendering them more or less invisible to Pakistani radar. One of the main downsides of the raid, however, was how soon the inhabitants of the compound might get tipped off by the sound of the approaching choppers. Even with noise-suppression devices on the stealth Black Hawks, they still made a very loud sound once they were flying in the immediate vicinity. Using stopwatches, the observers found that they could hear the "audio signature" of the helicopters when the aircraft were about a minute away from the target. McRaven had advertised it could be more like two minutes, because wind conditions would affect how the sound traveled.

During the rehearsals, the two helicopters flew toward the compound replica, dropped the SEAL teams in ninety seconds, and were quickly gone. Methodically, the SEALs practiced sweeping the compound and, as they were finishing, around ten minutes later, the helicopters swept in again to pick them up.

In the decade since 9/11, the SEALs had done many hundreds of building "take-downs" in hostile environments and had encountered pretty much every type of surprise possible: armed women, people with suicide jackets hidden under their pajamas, insurgents hiding in "spider holes," and even buildings entirely rigged with explosives. The SEALs had to assume they might encounter any one of these types of threats at the Abbottabad compound. As a result, what became known as the "McRaven option" was constantly "red-teamed," a formal process by the SEALs to identify potential flaws in the plan. "McRaven had a backup for every possible failure, and a backup to the failure of the backup, and a backup to the failure of the backup of the backup. It was a multilayered set of plans," recalls Michèle Flournoy.

When the SEALs on the strike team were finally informed who their target was, a great cheer went up; there was no ambiguity about the purpose of their mission, or about the commitment of the men who were undertaking it.

The SEAL teams rehearsed again for a week in mid-April, in the high deserts in Nevada, which replicated the likely heat conditions and the elevation of Abbottabad, which sits at four thousand feet. This time they rehearsed the entire mission from nighttime takeoff to the return to base more than three hours later. Again, Olson, McRaven, Vickers, and Bash observed the rehearsal, this time joined by Admiral Mullen. The observers were taken into a hangar, where the SEALs walked them through a "rehearsal of concept" drill using a cardboard model of the compound. The SEAL teams then flew off in their helicopters for about an hour. When they returned, the outside observers, now wearing night vision goggles, watched them as they assaulted the compound. During this rehearsal, wind conditions forced the helicopters to arrive at the target from an unexpected direction. This reminded the observers that no matter how many times the assault was rehearsed, there were still going to be some "game-time" decisions to make. The rehearsals also showed that the whole operation on the ground could be conducted in under thirty minutes—the amount of time the Pentagon had determined that the SEALs would have before they were interrupted by the arrival of Pakistani security forces.

Mullen had a great deal of faith in McRaven, whom he had

known since the younger officer was a navy captain a decade earlier. At that time, McRaven had received rave reviews about his work in the Bush White House. As chairman of the Joint Chiefs, Mullen had made it a point on his frequent trips to Afghanistan to drop in at the JSOC operations center at Bagram Air Base, outside Kabul, typically around midnight, when the SEAL missions were in full swing. As a result, Mullen had a high degree of confidence in the skills of the SEALs, which was reaffirmed when he observed their rehearsal of the Abbottabad raid. "If I am going to send somebody in to die," Mullen explains, "I want to know as much about it as I possibly can. I also had the opportunity to look the men in the eye. Every single one of them. Personally. I also felt an obligation to understand as much as I could. So when you are sitting around the table with the president I could say, 'I have confidence and here's why. Here is what I watched. Here are the details.'"

Following the rehearsals, McRaven went to the White House to give Obama and his top national security advisors his assessment of the plausibility of the mission. Tony Blinken says of McRaven, "First of all, it helps that he's from central casting. He looks and sounds the part, so he inspires confidence, but you also got the very strong impression that this was not a guy who was going to be blustering or bragging. This was a guy who was going to give his very honest assessment, and so when he did, he had a lot of credibility, and it also created a tremendous amount of reassurance. And basically what McRaven told us was after they modeled this, and gamed it, and rehearsed it, he said, 'We can do this.'"

At one point, when he was outlining the Abbottabad helicopter raid to Obama and his war cabinet, McRaven said, "In terms of difficulty, compared to what we're doing on a nightly basis in Afghanistan, what we're doing in Iraq, this is not among the most difficult missions technically. The difficult part was the sovereignty issue with Pakistan and flying for a long stretch of time over Pakistani airspace."

As the raid planning began to gel, White House officials had to think through what would happen if bin Laden was captured. Since bin Laden had repeatedly said he would rather die a "martyr" than end up in American captivity, this scenario was regarded as quite unlikely. In 2004, bin Laden's former bodyguard Abu Jandal had told *Al-Quds Al-Arabi* newspaper, "Sheikh Osama gave me a pistol. . . . The pistol had only two bullets, for me to kill Sheikh Osama with in case we were surrounded or he was about to fall into the enemy's hands so that he would not be caught alive. . . . He would become a martyr, not a captive, and his blood would become a beacon that would arouse the zeal and determination of his followers." In a tape posted to Islamist websites two years later, bin Laden confirmed his willingness to be martyred: "I have sworn to only live free. Even if I find bitter the taste of death, I don't want to die humiliated or deceived." Still, if bin Laden were to conspicuously surrender, the rules of engagement the SEALs adhered to meant that he would have to be taken into custody.

In case that happened, arrangements were made to have a high-value-detainee interrogation group, consisting of lawyers, interpreters, and experienced interrogators, standing by at Bagram Air Base in Afghanistan. Together with bin Laden, this group would fly to the aircraft carrier USS *Carl Vinson*, which would be cruising off the coast of Pakistan in the Arabian Sea, where al-Qaeda's leader would then be interrogated for some unspecified length of time.

The principals met again with the president on April 12 and 19. Panetta told Obama that the intelligence community had reached a point of diminishing returns with regard to what it could learn about the compound. They were seeing "the pacer" almost every day but could not say definitively it was bin Laden. But to try to achieve greater certainty by using a human spy close to the compound would greatly increase the risk of detection. Tony Blinken says, "There was always the tension between wanting to be more certain about bin Laden's presence and the danger that pushing the envelope on trying to establish his presence beyond a reasonable doubt would compromise what we were doing." At the April 19 meeting, President Obama gave a provisional go-ahead for the SEAL raid. The president asked McRaven how much notice he would need to set the operation in motion. McRaven replied, "I'll need four hours." Obama said, "I'll give you twenty-four." Some senior administration officials took this as a sign that Obama was now leaning toward doing the raid.

At the White House, intense secrecy continued to surround the planning for Abbottabad; no more than a dozen officials knew about it. Ben Rhodes, Obama's strategic communications advisor, had noticed that over the past months there had been a series of meetings in the Situation Room, the topics of which were not listed on the manifest, and that the cameras that were usually on in the room had been turned off. "I wasn't the only one who noticed this set of meetings, but nobody wanted to talk about that, right, because you don't want to talk about the meeting you are not invited to," Rhodes recalls. Over the course of many months there were twenty-four interagency meetings to discuss the ripening intelligence picture at the Abbottabad compound. These discussions were described on attendees' calendars as "non-meetings." No "seconds" could attend and no "read-ahead" memos were prepared, even though they are customary for meetings of the president's national security staff.

By mid-April, in order to develop and rehearse the various COAs, the universe of people who were being read into the bin Laden operation was growing, although the intelligence was highly compartmentalized and many who worked on the operation were apprised of few details. John Brennan, Obama's top counterterrorism aide and the former CIA station chief in Saudi Arabia, started planning for the possibility that the bin Laden intelligence might leak, which meant bringing Rhodes into the secret. Rhodes would be able to run interference with the press if that became necessary. Rhodes recalls, "In the past I have had to engage newspaper editors and say, 'Please don't run this, and here's why.' And Brennan wanted somebody who knew how to do that in case it leaked."

On 9/11, Rhodes, then in his early twenties, had been working in Brooklyn and had an unobstructed view of the World Trade Center towers coming down. He remembers the moment when Brennan briefed him about bin Laden: "I felt the enormous weight of the information I'd been told. When you're in this job, you learn a lot of secrets, but this was different. It's Osama bin Laden, after all, and you're anxious about it, you're excited about it, you're nervous about it. The inclination is to want to discuss that with people, but you really had to be in the utmost vigilance about protecting this information."

Brennan, Rasmussen, of the NSC staff, and McDonough, Obama's deputy national security advisor, had developed a "playbook" for the various scenarios that might happen during and after the raid. They started compiling it weeks before the president had made a final decision about what to do in Abbottabad, because all along he had guided them by saying, "Keep preparing. I haven't made a decision, but keep all the options moving forward. And have them fully developed." They were aware that once the Abbottabad operation was under way, they would have to be able to flip a switch immediately and have well-thought-out options ready for all the diplomatic maneuvers and public statements for any one of the multiple scenarios that might happen at Abbottabad. They asked Rhodes to help them to think about the strategic messaging that would follow each one of those scenarios.

The first was that the SEALs went into the compound and the operation was relatively clean and they got bin Laden. The messaging for that eventuality wasn't too complicated.

The second scenario was that the SEALs went in, bin Laden wasn't there, and they left cleanly. In this case, there would be no messaging at all, as the Obama administration stance would be to say nothing, and the hope was that the Pakistanis wouldn't say anything either.

The third scenario was that the SEALs found bin Laden but got into a firefight with the Pakistani army, or that lots of civilians were killed. Or even worse, there was a firefight and civilian casualities and bin Laden wasn't even there. This would cause outrage in the Muslim world and severe political backlash at home. Rhodes says, "So, for all the options that involved him not being there, where it wouldn't be deniable, a lot of work was put into: How would we explain how we thought this was good enough to do? So we had to come up with a very public version of our intelligence case, because we would have to justify why we took this incredible risk even if he wasn't there."

Rhodes started working with CIA spokesman George Little, the only other "communicator" read into the Abbottabad intelligence, to prepare an unclassified version of the bin Laden case that could be made available to the media and the public should the Abbottabad operation no longer be covert. Little, a tall, bespectacled intelligence officer with a PhD in international relations, worked up a sixty-six-page document that included diagrams of the compound.

In mid-April, John Brennan called Mike Leiter, director of the National Counterterrorism Center (NCTC), on a secure video teleconference line from the White House and said, "Mike, we want someone to come out and brief you on the compound where we think bin Laden might be."

"Who else can I tell?" Leiter asked Brennan, masking his irritation that he hadn't been told about this development earlier.

"No one."

"What are you looking for me to do, then?" Leiter asked.

"I mostly want you to think about threats to the homeland that could come out of a successful raid," Brennan said.

Mike Leiter is a blunt, fast-talking former federal prosecutor and naval aviator. When he attended Harvard Law School, he was the president of the *Harvard Law Review,* a position Barack Obama had held a few years earlier. Before running the NCTC, Leiter had worked for the congressional commission that examined the intelligence debacle surrounding the supposed weapons of mass destruction in Iraq, and had written much of its final report. The experience of delving into the intelligence failures that led to the Iraq War colored Leiter's reaction to the bin Laden intelligence.

"I had seen enough failures in this world that I wasn't going to get excited," he says. He still remembered when Agency officials had told Obama how pumped they were to have a real lead on Ayman al-Zawahiri, and it turned out instead to be an al-Qaeda double agent/suicide bomber who killed seven CIA employees.

After Leiter had been fully briefed, his gut told him that there was a decent chance bin Laden was living in the compound, but there were aspects of the case that bothered him. It was puzzling that there were no guards at the compound. And some of the women and children living there occasionally traveled for extended periods around Pakistan to visit family members. When the women and children traveled from Abbottabad, they carried their cell phones, which seemed a significant breach of bin Laden's otherwise strin-gent operational security.

In Leiter's mind, the bin Laden case was far from a "slam dunk." Leiter was also not persuaded by the claimed regularity with which things occurred or didn't occur at the compound. Some officials were saying that there was no phone communication in and out of the compound, but when you drilled into the details of the case, the NSA was finding new cell phones at the compound. And Leiter was also concerned by the gaps in the "coverage" of the compound. There were no eyes on the compound 24/7, either by the Pakistani agents on the ground or by the spy satellites high above it.

On Saturday, April 23, Leiter went to the White House to meet with Brennan, enumerated the gaps that he saw, and suggested that he put together a Red Team of analysts who would be tasked to come up with alternative explanations for the intelligence that had been gathered. Brennan pointed out that a Red Team of analysts from the CIA had already analyzed the data. Leiter countered that these analysts were too invested in the case to be completely dispas-sionate.

"I don't think that is sufficient if this is successful or a failure," he said to Brennan. "Certainly if this is a failure, John, you want a record that this was really done well. And even if it is successful, you still want to be able to stand up and say, 'We did this really care-fully.' John, you don't want to have a WMD commission come back and say, 'You didn't red-team this one.' I wrote that chapter, John."

Brennan agreed that the Red Team was a good idea, instructing Leiter, "Talk to Michael [Morell], and if you guys agree, great. If not, come talk to me." Leiter then went to see Tom Donilon, the na-tional security advisor, a disciplined and demanding lawyer who ran a tight ship for Obama at the National Security Council. Closing the door to his office, Donilon asked Leiter, "So, what do you think?" Leiter replied, "The thing you can't predict is, you can always have some aircraft accident. I was an aviator. Flying at night in a new place—that is where you are going to have a problem." Leiter then walked Donilon through the concerns he had about the intelligence case. Donilon was also puzzled by the women and children leaving the compound and was more dubious about the case than Brennan, who was by now convinced that bin Laden was living at the compound. If this operation went wrong, Donilon was ultimately going to have to take much of the heat for it; he was enthusiastic about the Red Team concept.

Leiter also stopped by the office of his friend Denis McDonough. McDonough, the deputy national security advisor, had worked as Obama's foreign policy advisor back when Obama was the junior senator from Illinois. McDonough told Leiter that if Obama green-lighted the operation in Abbottabad, it was scheduled to go down the next weekend, on Saturday night. That happened to be the same night that Leiter was getting married to Alice Brown, in front of 250 guests at Meridian House, fifteen blocks north of the White House. "Denis, are you fucking kidding me?" exclaimed Leiter. "This weekend? This weekend!" McDonough, a taciturn Minnesotan, assured him he wasn't kidding.

The ideal time to do the helicopter assault was when there was no illumination from the moon. That would help to ensure that the Night Stalkers of the 160th Special Operations Aviation Regiment, who would fly the choppers over the Afghanistan-Pakistan border using night vision goggles (NVG), could do so without the Pakistanis noticing. A moonless night would also give the SEALs a considerable advantage, as they would be wearing NVGs as they stormed the compound. There would be no moon at all over Pakistan on the following Saturday, April 30. A Saturday night seemed ideal because it was the time of week when the CIA observed the lowest level of Pakistani military activity. The next moonless night would not be until June 1, and by then the weather would be significantly hotter, which might affect how well the choppers could fly. Even more pressingly, the longer they waited, the greater the possibility of a leak.

At 7:00 a.m. on Monday, April 25, Leiter talked to Michael Morell at the CIA. Before Leiter could even get to why they needed a Red Team, Morell said, "Absolutely, I think it's a great idea. We need to do it."

Leiter selected two analysts from the National Counterterrorism Center with deep knowledge of al-Qaeda: Richard (a pseudonym), who had more than two decades of counterterrorism work under his belt and was widely respected in the intelligence community, and Rose (a pseudonym), an in-the-weeds analyst in her mid-thirties. Two CIA analysts who had played no role in developing the bin Laden intelligence were also added to the group. Leiter told them they had forty-eight hours to come up with alternative hypotheses about who could be at the compound, supported by the best arguments they could come up with.

Leiter's team explored three alternative hypotheses about the Abbottabad compound: First, it was associated with bin Laden, but he wasn't there now. Second, the compound was the residence of a leader in al-Qaeda, but not bin Laden. Third, the Kuwaiti had long since left al-Qaeda and was now working for some unidentified criminal.

The analysts found that the first hypothesis was the most likely. The likelihood that the compound was home to a high-value target (HVT) in al-Qaeda other than bin Laden was significantly lower, because bin Laden's deputy, Ayman al-Zawahiri, was not known to be living in this part of Pakistan, while the Kuwaiti had never had any connection to Zawahiri, nor did the number of wives and children in the compound match up with what was known about Zawahiri's family. Could it be some other al-Qaeda HVT who was not known to the intelligence community? Leiter says this was considered unlikely. "We actually thought we had a pretty good handle on all the HVTs. This is what everyone was doing for ten years." The possibility that it was a criminal unconnected to al-Qaeda living at the compound was also considered unlikely, given the historical connections that the Kuwaiti had to al-Qaeda's leader.

At the end of this exercise, Richard was on the low end of the Red Team analysts, with only 40 percent confidence that bin Laden was living at the compound, while one of the CIA analysts was on the high end, with an estimate in the 60 percent range. Still, all the analysts concluded that none of the alternative hypotheses was as likely as the theory that it was bin Laden at the compound.

As the Red Team was finalizing its work on Wednesday, April 27, the White House posted online the president's long-form 1961 birth certificate from the state of Hawaii. So-called birthers, including the publicity-hungry billionaire Donald Trump, had made a political issue out of Obama's citizenship, claiming that he was not actually born in the United States, which would make him ineligible to be president. Obama said he had released the document to try to end the "silliness" about his place of birth, which was distracting the country from more serious issues. The day before the release of Obama's birth certificate, the SEAL teams had already left their base on the coast of Virginia to fly to Bagram Air Base in Afghanistan.

Michèle Flournoy and Mike Vickers decided to make a last-ditch effort to get Robert Gates to back the raid. In Gates's office at the Pentagon, Flournoy and Vickers walked their boss through the raid and its risks and the measures that had been taken to mitigate those risks. Gates seemed to be persuaded, but after four and a half decades in government, he had long mastered how to play his cards close to the vest.

On the other side of the world, the CIA spies on the ground in Abbottabad contacted their bosses in Virginia with the news that the Kuwaiti's wife, Mariam, as well as their four children, had just returned from one of their frequent trips around Pakistan to visit family, and they were all now back at the Abbottabad compound. Some intelligence officials continued to puzzle over this: If bin Laden was really there, why would he risk letting these folks visit their relatives?

12 THE DECISION

ON THURSDAY, APRIL 28, the day following the release of Obama's birth certificate, Leiter presented the findings of the Red Team to the president and his war cabinet. "Bottom line is, the Red Team did not find anything or conclude anything revolutionary or new from what the previous team had," Leiter told them.

For those who were in favor of the raid, such as Michèle Flournoy and Mike Vickers, the Red Team findings didn't alter their views. "It really didn't change anything," explains Vickers. "People's estimates before this ranged from maybe sixty to eighty percent believing that bin Laden was there. And then the Red Team, a couple of them came back and said sixty percent, and one guy said forty percent, but he said his forty percent was better than any other explanation."

Leiter addressed Obama directly, saying, "Even if you're at the forty percent low end of this range, Mister President, that's still about thirty-eight percent better than we've been for ten years."

Still, that one estimate of 40 percent was discomfiting to some.

John Brennan recalls, "Some of us thought, 'Whoa! We thought the prospects were higher that he was in there.' And the president recognized that when people were saying, 'Well, there's only 40 percent of a chance,' that some people were going to get a little bit soft on this."

Ben Rhodes says, "There was a deflation in the room, because what you're looking for as you're getting closer to the call is greater certainty, not less. So essentially it played into all the fears that people had about what could go wrong. Is it worth the risk?"

Similarly, Tony Blinken says, "I think, if anything, the Red Team actually brought down the level of certainty; the positive ID percentage was higher before the Red Team got done. So I think we went from maybe seventy/thirty or sixty-five/thirty-five to fifty-five/forty-five or even fifty/fifty."

Director of National Intelligence James Clapper, who had spent more than four decades in the intelligence business, says the discussion of exact percentages gave the impression of precision, but "in the end it was subjective. It didn't matter whether the percentage of confidence was 40 percent or 80 percent. It seemed like the closer you were to working the problem, the in-the-trenches analysts who were really doing the legwork here, doing the grunt work, were very confident. And as you got concentric circles away from them, the confidence sort of went down." Clapper personally felt "it was the most compelling case we had had in ten years. And sure, it would've been nice to have somebody inside the compound—the maid or the cook we could've recruited—someone who could say, 'Yeah, that's him and that's who's there.' Well, we didn't have that."

For those who were inclined to oppose the raid, such as Defense Secretary Robert Gates, the Red Team analysis confirmed their doubts. Gates said, "I think this Red Team is really an outstanding piece of work, and I find it very persuasive." Persuasive, in other words, that bin Laden might well not be living in the Abbottabad compound.

CIA director Leon Panetta spoke up, saying firmly, "When you put it all together, we have the best evidence since Tora Bora, and that makes it clear we have an obligation to act. If I thought delaying this could produce better intelligence, that would be one thing, but because of the nature of the security at the compound, we're probably at the point where we have got the best intelligence we can get. It's now time to make a decision not about whether or not we should do something about it, but *what* to do about it. We've come this far. There's no turning back. We have enough information such that the American people would want us to act."

At the conclusion of this lengthy discussion, Obama summed up the case: "All right, guys. In the end, it's fifty-fifty that he's there."

Leiter had also been tasked to think through what kind of reaction an assault on the Abbottabad compound might cause overseas and at home. Overseas, the worst case was that the U.S. embassy in Pakistan, one of the largest in the world, would be overrun by protestors and that Pakistani security forces would do little to stop them—a replay of what had happened in 1979, when the embassy building in Islamabad was attacked by an angry mob and burned to the ground. Leiter and his team also looked at the possible threats from "homegrown" terrorists, who might attack U.S. military installations or government buildings when they heard the news of bin Laden's death. Leiter briefed both these worst-case scenarios to everyone in the room.

Obama gave everyone ample opportunity to speak. Toward the end of the meeting, the president methodically went around the room and asked everyone, "Where are you on this? What do you think?" So many officials prefaced their comments with the words

"Mister President, this is a very hard call" that the Situation Room began to fill with laughter, the only moments of levity in a tense two-hour meeting.

Joe Biden, who had been elected to the U.S. Senate when Obama was eleven, and had been chairman of the Senate Foreign Relations Committee before becoming vice president, was worried about the local fallout from the raid: a possible firefight with the Pakistanis or an incident at the U.S. embassy in Islamabad. "We need greater certainty that bin Laden is there," he advised. "The risks to the Pakistan relationship and its importance are such that we need to know more before acting." Referring to the earlier discussion of percentages and close calls, Biden said, "You know, I didn't know we had so many economists around the table." Biden concluded, "We owe the man a direct answer. Mister President, my suggestion is: Don't go."

Robert Gates continued to be skittish about the raid, saying, "There is a degree of risk associated with the raid option that I am uncomfortable with. An option of some kind of precision strike, I would be more comfortable with that." Gates again raised the Operation Eagle Claw and Black Hawk Down incidents, as he had repeatedly during earlier meetings with Obama. The secretary of defense reminded Obama's war cabinet that he had been in the White House the night the Eagle Claw mission imploded.

Gates and Biden pointed out that a raid in Abbottabad would likely cause a permanent rupture in America's relations with Pakistan, and that would mean the end of both the land and air corridors across Pakistan that were critical to the resupply of the 100,000 American soldiers in neighboring Afghanistan. It would also mean an end to the Pakistanis' grudging acquiescence to the use of their territory to launch drone strikes—attacks that had proven devastating to the leadership of al-Qaeda in Pakistan's tribal regions.

With both Gates and Biden still leery of the largely circumstantial intelligence and the toll that a raid would place on the critical U.S.-Pakistani relationship, that made two out of the three most-senior officials in Obama's cabinet against the SEAL helicopter assault.

Obama's top military advisor, Admiral Mike Mullen, had never prepared a presentation for the president with as much care as the one he now delivered. Using a pack of a dozen slides with notes on them, Mullen walked Obama through the final brief of the raid plan. Mullen said he had attended the full-scale rehearsal of the raid and that "Bill's [McRaven's] team can do this." Mullen's strong advocacy of the raid was unusual, because Gates and he were usually in lockstep on key national security issues, as they had been about mounting a large-scale counterinsurgency campaign in Afghanistan. Now Obama's secretary of defense and his chairman of the Joint Chiefs were advocating different courses of action.

General Cartwright was still in favor of deploying a tiny drone-fired munition to take out bin Laden, an option that remained on the table during the April 28 meeting. The smallest bomb commonly dropped by the U.S. Air Force was five hundred pounds. The kind of device Cartwright was advocating was minute by comparison, and was known as a small tactical munition. For the past three years, Raytheon had been developing such a weapon, a thirteen-pound "smart" bomb that was two feet long and steered by a GPS-guided system. But this tiny bomb came with a raft of potential problems. Such a weapon had never before been fired in combat, and because it was GPS-guided, it was a "fire and forget" device whose targeting could not be adjusted while it was in flight, as that of a laser-guided bomb could be. What if this experimental weapon failed to detonate? Or missed? Or took out the wrong guy on the compound? Or even exploded at the target but failed to kill him? Any of these scenarios would be a replay of the August 1998 cruise missile attacks

THE DECISION

Bill Clinton had ordered to kill bin Laden after al-Qaeda bombed the two U.S. embassies in Africa. The cruise missiles missed bin Laden and helped turn him into a global celebrity.

Hillary Clinton gave a long, lawyerly presentation that examined both the upsides and the downsides of the raid option. It wasn't clear where she was going with it until she summarized it: "It's a very close call, but I would say: Do the raid." Clinton says, "I made a long presentation because the president is a very thoughtful, analytical decision maker, and he is more likely to listen to an argument that is not filled with passion and emotion. So I wanted to lay out in a very methodical way the pluses and the minuses as I understood them of the various options. And then to conclude that, given what was at stake, this was one of the moments that I thought called for a decision, despite the risk."

When it was his turn to address Obama, Leiter said, "Mister President, my first choice would be that we wait and collect more [intelligence], but I am being told by the operators there is nothing more that can be collected without excessive risk. And I can't second-guess them on that." Leiter also endorsed the use of the drone-fired munition because he thought the political risks of such an attack were so much lower than those associated with the raid.

Leon Panetta, who had been Bill Clinton's chief of staff and before that a nine-term congressman, knew a thing or two about the realities of politics. He delivered a persuasive political argument in favor of the raid and of doing it as soon as feasible. "I've always used the test, Mister President, as somebody that's been in public office: What would the average American say if he or she knew what we were talking about? And I think if you told the average American—we have the best intelligence we've had since Tora Bora, we have the chance to get the number one terrorist in the world who

attacked us on 9/11—I think that they would say 'we gotta go.'"
Hillary Clinton voiced a related point: enough people already knew
about the bin Laden intelligence that it would eventually leak.

John Brennan, Obama's top counterterrorism advisor, urged a go
on the raid. He had already told the president privately that the CIA
officials who had developed the intelligence on Abbottabad were
"the people that have been following bin Laden for fifteen years.
This has been their life's work, this has been their life's journey, and
they feel it very much in their gut that bin Laden is at that compound. I feel pretty good, if not certain, that bin Laden is at that
compound."

Denis McDonough, the deputy national security advisor, and his
boss, Tom Donilon, were also supportive of the raid. Ben Rhodes,
Michèle Flournoy, Tony Blinken, Mike Vickers, Robert Cardillo,
and Nick Rasmussen all endorsed the raid, as did the director of
national intelligence, Jim Clapper, who said, "It is the option most
fraught with risk, but in my view the most important thing for this
is that we have eyes and ears and brains on the ground."

Obama listened to the counsel of his senior advisors intently, but
kept his own views to himself. One of the officials in the room who
had attended countless meetings with the president observes, "He's
very hard to read. He's an introverted guy. He's a thinker." As the
meeting wound up, at around 7:00 p.m., the president said, "This
is a close call and not one that I'm ready to make now. I need to go
think about this. I'm going to sleep on it. I'll give an order in the
morning." Obama felt that those who had voiced doubts about the
intelligence case and raid option had helped improve the operational
planning for the raid, particularly the ability of the SEALs to fight
their way out of Abbottabad, if it came to that.

Obama wrestled with the options, knowing that the burden of

this decision was going to be on his shoulders for the rest of his life. He felt that "the most difficult part is always the fact that you're sending guys into harm's way. And there are a lot of things that could go wrong. I mean there're a lot of moving parts here. So my biggest concern was, if I'm sending those guys in and Murphy's Law applies and something happens, can we still get our guys out? So that's point number one. Point number two, these guys are going in in the darkest of night. And they don't know what they're going to find there. They don't know if the building is rigged. They don't know if there are explosives that are triggered by a particular door opening. So huge risks that these guys are taking." Despite those risks, Obama decided to forgo the drone option: "I thought it was important if we were going to go into a sovereign country, that we had to have some proof that in fact it was bin Laden, rather than just firing a missile into a compound." Also, while this may have been a fifty-fifty intelligence case, Obama had 100 percent confidence in McRaven and the SEALs' ability to execute the mission.

Obama knew the stakes were high: "Obviously I knew that if we were unsuccessful, there was the potential for not only loss of life—the incredibly brave SEALs who were going in—but also there would be huge geopolitical ramifications." Obama couldn't help wondering, "What if the mysterious pacer was a prince from Dubai just keeping a low profile?"

Obama has always been a risk taker, albeit a highly disciplined one. After all, he took on Hillary Clinton, a supposed shoo-in for the Democratic nomination for president, after he had served only two years in the Senate. In 2009, President Obama, previously the "antiwar" candidate, tripled the number of troops in Afghanistan over what President Bush had deployed there. When Egyptians rose up against their octogenarian dictator, Hosni Mubarak, in February

2011, Obama, against the advice of nearly his entire cabinet—who argued "better the devil you know"—called Mubarak and told him it was time to step down. In March 2011, as Moammar Gadhafi moved to exterminate the burgeoning opposition movement in Libya, Obama went within days to the United Nations and NATO and set in motion the military campaign that toppled the Libyan dictator, a campaign for which he was roundly criticized by both the Left and the Right. Both Gates and Biden had advised Obama against getting involved in Libya.

Despite Biden's warnings about the irreparable damage to the U.S.-Pakistani relationship that a raid in Abbottabad might cause, Obama felt that whatever happened as a result of the raid, the American relationship with Pakistan could absorb the blow, particularly if efforts to repair the damage were made right away. And as for those who argued that the best approach was to wait and gather more certain intelligence, Obama had concluded by mid-April that the intelligence case was never going to be certain. Now that the circle of knowledge about Abbottabad had expanded, there was also the real risk that if they waited for the next favorable lunar cycle to mount the raid, word could trickle out about the Abbottabad compound, and there might not be another opportunity to find bin Laden.

Obama rolls the dice after considerable deliberation, but roll them he does. With Osama bin Laden as the prize, Obama was prepared to ignore the advice both of his vice president and his secretary of defense and roll the dice one more time. Obama says, "Even though I thought it was only fifty-fifty that bin Laden was there, I thought it was worth us taking a shot. . . . And the reason that I concluded it was worth it was that we have devoted enormous blood and treasure in fighting back against al-Qaeda, ever since 2001. And even before with the embassy bombing in Kenya. And so part of what was in my mind was all those young men that I visited who are still fighting in Afghanistan, and the families of victims of terrorism that I talk to. And I said to myself that if we have a good chance of not completely defeating, but badly disabling al-Qaeda, then it was worth both the political risks as well as the risks to our men."

On Friday, April 29, at 8:20 a.m. in the White House Diplomatic Reception Room, Obama gathered Donilon, McDonough, Brennan, and Chief of Staff Bill Daley in a semicircle around him. "Is there anything new?" he asked. "Have you guys changed your mind about the raid?" The advisors all told him they believed it was the right thing to do and strongly recommended he go forward with it.

Obama said simply, "I've considered the decision: It's a go. And the only thing that makes it not a go is if Bill McRaven and his folks believe that either weather or conditions on the ground increase the risk to our forces." Obama instructed Donilon to issue the orders that would set in motion the operation. Donilon says, "I've been in Washington a long time. This is the third president I have served. I first came to work in the White House in June of 1977, and those moments still really strike me, that we ask one person in our system to make these incredibly difficult calls on behalf of three hundred million Americans."

Tony Blinken heard the news shortly afterward. "I thought, 'Man, that is a gutsy call.' First, we don't know for sure bin Laden is there; the evidence is circumstantial. Second, most of his most senior advisors had recommended a different course of action. I remember when he left the meeting the previous day, I was not convinced he was going to do it. Leaving that meeting, I think a lot of people had visions of Jimmy Carter in their heads."

Directly after giving the "go" order for Abbottabad, Obama boarded Marine One at 8:30 a.m. with his family for the short hop to Andrews Air Force Base, where they then took Air Force One down to Tuscaloosa, Alabama, one of the cities hardest hit by a week of tornadoes that had touched down across eight states. "I've never seen devastation like this," said Obama, standing in the rubble in Tuscaloosa.

Meanwhile, Donilon signed an official authorization for the Abbottabad operation. Around the same time, officials at the American consulate in the northwestern city of Peshawar—not far from the tribal areas where al-Qaeda and a number of Taliban groups were headquartered—were told to evacuate. This evacuation order was framed as having to do with recent kidnapping threats, but was actually because of the impending operation.

That afternoon, Obama flew to Kennedy Space Center in Florida, where he met with Representative Gabrielle Giffords, the Arizona congresswoman who was slowly recovering from being shot in the head by a deranged man. Obama was attending the launch of the space shuttle *Endeavor*, which was commanded by Giffords's husband, Mark Kelly. That evening, Obama gave the commencement address at Miami Dade College, returning to the White House at 11:30 p.m.

At the JSOC headquarters in Afghanistan at Bagram Air Base, just north of Kabul, Admiral McRaven gave a tour to a visiting "codel," a delegation of visitors from Congress. He gave no hint that he was just about to launch the most important operation of his life.

Throughout the long day in Alabama and Florida, Obama kept his game face on. He said later that the Abbottabad operation "was weighing on me, but, you know, something I said during the campaign that I've learned over and over again in this job, is the presidency requires you to do more than one thing at a time."

One of those things was to attend the White House Correspondents' Dinner on Saturday evening—the nearest thing to Oscar night that dowdy Washington, D.C., has to offer. It is an annual tradition going back decades in which the president and pretty much every other important official in the administration—as well as many who like to think of themselves as important—gather with the Washington press corps for a black-tie dinner. Adding a little tinsel to the proceedings, New York media moguls attend, and a sprinkling of Hollywood stars and business heavyweights fly in for the night. The evening's entertainment generally consists of a comic who gently roasts politicians on both sides of the aisle, while the president takes a few pot shots of his own at his critics and the press.

Unbeknownst to the Washington press corps, the 2011 Correspondents' Dinner had been the subject of intense discussions in the Situation Room in recent days. Should the Abbottabad operation be delayed until after the dinner? There was sound reason to consider this idea, because if the raid went badly, the plan was to try to keep it a covert action and not acknowledge it, but you couldn't do that very well if just about all the senior national security officials attending the dinner suddenly got up and left to deal with the fallout from a botched raid. Similarly, if the president canceled his appearance at the dinner at the very last minute, the press corps would surely sense that something was up and start digging into what had caused the cancellation. Officials discussed how they might throw the press off the scent by simply announcing that the president had the flu. The counterargument was that if the Obama administration delayed the operation and then it came out that they had missed an opportunity to get bin Laden because of the dinner, it would be a public relations disaster of biblical proportions.

Obama was reluctant to consider moving the Abbottabad operation until after the Correspondents' Dinner. "The only thing that was going to drive the 'go' or 'no go' on this mission were the mission requirements of the SEALs in the field," he said. By Friday night, the discussion about what to do about the dinner was rendered moot, as it was predicted that there was going to be excessive cloud cover in northern Pakistan the following evening. McRaven decided to push the mission back twenty-four hours, to Sunday night.

On Saturday afternoon, during a break from rehearsing his speech for the Correspondents' Dinner, Obama called McRaven for a final status check, as it was by now late Saturday night in Afghanistan. During a twelve-minute phone call, McRaven affirmed that they were ready to go. The president concluded the call, saying, "I couldn't have any more confidence in you than the confidence I have in you and your force. Godspeed to you and your forces. Please pass on to them my personal thanks for their service and the message that I personally will be following this mission very closely."

Operation Neptune Spear was now a go. The name given to the mission was a nod to the trident wielded by Neptune, the mythological god of the sea, that appears on the badge awarded to all those who qualify as SEALs.

At 7:00 p.m. Saturday, Barack and Michelle Obama showed up as scheduled at the cavernous banquet hall of the Washington Hilton, the president in black tie and the first lady in a brown silk sleeveless gown with a plunging neckline. At the back of his mind, Obama was turning over the details of the Abbottabad operation, but he still managed to deliver a hilarious after-dinner monologue centered largely on the faux controversy about whether he was actually an American citizen. In the audience was Donald Trump, the blowhard billionaire who had been especially vocal in questioning the president's citizenship, and who hosted the NBC reality show *Celebrity Apprentice*. Obama began his monologue by saying, "My fellow Americans . . . Donald Trump is here tonight! Now, I know that he's taken some flak lately, but no one is happier, no one is prouder to put this birth certificate matter to rest than 'the Donald.' And that's because he can finally get back to focusing on the issues that matter—like, did we fake the moon landing? . . . But all kidding aside, obviously, we all know about [Donald Trump's] credentials and breadth of experience. For example—no, seriously, just recently, in an episode of *Celebrity Apprentice*—at the steakhouse, the men's cooking team did not impress the judges from Omaha Steaks. And there was a lot of blame to go around. But you, Mister Trump, recognized that the real problem was a lack of leadership. And so ultimately, you didn't blame Lil' Jon or Meatloaf. You fired Gary Busey. And these are the kind of decisions that would keep me up at night. Well handled, sir. Well handled." Trump listened to the president's deft skewering with a pained smirk.

Laughing along at the dinner were many of the key players in the impending bin Laden operation: Leon Panetta, Robert Gates, Tom Donilon, Admiral Mike Mullen, Mike Vickers, and White House chief of staff Bill Daley. The emcee of the dinner, comedian Seth Meyers, at one point made a joke about the long hunt for bin Laden. "People think bin Laden is hiding in the Hindu Kush," quipped Meyers, "but did you know that every day from 4 to 5 p.m. he hosts a show on C-SPAN?" Obama let rip a big guffaw at that one.

ABC News anchor George Stephanopoulos had gotten wind of the fact that, somewhat unusually, the White House was going to be closed to all tours the following day. Chatting with Bill Daley, Stephanopoulos quizzed him: "You guys have got something big going on over there?" Daley was momentarily spooked, but recovered, saying blandly, "Oh no. It's just a plumbing issue," which seemed to satisfy Stephanopoulos.

A few blocks away, at the historic Meridian House, Mike Leiter was married to Alice Brown. The judge conducting the ceremony was Laurence Silberman, who had led the commission that examined why the CIA had mistakenly concluded that Saddam Hussein had reconstituted his weapons of mass destruction. In less than twenty-four hours the CIA would have a chance to wipe away the memory of that grim chapter in its history. Or it might be embarrassed again.

13 DON'T TURN ON THE LIGHT

JUST AFTER MIDNIGHT, the residents of the bin Laden compound were startled awake by the strange sounds of explosions nearby. Bin Laden's daughter Maryam, age twenty, rushed upstairs to his top-floor bedroom to ask what was going on. "Go downstairs and go back to bed," he told her.

Then bin Laden told his wife Amal, "Don't turn on the light." It was a pointless admonition. Someone—it is still not clear exactly who—had taken the sensible precaution of turning off the electricity feeding the neighborhood, thus giving the SEALs a large advantage on that moonless night. Indeed, those would be the last words Osama bin Laden would ever utter.

SIX HOURS EARLIER, around 8:00 a.m. Eastern Time on Sunday, May 1, Obama's national security staffers had begun arriving at the White House. Some of them drifted over to a nearby Starbucks to get caffeinated for what was obviously going to be a very long day.

One or two of them were a little the worse for wear from having attended the White House Correspondents' Dinner the night before. Deputy National Security Advisor Denis McDonough had gone to his friend Mike Leiter's wedding. After a late night—"It was my wedding, for God's sake!"—Leiter, who had already postponed his honeymoon, told his new bride he had to go to the White House for some important meetings. "I might not be back for a while. I can't tell you why. You'll understand later," he said. Leon Panetta got up early that morning. While shaving he looked at himself in the mirror and thought, "The next time I look in this mirror, we will have accomplished something significant, or I will have to be explaining myself to a lot of people."

The nation's top security officials were careful to project a show of business as usual. As was his habit, Panetta, a committed Catholic, attended Sunday Mass. At about 9:45 a.m., President Obama left the White House for his usual round of golf at Andrews Air Force Base, but he played only nine holes. At 10:00 a.m. the "deputies" meeting began. The subcabinet officials assembled there each had thick briefing books that featured options labeled "branches" and "sequels," covering pretty much every contingency that might arise during Operation Neptune Spear.

At around noon, the principals of Obama's cabinet began arriving at the White House. So as not to attract attention, the armor-plated limos of cabinet officials such as Hillary Clinton were not parked in their usual spots near the West Wing, where the inquisitive White House press corps might notice them. The White House had canceled all tours so that tourists wouldn't see all the unusual comings and goings. Katie Johnson, the president's personal secretary, had scheduled a White House tour for the stars of the movie *The Hangover*, who were in town for the Correspondents' Dinner, and she asked Ben Rhodes if he could grant an exception. Rhodes told her it wouldn't be possible.

The White House national security team had set up secure communications in the Situation Room, connected to Admiral McRaven, who was by now in Jalalabad, in eastern Afghanistan. The "Sit Room" was also in secure communication with Panetta's offices at CIA headquarters and with the Ops Center in the Pentagon, where General Cartwright was monitoring all the intelligence feeds coming in from the field and had a team of some thirty officers standing by to respond to any contingency.

Cartwright's team had created an operational matrix that covered any likely eventuality: a helicopter going down, bin Laden taken alive, a dead bin Laden, an injured bin Laden, and someone other than bin Laden living at the compound. Cartwright's biggest concern was that Pakistan's premier military academy was less than a mile away from the compound. Might a large force of Pakistani soldiers be up at night for some reason and stumble on the operation? This could lead to a shootout with the Pakistanis. Not good. If Pakistani troops did suddenly appear in force, the plan was for the SEALs to try to avoid a firefight and to sit tight in the compound while senior U.S. military officials in Washington tried to negotiate their safe passage. But the SEALs had enough firepower and backup with the quick reaction force (QRF) on the Chinooks that they could fight their way out, if it came to that.

At 1:00 p.m. Eastern Time, as night fell seven thousand miles to the east, in Pakistan, Obama's war cabinet began to gather in the Sit Room. Across the Potomac River, in Langley, Virginia, Panetta was in a spacious conference room on the top floor of CIA headquarters. The room had been transformed into a command center, with maps on the walls, computers monitoring the operation, and two large screens with secure video streams, one linked to the Situation Room, the other to Admiral McRaven in Jalalabad.

"What do you think?" Panetta asked CIA Deputy Director Michael Morell.

"I won't be surprised if bin Laden is there. And I won't be surprised if he isn't there," Morell said.

"That's where I am," Panetta agreed.

Also observing the operation at the CIA was Admiral Eric Olson, a veteran of the Black Hawk Down incident in Somalia in 1993, now the overall commander of Special Operations. Olson had been awarded the Silver Star for "conspicuous gallantry" in Somalia and was keenly aware of how a U.S. helicopter assault in a foreign city could go badly wrong.

The CIA director narrated developments to the officials at the White House as he heard them from McRaven. Panetta was in nominal control of the operation so that it would remain covert and so that the White House would preserve "deniability" should bin Laden not be at the compound and the raid go undetected by the Pakistanis. But the CIA's "command and control" of the operation was a fiction; the real commander was McRaven.

At 1:22 p.m., Panetta ordered McRaven to perform the raid, telling him, "Go in there and get bin Laden, and if bin Laden isn't in there, get the hell out!"

At 2:00 p.m., Obama returned from his golf game and went straight to the Sit Room for the final meeting with his national security team as Operation Neptune Spear commenced. At 2:05 p.m., Leon Panetta began one more overview of the operation.

It was now just past 11:00 p.m. in Abbottabad, and the bin Laden household was in bed. And given the time difference between Pakistan and Afghanistan, it was just past 10:30 p.m. in Jalalabad, where the U.S. Navy SEAL team, consisting of twenty-three "operators" and an interpreter—a "terp," in military parlance—were readying themselves to board two Black Hawk choppers. The helicopters would carry them more than 150 miles to the east, perhaps to confront the man responsible for the deadliest mass murder in American history. The men carried small cards filled with photos and descriptions of bin Laden's family and the members of his entourage who were believed to be living at the compound. Also along for the operation was a combat dog named Cairo, wearing body armor just like his SEAL teammates.

Half an hour later, at about 11:00 p.m. local time, the two Black Hawks took off from the Jalalabad airfield, heading east toward the Pakistani border, which they would cross in about fifteen minutes. The MH-60 choppers were modified so as to remain undetected by Pakistani radar stations, which were in "peacetime" mode, unlike the radar facilities on the border Pakistan shared with its longtime enemy India, which were always on heightened alert. Painted with exotic emulsions designed to help them evade radar, the modified MH-60s also gave off a low heat "signature" in flight, and their tail rotors had been designed to make them less noisy and less susceptible to radar identification. On top of that, the helicopters flew "nap-of-the-earth," which means perilously low and very, very fast—only a few feet above the ground, driving around trees and hugging the riverbeds and valleys that penetrate the foothills of the Hindu Kush mountain range. This also made them harder to detect by radar. After crossing the Pakistani border, the choppers swung north of Peshawar and its millions of residents and eyeballs. The total flight time to the target was about an hour and a half.

The secrecy surrounding the bin Laden raid was so intense that of the 150,000 American and NATO soldiers in Afghanistan, the only one who had been briefed about the operation was their overall commander, General David Petraeus, who had received a heads-up three days earlier. As on most nights in Afghanistan, there were some dozen Special Forces operations launching that night to capture or kill militant commanders. The bin Laden raid was different not only because of the target but also because it was taking place in a country that the United States was nominally allied to but that had not been notified of the operation.

Shortly before midnight, Petraeus strolled into the ops center in NATO headquarters and asked everyone except one officer to leave. He then opened up a classified chat room on a computer that allowed him to monitor the operation. If needed, Petraeus was ready to order U.S. aircraft in Afghanistan to respond to Pakistani jets trying to intercept or even attack the American helicopters now entering their airspace.

Once the two Black Hawks were inside Pakistan's airspace, three bus-size Chinook helicopters took off from the Jalalabad airfield. One landed just inside the Afghan border with Pakistan, and two flew on to Kala Dhaka, in the mountainous region of Swat, about fifty miles northwest of Abbottabad, landing on a flat beachlike area on the banks of the broad Indus River. This part of northern Pakistan was barely populated and wasn't controlled by either the Taliban or the Pakistani government. On these two Chinooks was the QRF, consisting of two dozen SEALs who would go forward if the SEALs on the Black Hawks encountered serious opposition when they landed at the compound. The Chinooks also carried bladders of fuel for the Black Hawks, which would need to be refueled on the flight back to Afghanistan.

ADJOINING THE WHITE HOUSE situation room, which can accommodate more than a dozen senior officials at a large, highly polished wooden table and a couple dozen more staffers on the "backbencher" seats around the walls, is a much smaller meeting room. Like the Sit Room, this conference room has secure video and phone communications, but it has only a small table and can comfortably accommodate only seven people. In this room was Brigadier General Marshall B. "Brad" Webb, a deputy commander of JSOC, dressed in a crisp blue air force uniform festooned with ribbons, monitoring the SEAL teams on the raid in real time on a laptop, together with another JSOC officer. On the video monitors of the small conference room, grainy video of the unfolding raid was fed in from a bat-shaped RQ-170 Sentinel stealth drone flying more than two miles above Abbottabad.

National Security Advisor Tom Donilon stopped by the small conference room and asked what the officers were doing. Told that they were getting ready to unplug their equipment and move it into the main Situation Room, Donilon said, "No, you're not. Shut this off. I don't want this going on." Donilon didn't want to leave anyone with the impression that the president was micromanaging a military mission for which he'd already approved the plan. The officers pointed out that if they shut down their equipment there would no longer be a way to communicate with McRaven. "Okay," Donilon said, "you have to keep it all in this room."

Next door, a debate was percolating in the Situation Room about whether the president should be monitoring the operation live as it happened. Leiter recalls, "The White House, as only the White House can, had an endless debate about whether or not the president should monitor in real time. What if something went wrong and the president said something or did something? I wasn't going to sit around and wait for the debate to be solved. I was going to watch the damn thing."

Leiter went into the small conference room to watch the feed from the stealth drone, and was soon followed by members of

Obama's cabinet. "Slowly, onesies and twosies, they kept poking their head in," Leiter recalls. Vice President Joe Biden drifted in, and then Robert Gates and Hillary Clinton, and suddenly the room was full, with many of Obama's top intelligence and counterterrorism officials jammed up against the wall or peering through the doorway to get a better look at the unfolding drama.

The debate about whether the president should be monitoring the operation was settled when Obama popped into the room and announced, "I need to watch this," and settled himself into a chair off to one side of the cramped room. Dozens of other officials at the CIA and the Pentagon also were monitoring the same video feed.

The men and women in the room were updated about each key milestone along the way as the helicopters entered Pakistan's airspace and headed toward Abbottabad. The tension was palpable. Leiter, who used to fly attack jets for the navy, says, "The only thing I can compare it to is landing a plane on an aircraft carrier at night." There was very little discussion, except every once in a while an official would ask for clarification of what was going on, such as "Why is that helo there? What are they doing now?" If he could, Webb answered the question immediately; otherwise he made a quick call to find out what was happening.

The Black Hawks approached Abbottabad from the northwest. Once the helicopters reached their destination, the carefully planned operation began to unravel. As the first chopper tried to land in the largest courtyard in the compound, it suddenly lost altitude. The combination of the additional weight of the stealth technology and the higher-than-expected temperatures in Abbottabad had degraded its performance, causing an aerodynamic phenomenon known as "settling with power," meaning an unexpectedly fast drop. When the SEALs had practiced the maneuver on a replica of the compound in the States, the compound's outer walls had been represented by chain-link fencing, whereas the actual walls were made of concrete. The thick walls likely gave more energy to the Black Hawk's rotor wash and contributed to the chopper's instability. Because of that instability, the tail of the craft clipped one of the compound walls, breaking off the critical tail rotor. Now the pilot could no longer control the chopper. Relying on his training, he avoided a potentially catastrophic crash by burying the helo's nose in the dirt in the large yard where the compound occupants grew crops. Because of his quick thinking, the SEALs on the chopper did not sustain serious injuries and, after gathering their wits about them, were able to clamber out of the downed bird.

The plan had been for both Black Hawks to drop off the two dozen men, lingering for only a couple of minutes before flying out to a distant rendezvous point, where they would then wait for the signal to return for the SEAL team at the end of the mission. The hope was that any curious locals would assume that the two choppers were visiting the nearby military academy. Now one Black Hawk was down and any chance that the mission might remain "deniable" to the media and public was gone. So was the element of surprise.

Obama grimly watched this all unfold on the grainy video feed being beamed back from the drone high above the compound. The feed clearly showed that the rotors of the first helicopter had stopped spinning. Then the second helicopter, instead of hovering and dropping some SEALs on the roof of the main compound building, simply disappeared out of the shot.

"We could see that there were problems initially with one of the helicopters landing. So right off the top, everybody, I think, was holding their breath. That wasn't in the script," says Obama. "And when our helicopter tail didn't get over the wall into the yard there and we knew that it was lost, which meant you had to bring in the standby helicopter for the extraction, those were really intense moments," echoes Secretary Clinton. "This was like any episode of *24* or any movie you could ever imagine."

General James Clapper, the director of national intelligence, was an old friend of Robert Gates, who was sitting in front of him, also transfixed by the footage of the chopper going down. Clapper looked over at Gates, who was ashen. "I know his heart was in his throat then," says Clapper. Clapper's deputy Robert Cardillo says, "I could almost hear heartbeats in the room." Vice President Biden fingered his rosary beads.

In Panetta's conference room at the CIA, now packed with some two dozen officials from the Agency, Joint Special Operations Command, and other parts of the intelligence community, there was silence as the footage of the downed helicopter flickered on the screen. A female analyst who had worked on the bin Laden account for years nervously piped up, "Is that good?"

In his Texas drawl, Admiral McRaven addressed Panetta without any discernible shift in tone, saying, "We will now be amending the mission. Director, as you can see, we have a helicopter down in the courtyard. My men are prepared for this contingency and they will deal with it." Within a matter of seconds, McRaven could see on his video feed of the operation that the SEAL team on the downed helicopter had made it out of the bird without any serious problems. About a minute later, McRaven said, "I'm pushing the QRF to the objective," meaning that the SEALs waiting in the Chinook about twenty minutes' flying time to the north of the compound would now scramble to get to Abbottabad.

Despite the contingency plans, some of the officials observing the chopper crash were haunted by the knowledge that it was after just this kind of mishap that an operation could spiral badly out of control. The deadliest battle in the history of the SEALs had taken place six years earlier, in Kunar, in eastern Afghanistan, where the

Taliban had ambushed a group of four SEALs, three of whom were killed. The mission that was launched to try to extricate the SEALs turned into a fiasco when one of the rescue helicopters went down, killing all eight SEALs and eight Special Operations aviators on board.

After the helicopter went down in the Abbottabad compound, Mullen's biggest concern "was that someone at the White House would reach in and start micromanaging the mission. It is potentially the great disadvantage about technology that we have these days. And I was going to put my body in the way to try to stop that. Obviously, there was one person I couldn't stop doing that, and that was the president." Obama let the mission proceed.

AT THE COMPOUND, three SEALs from the downed chopper ran across the small field where the Black Hawk had crashed and opened a door on one of the inside walls of the compound, leading to a self-contained annex area. There they found the simple garage where the Kuwaiti parked his jeep and van and the one-story building where he lived with his family. The Kuwaiti poked his head out from behind a metal gate in this building, and the SEALs shot him twice in the chin, killing him. They also wounded the Kuwaiti's wife with a shot to her right shoulder. Their silenced weapons made little noise. (The courier's AK-47 was later found by his bedside. It seems unlikely that he fired it, given its location and the fact that no casings from such a weapon were later found at the scene.)

Meanwhile, the second Black Hawk pilot had seen what happened to the first chopper and shifted gears. Plan A had been to hover above the roof of bin Laden's bedroom so that a few SEALs could fast-rope down onto it and surprise bin Laden while he slept. Now the pilot opted for Plan B: the safer course of settling the bird down just outside the compound walls in a field of crops. A small group of SEALs jumped out, four of them to secure the outside perimeter of the compound, together with the interpreter and Cairo, a Belgian Malinois, similar to a German shepherd. The dog would track any "squirters," or people trying to escape from the compound, and would discourage inquisitive neighbors from getting too close. Most Muslims consider dogs to be "unclean" and are wary of them, in particular attack dogs such as Cairo. Cairo had also been trained to hunt for any hidden chambers or vaults inside the compound that might be hiding bin Laden. The remaining eight SEALs on the second chopper jumped out and set an explosive charge on a solid metal door on one of the compound's exterior walls, but when the gate was blown off its hinges, they were greeted by the sight of a large brick wall—a dead end. Soon after that, their colleagues from the downed chopper let them in through the main gate of the compound, saving them the trouble of blowing through the massive, thick exterior wall.

Up in his top-floor bedroom, bin Laden had become a victim of his own security arrangements. The few windows ensured that no one could look in to see him, but now it was impossible for him to see what was going on outside the small room he shared with his beloved Amal. Dressed in tan *shalwar kameez* robes, the leader of al-Qaeda just waited in the dark in silence for about fifteen minutes, seemingly mentally paralyzed as the Americans stormed his last refuge. With no moon and the electricity out, it was pitch black, which must have added to his confusion. Sewn into his clothing were several hundred euros and two phone numbers, one for a cell phone in Pakistan and another for a call center in Pakistan's tribal regions. This was the extent of bin Laden's escape plan, and it wasn't going to be of much help to him now.

Three SEALs went from the Kuwaiti's one-story building through a metal gate in a wall inside the compound and found themselves in a grassy courtyard in front of the main house. The SEALs entered the ground floor. On their left was a bedroom where they shot Abrar, the Kuwaiti's brother, and his wife, Bushra, killing them both. They were unarmed. At this point, the officials at the White House could no longer see what was going on, as the drone flying high above the compound was feeding back video only of the exterior of the bin Laden residence. Obama remembers, "We were really in a blackout situation and it was hard for us to know what exactly was taking place. We knew that gunshots were taking place, and we knew some explosions were taking place."

The SEAL team had no idea what the layout of the floors inside bin Laden's house might be. As they moved deeper inside, they passed a kitchen and two large storage rooms. Near the back of the house, which had a bunker-like feel, was a stairwell. Blocking their way to the upper two floors was a massive, locked metal gate. The SEALs blasted their way through this gate with the breaching materials they were carrying.

Leiter says that he was concerned that the house might be booby-trapped with bombs, a technique al-Qaeda had perfected in Iraq: "I kept waiting for some big explosion from the house that just made everything sink." Brennan was also anxious: "Might there be a quick reaction force that bin Laden may have had, security that we didn't know about?"

As the SEALs ran up to the second floor, they encountered bin Laden's twenty-three-year-old son, Khalid, whom they shot on the staircase. He appears to have been unarmed. Knots of children were now gathering on the stairs and landings of the bin Laden residence.

On a shelf in his bedroom were the AK-47 and Makarov machine pistol that were bin Laden's constant companions, but he didn't reach for them. Instead, he opened a metal gate, which blocked all access to his room and could be opened only from the inside, and quickly poked his head out to see what the commotion was. He was immediately spotted by the SEALs, who bounded up the next flight of stairs. At this point, unless bin Laden walked out of his bedroom with his hands up and said, "I surrender," there was no chance that he would be taken alive. Retreating inside, bin Laden made the fatal error of not locking this gate behind him, allowing the SEALs to run past it into a short hallway. They then turned right into his bedroom.

Hearing the sounds of strange men rushing into their room, Amal screamed something in Arabic and threw herself in front of her husband. The first SEAL who charged into the room shoved her aside, concerned she might be wearing a suicide bomb vest. Amal was then shot in the calf by another of the SEALs and collapsed unconscious onto the simple double mattress she shared with bin Laden. Bin Laden was offering no resistance when he was dispatched with a "double tap" of shots to the chest and his left eye. It was a grisly scene: his brains spattered on the ceiling above him and poured out of his eye socket. The floor near the bed was smeared with bin Laden's blood.

For all his bluster that he would go down fighting and his bodyguards would shoot him if he were ever found by the Americans, when the moment finally came, bin Laden went out not with a bang but with a whimper. The fifty-four-year-old bin Laden may have grown complacent or tired during his decade on the run; he had no real escape plan, and there was no secret passageway out of his house. Perhaps he expected some kind of warning that never came. Or perhaps he knew that a firefight inside the enclosed spaces of his house would likely end up killing some of his wives and children. After all, the SEALs shot to kill or to wound most of the adults they encountered in the compound, killing four men and one woman and wounding two other women. Of the eleven adults in the compound that night—which included three of bin Laden's older children: Khalid, Maryam, and Sumaiya—a total of seven were shot in the space of a quarter of an hour.

On the audio feed, McRaven heard the SEAL team give the code word *Geronimo*. Each step of the operation had been labeled with a letter of the alphabet, and *G* meant that bin Laden was "secured." McRaven relayed the word *Geronimo* to the White House. But this was ambiguous: Was bin Laden captured or dead? So McRaven asked the SEAL ground force commander, "Is he EKIA [Enemy Killed in Action]?" A few seconds later, the answer came back: "Roger, Geronimo EKIA." Then McRaven announced to the White House, "Geronimo EKIA."

There were gasps in the Situation Room, but no whoops or high fives. The president quietly said, "We got him, we got him."

It was still the middle of the night in Pakistan, and the SEALs were able to see only through the murky, pixilated green light of night vision goggles. McRaven came on the line again to say, "Look, I've got a Geronimo call, but I need to tell you it's a first call. This is not a confirmation. Please keep your expectations managed a little here. Most operators when they are on a mission their adrenaline is sky high. Yes, they are professional, but let's not count on anything until they get back and we have some evidence." McRaven also pointed out, "We've got SEALs on the ground without a ride."

The SEALs' next task was to blow up the downed helicopter crammed with secret avionics and clad in stealth technology. Then they had to get out of Pakistan without encountering Pakistani forces on the ground or in the air. Everyone following the operation knew that there was much that could still go wrong. Obama says, "All of us, I think, took pause, not wanting to get too excited: Number one because they're operating in pitch darkness and identification could not be certain. Number two, our guys still weren't out of there."

Leiter says, "We were just amazed by the lack of a Pakistani response. It was, even by Pakistani standards, remarkably slow." Belatedly, the Pakistanis did scramble two F-16s. Leiter, who had logged hundreds of hours of flight time in attack jets, was not especially concerned, knowing that Pakistani pilots didn't have much nighttime flying capability. "I had some appreciation for the Pakistanis' ability to find two helicopters flying near the ground at night with no airborne command and control," Leiter says. "An American F-16 couldn't have found them in the time they needed to. It was just a non-risk. Some people were more nervous than I was." Leiter was, however, concerned that the Pakistan military might interpret the mysterious choppers flying around Abbottabad as an incursion by the Indian air force and was relieved when the Pakistani F-16s started flying away from the Indian border.

The SEALs grabbed bin Laden's body and dragged it down the stairs of his residence, leaving a trail of bloody skid marks, all under the watchful eyes of Safia, bin Laden's twelve-year-old daughter. The bodies of the three other men killed by the SEALs, the courier and his brother and Khalid bin Laden, lay scattered around the compound, blood oozing from their noses, ears, and mouths. Next to her husband was Bushra, the wife of the courier's brother, also dead.

Outside the compound, the interpreter waved off curious neighbors who had started to gather, telling them in the local language that a security operation was going on and they should go home. In the twenty-three minutes after they killed bin Laden, some SEALs wired the disabled chopper with explosives, while others gathered up the many computers, cell phones, and thumb drives that littered bin Laden's residence, which might shed light on the inner workings of al-Qaeda and its plans for future terrorist attacks. The SEALs also rounded up the more than a dozen women and children, who were distraught and wailing, and moved them out of the way so that they could safely blow up the downed helicopter.

The SEALs had expected they might find twenty-one-year-old Hamza bin Laden, one of the older sons of al-Qaeda's leader, at the compound. They were carrying the cards that had detailed information about the adults they might encounter at the bin Laden residence, including Hamza, who had appeared in al-Qaeda propaganda videos while he was a child and had spent much of the decade after 9/11 in Iran. Hamza was known to have returned to Pakistan in the summer of 2010. Could he have escaped during the raid? That seems implausible, given the presence of twenty-three SEALs at the compound, four of whom were patrolling the perimeter with a dog trained to apprehend anyone escaping, while high overhead a U.S. drone monitored the raid. More likely, Hamza had never made it to Abbottabad and was living instead in Pakistan's tribal regions with other al-Qaeda members.

One of the SEAL operators took a photo of bin Laden's face and uploaded the picture to a server. It was sent on to Washington, where two separate teams of facial recognition experts were standing by to compare the picture of the dead bin Laden to existing photographs of him and provide a relatively quick, though not completely foolproof, confirmation that it was al-Qaeda's leader. DNA testing was the only way to identify him with complete certainty, but that would take longer. SEALs extracted samples of tissue from bin Laden's body and placed them in vials for DNA analysis. One set of vials would go with bin Laden's body on the backup Chinook that had just arrived at the compound, and another set would go on the working Black Hawk for the flight back to Afghanistan.

The Chinook picked up the dozen men from the disabled bird, and all the material seized from the compound—about one hundred thumb drives, DVDs, and computer disks, plus computer hard drives, five computers, and a number of cell phones. Bin Laden's body was also loaded onto the Chinook. The decision had already been made that his wives and children would be left behind.

In Washington, the officials watching the video feed from the stealth drone could see the two distinctive large rotors of a Chinook helicopter coming into the frame. That was the Chinook carrying the QRF arriving at the compound. The officials could also now see the SEAL teams on the ground gathering outside the wall of the compound waiting to board the chopper for the flight back to base. The video feed then showed a massive fireball as the downed helicopter was blown up. It was "like a Jerry Bruckheimer movie," says one official, who watched in awe. Then the Chinook took off from the Abbottabad compound and flew out of the drone's field of vision. At the CIA command center there were high fives all around and fist bumping.

Obama said later that the time the SEALs spent at the compound "was the longest forty minutes of my life, with the possible exception of when [my daughter] Sasha got meningitis when she was three months old, and I was waiting for the doctor to tell me that she was all right."

On the way out of Abbottabad, the Chinook and the Black Hawk separated, making them harder to detect as they headed toward Afghanistan. Both flew more direct routes than they had on the way into Pakistan, since speed rather than stealth was now of the essence, and the Black Hawk still needed to take on fuel at the refueling point inside Pakistan. Obama told his national security team, "Inform me as soon as our helicopters are out of Pakistani airspace."

At about 2:00 a.m. local time, 6:30 p.m. back in Washington, the Chinook landed back at the base in Jalalabad; the entire operation had taken a little over three hours. The CIA station chief in Afghanistan, a leading bin Laden analyst, and Admiral McRaven all quickly inspected bin Laden's corpse. They stretched the body out to its full length but didn't have a tape measure to confirm that the corpse measured six feet four, the height of the al-Qaeda leader, so a SEAL of roughly the same height lay down next to the body. The height was a match.

When McRaven spoke to Obama, he jokingly apologized for the downed stealth helicopter, saying, "Well, sir, I guess I owe you sixty million dollars."

"Let me get this straight, Bill. I just left a sixty-million-dollar helicopter in Pakistan and you don't have a buck ninety-nine for a tape measure?" Obama shot back.

Obama remembers, "It wasn't really until Bill McRaven personally saw the body that we confirmed that it was bin Laden." Shortly after this confirmation, the CIA's director for science and technology called into the Situation Room, reaching CIA chief of staff Jeremy Bash. "I have the results of the eight-point facial analysis on bin Laden," he said. The CIA official walked Bash through the basis of his analysts' confidence that the photo was a good match for bin Laden: "The length of his nose, the distance between his upper eyelid and his lower eyebrow, the shape of the ear, cartilage—they all match." Bash scribbled notes furiously and handed them to Panetta. Panetta began reading them out to Obama, saying, "We've gotten the facial analysis, and it matches. We believe it's bin Laden with ninety-five percent confidence." Cheers went up in the CIA conference room, and champagne bottles were soon discreetly uncorked in a number of Agency offices.

Should the president go out and announce bin Laden's death publicly that night? After all, there was still a 5 percent chance that it wasn't bin Laden. Obama's initial reaction was, "That's not good enough for me. I'm not going out to the American public with one chance in twenty of being wrong." Some of Obama's top cabinet officials urged that a public statement be delayed until the DNA test-ing was completed, in a day or so. Others said, "Mr. President, this isn't going to hold. It's going to leak. You have to make a statement." Obama said, "No, no, there's no news until I say so. People can leak all they want. But it's not news until I say something."

A photo of the dead al-Qaeda leader was then passed around the Situation Room, and Obama looked it over carefully. Leiter and Brennan looked at each other and said, "It's bin Laden." General Clapper remembers, "The pictures were kind of gruesome, but it was him. I was sure it was him." A White House official recalls, "There was a hole right around one of his eyes and it took off a chunk of his head, but it looked like Osama bin Laden, except for the fact that the beard was shorter and darker. It seemed like the beard had been dyed black and was a little shorter than the long gray beard in all the famous pictures of him walking around." Leiter remembers thinking, "I don't need facial recognition. It's bin Laden with a hole in his head—immediately recognizable. Holy shit! We just killed bin Laden!"

14 AFTERMATH

PAKISTANI SECURITY OFFICIALS began arriving at the Abbottabad compound within a few minutes after the SEALs had left. The officials could hear the sound of helicopters fading into the distance. They found a chaotic scene. First, they saw the burning helicopter, which they reported to the military. Perhaps, they thought, this was a Pakistani training mission gone badly wrong. Then, making their way through the compound gate, the officials came across a wounded woman. She was the courier's wife, Mariam. Speaking in Pashto, a local language, she said, "I am from Swat. My husband has been killed. If you go inside, there are many Arabs who have been killed."

Inside the main residence, the officials found several women screaming and shouting, and fourteen children, all handcuffed. They also found four dead bodies, two in the annex building and two on the ground floor of the main building. On the top floor bin Laden's youngest wife, Amal, lay unconscious on the bed, wearing an *abaya* (a loose black robe) as if she had been planning to go out. Shattered glass was everywhere. One of the older women told the officials in English, "They have killed and taken away Abu Hamza [the father of Hamza]." One of the officials asked, "Well, who is Abu Hamza?" She replied, "Osama bin Laden. They've killed the father of my son."

Bin Laden's twelve-year-old daughter, Safia, also spoke, saying, "I am Saudi. Osama bin Laden is my father." The Pakistanis took bin Laden's three wives and his children into custody and placed them under house arrest while they were debriefed by Pakistani military intelligence investigators.

One of the first journalists to arrive at the compound was Ihsan Khan, the local correspondent for the Voice of America's Pashto service. Khan, a dogged reporter in a part of the world where that can get you in trouble, had been dozing at home when he was awakened by a quite unusual sound: a helicopter flying over the city at about 12:45 a.m. This was the backup Chinook flying in to replace the downed Black Hawk. The distinctive sound of a helicopter flying overhead at night was something Khan hadn't heard once during the seven years he had lived in the city, even during the relief efforts in the region following the devastating 2005 earthquake that killed some seventy-five thousand people.

Khan called some buddies to see what was going on. They didn't know. Then, about twenty minutes later, at 1:05 a.m., Khan heard a huge explosion. This was the sound of the downed chopper being blown up. Khan leapt out of bed and dialed the local police. The line was busy. He made further calls and was told that a helicopter had just crashed. He rushed outside his house and saw a large fireball that looked to be about a mile away.

Whatever was going on was clearly news. Nothing ever happened in Abbottabad! It was one of the most peaceful cities in Pakistan. Khan dashed off an e-mail to his editor at VOA in Washington:

"A helicopter crashed down in sensitive area Kakul of Abbottabad. Before the incident heavy firing and blasts were heard by the locals. Officials have confirmed the heli crash but casualties and reasons haven't been disclosed. I am gathering further details and will be ready for live report. Please call me before the morning bulletin, if possible."

He then rushed to the location of the fireball, in the Bilal Town neighborhood. When he reached the compound, he found that the police had already cordoned it off. Locals told him that the electricity in the neighborhood had been switched off, and that this had not been a regularly scheduled "load shedding." Neighbors also told Khan that just before one of the helicopters had landed at the compound—very likely the backup Chinook—someone on the ground had wielded a colored laser light, flashing it near the compound to guide the helicopter in to land.

Back at the White House, Obama's team realized that, because of the helicopter crash, the bin Laden operation would not remain secret for long. The officials monitoring the feed from the stealth drone could already see people on the rooftops of buildings in Abbottabad talking on cell phones. And the NSA was already—within an hour of the raid—picking up conversations by local officials in Abbottabad about what had just happened at the mysterious "Arab house." Ben Rhodes was beginning to receive reports that Pakistani media were at the compound filming the aftermath of the raid and interviewing neighbors. Some Pakistani journalists were already speculating that the helicopter that went down was from a "foreign power," and soon the daytime news cycle in Pakistan would begin and Pakistan's raucous and conspiracy-minded media would have a field day with the story. Rhodes says, "Some of us were eager for the president to go out that night and speak to the world, because we were concerned about the story kind of beginning to dribble out sideways."

The debate that had percolated for months about how best to handle the Pakistanis bubbled up again in the Situation Room. Who should call the Pakistani leadership? And what should that person say? Pakistan is nominally controlled by its civilian government, but the military in fact controls all aspects of its national security policy. It would send the wrong signal for Obama to make the call to the most powerful man in Pakistan, chief of army staff General Ashfaq Parvez Kayani. Should Hillary Clinton call him, or should it be Admiral Mullen, who had put in more face time with Kayani than anyone in the White House? Mullen was pushing for a quick decision, saying, "We gotta call!"

Kayani and Mullen had developed a real friendship over the more than two dozen visits to Pakistan that Mullen had made during the past four years to try to shore up the ever-fragile Pakistani-American alliance. Kayani, an analytical thinker not given to bluster, had studied at the U.S. Army Command and General Staff College in Ft. Leavenworth, Kansas, and while he was certainly a proud Pakistani nationalist, he was not reflexively anti-American. Indeed, he had led the effort on the Pakistani military side to cement a "strategic partnership" with the United States over the previous couple of years.

Mullen knew it was important to try to reach Kayani before his generals spoke with him, because it would give Kayani the opportunity to take some ownership of what had happened, rather than leaving him to say that he had had no idea what was going on. The Pakistanis might also think that the events in Abbottabad were part of an attack by their traditional enemy India, and the Obama administration had to make sure that they understood the truth of the matter as soon as possible to avoid any conflict between the two nuclear-armed states.

A dog similar to Cairo, the Belgian Malinois brought by the SEALs on the bin Laden raid, jumps out of an aircraft with his Special Forces partner during a training drill. TECH. SGT. MANUEL J. MARTINEZ, U.S. AIR FORCE/DOD

Prospective Navy SEALs endure grueling training drills such as this one, in which recruits are shackled hand and foot in a deep pool. RICHARD SCHOENBERG

NAME: USAMA BIN LADIN
ALIASES: SHAYKH
SIGNIFICANCE:
POSSIBLE DESCRIPTION

- NATIONALITY: ARAB/SAUDI
- AGE: 54
- HT: 6'4" – 6'6"
- WT: ~160 LBS
- EYES: BROWN
- HAIR: BROWN
- CLOTHING: 3RD MALE OBSERVED ON CMPD ALWAYS WEARS LIGHT COLORED
  SHAWAL KAMEEZ WITH A DARK VEST. OCCASIONALLY
  WEARS LIGHT COLORED PRAYER CAP.
FAMILY MEMBERS: CMPD AC1, COURTYARD A, 2ND AND 3RD FLOOR
- 1ST WIFE: AMAL AL FATTAH AL SADAH (28 YRS OLD)
- DAUGHTER: SAFIYAH (9YRS OLD)
* 2 UNIDENTIFIED CHILDREN BORN SINCE 2011 (UNK IF IN "A" COMPOUND

- 2ND WIFE: SIHAM ABDULLAH BIN HUSAYN AL SHARIF (54 YRS OLD)
- SON: KHALID (23 YRS OLD)
- DAUGHTERS: MIRIAM (20 YRS OLD), SUMAYA (16 YRS OLD)

- 3RD WIFE: KHAYRIYA HUSAYN TAHA SABIR aka UMM HAMZA (62 YRS OLD)
- SON: HAMZA (21 YRS OLD)
  - WIFE: MARYAM
  - SON: USAMA (4 YRS OLD)
  - DAUGHTER: KHAYRIYA (1 YR OLD)
* 3RD WIFE KHAYRIYA AND SON RELEASED FROM IRANIAN CUSTODY IN JUL
2010

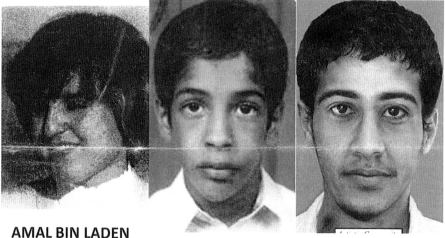

AMAL BIN LADEN
WIFE

KHALID
SON

Card identifying bin Laden family members carried by the U.S. Navy SEALs who raided the compound in Abbottabad on May 1, 2011. COURTESY OF CHRISTINA LAMB

NAME: IBRAHIM SAID AHMAD ABD AL HAMID
ALIASES: ARSHAD, ASIF KHAN, TARIQ, HAJI NADEEM, SARDAR ASHAD
(OWNER OF AC1)
SIGNIFICANCE: COURIER AND ASSESSED
                 AS ONE OF 3 INDIVIDUALS
                 RESPONSIBLE FOR HVT #1s CARE
POSSIBLE DESCRIPTION

NO PHOTO

- NATIONALITY: ARAB/KUWAITI
- AGE: 32
- HT: 5'9" – 5'11"
- WT: UNK
- EYES: UNK
- HAIR: UNK
- SKIN: UNK
- CLOTHING: TYPICALLY A WHITE SHAWAL KAMEEZ
- OTHER: MOVED FROM MARDAN CITY TO TARGET CMPD IN 2006 WITH
             BROTHER ABRAR
FAMILY MEMBERS: CMPD AC1, COURTYARD C
  - WIFE: MARYAM (31 YRS OLD)
  - SONS: KHALID (5-7 YRS OLD), AHMAD (1-4 YRS OLD), HABIB (18 MONTHS)
  - DAUGHTER: RAHMA (8 YRS OLD)
* WIFE AND KIDS RETURNED TO C CMPD ON 28 APR 2011
  - BROTHER: ABRAR
  - FATHER: AHMAD SAID (DECEASED)
  - MOTHER: HAMIDA AHMAD SAID (46 YRS OLD)

NAME: ABRAR AHMAD SAID ABD AL HAMID
ALIASES: ARSHAD, ASIF KHAN,
SARDAR ASHAD (OWNER OF AC1)
SIGNIFICANCE: FACILITATOR FOR HVT #1
POSSIBLE DESCRIPTION

- NATIONALITY: ARAB/KUWAITI
- AGE: 33
- HT: UNK
- WT: UNK
- EYES: UNK
- HAIR: DARK
- SKIN: UNK
- CLOTHING: WEARS GLASSES
- OTHER: MOVED FROM MARDAN CITY TO TARGET CMPD IN 2006 WITH
             BROTHER ABRAR
FAMILY MEMBERS: CMPD AC1, COURTYARD A, FIRST FLOOR
  - WIFE: BUSHRA (~30 YRS OLD)
  - SONS: IBRAHIM (4 MONTHS), ABD AL RAHMAN (1-4 YRS OLD), MUHAMMAD
(6-7 YRS OLD, ATTENDS MADRASSA AWAY FROM FAMILY)
  - DAUGHTER: KHADIJA (1-4 YRS OLD)
  - BROTHER: ABU AHMAD
  - FATHER: AHMAD SAID (DECEASED)
  - MOTHER: HAMIDA AHMAD SAID (46 YRS OLD)

The other side of the card featured detailed information about "the Kuwaiti," his
brother, and their families. COURTESY OF CHRISTINA LAMB

The quiet, hilly city of Abbottabad, where Osama bin Laden resided for more than five years. AP PHOTO/ANJUM NAVEED

The high, opaque windows of the top floor, where bin Laden and his youngest wife lived, can be seen in this image of the family's three-story house.
AP PHOTO/AQEEL AHMED

The kitchen garden in which bin Laden, dubbed "the pacer" by CIA analysts, often took walks during the day.
PAKISTAN STRINGER/REUTERS

02-May-11 05:44

Bin Laden wrapped in a blanket and sitting on the floor of a room in his Abbottabad compound watching a video of himself on TV.
DEPARTMENT OF DEFENSE

The Pakistani television network Geo News shows the burning wreckage of the crashed U.S. stealth helicopter on the night bin Laden was killed.
AP PHOTO/GEO TV

امریکی صدر اوباما نے اسامہ بن لادن کی ہلاکت کی تصدیق کردی

SIVE   EXCLUSIVE   GEO EXCLU

حسن عسکری   سینیر تجزیہ کار

اسامہ ابٹ آباد میں فوجی آپریشن میں مارا گیا، اوباما

OBAMA SAYS JUSTICE HAS BEEN DONE   09 02

The tail portion of the crashed U.S. stealth helicopter rests against an outer wall of the bin Laden compound on the morning after the raid.
PAKISTAN STRINGER/
REUTERS

The 97,000-ton aircraft carrier USS *Carl Vinson*, from which bin Laden's corpse was dropped into the Arabian Sea.
UNITED STATES NAVY

General Ashfaq Parvez Kayani, the chief of staff of the Pakistan army and the most powerful man in the nation. Having helped to forge a "strategic partnership" with the U.S., he felt betrayed that no one in the U.S. government had warned him of the raid on the Abbottabad compound.
AAMIR QURESHI/AFP/GETTY IMAGES

The three children at left, Fatima, age five; Abdullah, age twelve; and Hamza, age seven, are grandchildren of bin Laden. The three on the right, Hussain, age three; Zainab, age five; and Ibraheem, age eight, are the youngest of bin Laden's twenty-four children. Hussain and Zainab were born while bin Laden was living in Abbottabad.
THE SUNDAY TIMES/NI SYNDICATION

A crowd built in front of the White House to cheer the news that bin Laden was dead. BILL CLARK/ROLL CALL

Activists of Jamaat-e-Islami Pakistan (JI) chanted slogans as they marched during an anti-U.S. protest on May 6, 2011, in Peshawar, condemning the operation that killed bin Laden. Protests like this one were limited to supporters of hardline religious groups and were not well attended.
A MAJEED/AFP/GETTY IMAGES

Bin Laden's successor as the head of al-Qaeda, Dr. Ayman al-Zawahiri, in a video released on November 16, 2011, in which he praises bin Laden for his kindness, generosity, and loyalty.

He used to remember the 19 (people) who attacked the idiot of the age, America.

The stars on the Memorial Wall at CIA headquarters represent Agency employees who were killed in the line of duty, including two dozen who died in the decade after 9/11. CIA

IN HONOR OF THOSE MEMBERS
OF THE CENTRAL INTELLIGENCE AGENCY
WHO GAVE THEIR LIVES IN THE SERVICE OF THEIR COUNTRY

Protesters wave Egyptian flags at Cairo's Tahrir Square on March 11, 2011. Bin Laden's men and his ideas were notably absent from the revolutions that roiled the Middle East in 2011. MAHMUD HAMS/AFP/ GETTY IMAGES

AFTERMATH

Lieutenant General Ahmad Shuja Pasha, the head of Pakistan's powerful military intelligence service, was working in his study late at night when someone called to say, "Sorry to hear about the helicopter crash." Pasha knew that Pakistani military helicopters didn't have night vision capabilities, so it would be strange if it were a Pakistani chopper. "Has one of our helicopters crashed?" he asked his men in a series of phone calls. "It was not ours," he was told.

General Kayani took a call from his director of military operations at about 1:00 a.m. The news was alarming: a helicopter had just crashed near a residential compound in Abbottabad in a region of the country that is thick with military installations and nuclear weapons facilities. Assuming that India might be trying to make a preemptive strike against Pakistan's nuclear facilities, General Kayani phoned the head of the air force and ordered him to scramble jets to intercept anyone who might be flying that night. Two American-made F-16s were scrambled from their base five hundred miles to the southwest of Abbottabad. Pakistan is quite large—twice the size of California—and the jets couldn't find the intruders.

Once the two helicopters carrying the SEALs and bin Laden's body had safely exited Pakistani airspace, the first person Obama called was his predecessor as president. George W. Bush was eating dinner at a restaurant in Dallas with his wife, Laura, when the Secret Service informed him that he would have a call coming in from the White House in twenty minutes. Bush went home quickly to take the call. When Obama told him the news, Bush congratulated him and the SEALs. Bush says, "I didn't feel any great sense of happiness or jubilation. I felt a sense of closure, and I felt a sense of gratitude that justice had been done." Obama also called Bill Clinton, the first American president to have tried to kill bin Laden, with the cruise missile strikes on Afghanistan in 1998 that had followed the attacks on the U.S. embassies in Africa. And he phoned close ally David Cameron, the British prime minister, whose country had also suffered at the hands of al-Qaeda, so that Cameron wouldn't be surprised by the news the following morning.

Cameron Munter, the U.S. ambassador to Pakistan, had known of the impending raid in advance but had discussed it with no one at his embassy. Now, in the wee hours of the morning, as he followed the progress of the raid, he stepped outside the embassy chancery in Islamabad and received an unexpected call on his cell phone. It was a senior Pakistani official, who said, "We understand there has been a helicopter crash in Abbottabad. Do you know anything about this?" Munter told the man he would get back to him. He did not do so, believing the first set of calls to the Pakistani leadership was best handled by President Obama and Admiral Mullen. Based on the bewildered reactions of Pakistani officials to the events of that night, it was obvious to Munter and the officials monitoring the situation in the White House that the Pakistanis had not had a clue about bin Laden's presence in Abbottabad.

Obama called Pakistan's president, Asif Ali Zardari, and told him the news. Zardari became emotional. His wife, Benazir Bhutto, the former Pakistani prime minister, had been assassinated by the Taliban four years earlier. Zardari told Obama, "I'm happy because these are the same types of people who killed my wife, and her people are my family, so I share in this."

Admiral Mullen then got through to General Kayani, on a secure line. "Congratulations," Kayani immediately said upon hearing the news about bin Laden. The conversation lasted a tense twenty minutes. Mullen told Kayani the outlines of what had happened in Abbottabad and said that the president was mulling over making a statement about the raid. Kayani said that he was concerned about the violation of Pakistani sovereignty and urged that Obama go out as soon as possible and explain what had happened. Soon it would be daylight in Pakistan, and there was a mysterious downed helicopter in the middle of Abbottabad that clearly didn't belong to Pakistan; the local press would be all over the story. Kayani said, "Our people need to understand what happened here. We're not going to be able to manage the Pakistani media without you confirming this. You can explain it to them. They need to understand that this was bin Laden and not just some ordinary U.S. operation."

Kayani, in effect, demanded that Obama publicly explain what had happened as soon as it was feasible to do so. Mullen walked back into the Situation Room and said, "Kayani has asked for us to go public," which swayed Obama to go forward. At about 8:15 p.m. the White House informed the Washington press corps that the president would be making an important announcement in two hours. Earlier in the day, the White House press office had called a "lid," meaning that the president was not going to do or say anything that would make news for the rest of the day and the White House press corps could go home, but now those same correspondents were told by administration officials, "Just get in!" Biden and Clinton started working the phones from little booths in the Situation Room complex, calling key members of Congress and important allies to give them a heads-up before the president made his public announcement about bin Laden's death. Gates, who had not supported the raid, was the first to leave the White House, at about 8:30 p.m. The rest of Obama's national security team settled in for what would be a long night.

Network journalists and pundits took to the airwaves speculating about what a speech by the president late on a Sunday night could possibly concern. Initially, they wondered whether the Libyan dictator Moammar Gadhafi might have been killed in the NATO operation Obama had set in motion two months earlier. A day earlier, members of Gadhafi's family had been killed in a NATO air strike in Libya. Gradually the speculation became more informed as some reporters learned that the announcement had something to do with bin Laden.

Rhodes had sat down before the raid to write the "We got bin Laden" speech for the president, but he was only a few lines in before he thought, "I can't do this. It'd jinx it; it doesn't feel right." Instead, he had building blocks of a potential speech ready to go. The most ticklish aspect of the speech was how to describe Pakistan's involvement. Rhodes explains, "We decided not to sugarcoat it and say that they had played a role, but it was factually true that some of the intelligence collection that led us to the compound and was associated with the compound was based on Pakistani cooperation. It was unwitting; they didn't know they were helping to find bin Laden, but they did share things with us that filled out our intelligence picture, so we felt confident saying Pakistani cooperation helped lead to this."

Obama told Rhodes that, for the speech, he wanted to go back to the events of 9/11, to emphasize that Pakistan had helped in the fight against al-Qaeda, to remind people of the large sacrifice that a decade of war had cost the American people in Iraq and Afghanistan, and to end with the idea that America could still do extraordinary things. Obama and Rhodes were both furiously editing the draft of the speech right up to the moment the president walked out to the East Room of the White House to deliver it.

As the Obama national security team left the Situation Room and the president was making some final edits to his remarks, TV screens in the White House were tuned to the regularly scheduled programming that the bin Laden announcement would soon interrupt. Tony Blinken noticed that on NBC, the show that was going to be interrupted was Donald Trump's *Celebrity Apprentice.* "You can't write this stuff," says Blinken.

Just before the president made his speech, Mike Vickers, who had worked marathon hours during the planning of the bin Laden operation, called his wife. "Turn on the TV. This is why I've been gone all weekend and what I've been so preoccupied with for months."

Director of National Intelligence James Clapper was one of the officials who walked from the Situation Room to the East Room with Obama in the minutes before he addressed the nation. On the walk over, Clapper heard the sounds of the cheering crowds that had started to gather in Lafayette Park, in front of the White House, brought there by the news that bin Laden might have been killed. "I knew this meant a lot to the country but I didn't know how powerful the reaction would be. I remember walking out and hearing, 'USA! USA! USA!' from Lafayette Park. And it was at that moment it hit me. This was huge," says Clapper.

At 11:35 p.m., Obama walked down the high-ceilinged formal corridor to the East Room and up to a lectern. Dressed in a dark suit and red tie, the president made brief and sober remarks: "Good evening. Tonight, I can report to the American people and to the world that the United States has conducted an operation that killed Osama bin Laden, the leader of al-Qaeda, and a terrorist who's responsible for the murder of thousands of innocent men, women, and children." Obama was careful to offer some praise to the Pakistanis: "It's important to note that our counterterrorism cooperation with Pakistan helped lead us to bin Laden and the compound where he was hiding. Indeed, bin Laden had declared war against Pakistan as well, and ordered attacks against the Pakistani people." Despite the late hour on a Sunday night, the speech drew more viewers than any other in Obama's presidency; some fifty-five million Americans tuned in to hear that bin Laden had been killed.

After the president's speech, as Panetta left the White House in his heavily armored vehicle with tinted windows, some in the crowds that had gathered in Lafayette Park were chanting, "CIA! CIA! CIA!" Mullen was struck by "the young people that were out there. The twenty-one-year-olds who had been ten or eleven when 9/11 occurred, and they were out there cheering." Walking out of the White House, Flournoy recalls hearing a familiar song and thinking, "What is that? And I realized that it was a crowd of American citizens who had spontaneously gathered in Lafayette Park, singing the national anthem, and at that point I welled up and I was actually crying walking out to my car. I had not expected that, and it was an overwhelming moment."

Half a world away, bin Laden's corpse was being prepared for burial. Considerable thought had gone into the disposal of the body of al-Qaeda's leader. Obama officials wanted to ensure that there would be no grave that could become a shrine. (Similarly, the Soviets went to great lengths to ensure that after Hitler committed suicide at the end of World War II, the location of his remains was kept a closely guarded secret.) Obama's national security team consulted with Islamic experts, who explained that the most important obligations for a proper Muslim burial were wrapping the washed body in a white cloth, having specific prayers recited over it by a Muslim man, and performing the burial within twenty-four hours. A sea burial might be permissible in certain circumstances, for instance, if a person died at sea and there was no way to get to land immediately.

Obama's counterterrorism advisors had had something of a dress rehearsal for the burial of bin Laden two years earlier with Saleh Ali Saleh Nabhan, a leader of al-Qaeda in Africa, who was killed by U.S. Navy SEALS in a helicopter raid on September 14, 2009, as he was driving south of the Somali capital, Mogadishu. The SEALS landed briefly to pick up Nabhan's body, and after they had confirmed his identity through DNA samples, he was buried at sea.

John Brennan, the former CIA station chief in Saudi Arabia, called Prince Mohammed bin Nayef, the powerful Saudi deputy minister of interior, telling him that the CIA had pretty much confirmed that U.S. forces had killed bin Laden in Pakistan. Brennan asked whether the Saudis wanted bin Laden's body returned to his homeland. If not, he said, the plan was to bury him at sea. Nayef offered his congratulations—al-Qaeda had tried to assassinate him more than once—and said he would inform King Abdullah. Brennan explained that if the king had any different ideas they'd need to know in a few minutes. Nayef told Brennan to go ahead with his plan.

A V-22 Osprey tilt-rotor aircraft transported bin Laden's body from Bagram Air Base in central Afghanistan to the USS *Carl Vinson*, which was cruising off the coast of Pakistan. Once the corpse was on board, procedures for a Muslim burial were followed. In a ceremony that took a little under an hour, bin Laden's body was washed and wrapped in a white winding sheet. The body was then placed in a bag with weights, and an officer read some religious remarks, which were translated into Arabic. Bin Laden's corpse was then deposited on a flat board, which was tipped up so that the body dropped into the sea. On May 2, at 11:00 a.m.—at 2:00 a.m. back in Washington—bin Laden was consigned to a watery unmarked grave in the vast Arabian Sea, a burial witnessed by only a small group on the flight deck of the great American warship. Al-Qaeda's leader was fifty-four.

Leading Islamic scholars quickly protested, among them Sheikh Ahmed el-Tayeb, the grand imam of Cairo's al-Azhar mosque, the Harvard of Sunni Islamic learning, who said, "Bin Laden's burial at sea runs contrary to the principles of Islamic laws, religious values, and humanitarian customs." Iraqi religious scholar Abdul-Sattar al-Janabi also opined, "It is almost a crime to throw the body of a Muslim man into the sea. The body of bin Laden should have been handed over to his family to look for a country or land to bury him."

Omar bin Laden, one of bin Laden's older sons, released a written statement on behalf of his siblings decrying his father's "sudden and unwitnessed burial at sea [which] has deprived the family of performing religious rights [sic] of a Muslim man."

One of the two DNA samples taken from bin Laden was analyzed at Bagram Air Base, and the information derived from that sample was sent electronically to Washington, while another sample was hand-carried to Washington for additional analysis. Using DNA material obtained from relatives of bin Laden, intelligence officials now determined with complete certainty that the corpse that had sunk down into the deep was indeed that of al-Qaeda's leader.

John Brennan, Obama's main counterterrorism advisor, gave a press conference the same day that bin Laden's body was buried at sea, in which he made a number of assertions about what had happened at the Abbottabad compound: that bin Laden had used a woman as a human shield, that he had reached for his weapons, and that he had died in a firefight with the SEALs. The White House quickly retracted all those statements, attributing them to the confusion and fog of a battle that had been fought at night on the other side of the world less than twenty-four hours earlier.

The administration also fumbled its initial announcement about the release of photos of the dead bin Laden. The day after al-Qaeda's leader was killed, Panetta told NBC News that soon images proving the death of bin Laden "would be presented to the public." But quickly the White House clarified that this wasn't the case. Obama, Gates, and Clinton all agreed that the gruesome pictures of bin Laden would be used by al-Qaeda to incite harm against Americans, while conspiracy theorists—people who might believe that somehow, somewhere, bin Laden was still alive, and that the official story was all a ruse—wouldn't be persuaded by the photographic proof anyway. It was "important for us to make sure that very graphic photos of somebody who was shot in the head are not floating around as an incitement to additional violence, as a propaganda tool," explained Obama. For those who doubted that al-Qaeda's leader was dead, Obama had a simple message: "The fact of the matter is, you will not see bin Laden walking on this earth again."

During the president's daily intelligence briefing a couple of days after the raid, there was discussion of the fact that the SEALs seemed to have planned for everything, except for bringing a tape measure to measure bin Laden's dead body. "You ought to give McRaven a gold-plated tape measure," suggested Tony Blinken. Obama said, "That's a great idea." Four days after the raid, when McRaven walked into the Oval Office to meet with the president, Obama said, "Hey, I've got something for you," and presented him with a tape measure mounted on a plaque.

The mass of materials picked up by the SEALs at the bin Laden compound was quickly transported back to Washington, where a task force of 125 people worked 24/7 quickly to triage anything related to al-Qaeda attack planning that could be found. Every available Arabic speaker in the intelligence community was "surged" to work on what became known as the "treasure trove" and to start churning out reports to law enforcement and the intelligence community about any threat information that needed to be flagged. Reviewing the trove, what struck James Clapper, the director of national intelligence, were the effects of years of self-imposed isolation on bin Laden. Clapper found bin Laden's musings about mass casualty attacks on the American transportation system or oil tankers in the Indian Ocean to be a mix of the serious and the nutty. "Some of it was operational, a lot of it was aspirational, and I thought quite a bit of it was delusional. It kind of reminded me of Hitler in the later stages of World War II; he's moving all these army groups around that didn't exist."

On May 3, Panetta told *Time* magazine what White House officials had discussed in their private deliberations: "It was decided that any effort to work with the Pakistanis could jeopardize the mission. They might alert the targets." This statement added considerable salt to open wounds in Pakistan. The first reaction of the Pakistani military to the bin Laden operation had been shock. Al-Qaeda and its allies in Pakistan had repeatedly targeted the Pakistani army, so that shock was also leavened with a certain amount of satisfaction at the senior levels of the military. Later on the day that bin Laden was killed, Generals Kayani and Pasha met with Marc Grossman, Obama's special representative to Afghanistan and Pakistan, and with the U.S. ambassador to Pakistan, Cameron Munter. Both Pakistani generals offered their congratulations to the American diplomats on the death of bin Laden.

But the good feelings did not last. The shock of bin Laden's death soon gave way to anger as the Pakistanis realized that the promised strategic partnership with the United States had brought, first, a dramatically increased number of drone strikes in Pakistan's tribal region, which were enormously unpopular, and second, the Raymond Davis affair, during which the military had expended considerable political capital to get Davis released from jail after he killed the two Pakistanis in Lahore. The unilateral American raid to kill bin Laden in the heartland of Pakistan now capped these developments. As the full implications of the bin Laden operation sank in, General Kayani asked himself, "How could my good friend Admiral Mullen not have told me about the raid?" Kayani and Mullen have rarely spoken since.

AFTERMATH

The raid was horribly embarrassing for the Pakistani military, which likes to regard itself—with some justification—as the most capable institution in Pakistan. If the Navy SEALs could waltz into the heart of Pakistan without the Pakistani military noticing or doing anything about it, what did this say about the army's ability to protect its crown jewels, its nuclear weapons, from seizure by Indian forces, or even the American military?

Popular anger toward the army was high in Pakistan, in particular toward General Kayani, who had been trying to build bridges to the Americans. Criticism of the army from all quarters, generally unthinkable in Pakistan, was rampant in the days after the raid. Kayani's and Pasha's jobs seemed to hang in the balance, as they were losing support both inside the army and from Pakistanis in general. Kayani worried that the army's image could shatter, and he told his closest colleagues that this was the worst week of his life.

In the past, General Pasha, the Pakistani intelligence chief, had requested of his American counterpart, Panetta, that if the CIA didn't trust the Pakistani government or military with some matter of great import, to tell at least him or Kayani or President Zardari, so that the Pakistanis would be able to save face by truthfully saying they had been informed. A soft-spoken, mild-mannered man of five foot seven, with deep black circles around his eyes, reflecting many sleepless nights, Pasha had played a key role in getting the CIA contractor Raymond Davis released from prison, negotiating directly with the victims' families so that they would accept the "blood money" for Davis's release. After the bin Laden raid, Pasha felt that the relationship with the United States was broken beyond repair.

This sentiment was shared in the U.S. Congress, where there was widespread outrage that bin Laden had been hiding in Pakistan, a country that had received billions of dollars in U.S. aid since 9/11 (never mind that most of this "aid" was in fact compensation to the Pakistan military for mounting military operations the U.S. had demanded it undertake against the Taliban along the Afghanistan-Pakistan border). Representative Mike Rogers, the Michigan Republican who chaired the House Intelligence Committee, said publicly, "I believe that there are elements of both the [Pakistani] military and intelligence service who in some way, both prior and maybe even current, provided some level of assistance to Osama bin Laden." Rogers offered no proof for this assertion, and the U.S. intelligence community's assessment within weeks of the Abbottabad operation was that there was, in fact, no official Pakistani complicity in bin Laden's sojourn in Abbottabad and that nothing in the treasure trove recovered from his compound provided any proof that bin Laden had support from Pakistani officials. Still, Rogers's view that the Pakistanis had helped shelter al-Qaeda's leader was commonplace both in the halls of Congress and in the U.S. media.

As was expected, on May 6, just days after bin Laden's death, al-Qaeda officially confirmed the death of its leader in a message posted to jihadist Internet forums where the group's media arm had regularly posted its propaganda in the past. The message promised revenge for bin Laden's "martyrdom." Al-Qaeda asserted that bin Laden's blood was "more precious to us and to every Muslim than to be wasted in vain. . . . We call upon our Muslim people in Pakistan, on whose land Sheikh Osama was killed, to rise up and revolt . . . to cleanse their country from the filth of the Americans who spread corruption in it." Very few people, including Pakistanis, paid any attention to this call. Indeed, the protests in Pakistan that followed bin Laden's death were minor, numbering at most a few hundred people.

The same day that al-Qaeda confirmed bin Laden's death, Obama and members of his national security team traveled to Ft. Campbell,

Kentucky, home to the 160th Special Operations Air Regiment that had flown the choppers on the bin Laden mission. Over the course of half an hour, in a small classroom on the base, the president was briefed by the men who had carried out the operation.

First to speak was the helicopter pilot who had flown the Black Hawk that went down. "These types of things have happened before," he said. "You can never account for exactly what the environment's going to be."

"Did the weather play a role?" Obama asked.

"The weather can impact the flight plan, and the weather was a little warmer than anticipated," said the pilot.

The SEAL team ground commander used a model of the compound and a red laser pointer to explain what had gone right and what had gone wrong on the mission from start to finish. The biggest problem was not correctly matching the wall that surrounded the compound in the life-size mock-ups they had used for rehearsals. The solid walls of the actual compound had caused turbulent aerodynamics for the first Black Hawk when it hovered to drop the SEALs into the courtyard, and had necessitated the chopper's "hard landing."

The SEAL commander said, "We're alive today because of what the helicopter pilot did. An incredibly difficult thing to do, to deal with this machine and get everybody out safely." He went on to say, "This is the end result of a ten-year effort. We've been at this for a decade, and we've gotten better over the course of ten years at doing this. We've done it in Afghanistan, we've done it in Iraq." The SEAL commander then reeled off a list of forward operating bases in Afghanistan that had been named after SEAL team operators who had died in the past decade. Then he turned to the Abbottabad operation, describing everyone's role, including that of the interpreter, who yelled at neighbors in Pashto and Urdu to stay back:

"If it weren't for that guy, who knows what could've happened." The commander went on to say, "If you took one person out of the puzzle, we wouldn't have the competence to do the job we did; everybody's vital. It's not about the guy who pulled the trigger to kill bin Laden, it's about what we all did together."

The president didn't ask any of the SEALs who had taken the shot that had killed bin Laden, and no one volunteered the information. He simply said, "This small group of people in this room is the finest fighting force in the history of the world."

The president asked to see Cairo, the dog that had accompanied the SEALs on the raid. The SEAL team commander warned the commander in chief, "Well, sir, I strongly advise you to have a treat, because this is a tough dog, you know." Cairo was presented to Obama, although a presidential petting was discouraged and the dog was wearing a muzzle.

To patch up matters with the Pakistanis, Senator John Kerry, one of the few American politicians with any credibility in Pakistan because of his role in pushing for aid for civilian projects in the country, traveled to Islamabad in mid-May. During a several-hour conversation with Generals Kayani and Pasha, Kerry discussed all the areas of tension between the two countries: Pakistan's support for elements of the Taliban, CIA operations in Pakistan, and the raid in Abbottabad. Kayani and Pasha demanded a halt to the CIA drone program in Pakistan. Kayani also told Kerry of the deep sense of betrayal he had felt over the Abbottabad operation and the enormous risks he had taken in embracing the Americans. Kerry told them that an end to the drone program was not in the cards and that no president in his right mind would have outsourced the bin Laden operation to another country after the failure to capture al-Qaeda's leader at Tora Bora.

Kerry was able to negotiate the return of the tail of the downed ultrasecret stealth helicopter from the raid. He also arranged for the CIA to get access to the Abbottabad compound and to question bin Laden's wives. While Kerry was still in the air on his way home, the CIA launched another drone strike into Pakistan's tribal regions. This seemed to be the Agency's not-so-subtle way of reminding both the Pakistanis and Kerry that it still ran the show in Pakistan.

The Pakistanis used female interrogators to debrief bin Laden's ultrareligious wives, but they said very little about their lives on the run or in Abbottabad. The leader of the wives was the oldest, sixty-two-year-old Khairiah. Investigators described her as "very hard, very difficult." Despite the comfortable house they were placed in, the wives told their Pakistani jailors they just wanted to go home. And when CIA officials finally interviewed bin Laden's wives, all three women were quite hostile to the Americans. At this point in the tortured U.S.-Pakistani relationship, there were very few things that both sides agreed upon; one of them was just how difficult bin Laden's wives were to deal with. Almost a year after bin Laden was killed, the Pakistani government announced that his three widows had been charged with "illegal entry" into Pakistan, for which they could be jailed for up to five years.

President Obama visited CIA headquarters in northern Virginia on May 20 to thank the intelligence community for its work on the bin Laden mission. Obama met privately with about sixty CIA officers and analysts who had been integral to the hunt for al-Qaeda's leader, and then spoke to some one thousand employees who jammed the lobby of the Agency's headquarters. "The work you did and the quality of information you provided made the critical difference," he said. The president also noted wryly, "And we did something really remarkable in Washington—we kept it a secret." The audience erupted with laughter, applause, and cheers.

EPILOGUE **THE TWILIGHT OF AL-QAEDA**

JUST AS WE CANNOT understand why the French army risked marching to Moscow during the frigid Russian winter of 1812 without comprehending the ambitions of Napoleon, we cannot understand al-Qaeda or 9/11 without Osama bin Laden. It was bin Laden who conceived of al-Qaeda during the waning days of the Soviet occupation of Afghanistan, and he was its unquestioned leader from its inception in Peshawar in August 1988 until the day he was killed, more than two decades later. And it was bin Laden who came up with the strategy of attacking the United States in order to end its influence in the Muslim world—a strategy that ultimately fared about as well as the march on Moscow did for Napoleon. Instead of forcing the United States to pull out of the Middle East as bin Laden had predicted it would after the 9/11 attacks, the United States, together with its allies, largely destroyed al-Qaeda in Afghanistan and later invaded Iraq, while simultaneously building massive American military bases in Muslim countries such as Kuwait, Qatar, and Bahrain.

If bin Laden's strategy of attacking the United States was largely a failure, his ideas may have more lasting currency, at least among a small minority in the Muslim world. Like many of history's most effective leaders, bin Laden told a simple story about the world that his followers—from Jakarta to London—found easy to grasp. In his telling there was a conspiracy by the West and its puppet allies in the Muslim world to destroy true Islam, a conspiracy led by the United States. Bin Laden very effectively communicated to a global audience this master narrative of a war on Islam led by America that must be avenged. A Gallup Poll in ten Muslim countries conducted in 2005 and 2006 found that 7 percent of Muslims said the 9/11 attacks were "completely justified." To put it another way, out of the estimated 1.2 billion Muslims in the world, about 100 million Muslims wholeheartedly endorsed bin Laden's rationale for the 9/11 attacks and the need for Islamic revenge on the West.

One of bin Laden's most toxic legacies is that even militant Islamist groups that don't call themselves al-Qaeda have adopted this ideology. According to Spanish prosecutors, the Pakistani Taliban sent a team of would-be suicide bombers to Barcelona to attack the subway system there in January 2008. A year later, the Pakistani Taliban trained an American recruit, Faisal Shahzad, for an attack in New York. Shahzad traveled to Pakistan, where he received five days of bomb-making training in the tribal region of Waziristan. Armed with this training, Shahzad placed a bomb in an SUV and tried to detonate it in Times Square on May 1, 2010, around 6 p.m. Luckily, the bomb malfunctioned, and Shahzad was arrested two days later.

The Mumbai attacks of 2008 showed that bin Laden's ideas about attacking Western and Jewish targets had also spread to Pakistani militant groups such as Lashkar-e-Taiba (LeT), which had previously focused only on Indian targets. Over a three-day period in late November 2008, LeT carried out multiple attacks in

Mumbai, targeting five-star hotels housing Westerners and a Jewish-American community center and killing 170 people.

And al-Qaeda's regional affiliates will also try to continue bin Laden's bloody work. Al-Qaeda in the Arabian Peninsula (AQAP) was responsible for attempting to bring down Northwest Flight 253 over Detroit on Christmas Day 2009 with a bomb hidden in the underwear of Umar Farouk Abdulmutallab, a Nigerian recruit. A year later, AQAP hid bombs in toner cartridges on planes bound for Chicago. The bombs were discovered only at the last moment at East Midlands Airport in the United Kingdom and in Dubai.

In September 2009, the Somali Islamist insurgent group Al-Shabaab ("the youth" in Arabic) formally pledged allegiance to bin Laden following a two-year period in which it had recruited Somali-Americans and other U.S. Muslims to fight in the war in Somalia. After it announced its fealty to bin Laden, Shabaab was able to recruit larger numbers of foreign fighters; by one estimate up to twelve hundred were working with the group by 2010. A year later, Shabaab controlled much of southern Somalia.

In Nigeria, a country with a substantial Muslim population, a jihadist group known as Boko Haram attacked the United Nations building in the Nigerian capital, Abuja, killing some twenty people in the summer of 2011. Since then the group has mounted a systematic campaign against Christian targets.

In 2008, there was a sense that Al-Qaeda in Iraq (AQI) was on the verge of defeat. The American ambassador to Iraq, Ryan Crocker, said, "You are not going to hear me say that al-Qaeda is defeated, but they've never been closer to defeat than they are now." Certainly AQI had lost its ability to control large swaths of the country and a good chunk of the Sunni population as it had in 2006, but the group proved surprisingly resilient, continuing to pull off large-scale bombings in central Baghdad. And in 2012, AQI sent foot soldiers into Syria to fight against the regime of Bashar al-Assad, who is from a Shia sect despised as heretics by the Sunni ultrafundamentalists who make up al-Qaeda.

These groups, as well as "lone wolves" inspired by bin Laden, will continue to attempt to wreak havoc, but their efforts will not precipitate a "clash of civilizations" as bin Laden had hoped to do on 9/11. Indeed, governments in Muslim countries from Jordan to Indonesia have taken aggressive actions against al-Qaeda and its affiliates, and al-Qaeda is now peddling an ideology that has lost much of its purchase in the Muslim world. In the two most populous Muslim nations—Indonesia and Pakistan—favorable views of bin Laden and support for suicide bombings dropped by at least half between 2003 and 2010. The key reason for this decline was the deaths of Muslim civilians at the hands of jihadist terrorists. Al-Qaeda and its allies have consistently targeted the vast majority of fellow Muslims who don't precisely share their views. The trail of dead civilians from Baghdad to Jakarta and from Amman to Islamabad in the decade after 9/11 was largely the work of al-Qaeda and its allies. That al-Qaeda and its allies defined themselves as the defenders of true Islam yet left so many Muslim victims in their wake was not impressive to many in the Islamic world.

Despite the abject failure of al-Qaeda's strategy on 9/11, a number of prominent writers, academics, and politicians in the West claimed that the attacks on Washington and New York were the beginning of a war with a totalitarian ideology similar to the murderous ideologies the United States had done battle with in the twentieth century. Certainly "Binladenism" shared some commonalities with National Socialism and Stalinism: anti-Semitism and anti-liberalism, the embrace of charismatic leaders, the deft exploitation of modern propaganda methods, and the bogus promise of utopia here on Earth if its programs were implemented. But Binladenism never posed anything like the existential threat that communism or Nazism did. Still, the conviction that "Islamofascism" posed as great a threat to the West as the Nazis or Soviets had was an article of faith for some. The influential neoconservative Richard Perle warned that the West faced "victory or holocaust" in its struggle with the Islamofascists. And the former CIA director James Woolsey became a constant presence on television news programs after 9/11, invoking the specter of World War IV.

But this was all massively overwrought. The Nazis occupied and subjugated most of Europe and instigated a global conflict that killed tens of millions. And the United States spent about 40 percent of its GDP to fight the Nazis, fielding millions of soldiers. Communist regimes killed 100 million people in wars, prison camps, enforced famines, and pogroms.

The threat posed by al-Qaeda is orders of magnitude smaller. Despite bin Laden's hyperventilating rhetoric, there is no danger that his followers will end the American way of life. In almost any given year, Americans are far more likely to drown accidentally in a bathtub than to be killed by a terrorist. Yet, few of us harbor an irrational fear of a bathtub drowning. Al-Qaeda's amateur investigations into weapons of mass destruction do not compare to the very real possibility of nuclear conflagration the world faced during the Cold War, and there are relatively few adherents of Binladenism in the West today, while there were tens of millions of devotees of communism and fascism.

Despite the relative insignificance of the threat posed by al-Qaeda and its allies, the War on Terror was a bonanza for the American national security industrial complex. On 9/11, the annual budget for all the U.S. intelligence agencies was about $25 billion. A decade later it was $80 billion; and by then almost a million Americans held Top Secret clearances, and six out of ten of the richest

THE TWILIGHT OF AL-QAEDA

counties in the United States were in the Washington, D.C., area. If the War on Terror was, in the end, as much about about bringing bin Laden to justice as anything else, it is sobering to observe that American intelligence agencies consumed half a trillion dollars on their way to that goal.

SIX WEEKS AFTER the death of bin Laden, al-Qaeda announced his successor, the dour Egyptian surgeon Ayman al-Zawahiri. The long-time deputy to bin Laden had his work cut out for him; his predecessor had gifted him a bit of a lemon. By the time bin Laden was killed, al-Qaeda was an ideological "brand" long past its sell-by date and an organization in deep trouble.

In the "treasure trove" of some six thousand documents retrieved by the SEALs from the bin Laden compound, there is ample confirmation of how profound al-Qaeda's problems had become. In memos he never dreamed would end up in the hands of the CIA, bin Laden advised other militant jihadist groups not to adopt the al-Qaeda moniker. On August 7, 2010, he wrote to the leader of the brutal Al-Shabaab militia in Somalia, telling him that Al-Shabaab should not declare itself publicly to be part of al-Qaeda because to do so would only attract enemies, as al-Qaeda's Iraqi affiliate had done, and would make it harder to raise money from rich Arab donors.

Clearly, even bin Laden understood that the shine was long gone from the al-Qaeda brand. At the same time, he was troubled by the fact that the Obama administration had solved a branding problem of its own because it had "largely stopped using the phrase 'the war on terror' in the context of not wanting to provoke Muslims because they feel that saying 'the war on terror' would appear to most people to be a war on Islam."

The spectacular set of self-inflicted mistakes by al-Qaeda's affiliate in Iraq played heavily on the minds of bin Laden and his top advisors. Among themselves, they grumbled that al-Qaeda's campaign of attacks against Iraqi Christians had not been sanctioned by bin Laden. And bin Laden urged his followers in Yemen not to kill members of the local tribes, a tactic that al-Qaeda had frequently employed in western Iraq, which had provoked a tribal uprising against al-Qaeda that began in 2006 and dealt a large blow to the group's fortunes in Iraq.

In October 2010, bin Laden wrote a forty-eight-page memo to one of his deputies that surveyed the state of al-Qaeda's jihad. He began on an optimistic note, observing that for the Americans it had been "the worst year for them in Afghanistan since they invaded," a trend he predicted would only be amplified by the deepening U.S. budget crisis. But bin Laden also worried that al-Qaeda's longtime sanctuary in Waziristan, in Pakistan's tribal areas, was now too dangerous because of the campaign of American drone strikes there. "I am leaning toward getting most of our brothers out of the area."

In the meantime, bin Laden advised his followers not to move around the tribal regions except on overcast days, when America's satellites and drones would not have as good of coverage of the area, and he complained that "the Americans have great accumulated expertise of photography of the region due to the fact they have been doing it for so many years. They can even distinguish between houses that are frequented by male visitors at a higher rate than is normal."

Bin Laden urged his followers to depart the tribal regions for the remote Afghan provinces of Ghazni, Zabul, and, in particular, Kunar, where he himself had successfully hidden after the Battle of Tora Bora, pointing out that the high mountains and dense forests of Kunar provided especially good protection from prying American eyes. Bin Laden fretted about his twenty-year-old son, Hamza, who had moved to the tribal regions in Pakistan after being released from house arrest in Iran, writing, "Make sure to tell Hamza that I am of the opinion he should get out of Waziristan. . . . He should move only when the clouds are heavy." Hamza should decamp for the tiny, prosperous Persian Gulf kingdom of Qatar, bin Laden advised.

In his final days, bin Laden became doubly cautious, sometimes even paranoid in his thinking. He instructed that Hamza should throw out anything he had taken with him from Iran as it might contain a tracking chip and that he should avoid the company of someone named Abu Salman al-Baluchi because he had associates tied to the Pakistani intelligence services. Bin Laden also provided elaborate instructions about how Hamza might evade the surveillance of the American drones by meeting members of al-Qaeda inside a particular road tunnel near Peshawar.

Bin Laden also reminded his deputies "that all communication with others should be done through letters" rather than by phone or the Internet. As a result, he had to wait up to two or three months for responses to his queries—not an efficient way to run an organization. Bin Laden also advised his lieutenants that when they kidnapped someone they should take many precautions during the negotiating process and throw away any bags of ransom money because they might contain tracking devices.

In his isolated final years, bin Laden even became an inveterate micromanager, admonishing his group in Yemen that its members should always refuel and eat heartily before they embarked on road trips so that they wouldn't have to stop at gas stations and restaurants that might be monitored by government spies. And he advised al-Qaeda's North African wing to plant trees so they could later use them as cover for their operations. It's safe to assume that this arboreal advice was simply ignored.

Above all, bin Laden strategized about how to improve his public image, observing that "a huge part of the battle is in the media." He instructed his media team: "The tenth anniversary of the 9/11 attack is coming and due to the importance to this date, the time to start preparing is now. Please send me your suggestions on this." He suggested reaching out to the correspondents of both Al Jazeera English and Al Jazeera Arabic and wondered if he could get a hearing on an American TV network: "We should also look for an American channel that can be close to being unbiased such as CBS." Perhaps in response to this call for action, one of his media advisors—believed to be the American al-Qaeda recruit Adam Gadahn—suggested that bin Laden take advantage of the 9/11 anniversary in 2011 to record a high-definition videotape that could be given to all the major American news networks except Fox News, which Gadahn said "lacks neutrality." It does not appear that bin Laden ever made such a tape.

Until the end, bin Laden remained fixated on mounting another large-scale attack on the United States, prodding one deputy, "It would be nice if you could nominate one of the qualified brothers to be responsible for a large operation against the U.S. It would be nice if you would pick a number of the brothers not to exceed ten and send them to their countries individually without any of them knowing the others to study aviation." Bizarrely, he complained that Faisal Shahzad, the American citizen of Pakistani heritage who had tried to blow up an SUV in Times Square, had broken the oath of allegiance he had sworn to the United States, and he tut-tutted that "it is not permissible in Islam to betray trust and break a covenant." This seeming aversion to recruiting U.S. citizens to carry out such attacks narrowed the available options. In any case, Zawahiri pushed back, telling bin Laden it was much more realistic to attack American soldiers in Afghanistan than civilians in the United States.

The fact was, bin Laden and his men hadn't mounted a successful terrorist attack in the West since the July 7, 2005, transportation bombings in London. The terrorist network's plots to set off bombs in Manhattan in 2009 and to mount Mumbai-style attacks in Germany a year later all fizzled out. And al-Qaeda never mounted a successful attack in the United States after September 11, 2001.

This significant record of failure predated the momentous events of the Arab Spring—events in which al-Qaeda's leaders, foot soldiers, and ideas played no role. Meanwhile, U.S. drone strikes had decimated the bench of al-Qaeda's commanders since the summer of 2008, when President George W. Bush had authorized a ramped-up program of attacks in Pakistan's tribal regions. After Zawahiri's ascension to the top job in al-Qaeda, a CIA drone killed Atiyah Abdul Rahman, who, as we have seen, acted as bin Laden's chief of staff for many years. The group could not easily replace someone with Rahman's long experience, or the many other leaders of the group who had been picked off by drones during Bush's last year in office and during the presidency of Obama.

Zawahiri is unlikely to turn things around for al-Qaeda. Far from being the inspiring orator that bin Laden was, Zawahiri is more like the pedantic, long-winded uncle who insists on regaling the family at Thanksgiving dinner with accounts of his arcane disputes with obscure enemies. During 2011, Zawahiri's half-dozen or so public disquisitions about the events of the Arab Spring were greeted by a collective yawn in the Middle East. Not only was Zawahiri a black hole of charisma, he was an ineffective leader who was not well regarded or well liked even by the various jihadist groups from his native Egypt.

The death of bin Laden eliminates the founder of al-Qaeda, which has only known one leader since its founding in 1988, and it also eliminates the one man who provided broad, largely unquestioned strategic goals to the wider jihadist movement. A wild card is that one of bin Laden's dozen or so sons—endowed with the iconic family name—could eventually rise to take over the terrorist group.

JIHADIST TERRORISM WILL NOT, of course, disappear because of the death of bin Laden, but it is hard to imagine two more final endings to the "War on Terror" than the popular revolts against the authoritarian regimes in the Middle East and the death of bin Laden.

We do not, of course, know the final outcome of the Arab revolutions, but there is very little chance that al-Qaeda or other extremist groups will be able to grab the reins of power as the authoritarian regimes of the Middle East crumble. But while al-Qaeda and its allies cannot take power anywhere in the Muslim world, these groups do thrive on chaos and civil war. And the whole point of revolutions is that they are inherently unpredictable even to the people who are leading them, so anything could happen in the coming years in Libya, Yemen, and Syria, and much is unpredictable in Egypt.

In Egypt, Islamist groups did very well in parliamentary elections after the dictator Hosni Mubarak was deposed. The Muslim Brotherhood and a Salafist party received about three quarters of the vote. These groups do not advocate violence, and al-Qaeda has long been critical of the Brotherhood for its willingness to engage in elections that members of al-Qaeda consider to be "un-Islamic." But certainly the Salafists in Egypt want a society that looks much more like the Taliban in pre-9/11 Afghanistan than the one envisaged by the Facebook revolutionaries who first launched the revolt against Mubarak.

Despite Zawahiri's shortcomings and the serious institutional problems he has inherited, there are some opportunities for him to help resuscitate al-Qaeda. As the early great promise of the Arab Spring recedes, it is likely that Zawahiri will try to exploit the regional chaos to achieve his central goal: establishing a new haven for al-Qaeda. The one place where he might be able to pull this off is Yemen. Like bin Laden, many of al-Qaeda's members have roots in Yemen, and U.S. counterterrorism officials have identified the al-

Qaeda affiliate there as the most dangerous of the group's regional branches. And the civil war now engulfing Yemen has already provided an opportunity for jihadist militants to seize towns in the south of the country. Surely al-Qaeda will want to build on this feat in a country that is the nearest analogue today to pre-9/11 Afghanistan: a largely tribal, heavily armed, dirt-poor nation scarred by years of war.

OSAMA BIN LADEN long fancied himself something of a poet. His compositions tended to the morbid, and a poem written two years after 9/11 in which he contemplated the circumstances of his death was no exception. Bin Laden wrote, "Let my grave be an eagle's belly, its resting place in the sky's atmosphere amongst perched eagles." But there was no spectacular martyrdom in the mountains among the eagles. Instead bin Laden died surrounded by his wives in a squalid suburban compound awash in broken glass and scattered children's toys and medicine bottles—testament to the ferocity of the SEALs' assault on his final hiding place. And on February 25, 2012, Pakistani authorities sent mechanized diggers to the compound that tore the complex down, erasing bin Laden's six-year sojourn in Abbottabad over the course of a weekend.

If there is poetry in bin Laden's end, it is the poetry of justice, and it calls to mind President George W. Bush's words to Congress just nine days after 9/11, when he predicted that bin Laden and al-Qaeda would eventually be consigned to "history's unmarked grave of discarded lies," just as communism and Nazism had been before them. President Barack Obama has characterized al-Qaeda and its affiliates as "small men on the wrong side of history."

For al-Qaeda, that history sped up dramatically, as bin Laden's body sank down into the deep.

BIBLIOGRAPHY

BOOKS

Feroz Ali Abbasi, Guantánamo Bay Prison Memoirs, 2002–2004. Author's collection.

Matthew M. Aid, *Intel Wars: The Secret History of the Fight Against Terror* (New York: Bloomsbury, 2012).

Charles Allen, *Soldier Sahibs: The Men Who Made the North-West Frontier* (London: Abacus, 2001).

Jonathan Alter, *The Promise: President Obama, Year One* (New York: Simon and Schuster, 2009).

Mir Bahmanyar with Chris Osman, *SEALs: The US Navy's Elite Fighting Force* (Oxford, United Kingdom: Osprey Publishing, 2008).

Nasser al-Bahri with Georges Malbrunot, *Dans l'Ombre de Ben Laden: Révélations de son garde du corps repenti* (Neuilly-sur-Seine, France: Éditions Michel Lafon, 2010).

Ken Ballen, *Terrorists in Love: The Real Lives of Islamic Radicals* (New York: Free Press, 2011).

Neal Bascomb, *Hunting Eichmann: How a Band of Survivors and a Young Spy Agency Chased Down the World's Most Notorious Nazi* (Boston: Houghton Mifflin Harcourt, 2009).

Peter Bergen, *Holy War, Inc.: Inside the Secret World of Osama bin Laden* (New York: Simon and Schuster, 2001).

Peter Bergen, *The Longest War: The Enduring Conflict between America and al-Qaeda* (New York: Free Press, 2011).

BIBLIOGRAPHY

Peter Bergen, *The Osama bin Laden I Know: An Oral History* (New York: Free Press, 2006).

Gary Berntsen and Ralph Pezzullo, *Jawbreaker: The Attack on Bin Laden and Al-Qaeda: A Personal Account by the CIA's Key Field Commander* (New York: Crown, 2005).

Peter Blaber, *The Mission, the Men, and Me: Lessons from a Former Delta Force Commander* (New York: Berkley Caliber, 2008).

Mark Bowden, *Black Hawk Down: A Story of Modern War* (New York: Grove Press, 2005).

Mark Bowden, *Guests of the Ayatollah: The Iran Hostage Crisis: The First Battle in America's War with Militant Islam* (New York: Grove Press, 2007).

Mark Bowden, *Killing Pablo: The Hunt for the World's Greatest Outlaw* (New York: Atlantic Monthly Press, 2001).

Charles H. Briscoe, Richard L. Kiper, and Kalev Sepp, *U.S. Army Special Operations in Afghanistan* (Boulder, Colorado: Paladin Press, 2006).

Paula Broadwell and Vernon Leob, *All In: The Education of General David Petraeus* (New York: Penguin Press HC, 2012).

Jason Burke, *The 9/11 Wars* (London: Penguin Books, 2011).

George W. Bush, *Decision Points* (New York: Crown, 2010).

Dick Cheney, *In My Time: A Personal and Political Memoir* (New York: Simon and Schuster, 2011).

Steve Coll, *Ghost Wars: The Secret History of the CIA, Afghanistan, and bin Laden, from the Soviet Invasion to September 10, 2001* (New York: Penguin, 2004).

Steve Coll, *The Bin Ladens: An Arabian Family in the American Century* (New York: Penguin, 2008).

George Crile, *Charlie Wilson's War: The Extraordinary Story of How the Wildest Man in Congress and a Rogue CIA Agent Changed the History of Our Times* (New York: Grove Press, 2007).

Henry A. Crumpton, "Intelligence and War in Afghanistan, 2001–2002," in *Transforming U.S. Intelligence*, eds. Jessica E. Sims and Burton Gerber (Washington, DC: Georgetown University Press, 2005).

Michael DeLong and Noah Lukeman, *A General Speaks Out: The Truth About the Wars in Afghanistan and Iraq* (Osceola: Zenith Press, 2004).

Douglas Feith, *War and Decision: Inside the Pentagon at the Dawn of the War on Terrorism* (New York: Harper Perennial, 2009).

Yosri Fouda and Nick Fielding, *Masterminds of Terror: The Truth Behind the Most Devastating Terrorist Attack the World Has Ever Seen* (New York: Arcade Publishing, 2003).

Tommy Franks, *American Soldier* (New York: HarperCollins, 2004).

BIBLIOGRAPHY

Jim Frederick, *Special Ops: The Hidden World of America's Toughest Warriors* (New York: Time, 2011).

Dalton Fury, *Kill Bin Laden: A Delta Force Commander's Account of the Hunt for the World's Most Wanted Man* (New York: St. Martin's Press, 2008).

Robert M. Gates, *From the Shadows: The Ultimate Insider's Story of Five Presidents and How They Won the Cold War* (New York: Simon and Schuster, 2006).

Fawaz Gerges, *The Rise and Fall of Al-Qaeda* (New York: Oxford University Press, 2011).

Bradley Graham, *By His Own Rules: The Ambitions, Successes, and Ultimate Failures of Donald Rumsfeld* (New York: PublicAffairs, 2009).

Eric Greitens, *The Heart and the Fist: The Education of a Humanitarian, the Making of a Navy SEAL* (New York: Houghton Mifflin Harcourt, 2011).

Imtiaz Gul, *The Most Dangerous Place: Pakistan's Lawless Frontier* (New York: Penguin, 2011).

Michael Hastings, *The Operators: The Wild and Terrifying Inside Story of America's War in Afghanistan* (New York: Blue Rider Press, 2012).

Thomas Hegghammer, *Jihad in Saudi Arabia: Violence and Pan-Islamism Since 1979* (New York: Cambridge University Press, 2010).

John Heilemann and Mark Halperin, *Game Change: Obama and the Clintons, McCain and Palin, and the Race of a Lifetime* (New York: Harper, 2010).

Zahid Hussain, *Frontline Pakistan: The Struggle with Militant Islam* (New York: Columbia University Press, 2008).

Seth Jones, *Hunting in the Shadows: The Pursuit of Al Qa'ida Since 9/11* (New York: W. W. Norton & Company, 2012).

Gilles Kepel, Jean-Pierre Milelli, and Pascale Ghazaleh, trans., *Al Qaeda in Its Own Words* (Boston: President and Fellows of Harvard College, 2008).

Ronald Kessler, *The CIA at War: Inside the Secret Campaign Against Terror* (New York: St. Martin's Press, 2003).

Jim Lacey, *A Terrorist's Call to Global Jihad: Deciphering Abu Musab Al-Suri's Islamic Jihad Manifesto* (Annapolis: Naval Institute Press, 2008).

Robert Lacey, *Inside the Kingdom: Kings, Clerics, Modernists, Terrorists, and the Struggle for Saudi Arabia* (New York: Viking Press, 2009).

Najwa bin Laden, Omar bin Laden, and Jean Sasson, *Growing Up bin Laden: Osama's Wife and Son Take Us Inside Their Secret World* (New York: St. Martin's Press, 2009).

Bruce Lawrence, *Messages to the World: The Statements of Osama bin Laden* (New York: Verso, 2005).

Brynjar Lia, *Architect of Global Jihad* (New York: Columbia University Press, 2008).

BIBLIOGRAPHY

Jane Mayer, *The Dark Side: The Inside Story of How the War on Terror Turned into a War on American Ideals* (New York: Anchor Books, 2008).

Terry McDermott and Josh Meyer, *The Hunt for KSM: Inside the Pursuit and Takedown of the Real 9/11 Mastermind, Khalid Sheikh Mohammed* (New York: Little, Brown, and Company, 2012).

William H. McRaven, *Spec Ops: Case Studies in Special Operations Warfare: Theory and Practice* (New York: Random House, 1996).

Pervez Musharraf, *In the Line of Fire: A Memoir* (New York: Free Press, 2006).

Richard Myers, *Eyes on the Horizon: Serving on the Front Lines of National Security* (New York: Threshold Editions, 2009).

Leigh Neville, *Special Forces in Afghanistan: Afghanistan 2001–2007* (Oxford, UK: Osprey Publishing, 2007).

Dana Priest and William M. Arkin, *Top Secret America: The Rise of the New American Security State* (New York: Little, Brown and Co., 2011).

Condoleezza Rice, *No Higher Honor: A Memoir of My Time in Washington* (New York: Crown, 2011).

Donald Rumsfeld, *Known and Unknown: A Memoir* (New York: Penguin Group, 2011).

Benjamin Runkle, *Wanted Dead or Alive: Manhunts from Geronimo to Bin Laden* (New York: Palgrave Macmillan, 2011).

Michael Scheuer, *Osama bin Laden* (New York: Oxford University Press, 2011).

Eric Schmitt and Thom Shanker, *Counterstrike: The Untold Story of America's Secret Campaign Against Al Qaeda* (New York: Times Books, 2011).

Gary Schroen, *First In: An Insider's Account of How the CIA Spearheaded the War on Terror in Afghanistan* (New York: Presidio Press, 2005).

Henry Schuster and Charles Stone, *Hunting Eric Rudolph: An Insider's Account of the Five-Year Search for the Olympic Bombing Suspect* (New York: Berkley Books, 2005).

Mitchell Silber, *The Al Qaeda Factor: Plots Against the West* (Philadelphia: University of Pennsylvania Press, 2012).

Jessica E. Sims and Burton Gerber, eds., *Transforming U.S. Intelligence* (Washington, DC: Georgetown University Press, 2005).

Michael Smith, *Killer Elite: The Inside Story of America's Most Secret Special Operations Teams* (New York: St. Martin's Press, 2011).

Ali Soufan, *The Black Banners: The Inside Story of 9/11 and the War Against al-Qaeda* (New York: W. W. Norton & Company, 2011).

Anthony Summers and Robbyn Swann, *The Eleventh Day: The Full Story of 9/11 and Osama bin Laden* (New York: Ballantine Books, 2011).

Camille Tawil, *Brothers in Arms: The Story of Al-Qa'ida and the Arab Jihadists* (London: Saqi Books, 2011).

BIBLIOGRAPHY

George Tenet, *At the Center of the Storm: My Years at the CIA* (New York: HarperCollins, 2007).

Hugh Trevor-Roper, *The Last Days of Hitler* (Chicago: University of Chicago Press, 1987).

Mark Urban, *Task Force Black: The Explosive True Story of the Secret Special Forces War in Iraq* (New York: St. Martin's Press, 2011).

Joby Warrick, *The Triple Agent: The al-Qaeda Mole Who Infiltrated the CIA* (New York: Doubleday, 2011).

Richard Wolffe, *Renegade: The Making of a President* (New York: Crown, 2009).

Bob Woodward, *Obama's Wars* (New York: Simon and Schuster, 2010).

Bob Woodward, *Plan of Attack* (New York: Simon and Schuster, 2004).

Andy Worthington, *Guantanamo Files: The Stories of the 759 Detainees in America's Illegal Prison* (London: Pluto Press, 2007).

Donald P. Wright, James R. Bird, Steven E. Clay, Peter W. Connors, Lieutenant Colonel Scott C. Farquhar, Lynn Chandler Garcia, and Dennis Van Wey, *A Different Kind of War: The United States Army in Operation Enduring Freedom (OEF), October 2001–September 2005* (Fort Leavenworth, KS: Combat Studies Institute Press, 2005).

Lawrence Wright, *The Looming Tower: Al-Qaeda and the Road to 9/11* (New York: Alfred A. Knopf, 2006).

Abdul Salam Zaeef, *My Life with the Taliban* (New York: Columbia University Press, 2010).

Ahmad Zaidan, *Usama Bin Ladin Without a Mask: Interviews Banned by the Taliban* (Lebanon: World Book Publishing Company, 2003).

DOCUMENTS

U.S. Government Documents

United States Navy, Admiral William H. McRaven, biography, United States Special Operations Command, updated August 8, 2011.

Defendants' exhibit 950 in *U.S. v. Moussaoui*, Cr. No. 01-455-A, "FBI's Handling of Intelligence Information Related to Khalid al-Mihdhar & Nawaf al-Hamzi," Department of Justice Inspector General's report by Glenn A. Fine, obtained via INTELWIRE.com.

Department of Defense, "Recommendation for Continued Detention Under DoD Control (CD for Detainee, ISN US9SA-000063DP(S)," October 30, 2008.

Department of Defense, Verbatim Transcript of Combatant Status Review Trial, Khalid Sheikh Mohammed, March 10, 2007, http://www.defenselink.mil/news/transcript_ISN10024.pdf.

BIBLIOGRAPHY

Department of Defense, Verbatim Transcript of Combatant Status Review Trial for ISN 10024, Khalid Sheikh Mohammed, March 10, 2007, http://www.defenselink.mil/news/transcript_ISN10024.pdf.

Department of Justice Office of Legal Counsel, "Memorandum for John A. Rizzo, Senior Deputy Council, Central Intelligence Agency," May 30, 2005, http://s3.amazonaws.com/propublica/assets/missing_memos/28O LCmemofinalredact30May05.pdf.

JTF-GTMO Detainee Assessment for Abdul Shalabi, ISN US9SA-000042DP, May 14, 2008.

JTF-GTMO Detainee Assessment for Abdul Rabbani Abu Rahman, ISN US9PK-001460DP, June 9, 2008.

JTF-GTMO Detainee Assessment for Abu al-Libi, ISN US9LY-010017DP, September 10, 2008.

JTF-GTMO Detainee Assessment for Ali Hamza Ismail, ISN US9YM-000039DP, November 15, 2007.

JTF-GTMO Detainee Assessment for Ammar al-Baluchi, ISN USSPK-010018D, December 8, 2006.

JTF-GTMO Detainee Assessment for Awal Gul, ISN US9AF-000782DP, February 15, 2008.

JTF-GTMO Detainee Assessment for Bashir Lap, ISN US9MY-010022DP, October 13, 2008.

JTF-GTMO Detainee Assessment for Faruq Ahmed, ISN US9YM-000032DP, February 18, 2008.

JTF-GTMO Detainee Assessment for Harun al-Afghani, ISN US9AF-003148DP, August 2, 2007.

JTF-GTMO Detainee Assessment for Ibrahim Sulayman Muhammad Arbaysh, ISN US9SA-000192D, November 30, 2005.

JTF-GTMO Detainee Assessment for Khalid Shaykh Muhammad, ISN US9KU-010024DP, December 8, 2006.

JTF-GTMO Detainee Assessment for Maad Al-Qahtani, ISN US9SA-000063DP (S), October 30, 2008.

JTF-GTMO Detainee Assessment for Mohammed al-Qahtani, ISN US9SA-000063DP, October 30, 2008.

JTF-GTMO Detainee Assessment for Muazhamza al-Alawi, ISN US9YM-000028DP, March 14, 2008.

JTF-GTMO Detainee Assessment for Riduan Isomuddin, ISN US9ID-010019DP, October 30, 2008.

JTF-GTMO Detainee Assessment for Riyad Atiq Ali Abdu al-Haj, ISN US9YM-000256DP, March 23, 2008.

JFT-GTMO Detainee Assessment for Salim Hamed (Salim Hamdan), ISN US9YM-000149DP, September 4, 2008.

BIBLIOGRAPHY

JTF-GTMO Detainee Assessment for Sultan al-Uwaydha, ISN US9SA-000059DP, August 1, 2007.

JTF-GTMO Detainee Assessment for Walid Said bin Said Zaid, ISN US9YM-000550DP (S), January 16, 2008.

Mitchell D. Silber and Arvin Bhatt, "Radicalization in the West: the Home-grown Threat," New York Police Department, 2007. www.nypdshield.org/public/.../NYPD_Report-Radicalization_in_the_West.pdf.

"National Commission on Terrorist Attacks Upon the United States Final Report" (Washington, DC, 2004) ("9/11 Commission Report").

National Defense University, Conflict Records Research Center, "Document contains al-Qaeda review of the 9/11 attacks on the United States one year later," undated (circa September 2002), AQ-SHPD-D-001-285, http://www.ndu.edu/inss/docUploaded/AQ-SHPD-D-001-285.pdf.

National Intelligence Council, "National Intelligence Estimate: The Terrorist Threat to the U.S. Homeland," July 2007, http://www.c-span.org/pdf/nie_071707.pdf.

Office of the Director of National Intelligence, "Declassified Key Judgments of the National Intelligence Estimate. Trends in Global Terrorism: Implications for the United States," April 2006, http://www.dni.gov/press_releases/Declassified_NIE_Key_Judgments.pdf.

Office of the Inspector General, "Report on CIA Accountability with Respect to the 9/11 Attacks," August 21, 2007, https://www.cia.gov/library/reports/Executive%20Summary_OIG%20Report.pdf.

United States Department of State, Bureau of Intelligence and Research (INR), "The Wandering Mujahidin: Armed and Dangerous," August 21–22, 1993.

United States Department of State, Bureau of Intelligence and Research, (INR), "Terrorism? Usama bin Ladin: Who's Chasing Whom?" July 18, 1996.

United States Department of the Treasury, "Treasury Targets Key Al-Qa'ida Funding and Support Network Using Iran as a Critical Transit Point," July 28, 2011, http://www.treasury.gov/press-center/press-releases/Pages/tg1261.aspx.

United States Senate, Committee on Foreign Relations, "Tora Bora Revisited: How We Failed to Get Bin Laden and Why It Matters Today," November 30, 2009.

United States Senate Select Committee on Intelligence, "Report on Prewar Intelligence Assessments on Postwar Iraq, together with additional views," February 12, 2004, http://intelligence.senate.gov/prewar.pdf.

United States Special Operations Command History (6th edition, 2008), http://www.socom.mil/SOCOMHome/Documents/history6thedition.pdf.

WikiLeaks, Cable from U.S. Secretary of State to U.S. Embassy in Islamabad dated October 9, 2008.

BIBLIOGRAPHY

Document Sets and Reports

Brian Fishman, "Redefining the Islamic State: The Fall and Rise of Al-Qaeda in Iraq," The New America Foundation, August 18, 2011, http://newamerica .net/publications/policy/redefining_the_islamic_state.

Holloway Report, August 23, 1980, http://www.gwu.edu/~nsarchiv/NSAEBB/ NSAEBB63/doc8.pdf.

"Nomination of Michael Leiter to be Director, National Counterterrorism Center," http://www.fas.org/irp/congress/2008_hr/leiter.pdf.

"Pervez Musharraf on U.S.-Pakistan Relations," Council on Foreign Relations, October 26, 2011, http://carnegieendowment.org/files/1026carnegie -musharraf.pdf.

"Report into the London Terrorist Attacks on July 7, 2005," Intelligence and Security Committee, May 2006, http://www.cabinetoffice.gov.uk/sites/ default/files/resources/isc_7july_report.pdf, pp. 12 and 15.

Camille Tawil, "The Other Face of al-Qaeda," trans. Maryan El-Hajbi and Mustafa Abulhimal, Quilliam Foundation, November 2010.

Katherine Tiedemann and Peter Bergen, "The Year of the Drone," New America Foundation, February 24, 2010, http://counterterrorism.newamerica .net/sites/newamerica.net/files/policydocs/bergentiedemann2.pdf.

Court Documents

Interrogation of al-Qaeda recruit Nizar Trabelsi, who was questioned in French in June 2002. The text of his interrogation was later provided in Italian to prosecutors in Milan investigating one of Trabelsi's associates. Documents acquired and translated by investigative journalist Leo Sisti of L'Espresso. Author's collection.

U.S. v. Ali Hamza Ahmad Suliman al Bahlul, May 7, 2008.

U.S. v. Moussaoui, Cr. No. 01-455-A, exhibit ST-0001.

U.S. v. Khalid Sheikh Mohammed et al. (Indictment in U.S. District Court for the Southern District of New York [S14] 93 Cr. 180 [KTD], December 14, 2009).

U.S. v. Najibullah Zazi, Eastern District of New York, 09-CR-663, Memorandum of law in support of the government's motion for a permanent order of detention (Via IntelWire).

SPEECHES BY WESTERN OFFICIALS

Dick Cheney, remarks, "Town Hall Meeting," CQ Transcriptions, October 19, 2004.

Henry A. Crumpton, speech at CSIS Smart Power Series, Washington, DC, January 14, 2008, http://csis.org/files/media/csis/press/080114_smart_ crumpton.pdf.

BIBLIOGRAPHY

Jonathan Evans, address to the Society of Editors, Manchester, England, November 5, 2007, http://www.homeoffice.gov.uk/about-us/news/security-speech-mi5?version=1.

Robert Gates, remarks, Kutzenov Naval Academy, St. Petersburg, Russia, March 21, 2011.

John McCain, speech after his win in the Wisconsin Primary, C-SPAN, February 19, 2008, http://www.c-spanvideo.org/appearance/290354897.

Admiral Michael Mullen, U.S. Navy Chairman of the Joint Chiefs of Staff, before the Senate Armed Services Committee, September 22, 2011, http://armed-services.senate.gov/statemnt/2011/09%20September/Mullen%20 09-22-11.pdf.

Barack Obama, "Address to the Nation on the Way Forward in Afghanistan and Pakistan," White House press release, December 1, 2009, http://www.whitehouse.gov/the-press-office/remarks-president-address-nation-way-forward-afghanistan-and-pakistan.

Barack Obama, at Democratic Debate, Los Angeles, CA, January 31, 2008, http://articles.cnn.com/2008-01-31/politics/dem.debate.transcript_1_hillary-clinton-debate-stake/29?_s=PM:POLITICS.

Barack Obama, "Obama's Nobel Remarks [transcript]," *New York Times*, December 10, 2009, http://www.nytimes.com/2009/12.

Barack Obama, speech at Woodrow Wilson Center, Washington, DC, August 1, 2007, http://www.cfr.org/us-election-2008/obamas-speech-woodrow-wilson-center/p13974.

"Transcript: the Republican Candidates Debate," *New York Times*, August 5, 2007, http://www.nytimes.com/2007/08/05/us/politics/05transcript-debate.html?pagewanted=all.

Paul Wolfowitz, Defense Department Briefing, December 10, 2001.

STATEMENTS BY AL-QAEDA LEADERS AND OTHER ALLIED MILITANTS

Abd al-Halim Adl, letter to Khalid Sheikh Mohamed: translation from Counterterrorism Center at West Point, Harmony Program, http://www.ctc.usma.edu/wp-content/uploads/2010/08/Al-Adl-Letter_Translation.pdf.

Abu Musab al-Suri, "The Call to Global Islamic Resistance," published on jihadist websites, 2004.

Osama bin Laden, "Letter to Mullah Mohammed Omar from bin Laden," Undated, AFGP-2002-600321. Available at http://www.ctc.usma.edu/posts/letter-to-mullah-mohammed-omar-from-bin-laden-english-translation.

Osama bin Laden, "Statement," October 7, 2001. Aired on Al Jazeera.

Osama bin Laden interview with Al Jazeera, 1998. Available via http://www.telegraph.co.uk/news/worldnews/asia/afghanistan/1358734/Ever-since-I-can-recall-I-despised-and-felt-hatred-towards-Americans.html.

BIBLIOGRAPHY

"Note to Zarqawi," November 12, 2005, available at http://www.ctc.usma .edu/wp-content/uploads/2010/08/CTC-AtiyahLetter.pdf.

"The Solution: A Video Speech from Usama bin Laden Addressing the American People on the Occasion of the Sixth Anniversary of 9/11—9/2007," SITE Group translation, September 11, 2007, http://counterterrorismblog .org/site-resources/images/SITE-OBL-transcript.pdf.

"Al-Zarqawi: The Second al-Qa'ida Generation," Fu'ad Husayn, *Al-Quds al-Arabi*, May 21–22, 2005.

NEWSPAPERS, MAGAZINES, JOURNALS, NEWS AGENCIES, AND BROADCAST NEWS

Newspapers

Al-Hayat, Al-Quds Al-Arabi, Asharq Al-Awsat, Australian, Chicago Tribune, Daily Times (Pakistan), *Dawn* (Pakistan), *Der Spiegel, Express Tribune, Friday Times, Guardian, Harvard University Gazette, Independent, International Herald Tribune, Los Angeles Times, McClatchy Newspapers, The News* (Pakistan), *New York Times, New York Daily News, Sunday Times, Telegraph, Wall Street Journal, Washington Post, Washington Times, Weekly Standard, USA Today*

Magazines

Al-Majallah (Saudi Arabia), *Atlantic Monthly, Bloomberg Business Week, Mother Jones, National Journal, New Republic, New Yorker, Newsweek, Rolling Stone, Time, Washingtonian, Wired*

Journals

Foreign Affairs, Foreign Policy, Security Studies

News Agencies

Agence France-Presse, Associated Press, Reuters, ProPublica

Broadcast News and Radio

ABC, Canadian Broadcasting Corporation, CBS, CNN, France24, Al Jazeera, Middle East Broadcasting Corporation, MSNBC, NBC, PBS, Radio Free Europe/Radio Liberty

DOCUMENTARIES

Canadian Broadcasting Corporation, *Al Qaeda Family*, February 22, 2004.

CNN, *In the Footsteps of bin Laden*, August 23, 2006.

History Channel, *Targeting Bin Laden*, September 6, 2011.

National Geographic, *The Last Days of Osama bin Laden*, November 9, 2011; *George W. Bush: The 9/11 Interview*, August 30, 2011.

NBC, "Inside the Terror Plot That 'Rivaled 9/11,'" *Dateline*, September 14, 2009.

BIBLIOGRAPHY

PBS, *Frontline*, "Dana Priest: Top Secret America" (2011); "Campaign Against Terror" (2002).

Laura Poitras, *The Oath*, Praxis Films (2010).

INTERVIEWS

Abdullah Anas
Abdel Bari Atwan
Hutaifa Azzam
Jeremy Bash
Khaled Batarfi
Noman Benotman
Gary Berntsen
Tony Blinken
John Brennan
Robert Cardillo
Glenn Carle
James "Hoss" Cartwright
Shamila Chaudhary
James Clapper
Hillary Clinton
Henry A. Crumpton
Dell Dailey
Robert Dannenberg
Khaled al-Fawwaz
Ari Fleischer
Michèle Flournoy
Yosri Fouda
Tommy Franks
Dalton Fury
Brad Garrett

Susan Glasser
Eric Greitens
Robert Grenier
Jamal Ismail
Art Keller
Jamal Khalifa
Ihsan Mohammad Khan
Khalid Khawaja
Khalid Khan Kheshgi
David Kilcullen
Osama bin Laden
Michael Leiter
David Low
Stanley McChrystal
Denis McDonough
John McLaughlin
Hamid Mir
Vahid Mojdeh
Philip Mudd
Michael Mullen
Asad Munir
Arturo Munoz
Muhammad Musa
Vali Nasr
Leon Panetta

David Petraeus
Paul Pillar
Mohammed Asif Qazizanda
Nick Rasmussen
Ben Rhodes
Robert Richer
Bruce Riedel
Michael Scheuer
Shabbir (Bin Laden neighbor)
Ali Soufan
Cindy Storer
Barbara Sude
Abu Musab al-Suri
Camille Tawil
Frances Fragos Townsend
Wisal al-Turabi
Michael Vickers
Junaid Younis
Rahimullah Yusufzai
Mohammed Zahir
Ahmad Zaidan
Juan Zarate

NOTES

PROLOGUE: A COMFORTABLE RETIREMENT

1 **Major Abbott was beloved:** For a description of Major James Abbott, see Charles Allen, *Soldier Sahibs: The Men Who Made the North-West Frontier* (London: Abacus, 2001), p. 205.

1 **"I remember the day":** Sebastian Abbot, "Pakistani Town Copes with Infamy After Bin Laden," Associated Press, May 24, 2011, www.guardian.co.uk/world/feedarticle/9661254.

2 **"City of Schools":** Khalid Khan Kheshgi, interview by author, Pakistan, July 2011.

2 **U.S. Special Forces soldiers were posted there:** Cable from U.S. Secretary of State to U.S. embassy in Islamabad dated October 9, 2008, obtained from WikiLeaks.

2 **The vacation high season begins:** Abbot, "Pakistani Town Copes with Infamy."

2 **Western adventurers:** Author's own observations during visit to Abbottabad, July 2011.

2 **wealthy Afghan refugees:** M Ilyas Khan, "Bin Laden Neighbours Describe Abbottabad Compound," BBC, May 2, 2011, www.bbc.co.uk/news/world-south-asia-13257338.

3 **The Kuwaiti purchased the land:** "Pakistani Owner of Bin Laden's Hideaway Aided Him," Associated Press, May 4, 2011, dailytimespakistan.com/pakistani-owner-of-bin-laden%E2%80%99s-hideaway-aided-him/.

3 **"very simple, modest, humble type of man":** Ibid.

NOTES

3   **"One of my students could have":** Junaid Younis, interview by author, Abbottabad, Pakistan, July 20, 2011.

3   **Locals estimate that:** Saeed Shah, "At End, Bin Laden Wasn't Running Al-Qaeda, Officials Say," *McClatchy Newspapers,* June 28, 2011, www .mcclatchydc.com/2011/06/28/v-print/116666/at-end-bin-laden-wasnt-running.html.

4   **No planning permission was sought for this addition:** Junaid Younis interview.

4   **exclusive use:** Christina Lamb, "Bickering Widows Blame Young Wife for Alerting US," *Sunday Times,* May 22, 2011, www.thesundaytimes .co.uk/sto/news/world_news/Asia/article631884.ece.

4   **rarely left the second and third floors:** Author interview with Pakistani intelligence officials, July 2011.

4   **only to take a walk:** Ibid.

4   **A makeshift tarpaulin:** Ibid.

4   **last for more than twelve hours:** Najwa bin Laden, Omar bin Laden, and Jean Sasson, *Growing Up bin Laden: Osama's Wife and Son Take Us Inside Their Secret World* (New York: St. Martin's Press, 2009), p. 173.

4   **quite adept at volleyball:** Khalad al-Hammadi, "Bin Ladin's Former 'Bodyguard' Interviewed on al Qaida Strategies," *al-Quds al-Arabi,* in Arabic, August 3, 2004.

5   **Nor was he suffering from debilitating kidney disease:** Ibid.

5   **Bin Laden's first wife:** Wisal al-Turabi, interview by Sam Dealey, Khartoum, Sudan, July 10, 2005.

5   **eventually agreed to her request:** bin Laden, bin Laden, and Sasson, *Growing Up bin Laden,* pp. 282 and 146.

5   **allowed her to take only three:** Ibid., p. 282.

5   **"I will never divorce you":** Ibid.

5   **Najwa left Afghanistan on September 9, 2001:** Ibid., p. 146.

6   **motivation to marry Khairiah:** Wisal al-Turabi interview.

6   **a man she believed to be a true holy warrior:** Lawrence Wright, *The Looming Tower: Al-Qaeda and the Road to 9/11* (New York: Alfred A. Knopf, 2006), p. 252.

6   **they had a boy:** bin Laden, bin Laden, and Sasson, *Growing Up bin Laden,* p. 298.

6   **Khairiah fled Afghanistan for neighboring Iran:** Mohammed Al Shafey, "Bin Laden's Family Under House Arrest in Iran," *Asharq al-Awsat,* December 23, 2009, www.asharq-e.com/news.asp?section= 1&id=19259.

NOTES

7   **not uncomfortable:** Lara Setrakian, "Osama Bin Laden's Teen Daughter Allowed to Leave Iran," ABC News, March 22, 2010, abcnews.go .com/Blotter/International/iran-releases-osama-bin-ladens-teenage-daughter/story?id=10169432#.TsWKlF1AIj8.

7   **militants abducted Heshmatollah Attarzadeh-Niyaki:** "Iran Says Rescued Diplomat Kidnapped in Pakistan," Reuters, March 30, 2010, uk.reuters.com/article/2010/03/30/uk-pakistan-iran-idUKTRE62T1 FU20100330.

7   **This was part of a deal:** Author interview with Pakistani intelligence officials, July 2011.

7   **Sometime during the blazing summer of 2010:** Christina Lamb, "Revealed: The SEALs' Secret Guide to Bin Laden Lair," *Sunday Times,* May 22, 2011, www.thesundaytimes.co.uk/sto/news/world_news/Asia /article631893.ece; author interview with Pakistani intelligence officials.

7   **Her one disappointment was:** Author interview with Pakistani intelligence officials.

8   **Siham's first son, Khalid:** In the spring of 2011, bin Laden and Siham were planning Khalid's marriage to the daughter of an al-Qaeda fighter who had been killed in Afghanistan a few years earlier. Siham also had two of her daughters living with her: Maryam, age twenty, and Sumaiyah, age sixteen. There had also been tragedies for bin Laden and Siham. Their third daughter, Khadija, had married an al-Qaeda fighter in Afghanistan in 1999 when she was only eleven, but had recently succumbed to an illness in Pakistan's tribal regions, while Khadija's husband had also died in an American drone strike. So now their four young children were living in the Abbottabad compound along with Grandpa Osama and Grandma Siham.

8   **Siham had been a student:** Mustafa al-Ansari, "Bin Ladin's Brother-in-Law to Al Hayah: 'My Sister Holds PhD: She Differs with Husband Usama Ideologically,'" *Al Hayat* online, May 26, 2011.

8   **Siham's parents opposed . . . went ahead:** Ibid.

8   **donated it all:** Ibid.

8   **often edit bin Laden's writings:** Ibid.

8   **"chained" to bin Laden:** Ibid.

9   **"She had to be religious":** Hala Jaber, "Finding Osama a Wife," *Sunday Times,* January 24, 2010, www.thesundaytimes.co.uk/sto/news/ world_news/article195679.ece.

9   **"really believed that being a dutiful and obedient wife":** Ibid.

9   **couched as coming from a businessman:** Mustafa al-Ansari, "Bin Laden's Yemeni Spouse, 'Amal,' Will Not Remarry Even If Asked by President Ali Saleh!" *Al Hayat,* Arabic, June 13, 2011.

NOTES

9   **"God has blessed it":** Ibid.

9   **a $5,000 dowry:** Jaber, "Finding Osama a Wife."

9   **"We agreed that":** al-Ansari, "Bin Laden's Yemeni Spouse."

10   **The women had their own, more modest party:** Jaber, "Finding Osama a Wife."

10   **Initially, bin Laden's other wives:** Nasser al-Bahri, *Dans l'Ombre de Ben Laden: Révélations de son garde du corps repenti* (Neuilly-sur-Seine, France: Éditions Michel Lafon, 2010), p. 201.

10   **traveled from Yemen to Afghanistan:** al-Ansari, "Bin Laden's Yemeni Spouse."

11   **"Thank you for this great upbringing":** Ibid.

11   **"go down in history":** Ibid.

11   **named her after the Safia:** Hamid Mir, interviews by author, Islamabad, Pakistan, May 11, 2002, and March 2005.

11   **another four children:** "Yemen Family of bin Laden Widow Demands Her Return," Agence France Presse, May 17, 2011, www.dailytimes .com.pk/default.asp?page=2011\05\18\story_18-5-2011_pg7_7.

11   **two while she:** Lamb, "Revealed: The SEALs' Secret Guide."

11   **"Marry and increase in number":** al-Ansari, "Bin Ladin's Brother-in-Law."

11   **"I don't understand why":** Abdullah Anas, interview by author, London, June 15, 17, and 20, 2005.

12   **For their meat consumption:** Shopkeeper Mohammed Rashid told BBC Urdu's Aijaz Mahar that two goats were delivered every week, presumably for slaughter and consumption. "What Was Life Like in the Bin Laden Compound?" BBC, May 9, 2011, www.bbc.co.uk/news/ world-south-asia-13266944.

11   **Milk came from:** Saeed Shah, "Pakistani Officers' Photos Show Blood, but Not Bin Laden," *McClatchy Newspapers*, May 4, 2011, www .mcclatchydc.com/2011/05/04/113699/pakistani-officers-photos-show.html.

12   **If neighborhood kids accidentally:** "Abbottabad Children Played by Bin Laden Compound," CNN, May 9, 2011, articles.cnn.com/2011-05-09/world/pakistan.bin.laden.children_1_bin-terror-leader-compound? _s=PM:WORLD.

12   **knock for ten or twenty minutes:** Ibid.

12   **would not give their names and were notably religious:** Stan Grant, interview with local child, *The Situation Room*, CNN, aired May 30, 2011, transcripts.cnn.com/TRANSCRIPTS/1105/30/sitroom.02.html.

NOTES

12   **electricity and gas bills:** Ihsan Mohammad Khan, interview by author, Abbottabad, Pakistan, July 21, 2011; review of the electricity and gas bills by author.

13   **didn't need air-conditioning:** Khaled al-Fawwaz, interview by author, London, April 1, 1997.

13   **compound had no running water:** Noman Benotman, interview by author, London, August 30, 2005.

13   **"You should learn to sacrifice everything":** Ibid.

13   **attended a madrassa:** Lamb, "Revealed: SEALs' Secret Guide."

13   **did not go to school:** Robert Booth, Saeed Shah, and Jason Burke, "Osama Bin Laden Death: How Family Scene in Compound Turned to Carnage," *Guardian*, May 5, 2011, www.guardian.co.uk/world/2011/may/05/bin-laden-death-family-compound.

13   **both academics:** al-Hammadi, "Osama's Former 'Bodyguard.' "

13   **taught them poetry:** Zaynab Khadr, interview by Terrence McKenna, Islamabad, Pakistan, "Al Qaeda Family," Canadian Broadcasting Corporation, "Maha Elsammah and Zaynab Khadr," February 22, 2004. Transcript available at www.pbs.org/wgbh/pages/frontline/shows/khadr/interviews/mahazaynab.html.

13   **delivered an address:** Author interview with Pakistani intelligence officials.

14   **bin Laden created a dedicated living space:** Wright, *The Looming Tower*, p. 251; Abu Jundal, "His Three Wives Lived in One House That Had Only One Floor. They Lived in Perfect Harmony,"; Khalid al-Hammadi, "Bin Laden's Former 'Bodyguard' Interviewed, *Al-Quds al-Arabi*, March 20 to April 4, 2004.

14   **exhaust system that was nothing more:** Author observations of Abbottabad compound.

14   **The third floor:** Author interview with Pakistani officials.

14   **"Husband and wife":** al-Hammadi, "Osama's Former 'Bodyguard.' "

14   **never raised his voice in anger:** bin Laden, bin Laden, and Sasson, *Growing Up bin Laden*, p. 41.

14   **close relationship with his mother:** Khaled Batarfi, interview by author, Jeddah, Saudi Arabia, September 5 and 9, 2005.

15   **A clue as to how the fifty-four-year-old:** JoNel Aleccia, "What Was in Medicine Chests at Bin Laden Compound?" MSNBC, May 6, 2011, sys12-today.msnbc.msn.com/id/42934673/ns/world_news-death_of_bin_laden/.

15   **herbs or other natural sources:** Jaber, "Finding Osama a Wife."

15   **about 12,000 rupees a month each:** Author interview with Pakistani intelligence official.

NOTES

15 **bought and sold gold bangles and rings:** Shah, "At End, Bin Laden Wasn't Running al-Qaeda": author interview with jewelry store owner in Rawalpindi, Pakistan, July 19, 2011.

15 **catch a glimpse:** Author interview with Pakistani intelligence officials.

15 **instructed her never to talk about him:** Tariq Iqbal Chaudhry, "Abbottabad Commission Interviews al-Kuwaiti's Wife," *The News*, November 13, 2011, www.thenews.com.pk/TodaysPrintDetail.aspx?ID= 77219&Cat=2.

16 **religious practices:** bin Laden, bin Laden, and Sasson, *Growing Up bin Laden*, p. 17.

16 **Al Jazeera television and BBC radio:** "Osama bin Laden Videos Released by Government," ABC News, May 8, 2011, abcnews .go.com/Blotter/osama-bin-laden-home-videos-released-pentagon/ story?id=13552384; Hamid Mir interview.

16 **wrapped in a blanket:** "Osama bin Laden Videos Released by Government."

17 **publicly referred to Obama as a "house Negro":** "Al Qaeda Leader Mocks Obama in Web Posting," CNN, November 19, 2008, articles .cnn.com/2008-11-19/us/obama.alqaeda_1_al-zawahiri-barack-obama-obama-s-muslim/2?_s=PM:US.

17 **Palestine, but also the environment and the global economy:** Author interview with Pakistani officials.

17 **And he voraciously read:** Statement transcript, ABC News, September 6, 2007, abcnews.go.com/images/ Politics/transcript2.pdf. These books very likely came from the two excellent English-language bookstores, Saeed Book Bank and Mr. Books, in the Pakistani capital, Islamabad, two hours' drive from Abbottabad.

CHAPTER 1: 9/11 AND AFTER

18 **"Our boys were shocked":** From John Miller interview with Osama bin Laden for PBS *Frontline*, May 1998, www.pbs.org/wgbh/pages/frontline /shows/binladen/who/interview.html.

18 **loved like a father:** For description of the attitudes of bin Laden's followers toward their leader, see JTF-GTMO Detainee Assessment for Abdul Shalabi, ISN US9SA-000042DP, May 14, 2008.

18 **boots on the ground:** In interviews with veteran *Al-Hayat* journalist Camille Tawil, former Libyan Islamic Fighting Group *shura* member Noman Benotman repeatedly quotes bin Laden and al-Qaeda leaders referring to U.S. troops as "cowards" and notes that bin Laden did not think the United States would send troops to Afghanistan in retaliation for an attack. Camille Tawil, "The Other Face of al-Qaeda,"

trans. Maryan El-Hajbi and Mustafa Abulhimal, Quilliam Foundation, November 2010, p. 15.

18 **feeble as the former Soviet Union:** See bin Laden interview with Al Jazeera, 1998, available via www.telegraph.co.uk/news/worldnews/asia/afghanistan/1358734/Ever-since-I-can-recall-I-despised-and-felt-hatred-towards-Americans.html.

19 **some of al-Qaeda's senior officials:** Saif al-Adel and Abu Hafs al-Mauritani in particular expressed reservations about the attacks, out of concern that they would bring a devastating American response and might not be religiously justified. See "National Commission on Terrorist Attacks Upon the United States Final Report" (Washington, DC, 2004) (hereafter "9/11 Commission Report"), pp. 251–52.

19 **inoculate himself against any anger:** Ibid., p. 252.

19 **Tunisian Belgian al-Qaeda assassins:** Gary Schroen, *First In: An Insider's Account of How the CIA Spearheaded the War on Terror in Afghanistan* (New York: Presidio Press, 2005), pp. 1–6.

19 **on Thursday, September 6:** "Osama Bin Laden Video Excerpts," BBC, December 14, 2001, news.bbc.co.uk/2/low/south_asia/1709425.stm.

19 **heard the welcome news:** Feroz Ali Abbasi, a British Ugandan militant living in an al-Qaeda camp, later wrote that he and others heard about the killing on September 9, while listening to the radio. Feroz Ali Abbasi, Guantánamo Bay Prison Memoirs, 2002–2004, author's collection.

20 **fervent hope and belief:** Based on author observations and study of bin Laden.

20 **six days a week:** George Tenet, *At the Center of the Storm: My Years at the CIA* (New York: HarperCollins, 2007), p. 207.

20 **the CIA's assessment:** Ibid., p. 242.

20 **planned to detonate:** Barbara Sude, interview by author, Washington, DC, December 16, 2009.

20 **"preparations for hijackings":** "Transcript: Bin Laden Determined to Strike in US," CNN, April 10, 2004, articles.cnn.com/2004-04-10/politics/august6.memo_1_bin-conduct-terrorist-attacks-abu-zubaydah?_s=PM:ALLPOLITICS.

20 **longest presidential vacation:** Jim VandeHei and Peter Baker, "Vacationing Bush Poised to Set a Record," *Washington Post*, August 3, 2005, www.washingtonpost.com/wp-dyn/content/article/2005/08/02/AR2005080201703.html.

20 **Morell gave the President's Daily Brief:** Author interview with U.S. intelligence official.

20 **Fleischer asked Morell:** Tenet, *At the Center of the Storm*, pp. 253–54.

NOTES

21 **"smells like Osama bin Laden":** Ari Fleischer, interview by author, New York, September 11, 2011.

21 **"kick their ass":** George W. Bush, *Decision Points* (New York: Crown Publishers, 2010), p. 128.

21 **"see the news today":** Proceedings of a military commission, *United States v. Ali Hamza Ahmad Suliman al Bahlul*, May 7, 2008, www .defense.gov/news/01%20al%20Bahlul-trans-Pages%201to%20333-Redacted.pdf; also see Jason Burke, *The 9/11 Wars* (London: Penguin Books, 2011), p. 24.

22 **bin Laden brushed aside Zawahiri's obsessive focus:** Noman Benotman, interview by author, London, United Kingdom, August 30, 2005.

22 **described his first meeting with bin Laden in 1997 as "beautiful":** Khalid Al-Hammadi, "Bin Laden's Former 'Bodyguard' Interviewed on Al Qaeda Strategies," *Al Quds Al Arabi*, in Arabic, August 3, 2004, and March 20–April 4, 2005.

22 **"a very charismatic person":** Excerpts from Shadi Abdalla's (alias Emad Abdulhadie) interviews with German authorities that took place between April 2002 (when he was arrested) and May 2003. Author's collection.

22 **tuned his radio to the BBC's Arabic service:** Peter Bergen, *The Osama bin Laden I Know: An Oral History* (New York: Free Press, 2006), p. 307; Burke, *The 9/11 Wars*, p. 24; also see Yosri Fouda and Nick Fielding, *Masterminds of Terror: The Truth Behind the Most Devastating Terrorist Attack the World Has Ever Seen* (New York: Arcade Publishing, 2003), p. 145.

22 **"the brothers have struck":** Fouda and Fielding, *Masterminds of Terror*, p. 144.

23 **"Reports from the United States":** Ibid.

23 **"be patient":** This is from a videotaped conversation between bin Laden and a Saudi supporter; see Bergen, *The Osama bin Laden I Know*, p. 283; "Bin Laden Rejoiced on Sept. 11," ABC News, December 13, 2001.

23 **"Patience! Patience!" . . . sadness for the brothers:** Anthony Summers and Robbyn Swann, *The Eleventh Day: The Full Story of 9/11 and Osama bin Laden* (New York: Ballantine Books, 2011), p. 362.

23 **Bin Laden was confident:** Al-Qaeda military leader Mohammed Atef (known as Abu Hafs al-Masri) told Al Jazeera and *Al-Hayat* journalist Ahmad Zaidan in late 2000 that the kind of attack they expected after the USS *Cole* bombing would be similar to the American attacks on Kosovo and Serbia, U.S. air strikes from bases in Central Asia and maybe Pakistan; see Michael Scheuer, *Osama bin Laden* (New York: Oxford University Press, 2011), p. 229; also see Ahmad Zaidan, *Usama Bin Ladin Without a Mask: Interviews Banned by the Taliban* (Lebanon: World Book Publishing Company, 2003).

NOTES

24   **Morell replied:** Author interview with senior U.S. intelligence official, Washington, DC; also Tenet, *At the Center of the Storm*, p. 254.

24   **Offutt Air Force Base:** "9/11 Commission Report," p. 325.

24   **"We knew it was al-Qaeda":** Author interview with U.S. intelligence official, Washington, DC.

25   **"looked, smelled, and tasted":** Tenet, *At the Center of the Storm*, p. 259.

25   **as many as sixty:** Office of the Inspector General, "Report on CIA Accountability with Respect to the 9/11 Attacks," August 21, 2007, www.cia.gov/library/reports/Executive%20Summary_OIG%20Report.pdf.

25   **relied on only some:** Ambassador Hank Crumpton, "Remarks at CSIS Smart Power Series," Washington, DC, January 14, 2008, csis.org/files/media/csis/press/080114_smart_crumpton.pdf.

25   **on September 17, Bush signed:** "John Rizzo: The Lawyer Who Approved the CIA's Most Controversial Program," PBS *Frontline*, September 6, 2011

25   **"I had never in my experience":** Ibid.

25   **"I want justice":** "Bush: Bin Laden 'Wanted Dead or Alive,'" CNN, September 17, 2001, articles.cnn.com/2001-09-17/us/bush.powell.terrorism_1_bin-qaeda-terrorist-attacks?_s=PM:US.

25   **received a messenger:** Jamal Ismail, interview by the author, Islamabad, Pakistan, March 2005.

26   **decade and a half ... aired on Al Jazeera:** Bergen, *The Osama bin Laden I Know*, pp. xxxiv and 2.

26   **"They have links":** Jamal Ismail interview.

26   **requested, to no avail:** David B. Ottaway and Joe Stephens, "Diplomats Met with Taliban on Bin Laden," *Washington Post*, October 29, 2001, www.infowars.com/saved%20pages/Prior_Knowledge/US_met_taliban.htm.

26   **"I will not hand over a Muslim":** Abu Walid al-Misri, *The History of the Arab Afghans from the Time of Their Arrival in Afghanistan Until Their Departure with the Taliban*, serialized in *Asharq Al-Awsat*, December 8–14, 2004.

26   **"Islam says that when":** Vahid Mojdeh, former Taliban official, interview by author, Kabul, Afghanistan, January 2005.

27   **telling Yusufzai:** Rahimullah Yusufzai, interview by author, Peshawar, Pakistan, September 1998 and June 29, 2003.

27   **Omar asked Yusufzai:** Ibid.

27   **Mullah Omar naïvely believed:** Abdul Salam Zaeef, *My Life with the Taliban* (New York: Columbia University Press, 2010), p. 149.

NOTES

27   **of Muslims everywhere:** John F. Burns, "Afghanistan's Professional Class Flees Rule by Ultra-Strict Clerics," *New York Times,* October 7, 1996.

27   **hundreds of cheering Taliban:** For an account of this event, see Norimitsu Onishi, "A Nation Challenged: A Shrine, a Tale of the Mullah, and Muhammad's Amazing Cloak," *New York Times,* December 19, 2001, www.nytimes.com/2001/12/19/world/a-nation-challenged-a-shrine-a-tale-of-the-mullah-and-muhammad-s-amazing-cloak.html.

28   **"a piece of red-hot coal":** Pamela Constable, "Tales of the Taliban: Part Tragedy, Part Farce," *Washington Post,* February 28, 2004.

28   **two giant Buddhas:** A description can be found in Carlotta Gall, "Afghans Consider Rebuilding Bamiyan Buddhas," *International Herald Tribune,* November 5, 2006, www.nytimes.com/2006/12/05/world/asia/05iht-buddhas.3793036.html.

28   **planned to destroy the Buddhas:** The Taliban also secretly destroyed all the statues in the Kabul Museum, smashing some 2,500 artifacts using sledgehammers. See Peter Bergen, "Taliban-Destroyed Buddhas May Never Be Restored," CNN.com, May 11, 2007, edition.cnn.com/2007/WORLD/asiapcf/05/10/afghan.buddhas/index.html.

28   **told a visiting delegation of Pakistani officials:** Pervez Musharraf, *In the Line of Fire: A Memoir* (New York: Free Press, 2006), p. 215.

29   **helping to wreck the statues:** Incident described during interrogation of al-Qaeda recruit Nizar Trabelsi, who was questioned in French in June 2002. The text of his interrogation was later provided in Italian to prosecutors in Milan investigating one of Trabelsi's associates. Documents acquired and translated by investigative journalist Leo Sisti of *L'Espresso,* author's collection. Alan Cullison, "Inside Al-Qaeda's Hard Drive," *The Atlantic,* September 2004, www.theatlantic.com/magazine/archive/2004/09/inside-al-qaeda-rsquo-s-hard-drive/3428/.

29   **called on bin Laden to leave:** John F. Burns, "Afghan Clerics Urge Bin Laden to Leave; White House Says Unacceptable," *New York Times,* September 20, 2001, www.nytimes.com/2001/09/20/international/20CND-PAK.html?pagewanted=all.

30   **"informed interrogator" approach:** Ali Soufan interview.

30   **The FBI 302s, the official summaries of these interrogations:** Abu Jandal, FD-302, Federal Bureau of Investigation, pp. 59–63 and 74–81. Author's collection.

30   **"dozens and dozens of people":** Ibid.

30   **picked out eight:** Ali Soufan, interview by author, New York, December 17, 2009.

31   **"how deeply resented the Arabs were":** Robert Grenier, interview by the author, Washington, DC, January 19, 2010.

NOTES

31   **"The Americans are coming" . . . "I will go back":** Ibid.

32   **Grenier thought:** Ibid.

32   **shuttled between:** Burke, *The 9/11 Wars*, p. 61.

32   **suffering from psychological problems:** Alan Cullison and Andrew Higgins, "Files Found: A Computer in Kabul Yields a Chilling Array of al-Qaeda Memos" and "Forgotten Computer Reveals Thinking Behind Four Years of al-Qaeda Doings," *Wall Street Journal*, December 31, 2001, both available via LexisNexis. See also Cullison, "Inside al-Qaeda's Hard Drive."

33   **Kandahar meeting with Mullah Mansour:** JFT-GTMO Detainee Assessment for Salim Hamed (Salim Hamdan), ISN US9YM-000149DP, September 4, 2008.

33   **quickly decamped:** JTF-GTMO Detainee Assessment for Bashir Lap, ISN US9MY-010022DP, October 13, 2008.

33   **surprise appearance:** Osama bin Laden, "Statement," October 7, 2001, aired on Al Jazeera.

33   **"As a Muslim":** Cited in Summers and Swan, *The Eleventh Day*, p. 165.

34   **lengthy interview on October 21:** Bruce Lawrence, *Messages to the World: The Statements of Osama bin Laden* (New York: Verso, 2005), p. 106; Osama bin Laden in Wright, *The Looming Tower*, p. 106; transcript of bin Laden's October 2002 interview with Al Jazeera's Tayseer Allouni, translated by CNN, February 5, 2002, archives.cnn.com/2002/WORLD/asiapcf/south/02/05/binladen.transcript/index.html.

34   **wasn't "newsworthy" . . . only post-9/11 television interview:** "Bin Laden's Sole Post–September 11 TV Interview Aired," CNN.com, February 5, 2002, archives.cnn.com/2002/US/01/31/gen.binladen .interview/index.html.

34   **It seems likely:** In early October, Qatar's leader, Sheikh Hamad bin Khalifa al-Thani, met with secretary of state Colin Powell in Washington. According to reports at the time, Powell and other officials expressed their concerns about Al Jazeera's coverage, and Powell had said publicly that Al Jazeera was "irresponsible" for broadcasting bin Laden's tapes. See "Press Institute Criticizes US Pressure on Qatari Al-Jazeera TV Station," Agence France Presse, October 8, 2001; also see "Al-Jazeera Not to Change Coverage of Afghan Events; Rejects U.S. Criticism," *Al-Watan* (BBC Monitoring Middle East), October 12, 2001. Cited in Congressional Research Service report: "The Al-Jazeera News Network: Opportunity or Challenge for U.S. Foreign Policy in the Middle East?" July 23, 2003, www.au.af.mil/au/awc/awcgate/crs/rl31889.pdf. CNN obtained the interview from another commercial broadcast network in the Middle East, which had downloaded it when it was transmitted over an unencrypted transponder from Kabul to Al Jazeera headquarters in Doha, Qatar.

NOTES

35 **"How about the killing of innocent civilians?":** Transcription of bin Laden's interview with Allouni.

35 **economic consequences:** Osama bin Laden in Wright, *The Looming Tower*, p. 112.

35 **he well understood:** "Osama bin Laden Video Excerpts," BBC, December 14, 2001, news.bbc.co.uk/2/low/south_asia/1709425.stm.

36 **natural choice:** Mir had interviewed bin Laden in 1997 and 1998. "The Man Who Interviewed Osama bin Laden . . . 3 Times," *The Independent*, March 9, 2009, www.independent.co.uk/news/media/press/the-man-who-interviewed-osama-bin-laden-3-times-1639968.html.

36 **blindfolded and bundled up:** Hamid Mir interview, May 11, 2002.

36 **fall of Kabul was only four days away:** "The Fall of Kabul," *NewsHour with Jim Lehrer*, November 13, 2001, www.pbs.org/newshour/bb/asia/afghanistan/kabul_11-13.html.

36 **Mir turned the tape recorder back on:** Hamid Mir interview, May 11, 2002, and March 2005; Summers and Swann, *The Eleventh Day*, p. 166.

36 **When Mir asked him:** Hamid Mir interview, May 11, 2002; Hamid Mir, "Osama Claims He Has Nukes: If US Uses N-arms It Will Get Same Response," *Dawn*, November 10, 2001, www.dawn.com/2001/11/10/top1.htm.

36 **"I wish to declare":** Mir, "Osama Claims He Has Nukes."

36 **Mir told Zawahiri:** Hamid Mir interview, May 11, 2002.

37 **two years earlier:** Cullison, "Inside Al-Qaeda's Hard Drive."

37 **summoned to Kabul in early November 2001:** Bootie Cosgrove-Mather, "Osama's Doc Says He Was Healthy," Associated Press, November 27, 2002, www.cbsnews.com/stories/2002/11/27/attack/main531070.shtml. Similarly, Ahmed Zaidan of Al Jazeera television, who interviewed bin Laden for two or three hours eight months before 9/11, says, "I didn't see anything abnormal"; Ahmad Zaidan, interview by author, Islamabad, Pakistan, March 2005. That was also the take of Baker Atyani of the Middle East Broadcasting Corporation, who'd met al-Qaeda's leader five months later. Atyani thought that bin Laden had put on weight and was in "good health"; Bakr Atyani, phone interview by author, Islamabad, Pakistan, August 22, 2005. Abu Jandal, the al-Qaeda leader's chief bodyguard up until 2000, recalled that his boss had a problem with his larynx because of inhaling napalm during the anti-Soviet jihad, which is why he needed to "drink a lot of water" when he spoke for long periods of time; see al-Hammadi, "Bin Laden's Former 'Bodyguard.'" Abdel Bari Atwan, who spent two days with bin Laden in Tora Bora in 1996, recalls, "He was in perfect health. He never complained about how high it was in the mountains, and it was freezing. He had dry mouth most of the time. I noted that he drinks a lot of water and

tea"; Abdel Bari Atwan, interview by author, London, June 2005. Bin Laden did have a variety of ailments, including low blood pressure and a foot wound that he sustained while fighting the Soviets in Afghanistan in the late 1980s, but although all these conditions were sometimes debilitating, none of them was life-threatening; see Bergen, *The Osama bin Laden I Know*, p. 320.

37 **"He was in excellent health":** "Doctor Says Bin Laden Was Healthy," Associated Press, November 28, 2002, articles.latimes.com/2002/nov/28/world/fg-doctor28.

38 **began arriving:** Gary Schroen, who led the CIA team that entered Afghanistan after 9/11, writes that he received word on October 17 that a Special Forces team had arrived in the country's north. Schroen, *First In*, p. 194.

38 **jihad against the Soviets:** The detainee assessment for Ali Hamza Ismail (also known as Ali al-Bahlul), bin Laden's media maven, notes that the last time Ismail saw bin Laden was a month before Ramadan (which started on November 17, 2001), in the company of Jalaluddin Haqqani, at Haqqani's house. See JTF-GTMO Detainee Assessment for Ali Hamza Ismail, ISN US9YM-000039DP, November 15, 2007.

38 **Haqqani was sure:** Aslam Khan, "Interview of Jalaluddin Haqqani," *The News*, October 20, 2001 (location of interview unknown).

38 **invited bin Laden to move into his territory:** JTF-GTMO Detainee Assessment for Awal Gul, ISN US9AF-000782DP, February 15, 2008.

38 **attended a memorial ceremony:** Burke, *The 9/11 Wars*, p. 61.

38 **met with tribal elders:** JTF-GTMO Detainee Assessment for Awal Gul.

38 **winding road to Jalalabad:** Gary Berntsen, interview by author, Washington, DC, October 27, 2009.

38 **A few days later:** Atef was killed sometime between November 14 and 16, 2001. His death, though initially reported to have come in a U.S. air strike, was later confirmed to have been the result of a drone strike. See Steven Morris and Ewen MacAskill, "Collapse of the Taliban: Bin Laden's Deputy Reported Killed: Mullah Omar About to Quit Stronghold of Kandahar," *Guardian*, November 17, 2001. Also GlobalSecurity .org, www.globalsecurity.org/security/profiles/mohammed_atef.htm.

39 **chief executive officer:** Feroz Ali Abbasi, Guantánamo Bay Prison Memoirs, 2002–2004, author's collection.

39 **working around the clock:** Author interview with U.S. intelligence officials, Washington, DC, June 6, 2003.

39 **"shocked us deeply":** Mohammad al-Tariri, "Former Member of Al-Qaeda Tells *Al-Hayat* About Living Through the Events of 9/11 at the Side of Al-Qaeda Leader Osama Bin Laden," *Al-Hayat*, September 20, 2006 (translated from Arabic).

NOTES

39   **made arrangements:** JTF-GTMO Detainee Assessment for Salim Hamed.

CHAPTER 2: TORA BORA

40   **pep talks:** Gary Berntsen interview.

40   **and a contingent of bodyguards:** "Moroccan Security Source Views Danger of Moroccans Released from Guantánamo," *Asharq Al-Awsat*, August 20, 2004. The detainee assessment for Mohammed al-Qahtani at Guantánamo Bay says that Qahtani saw bin Laden in Tora Bora four or five days before Ramadan began on November 17. See also JTF-GTMO detainee assessment for Mohammed al-Qahtani, ISN US9SA-000063DP, October 30, 2008.

40   **several offenses by the Russians:** Mohammad Asif Qazizanda, a mujahideen commander based at Tora Bora, interview by author, Jalalabad, Afghanistan, July 4, 2004.

41   **more than six months to build:** Hutaifa Azzam, interview by author, Amman, Jordan, September 13, 2005.

41   **"I really feel secure":** Abdel Bari Atwan, interview by author, London, June 2005.

41   **took his older sons:** bin Laden, bin Laden, and Sasson, *Growing Up Bin Laden*, p. 73.

41   **subsistence diet:** Ibid., p. 186; also pp. 160–61.

41   **Even honored guests:** Abdel Bari Atwan interview.

41   **During the 1987 Jaji engagement:** For a description of the battle of Jaji and the impact it had on bin Laden and his following, see Bergen, *The Osama bin Laden I Know*, pp. 50–60.

42   **bin Laden had dispatched:** *U.S. v. Khalid Sheikh Mohammed et al.*, Indictment in U.S. District Court for the Southern District of New York (S14) 93 Cr. 180 (KTD), December 14, 2009.

42   **digging trenches and tunnels:** Detainee Yasin Muhammad Salih Mazeeb Basardah told his interrogators that Saudi Sultan al-Uwaydha allegedly went to Tora Bora three weeks before bin Laden arrived, to prepare matters for him; see JTF-GTMO Detainee Assessment for Sultan al-Uwaydha, ISN US9SA-000059DP, August 1, 2007. Another detainee (and Uwaydha's uncle), Abdul Rahman Shalabi, was reportedly also at Tora Bora preparing for bin Laden's arrival, by digging tunnels, setting up security, and moving stockpiled food. See JTF-GTMO Detainee Assessment for Abdul Shalabi, ISN US9SA-000042DP, May 14, 2008.

42   **stream of intelligence reports:** Gary Berntsen interview.

42   **"multiple hits":** Gary Berntsen, e-mail to author, November 24, 2009.

NOTES

42   **fed into an electronic map that overlaid data:** Henry A. Crumpton, "Intelligence and War in Afghanistan, 2001–2002," in *Transforming U.S. Intelligence,* eds. Jessica E. Sims and Burton Gerber (Washington, DC: Georgetown University Press, 2005), p. 172; Henry A. Crumpton, interview by author, Washington, DC, November 2009.

42   **the CIA now predicted:** United States Special Operations Command, "History of United States Special Operations Command," 6th ed., 2008, p. 97, www.socom.mil/SOCOMHome/Documents/history6thedition .pdf.

43   **"grave mistake and taboo":** JTF-GTMO Detainee Assessment for Muhammad al-Qahtani, ISN US9SA-000063DP (S), October 30, 2008.

43   **Bin Laden was convinced:** Faiza Saleh Ambah, "Out of Guantánamo and Bitter Toward Bin Laden," *Washington Post,* March 24, 2008, www.washingtonpost.com/wp-dyn/content/article/2008/03/23/ AR2008032301594.html.

43   **somehow to duplicate:** Peter Bergen, "The Battle for Tora Bora," *New Republic,* December 22, 2009, www.tnr.com/article/the-battle-tora-bora. The battle is reconstructed here based on interviews with two American generals who directed the war in Afghanistan, the U.S. ground commander at Tora Bora, three Afghan ground commanders, and three CIA officials deeply involved in the battle; accounts by eyewitnesses that were subsequently published on jihadist websites; recollections of more than a dozen captured survivors who were later questioned by interrogators or reporters; discussions with a CIA officer who interrogated al-Qaeda members who survived Tora Bora; an official history of the Afghan War by U.S. Special Forces Operations Command; an investigation of the Tora Bora battle by the Senate Foreign Relations Committee; and visits to the battle sites themselves.

43   **thirty square miles:** The Special Operations Command history of the battle says the battle area was ten kilometers by ten kilometers, United States Special Operations Command History, p. 95.

43   **skirmishes:** See Burke, *The 9/11 Wars,* p. 64.

43   **intense U.S. bombing:** Tenet, *At the Center of the Storm,* p. 226.

43   **snow was falling steadily:** Weather observations from a personal log kept by a Delta operator on the ground at Tora Bora, in e-mail to author, August 6, 2009.

44   **seemed preoccupied mostly:** Andrew Selsky, "Yemeni Says Bin Laden Was at Tora Bora," Associated Press, September 7, 2007, www .usatoday.com/news/topstories/2007-09-07-3032626105_x.htm.

44   **traveled into Tora Bora:** JTF-GTMO Detainee Assessment for Riyad Atiq Ali Abdu al-Haj, ISN US9YM-000256DP, March 23, 2008.

NOTES

44 **borrowed $7,000:** JTF-GTMO Detainee Assessment for Harun al-Afghani, ISN US9AF-003148DP, August 2, 2007.

44 **growing certainty:** Paul Wolfowitz, Defense Department Briefing, December 10, 2001.

44 **"We were hot":** Michael DeLong and Noah Lukeman, *A General Speaks Out: The Truth About the Wars in Afghanistan and Iraq* (Osceola: Zenith Press, 2004) p. 57.

44 **"was equipped to go to ground there":** "Transcript of Cheney interview," ABC News, November 29, 2001, abcnews.go.com/Primetime/story?id=132168&page=1.

44 **about seventy:** Dalton Fury, *Kill Bin Laden: A Delta Force Commander's Account of the Hunt for the World's Most Wanted Man* (New York: St. Martin's Press, 2008), p. xx; and e-mail from Fury to author, December 8, 2009.

45 **least expect them:** Dalton Fury, e-mail to author, January 15, 2011.

45 **turned down:** Fury, *Kill Bin Laden*, p. 76.

45 **somewhat effective mortar barrages:** Author interview with Tora Bora battle participant, Washington, DC, 2009.

45 **Arab and Pakistani militants:** Mohammed Zahir, interview by author, Jalalabad, Afghanistan, summer 2003.

45 **"They fought very hard":** Muhammad Musa, interview by author, Jalalabad, Afghanistan, June 2003.

45 **buoyed by the fact that:** Robert Lacey, *Inside the Kingdom: Kings, Clerics, Modernists, Terrorists, and the Struggle for Saudi Arabia* (New York: Viking Press, 2009), p. 322. Lacey explains how Saudis cherish the story of the Battle of Badr.

45 **bombing began, and continued around the clock:** Osama bin Laden, "Message to Our Brothers in Iraq," Al Jazeera, February 11, 2003 (translated by ABC News).

45 **seven hundred thousand pounds of American bombs:** Tenet, *At the Center of the Storm*, p. 226.

46 **wrote out nineteen death certificates:** Ayman al-Zawahiri, "Days with the Imam #1," obtained via Jihadology.net; "Osama Bin Laden Was Tender and Kind, Zawahiri Says," BBC, November 15, 2011, www.bbc.co.uk/news/mobile/world-us-canada-15750813.

46 **observe the Ramadan breaking of the fast:** United States Special Operations Command History, p. 97; also see Fury, *Kill Bin Laden*, p. 239.

46 **the evening of December 3 . . . eight hundred elite:** Gary Berntsen and Ralph Pezzullo, *Jawbreaker: The Attack on Bin Laden and al-Qaeda: A Personal Account by the CIA's Key Field Commander* (New York: Crown, 2005), p. 299; Henry A. Crumpton interview.

NOTES

46 **Berntsen's boss:** Henry A. Crumpton interview.

46 **"100 percent" ... Franks pushed back:** Ibid.; also General Tommy Franks, e-mail to author, November 24, 2009.

46 **Rumsfeld didn't ask Franks:** Donald Rumsfeld, *Known and Unknown: A Memoir* (New York: Penguin Group, 2011), pp. 402–3.

46 **Franks also believed:** "Campaign Against Terror," PBS *Frontline*, June 12, 2002, www.pbs.org/wgbh/pages/frontline/shows/campaign/interviews/franks.html.

46 **Crumpton had repeatedly warned:** Henry A. Crumpton interview.

46 **Bush even asked Crumpton directly:** Tenet, *At the Center of the Storm*, p. 227.

47 **suggested dropping GATOR antipersonnel mines:** Fury, *Kill Bin Laden*, p. 78.

47 **directed laser beams:** Ibid., p. 76.

47 **the latest intelligence:** United States Special Operations Command History, p. 98.

47 **"awakened to the sound":** The statement was posted to Al Neda, al-Qaeda's website at the time, on September 11, 2002.

47 **intercept from Tora Bora:** Fury, *Kill Bin Laden*, p. 173.

47 **Afghan soldiers said:** United States Special Operations Command History, p. 99.

47 **Wolfowitz ... told reporters:** Wolfowitz, Defense Department Briefing, December 10, 2001.

47 **He told his men he was leaving them:** See JTF-GTMO Detainee Assessment for Faruq Ahmed, ISN US9YM-000032DP, February 18, 2008.

48 **suggested a cease-fire:** Committee on Foreign Relations, U.S. Senate, "Tora Bora Revisited: How We Failed to Get Bin Laden and Why It Matters Today," November 30, 2009, p. 11.

48 **bin Laden addressing his followers:** Dalton Fury, e-mail to author, December 8, 2009.

48 **kept a careful log:** Dalton Fury, phone interview by author, November 23, 2009.

49 **would be treated like antigens:** DeLong and Lukeman, *A General Speaks Out,* p. 56.

49 **made the case:** Milton Bearden, "Afghanistan: Graveyard of Empires," *Foreign Affairs* (November/December 2001), www.foreignaffairs.com/articles/57411/milton-bearden/afghanistan-graveyard-of-empires.

49 **At this stage:** At that time, three soldiers had been killed, while on November 19, 2001, four journalists were killed. On U.S. ca-

NOTES

sualties, see www.icasualties.org/OEF/Fatalities.aspx; on journalist deaths, see Claire Cozens, "Swedish TV Cameraman Killed in Afghanistan," *Guardian*, November 27, 2001, www.guardian.co.uk/media/2001/nov/27/terrorismandthemedia.afghanistan.

49 **not a single American had died in combat:** Patrick T. Reardon, "As Bodies Pile Up, Support Can Slip," *Chicago Tribune*, March 30, 2003, www.globalsecurity.org/org/news/2003/030330-public-opinion01.htm.

49 **"look for options in Iraq":** Tommy Franks, *American Soldier* (New York: HarperCollins, 2004), p. 315.

49 **"What the fuck are they talking about?":** Bob Woodward, *Plan of Attack* (New York: Simon and Schuster, 2004), p. 8.

49 **an eight-hundred-page document:** Ibid.

49 **Franks then rebriefed:** Franks, *American Soldier*, pp. 329–42.

49 **explained why he did not send more U.S. soldiers:** Tommy Franks, e-mail to author, November 24, 2009.

50 **"There was no question":** Dell Dailey, interview by author, Washington, DC, October 2011.

50 **"No fucking way":** Ibid.

51 **traveled up to Bagram Air Base:** Ibid.

51 **Susan Glasser . . . recalled:** Susan Glasser, e-mail to author, December 9, 2008.

51 **about two thousand American troops:** Drew Brown, "U.S. Lost Its Best Chance to Decimate al-Qaida in Tora Bora," Knight-Ridder Washington Bureau, October 14, 2002; U.S. Special Operations Command History, p. 98, which describes a reinforced company of the Tenth Mountain being at Bagram and Mazar-e-Sharif. The Senate Foreign Relations Committee report, on page 17, explains that it was the Fifteenth and Twenty-sixth Marine Expeditionary Units; foreign.senate.gov/imo/media/doc/Tora_Bora_Report.pdf.

51 **less than a week:** Peter Krause, "The Last Good Chance: A Reassessment of U.S. Operations at Tora Bora," *Security Studies* 17, no. 4 (October 2008): 657; Stanley McChrystal interview.

51 **logistically difficult:** Donald P. Wright, James R. Bird, Steven E. Clay, Peter W. Connors, Lieutenant Colonel Scott C. Farquhar, Lynn Chandler Garcia, and Dennis Van Wey, *A Different Kind of War: The United States Army in Operation Enduring Freedom (OEF), October 2001– September 2005* (Fort Leavenworth, KS: Combat Studies Institute Press, 2005), p. 128.

51 **President Bush was never asked:** Condoleezza Rice, *No Higher Honor: A Memoir of My Time in Washington* (New York: Crown Pub-

292

NOTES

lishers, 2011), p. 119. In former vice president Dick Cheney's lengthy autobiography, *In My Time: A Personal and Political Memoir* (New York: Simon and Schuster, 2011), there is no discussion at all of Tora Bora.

52 **Bush confirms:** Bush, *Decision Points*, p. 202.

52 **only some three hundred:** Henry A. Crumpton, speech at CSIS Smart Power Series, Washington, DC, January 14, 2008, csis.org/files/media/csis/press/080114_smart_crumpton.pdf.

52 **a group of more than two dozen:** This group of bodyguards came to be known as the "dirty thirty." See, for instance, JTF-GTMO Detainee Assessment for Muazhamza al-Alawi, ISN US9YM-000028DP, March 14, 2008.

52 **one of bin Laden's sons:** "Moroccan Security Source Views Danger of Moroccans Released from Guantánamo," *Asharq Al-Awsat*, August 20, 2004.

52 **Bin Laden went to say good-bye:** "Al-Qaida Head Recalls 'Human Side' of Bin Laden," Associated Press, November 15, 2011, www.cbsnews.com/8301-501713_162-57325424/al-qaida-head-recalls-human-side-of-bin-laden/.

52 **Accompanied by some of his guards:** "Moroccan Security Source Views Danger of Moroccans Released from Guantánamo."

52 **a final testament:** Osama bin Laden, "The Will of One Seeking the Support of Allah Almighty, Usama Bin Laden," *Al-Majallah* (a Saudi magazine), December 14, 2001, www.fas.org/irp/world/para/ubl-fbis.pdf, p. 222.

53 **to rest:** JTF-GTMO Detainee Assessment for Awal Gul, ISN US9AF-000782DP, February 15, 2008.

53 **went by horse:** Ibid.

53 **bin Laden released a video:** Osama bin Laden videotape, Al Jazeera, December 27, 2001.

53 **bemoaning the fate:** Muhammad al-Shafey, "A Site Close to al-Qaeda Posts a Poem by bin Laden in Which He Responds to His Son Hamzah," *Asharq Al-Awsat*, June 16, 2002.

53 **Bush was incensed:** Author interview with U.S. intelligence official.

53 **"wild claim":** "Candidates Bid for Voter Turnout," CNN.com, October 26, 2004, articles.cnn.com/2004-10-25/politics/election.main_1_tora-bora-bin-afghan-forces?_s=PM:ALLPOLITICS.

53 **"absolute garbage":** "Richard B. Cheney Delivers Remarks at a Town Hall Meeting," *CQ Transcriptions*, October 19, 2004.

NOTES

CHAPTER 3: AL-QAEDA IN THE WILDERNESS

55 **The group's bylaws:** Translated by West Point's Combating Terrorism Center, April 18, 2002, AFGP-2002-600849, www.ctc.usma.edu/wp-content/uploads/2010/08/AFGP-2002-600849-Trans.pdf.

56 **"I was very upset":** Sebastian Rotella, "Al Qaeda Crosses the Ts in Terrorist," *Los Angeles Times*, April 16, 2008, articles.latimes.com/2008/apr/16/world/fg-qaedaculture16.

56 **splurged on an expensive fax machine:** Cullison, "Inside Al-Qaeda's Hard Drive."

56 **a letter to Khalid Sheikh Mohammed:** Letter from Abd al-Halim Adl to "Mukhtar," translation from Combating Terrorism Center at West Point, Harmony Program, www.ctc.usma.edu/wp-content/uploads/2010/08/Al-Adl-Letter_Translation.pdf.

56 **Abu Musab al-Suri:** Abu Musab al-Suri's real name is Mustafa Setmariam Nasar.

57 **"We are passing through":** Jim Lacey, *A Terrorist's Call to Global Jihad: Deciphering Abu Musab Al-Suri's Islamic Jihad Manifesto* (Annapolis, MD: Naval Institute Press, 2008), pp. 29 and 40.

57 **Suri wrote that:** Ibid., p. 100.

57 **"America destroyed":** Abu Musab al-Suri, "The Call to Global Islamic Resistance," published on jihadist websites, 2004.

58 **"Targeting America":** "Document Contains Al-Qaeda Review of the 9/11 Attacks on the United States One Year Later," undated (circa September 2002), AQ-SHPD-D-001-285, The Conflict Records Research Center, National Defense University, www.ndu.edu/inss/docUploaded/AQ-SHPD-D-001-285.pdf.

58 **"The giant American media":** Ibid.

58 **"Our ultimate objective":** Fu'ad Husayn, "Al-Zarqawi: The Second al-Qa'ida Generation," Al-Quds Al-Arabi, May 21–22, 2005. Husayn is a Jordanian journalist who received information from three people close to al-Zarqawi, including Saif al-Adel.

59 **Greystone:** "Dana Priest: Top Secret America 'Is Here to Stay,'" PBS *Frontline*, September 6, 2011, www.pbs.org/wgbh/pages/frontline/iraq-war-on-terror/topsecretamerica/dana-priest-top-secret-america-is-here-to-stay/.

59 **dozens of whom:** Peter Bergen and Katherine Tiedemann, "Disappearing Act: Rendition by the Numbers," *Mother Jones*, March 3, 2008, motherjones.com/politics/2008/03/disappearing-act-rendition-numbers.

59 **"The consensus of the experts":** "John Rizzo: The Lawyer Who Approved CIA's Most Controversial Programs," PBS *Frontline*, September 6,

NOTES

2011, www.pbs.org/wgbh/pages/frontline/iraq-war-on-terror/topsecret
america/john-rizzo-the-lawyer-who-approved-cias-most-controversial-
programs/.

59 **when the CIA discovered:** Douglas A. Frantz, "Nuclear Secrets:
Pakistan Frees 2 Scientists Linked to Bin Laden Network," *New York
Times,* December 17, 2001, www.nytimes.com/2001/12/17/world/
nation-challenged-nuclear-secrets-pakistan-frees-2-scientists-linked-
bin-laden.html.

59 **six weeks after 9/11:** Richard Myers, *Eyes on the Horizon: Serving on the
Front Lines of National Security* (New York: Threshold Editions, 2009),
p. 193.

60 **drawer of his desk:** Dave Montgomery, "For Bush, Getting Bin Laden
Was 'Unfinished Business,'" *McClatchy Newspapers,* May 2, 2011, www
.mcclatchydc.com/2011/05/02/113562/for-bush-getting-bin-laden-was
.html.

60 **in the form of a pyramid:** Ari Fleischer interview.

60 **call on his cell:** Ahmed Zaidan, interview by author, Islamabad, Pakistan, July 15, 2011.

61 **On the tape:** "Bin Laden's Message," Al Jazeera, November 12,
2002, translated by BBC Monitoring, news.bbc.co.uk/2/hi/middle_
east/2455845.stm.

61 **Chitral . . . length of time it seemed to take:** Author interview with
U.S. military intelligence official, 2006.

62 **living in Karachi:** JTF-GTMO Detainee Assessment for Abdul Rabbani Abu Rahman, ISN US9PK-001460DP, June 9, 2008.

62 **Adel authorized:** Author interviews with senior Saudi counterterrorism
officials, 2009.

62 **laid out in detail:** This interview formed the basis for Yosri Fouda and
Nick Fielding, *Masterminds of Terror: The Truth Behind the Most Devastating Terrorist Attack the World Has Ever Seen* (New York: Arcade Publishing, 2003).

62 **twenty packages of passports:** See JTF-GTMO Detainee Assessment
for Abdul Rabbani Abu Rahman.

62 **routinely handling:** See JTF-GTMO Detainee Assessment for Ammar
al-Baluchi, ISN USSPK 010018D, December 8, 2006.

63 **KSM planned a second wave:** JTF-GTMO Detainee Assessment for
Khalid Shaykh Muhammad, ISN US9KU-010024DP, December 8,
2006.

63 **"I am with KSM":** Scott Shane, "Inside a 9/11 Mastermind's Interrogation," *New York Times,* June 22, 2008, www.nytimes.com/2008/06/22/
washington/22ksm.html.

NOTES

63 **addressed to family members in Iran:** Asad Munir, interview by author, Islamabad, Pakistan, July 19, 2011.

63 **20-gigabyte hard drive:** JTF-GTMO Detainee Assessment for Ibrahim Sulayman Muhammad Arbaysh, ISN US9SA-000192D, November 30, 2005.

64 **passport photos of operatives:** U.S. Department of Defense, Verbatim Transcript of Combatant Status Review Trial, Khalid Sheikh Mohammed, March 10, 2007, www.defenselink.mil/news/transcript_ISN10024.pdf.

64 **called for attacks against Western countries:** "Robertson: Purported Bin Laden Tapes a 'Two Pronged Attack,'" CNN.com, October 20, 2003, www.cnn.com/2003/WORLD/meast/10/18/otsc.robertson/.

64 **British consulate in Turkey:** "Istanbul Rocked by Double Bombing," BBC News, November 20, 2003, news.bbc.co.uk/2/hi/europe/3222608.stm.

64 **on their way to work in Madrid:** "Madrid Train Attacks," BBC News, news.bbc.co.uk/2/shared/spl/hi/guides/457000/457031/html/.

64 **"If that were true":** Gilles Kepel, Jean-Pierre Milelli, and Pascale Ghazaleh, trans., *Al Qaeda in Its Own Words* (Boston: President and Fellows of Harvard College, 2008), pp. 71 and 75.

64 **called for attacks on Saudi oil facilities:** Craig Whitlock and Susan Glasser, "On Tape, Bin Laden Tries New Approach," *Washington Post,* December 17, 2004, www.washingtonpost.com/wp-dyn/articles/A3927-2004Dec16.html.

64 **rash of attacks:** Joel Roberts, "Al Qaeda Threatens More Oil Attacks," CBS News, February 25, 2006, www.cbsnews.com/stories/2006/02/27/world/main1346541_page2.shtml.

64 **few al-Qaeda operatives threw away:** Interview with General Michael Hayden by Tresha Mabile for *National Geographic's Last Days of Osama bin Laden,* September 6, 2011.

64 **newly emerging geolocation technologies:** Robert Dannenberg, interview by author, New York, December 17, 2009.

64 **Swiss cell phone SIM cards:** Don Van Natta Jr. and Desmond Butler, "How Tiny Swiss Cellphone Chips Helped Track Global Terror Web," *New York Times,* March 4, 2004, www.nytimes.com/2004/03/04/world/how-tiny-swiss-cellphone-chips-helped-track-global-terror-web.html?pagewanted=all&src=pm.

65 **Silicon Valley outfit:** Ashlee Vance and Brad Stone, "Palantir, the War on Terror's Secret Weapon," *Bloomberg BusinessWeek,* November 22, 2011, www.businessweek.com/magazine/palantir-the-vanguard-of-cyberterror-security-11222011.html.

65 **"targeter"**: Joby Warrick, *The Triple Agent: The al-Qaeda Mole Who Infiltrated the CIA* (New York: Doubleday, 2011), pp. 106 and 68.

65 **"digital exhaust"**: Phil Mudd, interview by author, Washington, DC, June 2, 2011.

65 **mushroomed from 340 to 1,500**: Ronald Kessler, *The CIA at War: Inside the Secret Campaign Against Terror* (New York: St. Martin's Press, 2003), p. 263.

65 **two serious assassination attempts**: Salman Masood, "Pakistani Leader Escapes Attempt at Assassination," *New York Times*, December 26, 2003, www.nytimes.com/2003/12/26/world/pakistani-leader-escapes-attempt-at-assassination.html.

65 **"We had so much trust"**: Asad Munir interview.

66 **handed over 369 suspected militants**: Pervez Musharraf, *In the Line of Fire: A Memoir* (New York: Free Press, 2008), p. 237.

CHAPTER 4: THE RESURGENCE OF AL-QAEDA

67 **Omar Khyam:** For more on Khyam's radicalization in Britain and the 2004 bomb plot, see Elaine Sciolino and Stephen Grey, "British Terror Trial Centers on Alleged Homegrown Plot," *International Herald Tribune*, November 26, 2006, www.nytimes.com/2006/11/26/world/europe/26iht-web.1026crevice.3665748.html?pagewanted=1.

67 **"had enough people"**: Mitchell Silber, *The Al Qaeda Factor: Plots Against the West* (Philadelphia: University of Pennsylvania Press, 2012), p. 96.

68 **inert material:** For a description of the "Operation Crevice" arrests, as the plot was dubbed by UK authorities, see ibid., pp. 83–107.

68 **enjoying his honeymoon:** Jane Perlez, "U.S. Seeks Closing of Visa Loophole for Britons," *New York Times*, May 2, 2007, www.nytimes.com/2007/05/02/world/europe/02britain.html?pagewanted=all.

68 **three-month visit to Pakistan:** "Report into the London Terrorist Attacks on July 7, 2005," Intelligence and Security Committee, May 2006, www.cabinetoffice.gov.uk/sites/default/files/resources/isc_7july_report.pdf, pp. 12 and 15.

68 **tasked him with launching an attack:** Mitchell D. Silber and Arvin Bhatt, "Radicalization in the West: The Homegrown Threat," New York Police Department, 2007, www.nypdshield.org/public/.../NYPD_Report-Radicalization_in_the_West.pdf, pp. 48–49.

68 **"today's heroes":** "London Bomber: Text in Full," BBC, September 1, 2005, news.bbc.co.uk/2/hi/uk_news/4206800.stm.

68 **Zawahiri himself then made an appearance:** "U.S., UK Investigate 'Bomber Tape,' " CNN.com, September 2, 2005, articles.cnn.com/2005-09-02/world/london.claim_1_al-jazeera-london-attacks-qaeda?_s=PM:WORLD.

NOTES

69   **The strike killed only local villagers:** Carlotta Gall et al., "Airstrike by US Draws Protests from Pakistanis," *New York Times*, January 15, 2006, www.nytimes.com/2006/01/15/international/asia/15pakistan .html?pagewanted=all.

69   **disparaging comments:** Hassan Fattah, "Qaeda Deputy Taunts Bush for 'Failure' in Airstrike," *New York Times*, January 31, 2006.

69   **"Sheikh Osama warned":** "Suicide Videos: What They Said," BBC, April 4, 2008, news.bbc.co.uk/2/hi/uk_news/7330367.stm.

70   **"would have rivaled 9/11":** Richard Greenberg, Paul Cruickshank, and Chris Hansen, "Inside the Terror Plot That 'Rivaled 9/11,'" *Dateline NBC*, September 14, 2009, www.msnbc.msn.com/id/26726987# .Tw9Q2V1AIj8.

70   **called for attacks on the Pakistani state:** "Bin Laden Tape Encourages Pakistanis to Rebel," Associated Press, September 20, 2007, www .usatoday.com/news/world/2007-09-20-al-qaeda-video_N.htm.

70   **more than fifty suicide attacks:** "Bomb Hits Pakistan Danish Embassy," BBC, June 2, 2008, news.bbc.co.uk/2/hi/south_asia/7430721 .stm.

70   **Saudi government surveyed:** Author discussions with Saudi officials, Riyadh, Saudi Arabia, 2009.

70   **secret PowerPoint briefing:** Evan Thomas, "Into Thin Air," *Newsweek*, September 3, 2007, www.thedailybeast.com/newsweek/2007/09/02/ into-thin-air.html.

70   **"Is that all there are?":** Ibid.

70   **"excellent idea":** "CIA Chief Has 'Excellent Idea' Where Bin Laden Is," CNN.com, June 22, 2005, articles.cnn.com/2005-06-20/us/goss .bin.laden_1_bin-ayman-sense-of-international-obligation?_s=PM:US.

70   **"A great deal of the resources":** Art Keller, interview by author, Albuquerque, New Mexico, February 13, 2007.

71   **"big surge":** Robert Grenier, interview by author, Washington, DC, February 18, 2009.

71   **"they were just all Iraq all the time":** David Kilcullen, interview by author, New York, November 20, 2009.

71   **"I couldn't go out myself":** Craig Whitlock, "In Hunt for bin Laden, a New Approach," *Washington Post*, September, 10 2008, www .washingtonpost.com/wp-dyn/content/article/2008/09/09/AR 2008090903404_3.html?nav=emailpage&sid=ST2008090903480.

71   **"We are zero for '07":** Warrick, *The Triple Agent*, p. 13.

71   **small, "compartmented":** Michael Leiter, interview by author, Washington, DC, August 29, 2011.

NOTES

72   **stopped seeking Pakistani officials' concurrence:** Author interview with Bush administration official, Washington, DC, 2009.

72   **from many hours to forty-five minutes:** Ibid.

72   **Hellfire missiles or JDAM . . . bombs:** "Reaper: A New Way to Wage War," *Time*, June 1, 2009, www.time.com/time/magazine/pdf/20090601drone.pdf.

72   **killed Abu Khabab al-Masri:** "Al-Qaeda Chemical Expert 'Killed,'" BBC, July 28, 2008, news.bbc.co.uk/2/hi/south_asia/7529419.stm.

72   **a fivefold increase:** See Katherine Tiedemann and Peter Bergen, "The Year of the Drone," *New America Foundation*, February 24, 2010, counterterrorism.newamerica.net/sites/newamerica.net/files/policydocs/bergentiedemann2.pdf.

72   **killed in the drone strikes:** See "Guard: Al Qaeda Chief in Pakistan Killed," CNN.com, September 9, 2011, edition.cnn.com/2008/WORLD/asiapcf/09/09/pakistan.alqaeda.killed/index.html; Pir Zubair Shah, "U.S Strike Is Said to Kill Qaeda Figure in Pakistan," *New York Times*, October 17, 2008, www.nytimes.com/2008/10/18/world/asia/18pstan.html; Ismail Khan and Jane Perlez, "Airstrike Kills Qaeda-Linked Militant in Pakistan," *New York Times*, November 22, 2008, www.nytimes.com/2008/11/23/world/asia/23rauf.html; Eric Schmitt, "2 Qaeda Leaders Killed in U.S. Strike in Pakistan," *New York Times*, January 8, 2009, www.nytimes.com/2009/01/09/world/asia/09pstan.html.

73   **"The whole time along":** Ari Fleischer interview.

73   **ground assaults in the tribal regions:** Eric Schmitt and Mark Mazzetti, "Bush Said to Give Orders Allowing Raids in Pakistan," *New York Times*, September 10, 2008, www.nytimes.com/2008/09/11/washington/11policy.html?pagewanted=all.

73   **attack a compound . . . housing militants:** Pir Zubair Shah, Eric Schmitt, and Jane Perlez, "American Forces Attack Militants on Pakistani Soil," *New York Times*, September 4, 2008, www.nytimes.com/2008/09/04/world/asia/04attack.html?_r=1&oref=slogin.

73   **"territorial integrity":** Stephen Graham, "Pakistan Army Chief Criticizes U.S. Raid," Associated Press, September 10, 2008, www.breitbart.com/article.php?id=D9346IB00&show_article=1.

CHAPTER 5: A WORKING THEORY OF THE CASE

74   **engraved on a wall:** Author observation.

75   **added to the honor roll:** Author observation.

75   **long oversaw:** The CIA's Alec Station was initially set up in December 1995 to keep track of bin Laden. It was disbanded in 2005. See Warrick, *The Triple Agent*, p. 94.

NOTES

75   **disappeared at the Battle of Tora Bora:** Accounts from two Guantá-
      namo Bay detainees indicate that, after the battle, bin Laden and his
      deputy, Ayman al-Zawahiri, escaped toward Jalalabad, where they
      stayed with Awal Gul. Gul died at Guantánamo in February 2011.
      See JTF-GTMO Detainee Assessment for Awal Gul, ISN US9AF-
      000782DP, February 15, 2008.

75   **"Elvis sightings":** Michael Scheuer, interview by author, Washington,
      DC, October 1, 2011.

75   **principal author of the highly classified President's Daily Brief:**
      Peter Bergen, *The Longest War: The Enduring Conflict Between America
      and al-Qaeda* (New York: Free Press, 2011), p. 48.

76   **identified as its author:** Ibid.

76   **Sude had the reputation:** David Low interview.

76   **"He was so weird looking":** Barbara Sude, interview by author, Wash-
      ington, DC, October 20, 2011.

76   **kill bin Laden or to capture him:** Ibid.

77   **"We wanted to make sure":** Robert Dannenberg interview.

77   **"They seem to have":** Michael Scheuer interview.

77   **critical to the spring 2002 arrest:** Warrick, *The Triple Agent*, p. 26.

78   **"If she bites your ankle":** Michael Scheuer interview.

78   **first strategic warning:** U.S. Department of State, Bureau of Intelli-
      gence and Research (INR), "The Wandering Mujahidin: Armed and
      Dangerous," August 21–22, 1993.

78   **a prescient analysis:** U.S. Department of State, Bureau of Intelligence
      and Research (INR), "Terrorism? Usama bin Ladin: Who's Chasing
      Whom?" July 18, 1996.

78   **balancing the demands:** Cindy Storer, interview by author, Washing-
      ton, DC, September 13, 2011.

78   **"She is really fast":** David Low, interview by author, Washington, DC,
      August 20, 2011.

79   **"You guys are crazy":** Roy Gutman, *How We Missed the Story: Osama
      bin Laden, the Taliban, and the Hijacking of Afghanistan* (Washington,
      DC: United States Institute of Peace Press, 2008), p. 170.

79   **Clarke says three times:** Richard Clarke, "The Dark Side," PBS *Front-
      line,* January 23, 2006, http://www.pbs.org/wgbh/pages/frontline/
      darkside/interviews/clarke.html

79   **as many as ten opportunities:** "CIA Insider Says Osama Hunt
      Flawed," CBS News, September 15, 2004, http://www.cbsnews.com/
      stories/2004/08/10/terror/main635038.shtml.

79   **the best chance to capture or kill:** "9/11 Commission Report," op. cit.,
      p. 137.

NOTES

80   **because of the concerns about the Emiratis:** John Diamond, *The CIA and the Culture of Failure: U.S. Intelligence from the End of the Cold War to the Invasion of Iraq* (Stanford, CA: Stanford University Press, 2008), pp. 316–318.

80   **In 1997, when I was a producer:** Author observations, near Jalalabad, Afghanistan, March 1997.

81   **the scanner wasn't working:** Ali Soufan, *The Black Banners: The Inside Story of 9/11 and the War Against al-Qaeda* (New York: W. W. Norton & Company, 2011), p. 99.

81   **"working theory of the case":** Author interviews with U.S. intelligence officials involved in the hunt for bin Laden.

81   **too dangerous:** Ibid.

81   **Bin Laden had known the patriarch:** Journalist and bin Laden chronicler Steve Coll recounts how Haqqani organized Arab volunteers for the anti-Soviet jihad in the 1980s, and operated in many of the same areas as bin Laden. See Steve Coll, *Ghost Wars: The Secret History of the CIA, Afghanistan, and bin Laden, from the Soviet Invasion to September 10, 2001* (New York: Penguin, 2004), p. 157.

81   **less and less likely:** Author interviews with U.S. officials involved in the hunt for bin Laden.

82   **welcomed back to Afghanistan:** When bin Laden arrived in Jalalabad (then controlled by Haji Qadir, a member of a Khalis faction) in 1996 from Sudan, he was quickly escorted to meet with Khalis himself. See Bergen, *The Osama bin Laden I Know*, pp. 158–59.

82   **believed by Pakistani intelligence:** Author interviews with U.S. counterterrorism officials.

82   **"Message to the American People":** "Bin Laden: 'Your Security Is in Your Own Hands,'" CNN.com, October 29, 2004, articles.cnn.com/2004-10-29/world/bin.laden.transcript_1_lebanon-george-w-bush-arab?_s=PM:WORLD.

82   **"I can still see the picture of bin Laden":** Frances Townsend, interview by author.

83   **"When there were videos":** Michael Scheuer interview.

83   **If plants were visible:** Author interview with senior counterterrorism official, Washington, DC, December 2011.

84   **a sequence in *Fahrenheit 9/11*:** "Al Jazeera, "Full Transcript of bin Laden's Speech," October 29, 2004, english.aljazeera.net/archive/2004/11/200849163336457223.html.

84   **recommended the works of Noam Chomsky:** SITE Group translation, September 11, 2007, counterterrorismblog.org/site-resources/images/SITE-OBL-transcript.pdf.

NOTES

84   **"We didn't necessarily think":** Barbara Sude interview.

84   **bragged to his girlfriend's father:** Neal Bascomb, *Hunting Eichmann: How a Band of Survivors and a Young Spy Agency Chased Down the World's Most Notorious Nazi* (Boston: Houghton Mifflin Harcourt, 2009), pp. 86–87.

84   **the operation to find Pablo Escobar:** The definitive account of the hunt for Pablo Escobar is in Mark Bowden, *Killing Pablo: The Hunt for the World's Greatest Outlaw* (New York: Atlantic Monthly Press, 2001).

85   **"You can throw all your phones away":** General Michael Hayden, interview for *Last Days of Osama bin Laden,* National Geographic Channel, aired November 9, 2011.

85   **Saudi media advisor:** Khaled al-Fawwaz, interview by author, London, April 1, 1997.

86   **assassination of Dzhokhar Dudayev:** Glenn Kessler, "File the Bin Laden Phone Leak Under 'Urban Myths,'" *Washington Post,* December 22, 2005, www.washingtonpost.com/wp-dyn/content/article/2005/12/21/AR2005122101994_pf.html.

86   **rookie cop:** Henry Schuster and Charles Stone, *Hunting Eric Rudolph: An Insider's Account of the Five-Year Search for the Olympic Bombing Suspect* (New York: Berkley Books, 2005), pp. 277–79.

87   **on a flight back home to Pakistan:** Tim Weiner, "U.S. Seizes Lone Suspect in Killing of 2 C.I.A. Officers," *New York Times,* June 18, 1997, www.nytimes.com/1997/06/18/world/us-seizes-the-lone-suspect-in-killing-of-2-cia-officers.html?ref=miramalkansi.

87   **habitually dressed:** Brad Garrett, interview by author, Washington, DC, November 2011.

87   **chasing the elusive Kansi:** Ibid.

88   **You can't trust the Pakistanis:** Ibid.

88   **sizable cash reward:** Ibid.

88   **no signals intelligence:** Peter Bergen, *Holy War, Inc.: Inside the Secret World of Osama bin Laden* (New York: Simon and Schuster, 2001), p. 4.

88   **"magic detainee":** Author interviews with U.S. counterterrorism officials involved in the hunt for bin Laden.

89   **"midlevel managers":** Ibid.

89   **"It was a reflection":** Philip Mudd, interview by author, Washington, DC, June 2, 2011.

89   **Mudd authored an influential memo:** Author interview with senior intelligence official, Washington, DC, November 2011.

90   **"If you sat around the table":** Philip Mudd interview.

90   **four "pillars":** Author interviews with U.S. counterterrorism officials involved in the hunt for bin Laden.

NOTES

90   **problem with this approach:** Author interview with senior U.S. intelligence official, Washington, DC, November 2011.

91   **"solid conclusions":** Ibid.

91   **increasingly easy for the CIA to dismiss:** Author interviews with senior U.S. counterterrorism officials.

91   **"was not making any new friends":** Ibid.

91   **"too big a footprint":** Ibid.

92   **might well be living with him:** Ibid.

92   **never developed any:** Author interview with senior U.S. counterterrorism official, Washington, DC, November 2011.

92   **safe houses in all the major cities:** bin Laden, bin Laden, and Sasson, *Growing Up bin Laden,* pp. 238–39.

92   **"probably in the outskirts of Islamabad":** Author interview with National Security Council official, Washington, DC, 2011.

93   **"We always hoped for a person":** Author interviews with counterterrorism officials involved in the hunt for bin Laden.

93   **highly compartmented . . . just not feasible:** Author interviews with U.S. intelligence officials involved in the hunt for bin Laden.

93   **"It was much easier":** Robert Dannenberg interview.

94   **created a composite:** Ibid.

94   **"never a sense":** Ibid.

CHAPTER 6: CLOSING IN ON THE COURIER

95   **believed that the sun revolved around the Earth:** Adam Zagorin and Michael Duffy, "Inside the Interrogation of Detainee 063," *Time,* June 20, 2005, www.time.com/time/magazine/article/0,9171,1071284-1,00 .html.

95   **dropped out of agricultural college:** JTF-GTMO assessment for Maad Al Qahtani, ISN US9SA-000063DP (S), October 30, 2008.

95   **fighting alongside the Taliban:** Ibid.

96   **Qahtani trained on the usual panoply:** See *U.S. v. Moussaoui,* Cr. No. 01-455-A, exhibit ST-0001.

96   **"ready for a mission":** JTF-GTMO Detainee Assessment for Maad Al Qahtani.

96   **"I'll be back":** Greg Miller and Josh Meyer, "Clues Missed on 9/11 Plotters," *Los Angeles Times,* January 27, 2004, articles.latimes.com/2004/jan/27/nation/na-terror27/2. Also see Michael Isikoff and Daniel Klaidman, "How the '20th Hijacker' Got Turned Away," *Newsweek,* January 26, 2004, www.thedailybeast.com/newsweek/2004/01/25/exclusive-how-the-20th-hijacker-got-turned-away.html.

NOTES

97   **arrested on December 15:** JTF-GTMO Detainee Assessment for Maad Al Qahtani.

97   **love of falconry:** Zagorin and Duffy, "Inside the Interrogation of Detainee 063."

97   **head-butting one of his interrogators:** Ibid.

97   **given drugs and enemas:** Neil A. Lewis, "Fresh Details Emerge on Harsh Methods at Guantánamo," *New York Times*, January 1, 2005.

97   **FBI official later noted:** Zagorin and Duffy, "Inside the Interrogation of Detainee 063."

97   **legal definition of torture:** Bob Woodward, "Guantanamo Detainee Was Tortured, Says Official Overseeing Military Trials," *Washington Post*, January 14, 2009, www.washingtonpost.com/wp-dyn/content/article/2009/01/13/AR2009011303372.html.

98   **after the weeks of abuse:** U.S. Department of Defense, "Recommendation for Continued Detention Under DoD Control (CD for Detainee, ISN US9SA-000063DP[S])," October 30, 2008.

99   **"Those guys were swashbucklers":** Michael Scheuer interview.

99   **gave them some useful information:** Musharraf, *In the Line of Fire*, p. 220.

99   **waterboarded 183 times:** Scott Shane, "Waterboarding Used 266 Times on 2 Suspects," *New York Times*, April 19, 2009, www.nytimes.com/2009/04/20/world/20detain.html.

99   **diapered and shackled:** Peter Finn, Joby Warrick, and Julie Tate, "How a Detainee Became an Asset: Sept. 11 Plotter Cooperated After Waterboarding," *Washington Post*, August 29, 2009, www.washingtonpost.com/wp-dyn/content/article/2009/08/28/AR2009082803874_pf.html.

99   **"retired":** Scott Shane, "Harsh Methods of Questioning Debated Again," *New York Times*, May 4, 2011, www.nytimes.com/2011/05/04/us/politics/04torture.html.

99   **senior CIA analyst Frederica traveled:** Jane Mayer, *The Dark Side: The Inside Story of How the War on Terror Turned into a War on American Ideals* (New York: Anchor Books, 2008), p. 273.

100   **When CIA officials interrogated Hambali:** JTF-GTMO Detainee Assessment for Riduan Isomuddin, ISN US9ID-010019DP, October 30, 2008.

100   **stayed in an al-Qaeda safe house:** Ibid.

100   **letter addressed to bin Laden:** "Letter May Detail Iraq Insurgency's Concerns," CNN.com, February 10, 2004, articles.cnn.com/2004-02-10/world/sprj.nirq.zarqawi_1_zarqawi-qaeda-senior-coalition?_s=PM:WORLD.

NOTES

100 **not clear if these techniques were actually employed:** Mark Hosenball and Brian Grow, "Bin Laden Informant's Treatment Key to Torture Debate," Reuters, May 14, 2011, www.reuters.com/article/2011/05/14/us-binladen-ghul-idUSTRE74D0EJ20110514. The confusion stems from ambiguity surrounding Ghul's detention and status, and the only mention of his treatment appears in a Department of Justice memo to the CIA regarding acceptable treatment of detainees, where it says that interrogators received approval to use "attention grasp, walling, facial hold, facial slap, wall standing, stress positions, and sleep deprivation." See U.S. Department of Justice, Office of Legal Counsel, "Memorandum for John A. Rizzo, Senior Deputy Council, Central Intelligence Agency," May, 30, 2005, p. 7, s3.amazonaws.com/propublica/assets/missing_memos/28OLCmemofinalredact30May05.pdf.

100 **traveled with al-Qaeda's leader:** JTF-GTMO Detainee Assessment for Maad Al Qahtani.

100 **the Kuwaiti was trusted by KSM:** Ken Dilanian, "Detainee Put CIA on bin Laden Trail," *Los Angeles Times,* May 5, 2011, articles.latimes.com/2011/may/05/nation/la-na-bin-laden-torture-20110505/2.

100 **the operational commander of al-Qaeda:** On al-Libi's role as operational commander, see JTF-GTMO Detainee Assessment for Abu al-Libi, ISN US9LY-010017DP, September 10, 2008.

100 **two serious but ultimately unsuccessful attempts:** Tim McGirk, "Can This Man Help Capture Bin Laden?" *Time,* May 8, 2005, www.time.com/time/magazine/article/0,9171,1058999,00.html.

101 **lacked melanin:** Musharraf, *In the Line of Fire,* p. 258.

101 **arrested in Pakistan:** JTF-GTMO Detainee Assessment for Abu al-Libi.

101 **handed over to the CIA:** Ibid. He was transferred to U.S. custody on June 6, 2005.

101 **he had been promoted to KSM's spot:** Ibid.

101 **Libi also told his interrogators:** Adam Goldman and Matt Apuzzo, "Phone Call by Kuwaiti Courier Led to bin Laden," Associated Press, May 3, 2011, abcnews.go.com/US/wireStory?id=13512344.

101 **made-up name:** Scott Shane and Charlie Savage, "Bin Laden Raid Revives Debate on Value of Torture," *New York Times,* May 3, 2011, www.nytimes.com/2011/05/04/us/politics/04torture.html.

102 **"If you were to ask me":** Robert Richer, interview by author, Washington, DC, October 6, 2011.

102 **Scrabble board:** Ibid.

102 **"Those guys gave a wealth of invaluable information":** Robert Dannenberg interview.

NOTES

102 **help in the hunt for bin Laden:** Author interviews with counterterrorism officials involved in the hunt for bin Laden.

103 **of real interest at the CIA:** Ibid.; also see Goldman and Apuzzo, "Phone Call by Kuwaiti Courier."

103 **his real name:** Lamb, "Revealed: The SEALs' Secret Guide."

103 **large family of brothers:** Author interviews with counterterrorism officials involved in the hunt for bin Laden.

103 **the Kuwaiti had died in the arms:** See JTF-GTMO Detainee Assessment for Walid Said bin Said Zaid, ISN US9YM-000550DP (S), January 16, 2008.

103 **"marginalized":** Barton Gellman and Thomas E. Ricks, "U.S. Concludes bin Laden Escaped at Tora Bora Fight," *Washington Post*, April 17, 2002, www.washingtonpost.com/ac2/wp-dyn/A62618-2002Apr16?language=printer.

103 **"As I would walk into the Oval Office":** Michael Hayden, interview for *The Last Days of Osama bin Laden*, National Geographic, aired November 9, 2011.

104 **"The president's questions were passed down to us":** Author interviews with counterterrorism officials involved in the hunt for bin Laden.

104 **warrant from a judge:** This story was first reported by James Risen and Eric Lichtblau, "Bush Lets U.S. Spy on Callers Without Courts," *New York Times*, December 16, 2005, www.nytimes.com/2005/12/16/politics/16program.html?pagewanted=all.

104 **pursuing bin Laden through his courier network:** Michael Hayden interview.

104 **"no bated-breath moment":** Author interviews with counterterrorism officials involved in the hunt for bin Laden.

105 **fixated on finding bin Laden:** Adam Goldman and Matt Apuzzo, "Meet 'John': The CIA's Bin Laden Hunter-in-Chief," Associated Press, July 5, 2011, www.msnbc.msn.com/id/43637044/ns/us_news-security/.

105 **Chuck's hair had gradually turned gray:** Author observation.

105 **done a thorough job:** "9/11 Commission Report," pp. 255–58, 534.

106 **Malaysian terror summit, on January 15, 2000:** Ibid., pp. 215 and 267.

106 **"Some fifty to sixty":** Office of the Inspector General, "Report on CIA Accountability with Respect to the 9/11 Attacks," August 21, 2007, www.cia.gov/library/reports/Executive%20Summary_OIG%20Report.pdf.

106 **had a visa ... flown to Los Angeles:** "9/11 Commission Report," p. 267.

106 **local phone directory:** Defendants' exhibit 950 in *U.S. v. Moussaoui*, Cr. No. 01-455-A, "FBI's Handling of Intelligence Information Related

NOTES

to Khalid al-Mihdhar and Nawaf al-Hamzi," Department of Justice Inspector General's report by Glenn A. Fine, obtained via INTELWIRE.
com, p. 29.

107 **"routine" notice:** Ibid., p. 54.

107 **"informing the FBI":** Office of the Inspector General, "Report on CIA Accountability." Also useful is Defendants' exhibit 950 in *U.S. v. Moussaoui*, p. 26 and generally.

CHAPTER 7: OBAMA AT WAR

108 **"We were told to evacuate":** Barack Obama's Speech at Woodrow Wilson Center, Washington, DC, August 1, 2007, www.cfr.org/us-election-2008/obamas-speech-woodrow-wilson-center/p13974.

108 **Obama thought she was vulnerable:** "I think I will be the Democrat who will be most effective in going up against John McCain, or any other Republican—because they all want basically a continuation of George Bush's policies—because I will offer a clear contrast as somebody who never supported this war, thought it was a bad idea." Barack Obama at Democratic Debate, Los Angeles, CA, January 31, 2008, articles.cnn
.com/2008-01-31/politics/dem.debate.transcript_1_hillary-clinton-debate-stake/29?_s=PM:POLITICS.

109 **"has protected or regenerated":** National Intelligence Council, "National Intelligence Estimate: The Terrorist Threat to the US Homeland," July 2007, www.c-span.org/pdf/nie_071707.pdf.

109 **met with his foreign policy advisors:** Ben Rhodes, interview by author, Washington, DC, August 15, 2011.

110 **Obama campaign's foreign policy critiques:** Author interviews with senior administration officials.

110 **"If we have actionable intelligence":** Obama's speech at Woodrow Wilson Center.

111 **"I find it amusing":** AFL-CIO Presidential Democratic Forum, Chicago, IL, August 7, 2007, www.msnbc.msn.com/id/20180486/ns/
msnbc_tv-hardball_with_chris_matthews/t/afl-cio-democratic-presidential-forum-august---pm-et/#.TwXh111AIj8.

111 **Clinton's most famous campaign ad:** Ariel Alexovich, "Clinton's National Security Ad," *New York Times*, February 29, 2008, thecaucus
.blogs.nytimes.com/2008/02/29/clintons-national-security-ad/.

111 **"Dr. Strangelove":** "Transcript: The Republican Candidates Debate," *New York Times*, August 5, 2007, www.nytimes.com/2007/08/05/us/
politics/05transcript-debate.html?pagewanted=all.

111 **"Will we risk the confused leadership":** "Transcript: John McCain Speech After His Win in the Wisconsin Primary," C-SPAN, February 19, 2008, www.c-spanvideo.org/appearance/290354897.

NOTES

112   **"John McCain likes to say"**: Jonathan Alter, *The Promise: President Obama, Year One* (New York: Simon and Schuster, 2009), p. 2.

113   **Obama approved the campaign**: Matthew M. Aid, *Intel Wars: The Secret History of the Fight Against Terror* (London: Bloomsbury, 2012), p. 119.

113   **a pair of CIA drone strikes**: R. Jeffrey Smith, Candace Rondeaux, and Joby Warrick, "2 U.S. Airstrikes Offer a Concrete Sign of Obama's Pakistan Policy," *Washington Post*, January 24, 2009, www.washingtonpost .com/wp-dyn/content/article/2009/01/23/AR2009012304189.html.

113   **"extraordinary efforts"**: "The Nobel Committee Explains Its Choice," *Time*, October 9, 2009, www.time.com/time/politics/article /0,8599,1929399,00.html.

113   **"surge" of thirty thousand troops**: "Remarks by the President in Address to the Nation on the Way Forward in Afghanistan and Pakistan," White House press release, December 1, 2009, www.whitehouse .gov/the-press-office/remarks-president-address-nation-way-forward-afghanistan-and-pakistan.

113   **forty-five drone strikes . . . reliable press reports**: See Peter Bergen and Katherine Tiedemann, "The Year of the Drone," New America Foundation, February 24, 2010, counterterrorism.newamerica.net/ sites/newamerica.net/files/policydocs/bergentiedemann2.pdf.

114   **"I face the world as it is"**: "Obama's Nobel Remarks [transcript]," *New York Times*, December 10, 2009, www.nytimes.com/2009/12/11/ world/europe/11prexy.text.html?pagewanted=all.

114   **his first intelligence briefings**: Bruce Riedel, interview by Tresha Mabile, Washington, DC, July 2011.

114   **three-day attack in Mumbai**: Somini Sengupta, "Dossier Gives Details of Mumbai Attacks," *New York Times*, January 6, 2009, www.nytimes .com/2009/01/07/world/asia/07india.html.

115   **"Most of these threats"**: Juan Zarate, interview by author, Washington, DC, 2010.

115   **"We need to redouble our efforts"**: "Obama on bin Laden: The Full *60 Minutes* Interview," CBS, May 8, 2011, www.cbsnews.com/8301-504803_162-20060530-10391709.html.

115   **"Where do you think Osama bin Laden is?"**: Bruce Riedel interview.

116   **"In order to ensure"**: Ken Dilanian, "In Finding Osama bin Laden, CIA Soars from Distress to Success," *Los Angeles Times*, May 8, 2011, articles .latimes.com/2011/may/08/nation/la-na-bin-laden-cia-20110508.

116   **It became embarrassing to bring nothing new**: Author interviews with U.S. counterterrorism officials involved in the hunt for bin Laden.

116   **late July of 2009**: Warrick, *The Triple Agent*, p. 117.

NOTES

117   **Balawi was arrested in early 2009:** Ibid., pp. 40–41.

117   **a short video clip:** Ibid., pp. 115–16.

117   **"golden source":** Ibid., p. 114.

117   **providing medical treatment:** Ibid., p. 126.

117   **"to conduct martyrdom operations":** John Marzulli, "Najibullah Zazi Pleads Guilty to Plotting NYC Terror Attack, Supporting al Qaeda," *New York Daily News*, February 22, 2010.

118   **first genuine al-Qaeda recruit:** Josh Meyer, "Urgent Probe Underway of Possible al Qaeda–linked Terror Plot," *Los Angeles Times*, September 21, 2009, articles.latimes.com/2009/sep/21/nation/na-terror-arrests21.

118   **pages of handwritten notes:** *U.S. v. Najibullah Zazi*, Eastern District of New York, 09-CR-663, memorandum of law in support of the government's motion for a permanent order of detention obtained via INTELWIRE.com.

118   **quick actions . . . "was acquired in Yemen":** "Yemen Can Carry Out Airstrikes Against al Qaeda," CNN.com, December 30, 2009, www.cnn.com/2009/WORLD/meast/12/30/U.S..yemen.strikes/index.html.

119   **"We dodged a bullet":** Jake Tapper, Karen Travers, and Huma Khan, "Obama: System Failed in a 'Potentially Disastrous' Way," ABC News, January 5, 2010, abcnews.go.com/print?id=9484260.

119   **arranged for the Jordanian doctor to slip over the border:** Warrick, *The Triple Agent*, p. 160.

119   **Forward Operating Base Chapman . . . December 30, 2009:** Ibid., p. 162.

119   **arranged for a cake to be made:** Ibid., p. 143.

119   **As he met with the CIA team:** Ibid., p. 179.

119   **"very personal for":** John Brennan, interview by author, Washington, DC, December 6, 2011.

120   **launched an unprecedented eleven:** Warrick, *The Triple Agent*, pp. 189–90.

120   **put more Agency officers on the ground:** Author interviews with National Security Council officials.

120   **"The CIA goes into a completely different mode":** Vali Nasr, interview by author, Washington, DC, May 31, 2011.

120   **almost four hundred U.S. officials:** Shamila Chaudhary, interview by author, Washington, DC, November 1, 2011.

121   **"all bets are off":** Bob Woodward, *Obama's Wars* (New York: Simon and Schuster, 2010), p. 365.

121   **Zardari pushed back:** Author interviews with National Security Council officials.

NOTES

CHAPTER 8: ANATOMY OF A LEAD

123   **the Kuwaiti was back in bin Laden's inner circle:** Bob Woodward, "Death of Osama bin Laden: Phone Call Pointed U.S. to Compound— and to 'the Pacer,' " *Washington Post,* May 6, 2011, www.washingtonpost .com/world/national-security/death-of-osama-bin-laden-phone-call- pointed-us-to-compound--and-to-the-pacer/2011/05/06/AFnSVaCG_ story.html; author interview with U.S. officials.

123   **at least an hour's drive:** Author interview with Pakistani intelligence official, July 2011.

123   **able to follow him as he drove home:** Author interview with senior U.S. intelligence official.

124   **phone or Internet service:** Mazzetti, Cooper, and Baker, "Behind the Hunt for Bin Laden"; author interview with U.S. intelligence officials.

124   **"Tell me about that fortress":** U.S. intelligence officer, interview with author, Washington, DC, December 20, 2011.

125   **"interested, but cautious":** History Channel, *Targeting Bin Laden,* September 6, 2011.

126   **"don't be afraid of making some of them kind of creative":** Author interview with U.S. intelligence official.

126   **"You are commanded to come out into the street":** Ibid.

126   **bogus vaccination program:** Saeed Shah, "CIA Organised Fake Vaccination Drive to Get Bin Laden's Family DNA," *Guardian,* July 11, 2011, www.guardian.co.uk/world/2011/jul/11/cia-fake-vaccinations-osama- bin-ladens-dna.

127   **"Closing In on Usama bin Ladin's Courier":** Author interview with U.S. counterterrorism officials involved in the hunt for bin Laden.

127   **"Anatomy of a Lead":** Goldman and Apuzzo, "Meet 'John': The CIA's bin Laden Hunter-in-Chief."

127   **"We had a group who weren't afraid":** Author interviews with U.S. counterterrorism officials involved in the hunt for bin Laden.

127   **friends and colleagues:** Ibid.

128   **alcoholic and a congenital liar:** Edward Helmore, "US Relied on 'Drunken Liar' to Justify War," *Guardian,* April 2, 2005.

128   **skeptical of this claim:** U.S. Senate Select Committee on Intelligence, "Report on Prewar Intelligence Assessments on Postwar Iraq, together with Additional Views," February 12, 2004, p. 87, intelligence.senate .gov/prewar.pdf.

128   **Matthew . . . a careful analyst:** Author interviews with U.S. counterterrorism officials involved in the hunt for bin Laden.

NOTES

128   **Kuwaiti even still working for al-Qaeda:** Ibid.

129   **"We put an enormous amount of work":** Ibid.

129   **"We kept explaining":** Ibid.

129   **"high confidence":** Ibid.

130   **religious school outside Abbottabad:** Lamb, "Revealed: The SEALs' Secret Guide."

131   **"pattern of life":** Author interviews with U.S. counterterrorism officials involved in the hunt for bin Laden.

131   **"non-alerting":** Author interview with former CIA operations officer posted in Pakistan after the 9/11 attacks.

132   **bin Laden's wives, children, and grandchildren:** Author interview with U.S. official.

132   **"the pacer":** Ibid.; also see Woodward, "Death of Osama bin Laden."

132   **"collection gaps" . . . local police on the payroll:** Author interviews with U.S. counterterrorism officials involved in the hunt for bin Laden.

134   **"We had pulled on a gazillion threads":** Ibid.

134   **"Oh, that's a bummer":** Denis McDonough, interview by author, Washington, DC, December 6, 2011.

134   **Brennan . . . pointed out:** Ibid.

135   **training police dogs:** "Part One of Series of Reports on bin Ladin's Life in Sudan," *Al Quds Al-Arabi*, November 24, 2001.

135   **"Seventy percent":** Author interview with U.S. counterterrorism officials involved in the hunt for bin Laden.

CHAPTER 9: THE LAST YEARS OF OSAMA BIN LADEN

136   **both in their early thirties:** Lamb, "Revealed: The SEALs' Secret Guide."

136   **rice, lentils, and other groceries:** Saeed Shah, "At End, bin Laden Wasn't Running al-Qaida, Officials Say," *McClatchy Newspapers*, June 29, 2011, www.mcclatchydc.com/2011/06/28/116666/at-end-bin-laden-wasnt-running.html.

136   **stomach upsets, colds and coughs:** Munir Ahmed, "AP Exclusive: Doc Recalls Kids from bin Laden Home," Associated Press, June 1, 2011.

136   **small white Suzuki Jeep and a red van:** Author observation of model of bin Laden compound.

137   **they worked in the transportation business:** Shabbir, a neighbor of bin Laden in Abbottabad, interview by author, Pakistan, July 20, 2011.

137   **they didn't help the poor:** Nahal Toosi and Zarar Khan, "Bin Laden's Neighbors Noticed Unusual Things," Associated Press, May 4, 2011.

NOTES

137 **father emigrated five decades earlier:** Zahid Hussain, "Investigators Track bin Laden Couriers," *Wall Street Journal*, June 1, 2011, online.wsj .com/article/SB10001424052702304563104576357601886423360. html; author interview with Pakistani intelligence official, July 2011.

137 **they could easily blend in:** Michael Isikoff, "How Profile of bin Laden Courier Led CIA to Its Target," NBC News, May 4, 2011, today.msnbc .msn.com/id/42906157/ns/today-today_news/t/how-profile-bin-laden-courier-led-cia-its-target/.

137 **small town of Hasan Abdal:** Author interview with Pakistani intelligence official, July 2011.

137 **plot carnage on a grand scale:** Peter Walker, "Osama bin Laden 'Closely Involved in al-Qaida Plots,'" *Guardian*, May 6, 2011, www .guardian.co.uk/world/2011/may/06/osamabinladen-al-qaida.

138 **heavy-handed and undiplomatic:** Sebastian Rotella, "New Details in the bin Laden Docs: Portrait of a Fugitive Micro-Manager," *ProPublica*, May 11, 2011, www.propublica.org/article/bin-laden-documents-portrait-of-a-fugitive-micro-manager.

138 **deep in the weeds of personnel decisions:** Author interview with U.S. intelligence official.

138 **issued instructions to his regional affiliates:** Lolita C. Baldor and Kimberly Dozier, "Source: Bin Laden Was Directing al-Qaeda Figures," Associated Press, May 7, 2011; author interview with Pakistani intelligence official, July 2011.

138 **Rahman also traveled to Iran:** U.S. Department of the Treasury, "Treasury Targets Key Al-Qa'ida Funding and Support Network Using Iran as a Critical Transit Point," July 28, 2011, www.treasury.gov/ press-center/press-releases/Pages/tg1261.aspx; also see Matt Apuzzo, "Atiyah Abd al-Rahman Dead: Al Qaeda Second in Command Killed in Pakistan," Associated Press, August 28, 2011, www.huffingtonpost .com/2011/08/27/atiyah-abd-al-rahman-al-qaeda-dead_n_939009 .html.

138 **Bin Laden reminded the leaders:** Author interview with Pakistani official, July 2011.

139 **Rahman wrote a seven-page letter:** Atiyah abd al-Rahman, "Note to Zarqawi," November 12, 2005, available at www.ctc.usma.edu/ wp-content/uploads/2010/08/CTC-AtiyahLetter.pdf; on Abdul al-Rahman's role in communicating with al-Qaeda in Iraq, see Brian Fishman, "Redefining the Islamic State: The Fall and Rise of Al-Qaeda in Iraq," New America Foundation, August 18, 2011, newamerica.net/ publications/policy/redefining_the_islamic_state.

139 **harmed the al-Qaeda brand:** Author interview with Pakistani official, July 2011.

NOTES

139   **scolding them for "fanaticism":** Fawaz Gerges, *The Rise and Fall of Al-Qaeda* (New York: Oxford University Press, 2011), p. 120.

139   **America was still their main enemy:** Ken Dilanian and Brian Bennett, "Osama bin Laden's Surrender Wasn't a Likely Outcome in Raid, Officials Say," *Los Angeles Times,* May 3, 2011, articles.latimes.com/2011/may/03/world/la-fg-bin-laden-us-20110504/2.

140   **not a sufficiently important target:** Rotella, "New Details in the bin Laden Docs"; Siobhan Gorman, "Petraeus Named in bin Laden Documents," *Wall Street Journal,* June 23, 2011, online.wsj.com/article/SB10001424052702304231204576404222056912648.html.

140   **al-Qaeda simply didn't have the resources:** Michael Leiter, interview by author, Washington, DC, August 29, 2011.

140   **attack the United States itself:** It should be noted that while bin Laden continued to emphasize large-scale attacks in the United States, he also supported the shift made by al-Qaeda in the Arabian Peninsula toward smaller attacks against American targets. See Kimberly Dozier, "Bin Laden Trove of Documents Sharpen US Aim," Associated Press, June 8, 2011, www.msnbc.msn.com/id/43331634/ns/us_news-security/t/bin-laden-trove-documents-sharpen-us-aim/.

140   **how many thousands of dead Americans:** Pierre Thomas and Martha Raddatz, "Osama bin Laden Operational Journal Among Evidence from SEAL Raid," ABC News, May 11, 2011, abcnews.go.com/Blotter/osama-bin-laden-diary-evidence-seal-raid/story?id=13581186.

140   **He mused about attacking trains:** Mark Mazzetti and Scott Shane, "Data Show Bin Laden Plots; C.I.A. Hid Near Raided Houses," *New York Times,* May 5, 2011, www.nytimes.com/2011/05/06/world/asia/06intel.html.

140   **disaffected African Americans and Latinos:** Greg Miller and Karen DeYoung, "Bin Laden's Preoccupation with U.S. Said to Be Source of Friction with Followers," *Washington Post,* May 11, 2011.

140   **Bryant Neal Vinas:** For more on Vinas, see Michael Powell, "U.S. Recruit Reveals How Qaeda Trains Foreigners," *New York Times,* July 23, 2009, www.nytimes.com/2009/07/24/nyregion/24terror.html?pagewanted=all.

140   **tenth anniversary of 9/11:** Siobhan Gorman, "Bin Laden Plotted New Attack," *Wall Street Journal,* July 15, 2011, online.wsj.com/article/SB10001424052702304521304576446213098582284.html.

140   **Christmas:** Dozier, "Bin Laden Trove of Documents Sharpen U.S. Aim."

140   **oil tankers . . . wider strategy:** Damien Pearse, "Al-Qaida Hoped to Blow Up Oil Tankers, Bin Laden Documents Reveal," *Guardian,* May 20, 2011, www.guardian.co.uk/world/2011/may/20/al-qaida-oil-tankers-bin-laden.

NOTES

141   **in touch with a group of Moroccan militants:** "Top Terrorist Had Ties to Düsseldorf Cell," *Der Spiegel*, May 6, 2011, www.spiegel.de/international/germany/0,1518,761101,00.html.

141   **in the fall of 2010:** Author interviews with U.S. national security officials, December 2010.

141   **Monotheism and Jihad Group:** Matt Apuzzo, "Osama Wanted New Name for al-Qaida to Repair Image," Associated Press, June 24, 2011, www.salon.com/2011/06/24/us_al_qaida_new_name/. Monotheism and Jihad was, somewhat ironically, the name of Abu Musab al-Zarqawi's terrorist group before it became al-Qaeda in Iraq. There was an earlier al-Qaeda in the Arabian Peninsula that was repressed by Saudi authorities; the new iteration of the group was announced in 2009, when al-Qaeda in the Southern Arabian Peninsula merged with its Saudi counterpart.

141   **did not reflect al-Qaeda's "values":** Rotella, "New Details in the bin Laden Docs."

142   **didn't know Awlaki:** Author interview with senior U.S. intelligence official.

142   **Bin Laden also offered strategic advice:** Greg Miller, "Bin Laden Document Trove Reveals Strain on al-Qaeda," *Washington Post*, July 1, 2011, www.washingtonpost.com/national/national-security/bin-laden-document-trove-reveals-strain-on-al-qaeda/2011/07/01/AGdj0GuH_story.html.

142   **half a dozen other key lieutenants:** Peter Bergen and Katherine Tiedemann, "Washington's Phantom War: The Effects of the U.S. Drone Program in Pakistan," *Foreign Affairs* (July/August 2011), www.foreignaffairs.com/articles/67939/peter-bergen-and-katherine-tiedemann/washingtons-phantom-war.

142   **"getting hammered":** Author interview with senior U.S. intelligence official.

142   **counterintelligence shop . . . particular worry:** Author interviews with Pakistani intelligence officials, July 2011; Greg Miller, "Bin Laden Document Trove."

143   **negotiate a grand alliance:** Jason Burke, "Osama bin Laden Tried to Establish 'Grand Coalition' of Militant Groups," *Guardian*, May 30, 2011, www.guardian.co.uk/world/2011/may/30/osama-bin-laden-militant-alliance.

143   **considered brokering some sort of deal:** Mark Mazzetti, "Signs That Bin Laden Weighed Seeking Pakistani Protection," *New York Times*, May 26, 2011, www.nytimes.com/2011/05/27/world/middleeast/27binladen.html.

NOTES

143   **in 2003 tried to assassinate Pakistan's president:** Salman Masood, "Pakistan Leader Escapes Attempt at Assassination," *New York Times,* December 26, 2003, www.nytimes.com/2003/12/26/world/pakistani-leader-escapes-attempt-at-assassination.html?pagewanted=all&src =pm.

143   **his battle was fought in the media:** "Letter to Mullah Mohammed Omar from bin Laden," undated, AFGP-2002-600321, available at www.ctc.usma.edu/posts/letter-to-mullah-mohammed-omar-from-bin-laden-english-translation.

144   **Kyoto agreement on global warming:** Osama bin Laden, "The Wills of the Heroes of the Raids on New York and Washington," videotape released September 11, 2011, transcript available at abcnews.go.com/images/Politics/transcript2.pdf.

144   **five audiotapes a year:** Mazzetti and Shane, "Data Show Bin Laden Plots."

144   **"catastrophe":** Inal Ersan, "Bin Laden Warns EU over Prophet Cartoons," Reuters, March 20, 2008, www.ft.com/intl/cms/s/0/08d9a978-f60e-11dc-8d3d-000077b07658.html#axzz1jqoWHZmu.

144   **bombed the Danish embassy in Islamabad:** Jane Perlez and Pir Zubair Shah, "Embassy Attack in Pakistan Kills at Least 6," *New York Times,* June 3, 2008, www.nytimes.com/2008/06/03/world/asia/03pakistan .html.

144   **recent Israeli invasion of Gaza:** "Bin Laden 'Tape' Calls Israel Offensive in Gaza a Holocaust," Associated Press, March 14, 2009, www .guardian.co.uk/world/2009/mar/14/osama-bin-laden-gaza-Israel.

144   **weighed in on France's decision:** Leela Jacinto, "Bin Laden Targets France, Blasts Burqa Ban and Afghan War," France24.com, October 28, 2010, www.france24.com/en/20101027-osama-bin-laden-terrorism-france-al-qaeda-burqa-ban.

145   **"We watch this great historic event":** Scott Shane, "In Message, Bin Laden Praised Arab Revolt," *International Herald Tribune,* May 18, 2011, www.nytimes.com/2011/05/19/world/middleeast/19binladen .html?gwh=BD6FB65DDBFB14D2218387E70809F0D5.

CHAPTER 10: THE SECRET WARRIORS

147   **three shots rang out:** Robert D. McFadden and Scott Shane, "In Rescue of Captain, Navy Kills 3 Pirates," *New York Times,* April 12, 2009, www.nytimes.com/2009/04/13/world/africa/13pirates.html?page wanted=all.

147   **Obama had authorized the use:** Ibid.

148   **Obama called:** Author interview with Department of Defense official, December 2011.

315

NOTES

148   **killing eight American servicemen:** Mark Bowden, "The Desert One Debacle," *The Atlantic*, May 2006, www.theatlantic.com/magazine/archive/2006/05/the-desert-one-debacle/4803/2/?single_page=true.

148   **A Pentagon investigation found:** Holloway Report, August 23, 1980, www.gwu.edu/~nsarchiv/NSAEBB/NSAEBB63/doc8.pdf.

149   **creation in 1980 of the Joint Special Operations Command:** Steven Emerson, "Stymied Warriors," *New York Times*, November 13, 1988, www.nytimes.com/1988/11/13/magazine/stymied-warriors.html.

149   **suspicious of the "snake eaters":** See for instance Michael Smith, *Killer Elite: The Inside Story of America's Most Secret Special Operations Teams* (New York: St. Martin's Press, 2011), p. 215.

149   **the debacle at Mogadishu:** See Mark Bowden, *Black Hawk Down: A Story of Modern War* (New York: Atlantic Monthly Press, 1999).

150   **sent some of its top trainers:** "9/11 Commission Report," p. 60.

150   **"You know it would scare the shit out of al-Qaeda":** Coll, *Ghost Wars*, p. 498.

150   **"I don't carry a brief":** Michael Scheuer interview.

150   **expressing his irritation:** Document 19, National Security Archives, George Washington University, www.gwu.edu/~nsarchiv/NSAEBB/NSAEBB358a/index.htm#19.

151   **Officials working for Rumsfeld:** Bradley Graham, *By His Own Rules: The Ambitions, Successes, and Ultimate Failures of Donald Rumsfeld* (New York: PublicAffairs, 2009), p. 369.

151   **"Somalia-ized":** Smith, *Killer Elite*, p. 233.

151   **"showstoppers" . . . "actionable intelligence":** Ibid.

151   **"brand-new Ferrari":** Richard Shultz Jr., "How Clinton Let al Qaeda Go," *Weekly Standard*, January 19, 2004, archive.frontpagemag.com/readArticle.aspx?ARTID=14524.

151   **asking General Schoomaker:** Smith, *Killer Elite*, p. 258.

151   **executive order:** Dana Priest and William M. Arkin, *Top Secret America: The Rise of the New American Security State* (New York: Little, Brown and Co., 2011), p. 236.

152   **didn't even acknowledge that JSOC existed:** Dexter Filkins, "Stanley McChrystal's Long War," *New York Times Magazine*, October 14, 2009, www.nytimes.com/2009/10/18/magazine/18Afghanistan-t.html?pagewanted=all.

152   **from a force of eighteen hundred:** Priest and Arkin, *Top Secret America*, p. 227; see generally Marc Ambinder and D. B. Grady, *The Command: Deep Inside the President's Secret Army* (John Wiley & Sons, ebook).

152   **Confederate Air Force:** U.S. intelligence official, interview by author, Washington, DC, December 2011.

NOTES

153 **if it was going to defeat al-Qaeda:** Spencer Ackerman, "How Special Ops Copied al-Qaida to Kill It," Danger Room, *Wired*, September 9, 2011, www.wired.com/dangerroom/2011/09/mcchrystal-network/all/1.

153 **Mohamed taught courses:** See Bergen, *Holy War, Inc.*, p. 132.

153 **During his leave from the army:** On Mohamed taking leave time to travel to Afghanistan, see ibid., pp. 132–33.

153 **manuals he had pilfered from Ft. Bragg:** Wright, *The Looming Tower*, p. 181.

153 **"flat and fast":** Author interview with former Special Operations officers.

153 **In the summer of 2004:** Ibid.

154 **to work at the CIA station in Baghdad:** Ibid.

154 **One of the senior leaders in the Pentagon:** Author interview with senior Department of Defense official.

154 **leased a couple of small aircraft:** Author interview with former Special Operations officers.

155 **"actionable intelligence":** Ibid.; also see Priest and Arkin, *Top Secret America*, pp. 244–55.

155 **"fight for intelligence":** Eric Schmitt and Thom Shanker, *Counterstrike: The Untold Story of America's Secret Campaign Against Al Qaeda* (New York: Times Books, 2011), p. 93.

155 **"divining rod":** Priest and Arkin, *Top Secret America*, p. 244.

156 **netting more leads for JSOC:** Author interview with National Security Council official.

156 **JSOC was "awesome":** Bob Woodward, "Why Did Violence Plummet? It Wasn't Just the Surge," *Washington Post*, September 8, 2008, www.washingtonpost.com/wp-dyn/content/article/2008/09/07/AR2008090701847.html?hpid=topnews.

156 **thirty-four task force members were disciplined:** Eric Schmitt and Carolyn Marshall, "In Secret Unit's 'Black Room,' a Grim Portrait of Detainee Abuse," *New York Times*, March 19, 2006, www.nytimes.com/2006/03/19/international/middleeast/19abuse.html?ei=5088&en=e8755a4b031b64a1&ex=1300424400&partner=rssnyt&emc=rss&pagewanted=all.

156 **McChrystal himself was one:** Scott Lindlaw and Martha Mendoza, "General Suspected Cause of Tillman Death," Associated Press, August 4, 2007, www.washingtonpost.com/wp-dyn/content/article/2007/08/03/AR2007080301868.html.

156 **half a dozen operations a month ... three hundred a month:** Author interview with senior U.S. intelligence official.

156 **"17-5-2":** Priest and Arkin, *Top Secret America*, p. 240.

NOTES

157   **McChrystal wrote to all his men:** Smith, *Killer Elite*, p. 276.

157   **20 of his men in Afghanistan and 250 in Iraq:** Priest and Arkin, *Top Secret America*, p. 238.

157   **twenty operations a month:** Author interview with senior U.S. Department of Defense official.

158   **hardest training in the world:** Eric Greitens, *The Heart and the Fist: The Education of a Humanitarian, the Making of a Navy SEAL* (New York: Houghton Mifflin Harcourt, 2011), pp. 144–63.

158   **swimming underwater for fifty yards:** Eric Greitens, interview by author, Washington, DC, August 2011.

158   **"We had some incredible people":** Ibid.

158   **"you are going to push people as hard as you possible can":** Ibid.

159   **divided into squadrons that are named by color:** Mir Bahmanyar with Chris Osman, *SEALs: The US Navy's Elite Fighting Force* (Oxford, UK: Osprey Publishing, 2008), p. 22.

159   **DevGru's base at Dam Neck:** Author observations of the base from a 2010 visit.

160   **potential to be Operation Eagle Claw all over again:** Schmitt and Shanker, *Counterstrike*, pp. 31–32.

160   **distinctive red motorcycle:** Author interview with senior U.S. intelligence official.

160   **A plan was developed to drop in thirty SEALs:** Evan Thomas, "Into Thin Air," *Newsweek*, September 2, 2007.

160   **Rumsfeld called off the raid:** Mark Mazzetti and David Rohde, "Amid U.S. Policy Disputes, Qaeda Grows in Pakistan," *New York Times*, June 30, 2008, www.nytimes.com/2008/06/30/washington/30tribal .html?pagewanted=all.

161   **On August 11, 2006:** See JTF-GTMO Detainee Assessment for Harun al-Afghani, ISN US9AF-003148DP, August 2, 2007.

161   **In July 2007, JSOC received intelligence:** Author interview with senior U.S. intelligence official.

161   **summit meeting of militants:** Ibid.; Eric Schmitt and Thom Shanker, "In Long Pursuit of Bin Laden, the '07 Raid, and Frustration," *New York Times*, May 5, 2011, www.nytimes.com/2011/05/06/world/ asia/06binladen.html?pagewanted=1&hp.

162   **smaller operation over the course:** Author interview with senior U.S. intelligence official.

CHAPTER 11: COURSES OF ACTION

163   **"I want to hear back from you":** Author interview with senior administration official, Washington, DC, August 2011.

NOTES

163   **"Let's make sure"**: John Brennan in *Targeting bin Laden.*

163   **"If we were going to embark"**: Barack Obama in *Targeting bin Laden.*

163   **someone on the fringes of al-Qaeda:** Chris Brummitt and Adam Goldman, "Indonesia: Terror Suspect Went to Meet bin Laden," Associated
Press, May 4, 2011, www.foxnews.com/world/2011/05/04/indonesia-
terror-suspect-went-meet-bin-laden/#ixzz1kCVvHPfP.

164   **"We have to act now"**: Adam Goldman and Matt Apuzzo, "AP Enterprise: The Man Who Hunted Osama bin Laden," Associated Press,
July 5, 2011, news.yahoo.com/ap-enterprise-man-hunted-osama-bin-
laden-040627805.html.

164   **"options to go against this compound"**: John Brennan in *Targeting bin
Laden.*

164   **CAD file:** Shane Harris, "Bin Laden Death Planned Out in Miniature,"
Washingtonian, May 5, 2011, www.washingtonian.com/blogarticles/
19328.html.

164   **two tiny toy cars:** Author observation of parts of the model.

164   **"That was a good vehicle"**: James Cartwright, interview by author,
Washington, DC, September 30, 2011.

165   **bring another person into the secret:** Michael Vickers, interview by
author, Washington, DC, November 15, 2011.

165   **known each other for three decades:** Ibid.

165   **Much of the public credit:** Author interview with senior U.S. intelligence official.

165   **well over two thousand a year by 2010:** Author interview with senior
Department of Defense official.

165   **soared from 35 percent to more than 80 percent:** Woodward, "Death
of Osama bin Laden."

166   **average age of Taliban commanders in Afghanistan declined:** Con
Coughlin, "Karzai Must Tell Us Which Side He's On in Afghanistan,"
Telegraph, November 18, 2010, www.telegraph.co.uk/comment/
columnists/concoughlin/8144423/Karzai-must-tell-us-which-side-hes-
on-in-Afghanistan.html.

166   **once a month in Afghanistan:** Craig Whitlock, "Adm. William McRaven: The Terrorist Hunter on Whose Shoulders Osama Bin Laden Raid
Rested," *Washington Post*, May 4, 2011.

166   **McRaven visited CIA headquarters:** Siobhan Gorman and Julian E.
Barnes, "Spy, Military Ties Aided bin Laden Raid," *Wall Street Journal*,
May 23, 2011, online.wsj.com/article /SB10001424052748704083904
576334160172068344.html.

166   **McRaven could see immediately:** Author interview with Pentagon
official.

NOTES

166   **"First of all, congratulations":** Author interview with U.S. intelligence official.

167   **"He's an experienced operator":** Ibid.

167   **tasked a navy captain:** Gorman and Barnes, "Spy, Military Ties Aided Bin Laden Raid."

167   **a covert, "deniable" operation:** Michael Vickers interview; Michael Leiter inverview.

167   **first floor of the CIA's printing plant:** Nicholas Schmidle, "Getting bin Laden," *New Yorker,* August 1, 2011, www.newyorker.com/reporting/2011/08/08/110808fa_fact_schmidle?currentPage=all.

167   **One plan was . . . nixed that plan:** Ibid.

168   **helped establish a Special Operations curriculum:** "Biography: Admiral William H. McRaven, United States Special Operations Command," updated August 8, 2011, http://www.navy.mil/navydata/bios/navybio.asp?bioid=401.

168   **one of the principal authors:** Ibid.

168   **McRaven's 1996 book:** William H. McRaven, *Spec Ops: Case Studies in Special Operations Warfare: Theory and Practice* (New York: Random House, 1996).

168   **the star is Jonathan Netanyahu:** "Of all the men studied so far no one exhibits as much leadership ability as Jonathan Netanyahu," McRaven writes in ibid., p. 342.

169   **read Machiavelli to relax:** Ibid., p. 345.

169   **It was a simple plan:** Author interview with Pentagon official.

169   **not the only "kinetic" . . . plan:** Author interview with senior Pentagon official.

169   **highest-ranking female . . . mother of three:** Emily Wax, "Michèle Flournoy, Pentagon's Highest-Ranking Woman, Is Making Her Mark on Foreign Policy," *Washington Post,* November 6, 2011, www.washingtonpost.com/lifestyle/style/Michèle-flournoy-pentagons-highest-ranking-woman-is-making-her-mark-on-foreign-policy/2011/10/27/gIQAh6nbtM_story.html. Three of the five key players at the Pentagon deeply involved in the bin Laden operation were raised in the decidedly unmilitary milieu of Hollywood: Michèle Flournoy's father was a cinematographer there, Michael Mullen's father was a Hollywood agent, and Michael Vickers's father was a set designer.

170   **range of options to consider:** James Cartwright interview.

170   **"We had a very serious debate":** Michèle Flournoy interview by author, Washington, DC, November 18, 2011.

171   **"fair-weather friend":** "Pervez Musharraf on U.S.-Pakistan Relations," Council on Foreign Relations, October 26, 2011, carnegieendowment.org/files/1026carnegie-musharraf.pdf.

NOTES

171   **Pakistan was a sanctuary for militant groups:** Statement of Admiral Michael Mullen, U.S. Navy Chairman of the Joint Chiefs of Staff, Before the Senate Armed Services Committee, September 22, 2011, armed-services.senate.gov/statemnt/2011/09%20September/Mullen%2009-22-11.pdf.

171   **a CIA contractor:** Greg Miller, "U.S. Officials: Raymond Davis, Accused in Pakistan Shootings, Worked for CIA," *Washington Post*, February 22, 2011, www.washingtonpost.com/wp-dyn/content/article/2011/02/21/AR2011022102801.html.

171   **called for the execution of Davis:** "Rallies Demand Public Execution of Davis," *Dawn*, February 12, 2011, www.dawn.com/2011/02/12/rallies-demand-public-execution-of-davis.html.

171   **about three-quarters of all NATO and U.S. supplies:** Muhammad Tahir, "Central Asia Stands to Gain as NATO Shifts Supply Lines Away from Pakistan," Radio Free Europe/Radio Liberty, March 22, 2011, www.rferl.org/content/central_asia_supply_lines_afghanistan/2345994.html.

172   **"So there was a big push":** Michèle Flournoy interview.

172   **work together to expand:** Remarks by Defense Secretary Robert Gates, Kuznetsov Naval Academy, St. Petersburg, Russia, March 21, 2011.

172   **"I didn't want to miss the opportunity":** Hillary Clinton, interview by author, Washington, DC, January 23, 2012.

172   **"decided that the potential":** Nick Rasmussen interview.

173   **On a Friday evening in late February:** Gorman and Barnes, "Spy, Military Ties Aided Bin Laden Raid."

173   **U.S. Marine aviator . . . Tony Blinken:** Yochi J. Dreazen, "Man Most Likely to Take Top Military Job Has Never Seen War," *The National Journal*, May 2, 2011.

174   **What was likely to be difficult:** Author interview with Pentagon official.

174   **"I think our folks":** Author interview with U.S. intelligence official.

174   **On March 14, 2011, Obama's war cabinet gathered:** Author interview with senior administration official, Washington, DC.

174   **force of the bombs would:** James Cartwright interview.

175   **"Some people said":** Tony Blinken, national security adviser to Vice President Joseph Biden, interview by author, Washington, DC, November 3, 2011.

175   **bin Laden might shelter in a vault . . . escape through a tunnel:** James Cartwright interview.

175   **Using thermal imaging, the NGA concluded:** Author interview with National Security Council official.

NOTES

175 **large streams course through the neighborhood:** Author observations during visits to Abbottabad, July 2011 and February 2012.

175 **Proponents of the raid option, who included Panetta:** Author interview with senior administration official.

175 **they could just leave and no one would ever know:** Ibid.

176 **General Cartwright, Obama's favorite general:** Author interviews with multiple senior administration officials.

176 **hit the mysterious "pacer":** Author interview with counterterrorism officials involved in the hunt for bin Laden; also see Woodward, "Death of Osama bin Laden."

176 **required a very high degree of precision:** Author interview with senior administration official.

176 **"chatter" about bin Laden's "martyrdom":** Ibid.

176 **"it was a system that had not been tested":** Michael Mullen, interview by author, Annapolis, MD, January 20, 2012.

176 **Michèle Flournoy was also one of the proponents of the raid:** Michèle Flournoy interview.

177 **"Mister President, we haven't thoroughly tested this out yet":** John Brennan in *Targeting bin Laden.*

177 **Obama observed, "Then you'd better get moving":** Author interview with U.S. official.

177 **a helicopter-borne assault team was a risky option:** Author interview with White House official.

177 **his comments didn't get much traction at the time:** Author interview with U.S. intelligence official; James Cartwright interview.

177 **many of the participants believed:** Author interview with U.S. intelligence official.

178 **"Everybody left those meetings":** Hillary Clinton interview.

178 **might end up getting killed in his Pakistani prison cell:** Mazzetti, Cooper, and Baker, "Behind the Hunt for bin Laden."

178 **it would require dropping thirty-two 2,000-pound bombs:** Author interview with senior U.S. intelligence official.

178 **Bombs might also fall short of the target:** Ibid.

179 **Obama peppered McRaven with questions:** Jake Tapper, "President Obama to National Security Team: 'It's a Go,'" ABC News, May 2, 2011, abcnews.go.com/blogs/politics/2011/05/president-obama-to-national-security-team-its-a-go/.

179 **one of the most skeptical of the president's advisers:** Michèle Flournoy interview.

NOTES

179   **"We finally left the White House at about 1:30 in the morning"**: Robert M. Gates, *From the Shadows: The Ultimate Insider's Story of Five Presidents and How They Won the Cold War* (New York: Simon and Schuster, 2006), pp. 154–55.

180   **"What if you have a helicopter crash?"** . . . **"Kool-Aid"**: Michèle Flournoy interview.

180   **any chance that the Pakistanis would be given a heads-up:** Author interview with senior U.S. intelligence official.

180   **"McRaven, in some of the earliest briefings, was very sensitive"**: Author interview with senior administration official.

180   **avoiding any kind of firefight:** Ibid.

181   **defensive perimeter . . . the intelligence case:** Ibid.

181   **"The premium is on the protection of our force"**: Ibid.

181   **ended up having some two dozen Navy SEALs in Pakistani custody:** Author interview with senior administration officials, Washington, DC.

181   **"That was a huge fundamental shift"**: Ibid.

182   **quick reaction force:** Ibid.

182   **"If we know we can find Number One or Number Two"**: Michael Mullen interview.

182   **forged a personal relationship:** Author interview with Pakistani official.

182   **"You have too many CIA agents in this country"**: Ibid.

182   **"shouting match"**: Jane Perlez, "Denying Links to Militants, Pakistan's Spy Chief Denounces U.S. Before Parliament," *New York Times*, May 13, 2011, www.nytimes.com/2011/05/14/world/asia/14pakistan.html.

182   **over the course . . . deep in the forests of North Carolina:** Schmidle, "Getting bin Laden."

183   **These rehearsals . . . "on target"**: Author interview with senior U.S. intelligence official.

183   **"audio signature" . . . McRaven had advertised it could be:** Ibid.

183   **During the rehearsals . . . the SEALs practiced:** Ibid.

183   **had encountered pretty much every type of surprise possible:** James Cartwright interview.

184   **"McRaven had a backup for every possible failure"**: Michèle Flournoy interview.

184   **a great cheer went up:** Eric Greitens interview.

184   **replicated the likely heat conditions:** Schmidle, "Getting bin Laden."

184   **this time joined by Admiral Mullen:** Author interview with senior U.S. intelligence official.

NOTES

184 **"rehearsal of concept" . . . "game time" decisions:** Ibid.

184 **the whole operation could be conducted in under thirty minutes:** Author interview with senior U.S. administration official.

185 **drop in at the JSOC operations center at Bagram:** Michael Mullen interview.

185 **"If I am going to send somebody in to die":** Ibid.

185 **"First of all, it helps that he's from central casting":** Tony Blinken interview.

185 **"In terms of difficulty":** Author interview with senior U.S. intelligence official.

186 **told the *Al-Quds Al-Arabi* newspaper:** Khalid al Hammadi, "Bin Laden's Former 'Bodyguard' Interviewed," *Al-Quds Al-Arabi*, August 3, 2004, and March 20 to April 4, 2004.

186 **willingness to be martyred:** The *Guardian* website has a useful chronology of statements by bin Laden and Zawahiri at www.guardian.co.uk/alqaida/page/0,,839823,00.html, where bin Laden's February 20, 2006, statement can be found.

186 **rules of engagement the SEALs adhered to:** Leon Panetta interview with *NBC Nightly News*, May 3, 2011, www.msnbc.msn.com/id/42887700/ns/world_news-death_of_bin_laden/t/transcript-interview-cia-director-panetta/#.TwHRIiNAYfU.

186 **consisting of . . . experienced interrogators:** James Cartwright interview. See also Eric Schmitt, Thom Shanker, and David E. Sanger, "U.S. Was Braced for Fight with Pakistanis in bin Laden Raid," *New York Times*, May 9, 2011, www.nytimes.com/2011/05/10/world/asia/10intel.html?emc=na#.

186 **would fly to the aircraft carrier USS *Carl Vinson*:** James Cartwright interview; Schmitt, Shanker, and Sanger, "U.S. Was Braced for Fight."

186 **point of diminishing returns:** Author interview with senior U.S. intelligence official.

187 **"There was always the tension between":** Tony Blinken interview.

187 **Obama gave a provisional go-ahead:** Gorman and Barnes, "Spy, Military Ties Aided bin Laden Raid."

187 **"not invited":** Ben Rhodes interview in *Targeting bin Laden*.

188 **"In the past I have had to engage newspaper editors and say":** Ben Rhodes interview.

188 **"I felt the enormous weight of the information I'd been told":** Ben Rhodes interview in *Targeting bin Laden*.

188 **"playbook" . . . "Keep preparing":** Author interview with senior administration official.

188 **able to flip a switch immediately:** Ibid.

NOTES

189 **"So, for all the options that involved him not being there":** Ibid.

189 **worked up a sixty-six-page document:** Author interview with U.S. intelligence official.

189 **In mid-April, John Brennan called Mike Leiter:** Michael Leiter interview.

190 **president of the *Harvard Law Review*:** *Harvard Gazette*, February 25, 1999, news.harvard.edu/gazette/1999/02.25/news.html.

190 **position that Barack Obama had held:** Fox Butterfield, "First Black Elected to Head Harvard's Law Review," *New York Times*, February 6, 1990, www.nytimes.com/1990/02/06/us/first-black-elected-to-head-harvard-s-law-review.html.

190 **worked for the congressional commission ... final report:** Testimony of former senator Charles S. Robb before the Senate Select Committee on Intelligence, "Nomination of Michael Leiter to Be Director, National Counterterrorism Center," p. 3, www.fas.org/irp/congress/2008_hr/leiter.pdf.

190 **"I had seen enough failures in this world":** Michael Leiter interview.

190 **there were aspects of the case that bothered him:** Ibid.

190 **In Leiter's mind ... gaps in the coverage:** Ibid.

191 **"I don't think that is sufficient if this is successful or a failure":** Ibid.

191 **Brennan agreed that the Red Team was a good idea:** Ibid.

191 **Leiter then went to see Tom Donilon:** Ibid.

192 **"Denis, are you fucking kidding me?":** Ibid.

192 **The ideal time to do the helicopter assault:** Author interview with senior U.S. intelligence official.

193 **the longer they waited, the greater the possibility of a leak:** Ibid.; James Cartwright interview.

193 **Morell said, "Absolutely, I think it's a great idea:** Michael Leiter interview.

193 **they had forty-eight hours:** Ibid.

193 **Leiter's team explored three alternative hypotheses:** Ibid.

193 **The analysts found that the first hypothesis was the most likely:** Ibid.

194 **"We actually thought we had a pretty good handle":** Ibid.

194 **none of the alternative hypotheses was as likely:** Ibid.

194 **posted online ... "silliness":** Alan Silverleib, "Obama Releases Original Long-Form Birth Certificate," CNN, April 27, 2011, edition.cnn.com/2011/POLITICS/04/27/obama.birth.certificate/index.html.

194 **the SEAL teams had already left their base:** Schmidle, "Getting bin Laden."

NOTES

CHAPTER 12: THE DECISION

196 **"Bottom line is":** Michael Leiter interview.

196 **"It really didn't change anything":** Michael Vickers interview.

196 **"Even if you're at the forty percent low end of this range":** Michael Leiter interview.

197 **"We thought the prospects were higher":** John Brennan in *Targeting bin Laden.*

197 **"There was a deflation in the room":** Ben Rhodes in *Targeting bin Laden.*

197 **"if anything, the Red Team actually brought down":** Tony Blinken interview.

197 **"I think this Red Team":** Michael Leiter interview.

198 **"the best evidence since Tora Bora":** Author interview with senior U.S. intelligence official. Also see Massimo Calabresi, "CIA Chief: Pakistan Would Have Jeopardized Operation," *Time*, May 3, 2011, swampland.time.com/2011/05/03/cia-chief-breaks-silence-u-s-ruled-out-involving-pakistan-in-bin-laden-raid-early-on/.

198 **Obama summed up the case:** Michael Leiter interview.

199 **"Mister President, this is a very hard call":** Ben Rhodes interview for *Targeting bin Laden.*

199 **Situation Room began to fill with laughter:** Interviews with senior administration officials.

199 **Joe Biden . . . was worried about the local fallout from the raid:** Ibid.

199 **Robert Gates continued to be skittish:** Ibid.; Michael Leiter interview; James Cartwright interview.

199 **Gates and Biden still leery:** Michael Leiter interview and interviews with senior administration officials.

200 **against the SEAL helicopter assault:** Tom Donilon interview for *Targeting bin Laden;* Mike Leiter interview.

200 **had never prepared . . . with as much care:** Michael Mullen interview.

200 **"Bill's [McRaven's] team can do this":** Ibid.

200 **a tiny drone-fired munition:** Author interviews with senior administration officials.

200 **a thirteen-pound "smart" bomb:** V. J. Hennigan, "Pentagon Seeks Mini-Weapons for New Age Warfare," *Los Angeles Times*, May 30, 2011.

201 **Hillary Clinton gave a long, lawyerly presentation:** Author interview with senior administration officials.

NOTES

201   **"Mister President, my first choice would be that we wait"**: Michael Leiter interview.

202   **"I've always used the test"**: Leon Panetta, interview by author, Washington, DC, February 16, 2012.

202   **Hillary Clinton voiced a related point**: Author interview with senior administration officials.

202   **John Brennan, Obama's top counterterrorism adviser, urged a go**: Michael Leiter interview.

202   **Ben Rhodes, Michèle Flournoy, Tony Blinken, Mike Vickers, Robert Cardillo, and Nick Rasmussen all endorsed the raid**: Author interviews with each of them.

202   **Obama listened to the counsel**: Tony Blinken interview.

202   **"This is a close call"**: Barack Obama interview for *Targeting bin Laden*.

202   **felt that those who had voiced doubts**: "Obama on bin Laden: The Full *60 Minutes* Interview."

203   **on his shoulders for the rest of his life**: John Brennan interview for *Targeting bin Laden*.

203   **"The most difficult part"**: "Obama on bin Laden: The Full *60 Minutes* Interview."

203   **"I thought it was important"**: Barack Obama in *Targeting bin Laden*.

203   **Obama had 100 percent confidence:** Author interview with administration officials, Washington, DC, August 2011.

203   **Obama knew the stakes were high**: Barack Obama in *Targeting bin Laden*.

203   **"What if the mysterious pacer was a prince from Dubai"**: "Obama on bin Laden: The Full *60 Minutes* Interview."

203   **tripled the number of troops in Afghanistan**: "Remarks by the President in Address to the Nation on the Way Forward in Afghanistan and Pakistan."

204   **called Mubarak and told him it was time to step down**: Jake Tapper, "After Thursday Speech, White House Pushed Mubarak: You Must Satisfy the Demonstrators in the Street," ABC News, February 11, 2011, abcnews.go.com/blogs/politics/2011/02/after-thursday-speech-white-house-pushed-mubarak-you-must-satisfy-the-demonstrators-in-the-street/; author interview with senior administration official.

204   **military campaign that toppled the Libyan dictator**: Paul Richter and Christi Parsons, "Obama Faces Growing Criticism for Libya Campaign," *Los Angeles Times*, March 21, 2011, articles.latimes.com/2011/mar /21/world/la-fg-us-libya-20110322.

NOTES

204   **Both Gates and Biden had advised Obama against:** Michael Hastings, "Inside Obama's War Room," *Rolling Stone*, October 13, 2011, www.rollingstone.com/politics/news/inside-obamas-war-room-20111013.

204   **word could trickle out:** Author interviews with senior administration oficials, Washington, DC, December 2011.

204   **"Even though I thought it was only fifty-fifty":** "Obama on bin Laden: The Full *60 Minutes* Interview."

205   **semicircle around him:** Tom Donilon in *Targeting bin Laden.*

205   **"I've considered the decision":** Ibid.

205   **"This is the third president":** Tom Donilon for *Targeting bin Laden,* unaired portion of his interview.

205   **"I thought, 'Man, that is a gutsy call'":** Tony Blinken interview.

206   **"I've never seen devastation like this":** "Obama on Tornado Devastation in the South: 'It's Heartbreaking,'" *Los Angeles Times*, April 29, 2011, latimesblogs.latimes.com/washington/2011/04/obama-visits-tornado-devastation.html.

206   **Donilon signed an official authorization:** Tom Donilon in *Targeting bin Laden.*

206   **were told to evacuate:** Saeed Shah, "U.S. Officials Escape bin Laden Revenge Bombing in Pakistan," *McClatchy Newspapers*, October 4, 2011, www.mcclatchydc.com/2011/05/20/v-print/114485/us-officials-survive-bomb-attack.html.

206   **Obama flew to Kennedy Space Center:** Devin Dwyer, "President Obama, Gabrielle Giffords Meet After Shuttle Launch Postponed," ABC News, April 29, 2011, abcnews.go.com/US/president-obama-gabrielle-giffords-meet-florida-scrubbed-shuttle/story?id=13478147#.Tx3niV1AIj8.

208   **McRaven decided to push the mission back:** Michael Leiter interview; Tom Donilon in *Targeting bin Laden.*

208   **during a break from rehearsing his speech:** Mazzetti, Cooper, and Baker, "Behind the Hunt for bin Laden."

208   **"I couldn't have any more confidence in you":** Jake Tapper, "President Obama to National Security Team: 'It's a Go,'" ABC News, May 2, 2011, abcnews.go.com/blogs/politics/2011/05/president-obama-to-national-security-team-its-a-go/.

208   **Obama was turning over the details:** "Obama on bin Laden: The Full *60 Minutes* Interview."

208   **a hilarious after-dinner monologue:** Transcript of Obama's Remarks at the Correspondents' Dinner, *Wall Street Journal*, May 1, 2011, blogs.wsj.com/washwire/2011/05/01/transcript-of-obamas-remarks-at-the-correspondents-dinner/.

NOTES

209 **comedian Seth Meyers, at one point made a joke:** Nick Carbone, "Obama's Poker Face: President Reacts to Bin Laden Joke at Correspondents' Dinner," *Time*, May 2, 2011, newsfeed.time.com/2011/05/02/obamas-poker-face-president-reacts-to-bin-laden-joke-at-correspondents-dinner/#ixzz1kKBJRvr5.

209 **Stephanopoulos quizzed him:** Marc Ambinder in *Targeting bin Laden.*

CHAPTER 13: DON'T TURN ON THE LIGHT

211 **"Go downstairs and go back to bed":** Author interview with Pakistani official familiar with the interrogation of bin Laden's wives.

211 **"Don't turn on the light":** Ibid.

211 **taken the sensible precaution of turning off the electricity:** Ihsan Mohammad Khan, interview by author, Abbottabad, Pakistan, July 21, 2011.

211 **staffers had begun arriving at the White House:** Author interview with senior administration officials.

212 **McDonough had gone to his friend Mike Leiter's wedding:** Michael Leiter interview.

212 **"It was my wedding" ... "I might not be back":** Ibid.

212 **attended Sunday mass:** Marc Ambinder in *Targeting bin Laden.*

212 **"deputies" meeting began ... each had thick briefing books:** Author interview with senior administration official.

212 **"branches" and "sequels":** Author interview with Pentagon official.

212 **the armor-plated limos:** Marc Ambinder in *Targeting bin Laden.*

212 **canceled all tours ... the movie *The Hangover:*** Ben Rhodes interview.

213 **secure communications in the Situation Room:** Ben Rhodes in *Targeting bin Laden.*

213 **team of some thirty officers:** James Cartwright interview.

213 **Cartwright's team ... biggest concern was:** Ibid.

213 **sit tight in the compound:** Author interview with senior administration official.

213 **could fight their way out:** Ibid.

213 **Obama's war cabinet began to gather in the Sit Room:** Mike Leiter interview.

213 **room had been transformed into a command center:** Calabresi, "CIA Chief: Pakistan Would Have Jeopardized Operation."

214 **"What do you think?" Panetta asked:** Author interview with senior intelligence official.

214 **Observing the operation at the CIA:** Eric Olson interview by Martha Raddatz, Aspen, Colorado, July 27, 2011, http://www.c-spanvideo.org/program/300735-1.

NOTES

214 **Panetta was in nominal control of the operation:** Author interview with U.S. intelligence official.

214 **At 1:22 p.m., Panetta ordered McRaven to perform the raid:** Ibid.

214 **At 2:05 p.m., Panetta began one more overview of the operation:** Mazzetti, Cooper, and Baker, "Behind the Hunt for bin Laden."

214 **twenty-three "operators" and an interpreter:** Schmidle, "Getting bin Laden."

215 **small cards filled with photos and descriptions:** Lamb, "Revealed: The SEALs' Secret Guide."

215 **combat dog named Cairo, wearing body armor:** Ben Forer, "Osama Bin Laden Raid: Navy SEALs Brought Highly Trained Dog with Them into Compound," ABC News, May 5, 2011, abcnews.go.com/US/osama-bin-laden-raid-navy-seals-military-dog/story?id=13535070#.TtaMrF1AIj8.

215 **at about 11:00 p.m. local time, the two Black Hawks took off:** Schmidle, "Getting bin Laden."

215 **in "peacetime" mode:** Irfan Ghauri, "Abbottabad Incursion: US Took Advantage of 'Peacetime Mode,'" *Express Tribune*, July 12, 2011, tribune.com.pk/story/207808/abbottabad-incursion-us-took-advantage-of-peacetime-mode/.

215 **gave off a low heat "signature" . . . flew "nap-of-the-earth":** Chris Marvin, former Black Hawk pilot, interview for *The Last Days of Osama bin Laden*, National Geographic Channel, November 9, 2011.

215 **flight time to the target was about an hour and a half:** Author interview with U.S. intelligence official.

215 **Petraeus, who had received a heads-up three days earlier:** Paula Broadwell and Vernon Loeb, *All In: The Education of General David Petraeus* (New York: Penguin Press, 2012), pp. 255–59.

216 **dozen Special Forces operations:** Ibid.

216 **Petraeus strolled into the ops center:** Ibid; David Petraeus, interview by Tresha Mabile, Washington, DC, August 2011.

216 **three bus-size Chinook helicopters:** Schmidle, "Getting bin Laden."

216 **Flew on to Kala Dhaka:** "OBL Operation: Helicopters Landed in Kala Dhaka Before Proceeding to Abbottabad," *Express Tribune*, May 14, 2011, tribune.com.pk/story/168573/osama-bin-laden-operation-helicopters-landed-in-kala-dhaka-before-proceeding-to-abbottabad/.

216 **more than a dozen senior officials:** Author observations.

217 **bat-shaped RQ-170 Sentinel stealth drone:** Greg Miller, "CIA Flew Stealth Drones into Pakistan to Monitor bin Laden House," *Washington Post*, May 17, 2011, www.washingtonpost.com/world/

national-security/cia-flew-stealth-drones-into-pakistan-to-monitor-bin-laden-house/2011/05/13/AF5dW55G_story.html.

217   **"The White House, as only the White House can":** Michael Leiter interview.

218   **"Slowly, onesies and twosies":** Ibid.

218   **"I need to watch this":** Schmidle, "Getting bin Laden."

218   **Dozens of other officials:** James Cartwright interview.

218   **"The only thing I can compare it to":** Michael Leiter interview.

218   **"Why is that helo there?":** Ibid.

218   **weight . . . and the higher-than-expected temperatures:** Author interview with former JSOC officer, Washington, DC.

218   **"settling with power":** Former Black Hawk pilot Chris Marvin in *The Last Days of Osama bin Laden.*

219   **outer walls had been represented by chain-link fencing:** Author interview with U.S. intelligence official.

219   **he avoided a potentially catastrophic crash:** Ibid.

219   **hope was that any curious locals would assume:** "Sources: Raiders Knew Mission a One-Shot Deal," Associated Press, May 17, 2011, www.navytimes.com/news/2011/05/ap-raiders-knew-mission-a-one-shot-deal-051711/.

219   **"We could see that there were problems":** Barack Obama in *Targeting bin Laden.*

219   **"And when our helicopter tail didn't get over the wall":** Hillary Clinton, interview by author, Washington, DC, January 23, 2012.

220   **Gates, who was ashen:** Author interview with senior administration official.

220   **"I know his heart was in his throat then":** James Clapper interview.

220   **nervously piped up, "Is that good?":** Author interview with U.S. intelligence official.

220   **"Director, as you can see, we have a helicopter down":** Ibid.

220   **"I'm pushing the QRF to the objective":** Ibid.

221   **deadliest battle in the history of the SEALs:** Laura Blumenfeld, "The Sole Survivor," *Washington Post,* June 11, 2007, www.washingtonpost.com/wp-dyn/content/article/2007/06/10/AR2007061001492_pf.html.

221   **three SEALs from the downed chopper:** Christina Lamb and Nicola Smith, "Geronimo! EKIA 38 Minutes to Mission Success," *The Australian,* May 9, 2011, www.theaustralian.com.au/news/world/geronimo-

ekia-38-minutes-to-mission-success/story-e6frg6so-1226052094513;
Philip Sherwell, "Osama bin Laden Killed: Behind the Scenes of
the Deadly Raid," www.telegraph.co.uk/news/worldnews/al-qaeda
/8500431/Osama-bin-Laden-killed-Behind-the-scenes-of-the-deadly-
raid.html.

222 **settling the bird down just outside the compound walls:** Schmidle,
"Getting bin Laden"; author interview with Pakistani official by author.

222 **secure the outside perimeter:** Author interview with NSC officials;
author interviews with U.S. intelligence officials.

222 **track any "squirters" . . . hunt for any hidden chambers:** Gardiner
Harris, "A bin Laden Hunter on Four Legs," *New York Times*, May 4,
2011, www.nytimes.com/2011/05/05/science/05dog.html.

222 **The remaining eight SEALs:** Author interview with Pakistani official.

222 **for about fifteen minutes:** Author interviews with senior Department
of Defense officials.

222 **Sewn into his clothing:** Author interview with U.S. intelligence official.

223 **shot Abrar, the Kuwaiti's brother, and his wife, Bushra:** Author interview with Pakistani officials.

223 **"We were really in a blackout":** Barack Obama in *Targeting bin Laden*.

223 **no idea what the layout of the floors:** Author interview with U.S. intelligence officials.

223 **"I kept waiting for some big explosion":** Michael Leiter interview.

223 **"Might there be a quick reaction force":** John Brennan in *Targeting
bin Laden*.

223 **Knots of children:** Dozier, "Bin Laden Trove of Documents Sharpen
US Aim."

224 **the AK-47 and Makarov machine pistol:** The AK-47 and the Russian-
made Makarov pistol will be installed at the CIA Museum, in Langley, VA.

224 **unless bin Laden walked out of his bedroom:** Author interview with
senior U.S. intelligence official.

224 **screamed something in Arabic:** Schmidle, "Getting bin Laden."

224 **shoved her aside:** Ibid.

224 **brains spattered:** Author observations at bin Laden compound in
Abbottabad.

224 **expected some kind of warning:** Interview with Leon Panetta, *Charlie
Rose*, PBS, September 6, 2011, www.defense.gov/transcripts/transcript
.aspx?transcriptid=4872.

225 **G meant that bin Laden was "secured":** Author interview with Pentagon official, February 10, 2012.

NOTES

225 **There were gasps in the Situation Room:** Ben Rhodes in *Targeting bin Laden.*

225 **no whoops:** Michael Leiter interview.

226 **blow up the downed helicopter crammed with secret avionics:** Author interview with Pentagon official.

226 **"We were just amazed":** Michael Leiter interview.

227 **blood oozing from their noses, ears, and mouths:** Reuters released photographs of three of the corpses.

227 **interpreter waved off curious neighbors:** CNN, May 12, 2011, Local Young Man: "We tried to go there and they pointed the laser guns on us, and said, 'No you can't go.' They were speaking Pashto so we thought they were from Afghanistan, not America."

228 **placed them in vials for DNA analysis:** Schmidle, "Getting bin Laden."

228 **the material seized from the compound:** Robert Windrem and Alex Johnson, "Bin Laden Aides Were Using Cell Phones, Officials Tell NBC," NBC News, www.msnbc.msn.com/id/42881728/ns/world_news-death_of_bin_laden/t/bin-laden-aides-were-using-cell-phones-officials-tell-nbc/#.TyBX1l1AIj8.

228 **high fives all around and fist bumping:** Author interview with counterterrorism officials involved in the hunt for bin Laden.

229 **Chinook and the Black Hawk separated . . . more direct routes:** Author interview with U.S. National Security official.

229 **Black Hawk still needed to take on fuel:** Author interview with senior administration official.

229 **At about 2:00 a.m. local time . . . the Chinook landed:** Ibid.

229 **all quickly inspected bin Laden's corpse:** U.S. intelligence official interview.

229 **"Well, sir, I guess I owe you sixty million dollars":** Author interview with senior intelligence official.

229 **Obama remembers, "It wasn't really until":** Barack Obama in *Targeting bin Laden.*

229 **"I have the results of the eight-point facial analysis on bin Laden":** Author interview with U.S. intelligence officials.

230 **Cheers . . . champagne bottles:** Ibid.

230 **"The pictures were kind of gruesome":** James Clapper interview.

230 **"There was a hole right around one of his eyes":** Author interview with senior administration official.

230 **"I don't need facial recognition":** Michael Leiter interview.

NOTES

CHAPTER 14: AFTERMATH

231 **Pakistani security officials began arriving:** Author interview with Pakistani official.

231 **"I am from Swat":** Asad Munir, former ISI official, interview by author, Pakistan, July 15, 2011.

232 **"They have killed and taken away Abu Hamza":** Ibid.

232 **daughter, Safia, also spoke:** Robert Booth, Saeed Shah, and Jason Burke, "Osama bin Laden Death: How Family Scene in Compound Turned to Carnage," *Guardian*, May 5, 2011, www.guardian.co.uk/world/2011/may/05/bin-laden-death-family-compound.

232 **awoken by a quite unusual sound:** Ihsan Mohammad Khan interview.

233 **"A helicopter crashed down":** Ihsan Khan e-mail to Voice of America in Washington, DC, May 2, 2011.

233 **not remain secret for long:** Author interview with U.S. intelligence officials.

233 **see people on the rooftops:** Ibid.

233 **picking up conversations by local officials:** Author interview with U.S. military official involved in the hunt for bin Laden.

233 **reports that Pakistani media were at the compound filming:** Ben Rhodes interview.

233 **"Some of us were eager for the president to go out":** Ibid.

234 **saying, "We gotta call!":** Michael Leiter interview.

234 **developed a real friendship:** Michael Mullen interview.

235 **"It was not ours":** Najam Sethi, "Operation Get OBL," May 6, 2011, *Friday Times*, www.thefridaytimes.com/06052011/page1.shtml.

235 **Kayani took a call . . . F-16s were scrambled:** Zahid Hussain, Matthew Rosenberg, and Jeremy Page, "Slow Dawn After Midnight Raid," *Wall Street Journal*, May 9, 2011.

235 **first person Obama called was his predecessor:** Author interview with senior administration official.

235 **"I didn't feel any great sense of happiness":** *George W. Bush: The 9/11 Interview*, National Geographic Channel, August 28, 2011.

236 **Munter had known of the impending raid:** Author interview with National Security Council official.

236 **It was a senior Pakistani official:** Author interview with U.S. official.

236 **bewildered reactions of Pakistani officials:** Michael Leiter interview; author interview with U.S. officials.

236 **Zardari told Obama, "I'm happy because":** Author interview with senior administration official.

NOTES

236 **"Congratulations," Kayani immediately said:** Ibid.

236 **lasted a tense twenty minutes:** Ibid.

236 **urged that Obama go out as soon as possible and explain:** Ibid.

237 **"Our people need to understand what happened here":** Ibid.

237 **"Just get in!":** Ed Henry, CNN White House correspondent, CNN, May 1, 2011.

238 **Gradually the speculation:** Geraldo Rivera, "Geraldo at Large," *Fox News,* May 1, 2011.

238 **he thought, "I can't do this. It'd jinx it":** Ben Rhodes interview.

238 **"We decided not to sugarcoat it":** Ibid.

238 **Obama told Rhodes that, for the speech:** Ibid.

239 **"You can't write this stuff":** Tony Blinken interview.

239 **"Turn on the TV":** Michael Vickers interview.

239 **"I remember walking out":** James Clapper interview.

239 **"Good evening. Tonight I can report":** "Full Text of Obama's Speech on bin Laden's Death," CBS, May 2, 2011, www.cbsnews.com/8301-503544_162-20058783-503544.html.

240 **some fifty-five million Americans:** Brian Stelter, "Obama's TV Audience Was His Largest," *New York Times,* May 3, 2011, www.nytimes.com/2011/05/04/arts/television/bin-laden-speech-drew-obamas-largest-audience-as-president.html.

241 **Nayef offered his congratulations:** Author interview with senior administration official.

241 **A V-22 Osprey tilt-rotor aircraft:** Schmidle, "Getting bin Laden."

241 **ceremony that took a little under an hour:** "DOD Background Briefing with Senior Defense Officials from the Pentagon and Senior Intelligence Officials by Telephone on U.S. Operations Involving Osama Bin Laden," May 2, 2011, www.defense.gov/transcripts/transcript.aspx?transcriptid=4818.

242 **hand-carried to Washington:** Author interview with senior administration official.

242 **Using DNA material obtained from relatives:** "DOD Background Briefing with Senior Defense Officials from the Pentagon and Senior Intelligence Officials by Telephone on U.S. Operations Involving Osama Bin Laden," May 2, 2011, www.defense.gov/transcripts/transcript.aspx?transcriptid=4818.

242 **made a number of assertions about what had happened:** "Transcript of White House Press Briefing on bin Laden's Death," *Wall Street Journal,* May 2, 2011, blogs.wsj.com/washwire/2011/05/02/transcript-of-white-house-press-briefing-on-bin-ladens-death/.

NOTES

242 **White House quickly retracted:** Robert Booth, "The Killing of Osama bin Laden: How the White House Changed Its Story," *Guardian*, May 4, 2011, www.guardian.co.uk/world/2011/may/04/osama-bin-laden-killing-us-story-change.

242 **"would be presented to the public":** "Transcript of Interview with CIA Director Panetta," NBC News, May 3, 2011, www.msnbc.msn .com/id/42887700/ns/world_news-death_of_bin_laden/t/transcript-interview-cia-director-panetta/#.TxclzV1AIj8.

242 **Obama, Gates, and Clinton all agreed:** "Obama on bin Laden: The Full *60 Minutes* interview," CBS News, May 8, 2011, www.cbsnews .com/8301-504803_162-20060530-10391709.html.

243 **"important for us to make sure":** Ibid.

243 **"The fact of the matter is":** Ibid.

243 **"You ought to give McRaven a gold-plated tape measure":** Tony Blinken interview.

243 **a tape measure mounted on a plaque:** Author interview with senior administration official.

243 **a task force of 125 people worked 24/7:** Author interview with senior U.S. intelligence official.

244 **"It was decided that any effort to work with the Pakistanis":** Calabresi, "CIA Chief: Pakistan Would Have Jeopardized bin Laden Operation."

244 **first reaction of the Pakistani military to the bin Laden operation:** Author interview with U.S. official.

244 **Both Pakistani generals offered their congratulations:** Author interview with U.S. official.

245 **horribly embarrassing for the Pakistani military:** Ibid.

245 **Criticism of the army from all quarters:** "Altaf Asks Military, Govt to Apologise Over US Raid," *Dawn*, May 5, 2011, www.dawn.com/2011/ 05/05/altaf-asks-military-govt-to-apologise-over-us-raid.html.

245 **this was the worst week of his life:** Author interviews with senior Pakistani military official and U.S. diplomatic official.

245 **at least him or Kayani or President Zardari:** Author interview with Pakistani military official.

245 **Pasha had played a key role:** Author interviews with U.S. officials.

245 **Pasha felt that the relationship with the United States:** Author interview with Pakistani official.

246 **"I believe that there are elements":** Eli Lake, "Rogers: Pakistani Intelligence Services Aided bin Laden," *Washington Times*, June 14,

NOTES

2011, www.washingtontimes.com/news/2011/jun/14/rogers-pakistan-military-intel-aided-bin-laden/.

246 **no official Pakistani complicity:** Michael Leiter interview; author interviews with multiple other intelligence officials.

246 **al-Qaeda officially confirmed the death of its leader:** Augustine Anthony, "Al-Qaeda Confirms Bin Laden Is Dead, Vows Revenge," Reuters, May 6, 2011, www.reuters.com/article/2011/05/06/us-obama-statement-idUSTRE74107920110506.

246 **The same day that al-Qaeda announced bin Laden's death:** Jake Tapper, Nick Schifrin, and Jessica Hopper, "Obama Thanks SEALs, Troops Back from Afghanistan," ABC News, abcnews.go.com/Politics/obama-seals-troops-back-afghanistan-job-well-done/story?id=13543148#.Txd JtV1AIj8.

247 **half an hour, in a small classroom:** Author interviews with senior administration officials.

247 **First to speak was the helicopter pilot:** Ibid.

248 **describing everyone's role, including that of the interpreter:** Ibid.

248 **"finest fighting force in the history of the world":** Ibid.

248 **"Well, sir, I strongly advise you to have a treat":** Ibid.

248 **discussed all the areas of tension:** Author interview with U.S. government official, Washington, DC.

249 **While Kerry was still in the air:** Ibid.

249 **"very hard, very difficult":** Author interview with Pakistani intelligence official involved in the interrogation of bin Laden's wives.

249 **President Obama visited CIA headquarters:** Transcript of President Obama's remarks to the intelligence community, May 20, 2011.

249 **"we kept it a secret":** Ibid.

EPILOGUE: THE TWILIGHT OF AL-QAEDA

250 **inception in Peshawar in August 1988:** Peter Bergen, *The Osama bin Laden I Know* (New York: Free Press, 2006), pp. 74–82.

251 **A Gallup Poll:** John Esposito and Dalia Mogahed, *Who Speaks for Islam? What a Billion Muslims Really Think* (New York: Gallup Press, 2007).

251 **sent a team of would-be suicide bombers to Barcelona:** Al Goodman, "11 on Trial Over Alleged Barcelona Terror Plot," CNN.com, November 13, 2009, http://edition.cnn.com/2009/WORLD/europe/11/12/spain.terror.trial/.

251 **trained an American recruit, Faisal Shahzad:** *United States of America v. Faisal Shahzad*, Plea, 10-CR-541 (MGC), United States District

Court, Southern District of New York, June 21, 2010, http://www
.investigativeproject.org/documents/case_docs/1435.pdf.

251 **LeT carried out multiple attacks in Mumbai:** Somini Sangupta, "Dossier Gives Details of Mumbai Attacks," *New York Times*, January 6, 2009, www.nytimes.com/2009/01/07/world/asia/07india.html.

252 **hid bombs in toner cartridges:** "Magazine Details al Qaeda Cargo Plane Plots," CNN.com, November 21, 2010, http://articles.cnn .com/2010-11-21/world/al.qaeda.magazine_1_cargo-plane-aqap-plane-crash?_s=PM:WORLD.

252 **formally pledged allegiance to bin Laden:** Katherine Houreld, "Somali Militant Group al-Shabaab Formally Joins Al-Qaeda," Associated Press, February 9, 2012, http://www.guardian.co.uk/world/2012/feb/09/somali-al-shabaab-join-al-qaida.

252 **up to twelve hundred were working:** Jane Ferguson, "Violent Extremists Calling Fighters to Somalia," CNN.com, April 27, 2010, http://articles.cnn.com/2010-04-27/world/somalia.al.shabaab_1_somali-american-transitional-federal-government-foreign-fighters?_s=PM:WORLD.

252 **Ryan Crocker, said:** Lee Keath, "Al Qaeda Is Close to Defeat in Iraq, US Ambassador Says," Associated Press, May 25, 2008, http://articles .boston.com/2008-05-25/news/29268149_1_shi-ite-sadr-city-maliki.

252 **AQI sent foot soldiers into Syria:** "US Official Says Al-Qaeda Involved in Syria," Al Jazeera, February 17, 2012, http://www.aljazeera .com/news/middleeast/2012/02/201221794018300979.html.

253 **favorable views . . . dropped by at least half:** "Terror Suspect Went to Meet bin Laden," Associated Press, May 4, 2011, www.foxnews .com/world/2011/05/04/indonesia-terror-suspect-went-meet-bin-laden/#ixzz1kCVvHPfP.

254 **warned that the West faced "victory or holocaust":** David Frum and Richard Perle, *An End to Evil: How to Win the War on Terror* (New York: Random House, 2003), p. 7. Also see Dana Milbank, "Prince of Darkness Denies Own Existence," *Washington Post*, February 20, 2009.

254 **invoking the specter of World War IV:** Charles Feldman and Stan Wilson, "Ex-CIA Director: US Faces 'World War IV,'" CNN.com, April 3, 2003, http://www.cnn.com/2003/US/04/03/sprj.irq.woolsey .world.war/; James Woolsey on CNN, June 2, 2002.

254 **a global conflict that killed tens of millions:** See generally *The Black Book of Communism* (Cambridge, MA: Harvard University Press, 1999).

254 **Americans are far more likely to drown:** In a typical year about three hundred Americans accidentally drown in their bathtubs, http://danger .mongabay.com/injury_death.htm.

255 **al-Qaeda announced his successor:** Saeed Shah, "Ayman al-Zawahiri Takes Over Al Qaeda Leadership," McClatchy, June 17, 2011, http://

www.sfgate.com/cgi-bin/article.cgi?f=/c/a/2011/06/16/MNLH1JUT 4A.DTL.

258 **set off bombs in Manhattan in 2009:** John Marzulli, "Najibullah Zazi Pleads Guilty to Plotting NYC Terror Attack, Supporting Al Qaeda," *New York Daily News*, February 22, 2010.

259 **Mumbai-style attacks in Germany:** "Terror Suspects 'Were Tipped Off,'" CNN.com, September 10, 2007, http://articles.cnn.com/2007-09-10/world/germany.terror_1_joerg-ziercke-terror-plot-training-camps?_s=PM:WORLD.

259 **ramped-up program of attacks:** Katherine Tiedemann and Peter Bergen, "The Year of the Drone," New America Foundation, February 24, 2010, http://counterterrorism.newamerica.net/sites/newamerica.net/files/policydocs/bergentiedemann2.pdf.

259 **a CIA drone killed Atiyah Abdul Rahman:** "Atiyah Abd al-Rahman Dead: Al Qaeda Second in Command Killed in Pakistan," Associated Press, August 28, 2011, http://www.huffingtonpost.com/2011/08/27/atiyah-abd-al-rahman-al-qaeda-dead_n_939009.html.

259 **one of bin Laden's dozen or so sons:** Douglas Farah and Dana Priest, "Bin Laden Son Plays Key Role in Al-Qaeda," *Washington Post*, October 14, 2003, http://www.washingtonpost.com/wp-dyn/content/article/2007/08/20/AR2007082000980.html.

260 **Islamist groups did very well:** "Two Islamist Parties Win Big in Egypt Election," CNN.com, January 21, 2012, http://articles.cnn.com/2012-01-21/africa/world_africa_egypt-elections_1_egypt-election-egyptian-election-conservative-al-nour-party?_s=PM:AFRICA.

261 **the most dangerous of the group's regional branches:** "Intel Chief: U.S. Faces Many Interconnected Foes," Associated Press, January 31, 2012, http://www.cbsnews.com/8301-201_162-57368904/intel-chief-u.s-faces-many-interconnected-foes/.

261 **"Let my grave be an eagle's belly":** Osama bin Laden, "Exposing the New Crusader War," on jihadist websites February 2003.

261 **sent mechanized diggers to the compound:** "Osama Bin Laden Compound Being Demolished in Pakistan," Reuters, February 25, 2012. http://www.guardian.co.uk/world/2012/feb/26/osama-bin-laden-compound-demolished.

261 **"history's unmarked grave of discarded lies":** "President Bush Addresses the Nation," *Washington Post*, September 20, 2001, http://www.washingtonpost.com/wp-srv/nation/specials/attacked/transcripts/bushaddress_092001.html.

261 **"small men on the wrong side":** Remarks by the President at United States Military Academy at West Point Commencement, West Point, New York, May 22, 2010.

ACKNOWLEDGMENTS

Nonfiction book writing is a strange combination of the intensely solitary—no one is going to write the book for you—and the profoundly collective. Andrew Lebovich worked on all phases of this project, performing and organizing research, fact-checking and footnoting the book, and translating French materials. Jennifer Rowland also performed and organized research, fact-checked and footnoted the manuscript, translated Arabic materials, and did the excellent photo research. It was my good luck to have two researchers as smart and well organized as Andrew and Jennifer to work on this book and to have worked with them on a daily basis at the New America Foundation. Andrew has gone on to work for a D.C.-based firm doing analysis on North Africa, and we will be hearing much more from him in the future.

The New America Foundation in Washington, D.C., has been my home for a decade. I am especially lucky to work there with its president, Steve Coll, who is invariably the smartest guy in the room and also the most self-effacing. His work ethic, integrity, and leadership are inspirational. Thanks also to my New America colleagues Patrick Doherty and Brian Fishman, who work with me in the national security program at New America. And thanks to Simone Frank, Danielle Maxwell, Troy Schneider, Stephanie Gunter, Faith Smith, and Rachel White, who help our program in numerous different ways. Thanks to interns Tristan Berne, Galen Petruso, Kelsy Greenwald, and Eric Verdeyen, who all helped with some of the research for the book. Thanks also to Christina Satkowski.

The author Ken Ballen, who is also a leading pollster in the Muslim world, read the manuscript carefully and had many important suggestions about how to improve it. Similarly, the security expert Andrew Marshall made key editorial

ACKNOWLEDGMENTS

observations about how to better conceptualize the book. Thanks to you both for your guidance and friendship.

The journalism of Nick Schmidle in the *New Yorker* and Kimberly Dozier and Adam Goldman at the Associated Press deserves special mention for the light it has helped to shed on the Abbottabad raid and the intelligence breakthroughs that led to it.

In Pakistan, I received invaluable help from Major General Nazir Butt and Commodore (ret.) Zafar Iqbal. Thanks to you both for your sage advice and friendship. Thanks also to Khalid Khan Kheshgi and Ihsan Khan.

Thanks also to the team at Free Press, who published my three previous books on al-Qaeda and bin Laden, which were the necessary foundations to write this book, and in particular my editor there, Dominick Anfuso. Thanks also to Will Sulkin and Stuart Williams, of the Bodley Head, who are publishing this book in the United Kingdom. Thanks also to Politikens Forlag in Denmark, the House of Books in Holland, Verlagsgruppe Random House GmbH in Germany, Cappelen Damm AS in Norway, and Publicações Dom Quixote, Lda., in Portugal for publishing this book in their respective countries.

At the White House, thanks to Ben Rhodes and Jamie Smith for the help you provided. At the Department of Defense, thanks to Doug Wilson, Dr. George Little, Carl Woog, Captain John Kirby, Tara Rigler, Bob Mehal, and Lieutenant Colonel James Gregory for the support you offered. At the CIA, thanks to Preston Golson, Cynthia Rapp, Jennifer Youngblood, and Marie Harf; at the National Counterterrorism Center, thanks to Carl Kropf; at the Office of the Director of National Intelligence, thanks to Shawn Turner and Mike Birmingham; at Special Operations Command, thanks to Ken McGraw; in the Office of the Vice President, thanks to Alexandra Kahan; at the State Department, thanks to Philippe Reines and Caroline Adler; at the Defense Intelligence Agency, thanks to Susan Strednansky; in Admiral Mullen's office, thanks to Sarah Chayes and to Sally Donnelly; in General McChrystal's office, thanks to Duncan Boothby and Samuel Ayres, and thanks also to Colonel Erik Gunhus in Afghanistan. Thanks to Lieutenant Colonel Patrick Buckley, Lieutenant Colonel Joel Rayburn, Ferial Govashiri, and Tommy Vietor.

At Nutopia Productions, thanks to Jane Root and Phil Craig, who made available the full transcripts of the White House interviews that they taped for their invaluable documentary *Targeting bin Laden,* which aired on the History Channel. Thanks to Christina Lamb of the *Sunday Times,* who made available the card that the SEALs carried the night of the raid, which is reproduced in this book. Thanks to Gene Thorp for the excellent maps. Thanks also to Keith Sinzinger.

Thanks to Anderson Cooper, Eric Greitens, and Steve Coll, three gentlemen whose work and character I greatly admire and who all looked over the manuscript. Thanks also to all those who agreed to be interviewed for the book. Those who agreed to go on the record can be found in the list of interviewees on page 273.

I have worked at CNN in one capacity or another since 1990 and am grate-

ACKNOWLEDGMENTS

ful to continue to work there today with so many of its excellent reporters, executives, producers, and editors, in particular Pamela Sellars, Richard Galant, Charlie Moore, and Anderson Cooper. Thanks also to Henry Schuster, now at CBS's *60 Minutes,* who has been a friend and colleague for a decade and a half.

Thanks to Storyhouse Productions and producer Simon Epstein for their work on the National Geographic documentary *The Last Days of Osama bin Laden,* which helped to inform this book. And a particular thanks to my wife, Tresha Mabile, who was the co-executive producer of the documentary and traveled to Pakistan when she was five months pregnant to produce it. At National Geographic Television, thanks to Michael Cascio, Kim Woodward, and Jack Smith, who made the documentary better.

Thanks to Marin Strmecki of the Smith Richardson Foundation and Nancy Chang of the Open Society Institute, for their funding of our work at the New America Foundation. Thanks also to Chip Kaye and Fareed Zakaria, who chair the advisory council for the national security program at New America and have been stalwart supporters. Thanks also to the other members of the advisory council, Anne-Marie Slaughter, Fred Hassan, Tom Freston, Bob Niehaus, and Chris Niehaus. Thanks also to Liaquat and Meena Ahamed.

Some of the reporting for this book first took shape in a number of magazines and newspapers. I am grateful to *The New Republic*'s former editor Franklin Foer for publishing my work and to the magazine's current editor, Richard Just, who made my pieces much better. Thanks to Cullen Murphy at the *Atlantic* and Wayne Lawson at *Vanity Fair,* Carlos Lozada at the *Washington Post,* Rick Stengel at *Time,* Alan Hunter at the *Sunday Times,* and Robert Colvile, Con Coughlin, and Sally Chatterton at the *Daily Telegraph.*

Thanks to the director Greg Barker, who has optioned this book for a theatrical-release documentary for HBO, and to producers John Battsek and Julie Goldman. I'm looking forward to seeing the results! Thanks also to Colin Callender and Marc Gordon of Playground Entertainment for their interest in this book.

Thanks to Susan Glasser, Blake Hounshell, and Benjamin Pauker of Foreign Policy for your collaboration on the AfPak Channel. Thanks to Chris Clifford and Shannon Calabrese of Keppler Speakers and Clark Forcey for your advice and help over the years. Thanks to Karen Greenberg at Fordham Law School's Center on National Security for your counsel and friendship.

My agent, Tina Bennett of Janklow & Nesbit, has been a joy to work with for the past decade, both as a friend and as an intellectual sounding board. Tina is widely and justly regarded as the best nonfiction agent in the business, and I consider myself very lucky to be one of the authors she represents. Also at Janklow, thanks to Svetlana Katz.

Thanks to the Bergen, Mabile, Gould, Takacs, and Coughlin families for all your support. In particular I want to thank my mother-in-law, Albertha Mabile, who came to stay with us in the first month when Pierre was born and helped to hold down the fort. You were indispensable. (How did you sleep last night?)

At Crown, thanks to the superb team of Molly Stern, David Drake, Annsley

ACKNOWLEDGMENTS

Rosner, Jay Sones, Julie Cepler, Matthew Martin, Robert Siek, Linda Kaplan, and Rachel Berkowitz. Special thanks to assistant editor Stephanie Chan, who worked diligently on the photo inserts. Copy editor Jenna Dolan made the book better and more accurate in innumerable small ways. And executive publicist Penny Simon brought much efficiency and good humor to the task of publicizing this book.

In many ways this book is a co-production with my wonderful editor, Rachel Klayman, who edited my first book about bin Laden, the manuscript of which I submitted to her a week or so before the 9/11 attacks. Rachel brought her ferocious intelligence to bear on this new project and also her great attention to detail, which was mandatory for a book that had to be researched, reported, and written in ten months. An "editor's editor," she worked with a great deal of care and thought on every line of this book. She did all this with much grace and humor despite the other significant projects she also had going on. I hope we can publish another book together soon!

Above all, thanks to my wife, Tresha Mabile. Thanks for reading this book many times over and discussing its contents with me far beyond what anyone could ask for. And thanks also for traveling to Pakistan with me to research the book when you were pregnant with Pierre. The book is dedicated to him, our most important joint project. I love him and you, a lot.

INDEX

Page numbers in *italics* refer to maps. Page numbers beginning with 273 refer to notes.

INDEX

finances of, 15, 44, 56, 62, 63–64,
140, 142–43

founding of, 21, 39, 123, 250, 257

globalization of, 89, 251–52

identified as source of 9/11 attacks,
24–25

information gleaned from Jandal on,
29–31

NIE on, 78, 109

pre-9/11, 55–56, 69

reduced threat to U.S. from, 254

religious fanaticism of, 45, 93, 126,
139

resurgence of, 54, 67–73, 109, 252,
258

rift between Taliban and, 31–32

tarnished by killing of Muslims, 139,
145–46, 253

training camps of, 30, 55, 57, 67, 69,
78, 89, 95–96, 105, 118, 251

twilight of, 254–57

al-Qaeda in the Arabian Peninsula
(AQAP), 137, 138, 141, 312

Al-Qaeda Senior Leadership (AQSL),
90

Al-Quds Al-Arabi, 186

Al-Shabaab, 114–15, 138, 255

American Airlines Flight 77, 9/11 crash
of, 23, 107

Analyst's Notebook, 64

analysts' task force (CIA), 17, 74–94,
99, 105, 129–30

assessment of family and associates
by, 76, 84, 90, 93

audio- and videotapes examined by,
82–83

books about bin Laden studied by,
91–92

communications examined by, 85,
90, 93–94

courier network examined by,
90–91, 94

degrees of certainty in, 133–35, 164

in Kuwaiti lead, 126–27

process of elimination in, 81–82

study of successful manhunts by,
84–88

women in, 77–78, 220

"working theory" of, 81

see also specific analysts

"Anatomy of a Lead," 127

Arab Spring, 144–45, 255–58

Army Rangers, 46, 148, 149, 156, 160

Assad, Bashar al-, 253

As Sahab, 68, 144

assassinations, attempted
assassinations, 6, 10–11, 19, 65,
72, 80, 86, 100, 140, 143, 236,
241

Atef, Mohammed, 37, 38–39, 56, 280,
285

Atlanta Olympics bombing, 86

Atta, Mohammed, 36, 96

Attarzadeh-Niyaki, Heshmatollah, 7

Atwan, Abdel Bari, 41, 284–85

audiotapes, 60–61, 82, 144, 145

Ausaf, 36

Awlaki, Anwar al-, 141–42

Aziz, Amer, 37

B-2 bombers, 1, 161–62, 173–75, 178

Bagram Air Base, 51, 154, 157, 185,
186, 194, 206, 241, 242–43

Bahlul, Ali al-, 21, 22

Bainbridge, USS, 147

Balawi, Humam al-, 117–20

Bali suicide bombings, 61, 63, 164

Baluchi, Abu Salman al-, 257

Bamiyan Buddhas, 28–29, 282

Barcelona, subway attack on, 251

Bash, Jeremy, 126, 174, 183, 184, 229

Batarfi, Ayman Saeed Abdullah, 43

BBC radio, 16, 22, 23

Bearden, Milton, 49

Beirut, 119

Bennett, Gina, 78

Bennett, Lansing, 86

Berntsen, Gary, 42, 46

Bhutto, Benazir, 236

INDEX

INDEX

INDEX

INDEX

dogs, 134–35, 159, 215, 222, 227, 248

Donilon, Tom, 115–16, 191–92, 202, 205–6, 209, 217

double agents, 127, 153, 190

drones, 72, 152, 154, 176, 179
   raid monitored by, 217, 223, 227, 228, 233

drone strikes, 59, 69, 72, 169, 173, 275, 285
   as Abbottabad operation option, 200, 203
   acceleration of, 72, 113, 121, 142
   in Pakistan's tribal regions, 5, 71, 72, 105, 113, 116, 120, 121, 142, 244, 249, 255

Dudayev, Dzhokhar, 86

Egypt, 22, 59, 145, 257–58

Eichmann, Adolf, 84

elections, U.S.:
   of 2004, 55, 64, 82
   of 2008, 108–12, 203

el-Tayeb, Sheikh Ahmed, 241

"Elvis sightings," 75, 91

Emanuel, Rahm, 115

Endeavor, 206

Enemy Killed in Action (EKIA), 225

Entebbe, raid at, 168–69

Escobar, Pablo, 84–85

F3EA (find, fix, finish, exploit, and analyse) sequence, 156

facial recognition analysis, 228, 229

Farenheit 9/11, 84

Fawwaz, Khaled al-, 85

Federal Bureau of Investigation (FBI), 29–30, 87
   lack of communication between CIA and, 25, 106

Fleischer, Ari, 20–21, 60, 73

Flournoy, Michèle, 169–72, 176–77, 180, 184, 194, 196, 202, 240, 318–19

Flynn, Michael T., 154

Franks, Tommy, 46–47, 49–50

Frederica (analyst; pseudonym), 77–78, 100

Fury, Dalton (pseudonym), 44, 47–48

Gadahn, Adam, 258

Gadhafi, Moammar, 113, 204, 237–38

Garrett, Brad, 87–88

Gates, Robert, 148, 172, 173, 179–80, 194, 197, 199–200, 204, 209, 218, 220, 237, 242

geolocation technology, 64, 122–23, 200

Germany, failed plan to attack, 141, 259

Ghailani, Ahmed Khalfan, 65

Ghul, Hassan, 100, 303

Giffords, Gabrielle, 206

Gilani, Yousuf Raza, 120

Glasser, Susan, 51

Goss, Porter, 70, 160

Great Britain, 1, 49, 57, 67, 69–70, 109, 141, 236, 257

Green Berets, 25, 48, 149

Greitens, Eric, 158

Grenier, Robert, 31–32, 71

Greystone program, 59

Grossman, Marc, 244

Growing Up bin Laden (Najwa and Omar bin Laden), 92

Guantánamo, xx, 97–98, 113, 286, 298

Gul, Awad, 52–53, 298

Habib, Khalid, 72

Hamzi, Nawaf al-, 25, 106–7

Haq, Amin ul-, 38, 99

Haq, Qazi Mahoof Ul, 3

Haqqani, Jalaluddin, 38, 81, 299

Haris, Abu, 72

Hawsawi, Mustafa al-, 23

Hayden, Michael, 71, 85, 103–4

INDEX

Heathrow airport, 63, 109
Hekmatyar, Gulbuddin, 81–82
helicopters, 51, 148–49, 176
   in Abbottabad raid, 177–86, 192,
      213–16, 218–22, 226–29, 231,
      232, 233, 235, 247, 249
Hell Week, 158
high value target (HVT), 193–94
hijackers, 30, 96
   CIA failure to watch-list, 106–7
   as revered by al-Qaeda, 23, 45
   twentieth, *see* Qahtani, Mohammed
      al-
Hitler, Adolf, 21, 114, 240, 244
Homeland Security Department, U.S.,
   69

Imperial Hubris (Scheuer), 17
India, 215, 226, 234, 235, 251
"informed interrogation" technique,
   30
"Inroads," 90
interrogations, 29–30, 59, 77, 93, 97–
   103, 114, 186, 286, 287, 298
Iran, 7, 24, 179
   al-Qaeda in, 159–60
   bin Laden family's house arrest in,
      6–7, 62, 138
Iraq, 24, 138, 157
   al-Qaeda (AQI) in, 89, 100, 137,
      138–39, 153, 156, 312
   invasion of, 49–50, 67, 250
   see also Iraq War
Iraqi, Abdul Hadi al-, 67, 68
Iraq War, 64, 67, 68, 117
   and alleged WMD, 127–28, 133,
      190, 210
   end of, 120, 165
   JSOC in, 153–58
   Obama on, 114
   U.S. resources directed at, 49–50,
      70–71, 109–10
ISI, 65–66
Islamabad, 25, 70, 92–93, 249

Ismail, Jamal, 25–26
Israel, 17, 24
   Eichmann tracked by, 84
   in Entebbe raid, 168–69
   Gaza invasion by, 144
   U.S. support for, 19–20

Jaji, Battle of, 41–42
Jalalabad, xx, xxi, 38, 40, 53, 213, 214,
   215, 216, 229, 298
Janabi, Abdul-Sattar al-, 242
Jandal, Abu (Nasser Ahmed Naser
   al-Bahri), 22, 29–30, 186, 284
Jeddah, attack on U.S. consulate in,
   61
Jemaah Islamiya, 63, 100
Jews, 11, 84
   see also Israel
jihad, 35, 57, 70, 86, 89, 141, 251–53,
   257
   of bin Laden, 5–6, 42, 52, 53
   history of, 56–57
Jihad, 26
John (analyst; pseudonym), 104–5,
   129, 133, 164
Johnson, Katie, 212
Joint Special Operations Command
   (JSOC), 50, 147–62, 217
   in Afghanistan, 165–66
   CIA cooperation with, 155, 160,
      166
   creation of, 148–49
   intelligence sharing by, 155
   McChrystal's Iraq War strategy for,
      153–58
   as operating outside bureaucracy,
      151–52, 154
   technological innovations of, 154–56
   work ethic of, 157
   see also specific units
Jordan, 117, 253
   hotel suicide bombings in, 139
journalists, 26–27, 41, 49, 51, 232–33,
   237

INDEX

Kabul, 28, 29–30, 32, 33, 36, 37, 38,
  42, 92, 157
Kandahar, 10, 13, 22, 26, 32–33, 39,
  51
Kansi, Mir Aimal, 86–87
Kappes, Steve, 71
Karachi, 23, 62–63, 100
Kayani, Ashfaq Parvez, 73, 181–82,
  234, 236–37, 244–45, 248
Keller, Art, 70
Kelly, Mark, 206
Kerry, John, 53, 82, 112, 248–49
Khadija (wife), 8–9
Khairiah (Um Hamza; wife), 6–7, 14,
  17, 231–32, 249
Khalis, Yunis, 38
Khan, Arshad (alias), 136
Khan, Ihsan, 232–33
Khan, Mohamed, 68
Khan, Tariq (alias), 136
Khartoum, 8, 78, 80, 135
Khost, 22
  suicide bombing at, 119, 127, 190
Khyam, Omar, 67–68
Kilcullen, David, 71
Kini, Usama Al-, 73
Kunar province, bin Laden's escape to,
  53, 55, 257
Kuwaiti, Abu Ahmed al- (Ibrahim
  Saeed Ahmed; the Kuwaiti), xx, 3,
  13, 14, 94, 103, 130
  Abbottabad lifestyle of, 15, 131,
    136–37
  alternative hypotheses about, 128–
    29, 193
  in bin Laden's communications with
    al-Qaeda, 136–37
  children of, 195
  CIA focus on, 95–107, 122–24,
    164
  death of, 221, 226, 231
  as key to finding bin Laden, 127
Kuwaiti, Abu Jafar al-, 47
Kuwaiti, the, see Kuwaiti, Abu Ahmed
  al-

Lashkar-e-Taiba (LeT), 120, 251
Leiter, Michael, 71, 189–93, 198, 201
  209–10, 212, 217–18, 226, 230
Libi, Abu Faraj al-, 90, 100–101,
  102–3, 160
Libi, Ibn al-Sheikh al-, 43, 65
Libya, 43, 113, 121, 138, 145, 204,
  237–38, 257
Little, George, 189
London, transportation system
  bombings in, 68–69, 109, 141,
  258
Low, David, 78

McCain, John, 110–11, 112, 305
McChrystal, Stanley, 152–58, 160
McDonough, Denis, 109, 188, 192,
  202, 205, 212
McFadden, Robert, 29–30
McRaven, William, 148, 165–69,
  173–74, 177, 179, 180–87, 200,
  203, 205, 206, 208, 213, 214,
  217, 220, 225–26, 229, 243
  six key principles of, 168–69
"McRaven option," 184
Maersk Alabama, 147
Madrid, commutation system attacks
  in, 64
Malaysia, 63, 106
Malik, Rehman, 120
Manhattan:
  failed attack on subway system in,
    117–18, 258–59
  failed Times Square bombing in, 251
maps, *xi–xiii*, 42
Mariam (Kuwaiti's wife), 15, 195, 221,
  231
Marines, U.S., 51, 149, 173
Masri, Abu Jihad Al-, 72
Masri, Abu Khabab al-, 72
Masri, Abu Zubair Al-, 72
Massoud, Ahmad Shah, 6, 19, 79
Matthews, Jennifer, 77–78, 119
Mattis, James N., 51

INDEX

INDEX

active involvement in Abbottabad
operation plans by, 163–65, 167,
172, 177–79, 181–82, 186, 187,
198, 202–4, 206, 207
in aftermath of Abbottabad raid,
233–34, 247–48, 249–50
as aggressive in war against al-
Qaeda, 112–21, 142, 203
on al-Qaeda, 259
bin Laden's hatred of, 16–17
bin Laden's plot to assassinate,
140
in birth certificate controversy, 194,
196, 208–9
on day of 9/11, 108
on day of raid, 212, 214, 217–20,
228–30
go-ahead for Abbottabad raid by,
187, 192, 204–6
in hunt for bin Laden, 92, 108–21,
133
inauguration of, 112, 113, 114–15
on national security, 109–12
Nobel Peace Prize of, 113, 114
perceived as antiwar, 112–13, 203
public announcement of bin Ladin's
death by, 230, 236–40, 233–34
as risk taker, 203–4
in 2008 election campaign, 108–12,
203
at White House Correspondents'
Dinner, 207–9
Oklahoma City, Federal Building
bombing in, 67–68
Olson, Eric, 183, 184, 214
Omar, Mullah, 19, 26–29, 31–32, 82,
143
160th Special Operations Air
Regiment, 149, 192, 247
Operation Eagle Claw (Desert One),
148–49, 160, 179, 199
Operation Neptune Spear, see
Abbottabad raid
*Osama bin Laden I Know, The: An Oral
History* (Bergen), 91–92

Osmani, Mullah Akhtar Mohammad,
31–32

"pacer," 132–33, 176, 186, 203
Pakistan:
al-Qaeda in cities of, 64, 66, 70, 92
al-Qaeda in tribal regions of, 2, 7,
62, 66, 68–69, 70, 81, 87–89, 92,
109, 116, 120, 142, 199, 227, 251
al-Qaeda's attacks on, 70, 143
in Battle of Tora Bora, 46–47
CIA presence in, 182
drone strikes in, 5, 71, 72, 105, 113,
119, 120, 121, 142, 244, 249, 255
ISI of, 65–66, 182
maps of, *xi–xiii*
media of, 232–33, 237
military of, 244–46
as not involved in Abbottabad
operation, 180–81
Obama's policy toward, 110–13
in response to Abbottabad raid, 226,
231, 236, 244–46
in sovereignty issue, 73, 170–72,
173–76, 185–86, 203, 236
strained relations between U.S. and,
73, 109–12, 120–21, 159, 160,
170–72, 173–76, 185–86, 199,
204, 226, 234, 244–46
and U.S. diplomatic strategy after
raid, 233–34, 244–46, 248–49
Panetta, Leon, 115–16, 120, 133–35
in Abbottabad operation planning,
124–26, 163–65, 167, 172–75,
182, 186, 198, 201, 209
in aftermath of raid, 240, 242, 244,
245
on day of raid, 212, 213–14, 220,
229
Pasha, Ahmad Shuja, 182, 235, 245,
248
Patek, Umar, 164
"pattern of life" analysis, 131
Patterson, Anne, 121

INDEX

INDEX

INDEX

WikiLeaks, xx, 98
Wolfowitz, Paul, 47
women:
  in analysts' task force, 76–79; *see also specific agents*
  cultural shift in CIA toward, 78–79
  Muslim, 2, 8, 9, 11, 14–15, 144, 249
Woodrow Wilson Center, Obama's speech at, 109–11
Woolsey, James, 254
World Trade Center, 9/11 attack on, 6, 20–21, 23, 35, 58, 189
World War II, 84, 144, 168, 241, 244

Yazid, Mustafa Abu al-, 142
Yemen, 4, 9, 12, 21, 22, 23, 29, 43, 56, 69, 81, 89, 96, 118, 119, 120, 121, 139, 142, 145
  al-Qaeda in the Arabian Peninsula in, 137, 141, 258
  as future base of al-Qaeda, 257–58

Younis, Juniad, 3
Yusufzai, Rahimullah, 26–27

Zaeef, Mullah Abdul Salam, 27
Zahir, Mohammed, 45
Zaidan, Ahmad, 60–61, 280, 284
Zaman, Hajji, 48
Zarate, Juan, 115
Zardari, Asif Ali, 121, 236, 245
Zarqawi, Abu Musab al-, 139, 156, 312
Zawahiri, Ayman al-, 17, 37, 40, 45, 52, 56, 69, 115, 117, 127, 138, 160, 190, 194, 258, 298
  as bin Laden's second in command, 21–22, 68–69, 89–90
  as successor to bin Laden, 254–57, 258
Zazi, Najibullah, 117–18
Zubaydah, Abu, 65, 77

ABOUT THE AUTHOR

CNN's Peter Arnett and Peter Bergen together with cameraman Peter Jouvenal
(at right) did the first television interview with Osama bin Laden in spring 1997.
They met al-Qaeda's leader in a mud hut in the mountains of eastern Afghanistan,
where this photograph was taken.

Peter Bergen is the author of three previous books about Osama bin
Laden and al-Qaeda. His first book, *Holy War, Inc.*, was a *New York
Times* bestseller and has been translated into eighteen languages.
His most recent book, *The Longest War*, also a *New York Times* best-
seller, won the Washington Institute's prize for the best book on
the Middle East of 2011. Bergen is CNN's national security analyst
and director of the national security studies program at the New
America Foundation. He is a contributing editor at the *New Republic*
and has worked as a correspondent for National Geographic Television, Discovery, and CNN. He has held teaching positions at the
Kennedy School of Government at Harvard University and at the
School of Advanced International Studies at Johns Hopkins University. His writing has appeared in the *New York Times, Washington*

Post, Wall Street Journal, Foreign Affairs, Atlantic, Rolling Stone, Time, Vanity Fair, and many other newspapers and magazines around the world. A member of the National Security Preparedness Group, a successor to the 9/11 Commission, he is also the editor of the AfPak Channel, which can be found at www.foreignpolicy.com/afpak. He has testified before several congressional committees about Afghanistan, Pakistan, and al-Qaeda. Bergen holds an MA in modern history from New College, Oxford University. He lives in Washington, D.C., with his wife, documentary producer Tresha Mabile, and their son, Pierre.

For more information, visit peterbergen.com.